Studying the Clinician

Studying the Clinician

JUDGMENT RESEARCH
AND
PSYCHOLOGICAL ASSESSMENT

Howard N. Garb

AMERICAN PSYCHOLOGICAL ASSOCIATION
WASHINGTON, DC

Published by
American Psychological Association
750 First Street, NE
Washington, DC 20002

Copies may be ordered from
APA Order Department
P.O. Box 92984
Washington, DC 20090-2984

In the UK and Europe, copies may be ordered from
American Psychological Association
3 Henrietta Street
Covent Garden, London
WC2E 8LU England

Typeset in Goudy by Monotype Composition Company, Baltimore, MD

Printer: Port City Press, Inc., Baltimore, MD
Cover Designer: Berg Design, Albany, NY
Technical/Production Editor: Susan Bedford

Library of Congress Cataloging-in-Publication Data
Garb, Howard N.
    Studying the clinician: judgment research and psychological
assessment / by Howard N. Garb.
        p.   cm.
    Includes bibliographical references and index.
    ISBN 1-55798-483-2 (acid-free paper)
    1. Psychiatry—Decision making.   2. Clinical psychology—Decision
making.   3. Psychodiagnostics.   4. Clinical competence.   I. Title.
RC455.2.D42G37   1998
616.89—dc21   97-47679
                                                               CIP

British Library Cataloguing-in-Publication Data
A CIP record is available from the British Library.

Printed in the United States of America
First Edition

To my parents,
Suzanne and Julius Garb

CONTENTS

PREFACE

This book describes research on psychodiagnosis, personality assessment, and neuropsychological assessment. Topics include the reliability and validity of judgments and decisions, the cognitive processes of clinicians, and the optimal use of computers for making judgments. Implications for training and clinical practice are described along with implications for the expert testimony of mental health professionals in legal settings.

This book was written primarily for students and professionals in psychology, but it should also be of interest to students and professionals in other mental health fields. When used as a text for a graduate-level course in psychological testing, the book may be paired with a book on psychometrics or one on the description and interpretation of specific psychological tests. The present book does not describe issues in test construction nor does it contain advice or instruction on the use of specific tests. This book can also be used as a text for a course on clinical judgment, clinical versus statistical prediction, and the use of structured interviews. A course on these topics can be offered as an alternative to a course on projective testing.

Because a theme of this book is that people's beliefs, preconceptions, and biases influence their judgments, it seems appropriate that I comment on my own personal and professional background. I was born in 1955, and I am White, married, and heterosexual. My family background is unusual because many of the relatives on one side of my family struggled with the pain of mental illness, whereas many of the relatives on the other side of my family were mental health professionals. One of my uncles died in a mental hospital as a young man after receiving electroconvulsive treatment. On the other side of my family, my mother, my aunts, and my uncle were all mental health professionals. Merton Gill, of Rapaport, Gill, and Schafer (1946) fame, was my grandfather's cousin. Because the members of one side of my family complained that "the doctors had killed" my uncle, it seems natural that I would wonder if mental health professionals are able to make appropriate judgments and treatment plans.

With regard to my professional background, I have been a full-time staff psychologist at the Pittsburgh V.A. Health Care System since 1984, for 12 years on an acute psychiatry unit and more recently as an outpatient therapist. I used to, but no longer, administer and interpret the House–Tree–Person projective technique and the Rorschach Inkblot Method. I do currently use objective personality tests. My treatment orientation has changed from psychodynamic to cognitive–behavioral. With regard to my biases, I strongly believe that clinical work should be guided by research.

I decided to write this book because I believe that clinicians and research investigators know little about research on judgment and decision making. The field has been fragmented because studies have been published in a multitude of journals by investigators from a number of fields, including clinical psychology, psychiatry, counseling psychology, neuropsychology, social work, and sociology. By synthesizing results from over 1,000 studies, I hoped to learn what issues have, and have not, been adequately addressed, and I hoped to be able to make recommendations for improving clinical practice.

Acknowledgments must be made. For their support and assistance in numerous ways, I wish to thank the following: from the Pittsburgh V.A. Healthcare System—Georgette Bellucci, Stephen Perconte, Daniel P. van Kammen, Jeffrey Peters, Hai Giap, John Rueda, Betsy Frantz, Alice Atkins, Jay Smith, and Peter Lazzarotti; from APA Books—Susan Bedford, Julia Frank-McNeil, Peggy Schlegel, Mary Lynn Skutley, and Evan R. Karachalios; my wife, Flora, and my children, Merrick and Leanna; my advisor from graduate school, Harry S. Upshaw, and my friend from graduate school days, Richard J. McNally; and for commenting on drafts of this book, William M. Grove and Jerry S. Wiggins. I would like to thank Will Grove in particular for making detailed and extensive comments.

HOWARD N. GARB

Studying the Clinician

INTRODUCTION

In this book, the focus is on clinicians, not patients. The judgments and decisions made by clinicians—not the judgments and decisions of patients—will be described.

Judgment research[1] in the area of psychological assessment is important for several reasons. For example, it is important for evaluating validity. Rather than evaluate the validity of a set of test scores, one can evaluate the validity of a set of judgments made by a clinician. In commenting on the history of psychometrics, Angoff (1988) observed

> Not until later did it come to be more fully understood that one does not validate a test, nor even the scores yielded by the test, but the interpretations and inferences that the user draws from the test scores, and the decisions and actions that flow from those inferences. (p. 24)

This concept of validity, which originated with Cronbach (1971), is now well accepted (American Psychological Association [APA], 1985, p. 9). Thus, judgment research is important for establishing the validity of psychological assessment.

Judgment research is also important because it can help clinicians make more accurate judgments. Improving the accuracy of judgments is the ultimate goal of judgment research. By learning about the validity of judgments, the cognitive processes of clinicians, and the use of computers

---

[1]The term *judgment research* is used in this volume to refer to research on both judgments and decisions.

to make judgments, we may be able to improve psychological assessment. For example, by learning about the conditions when biases and errors are likely to occur, clinicians may become more adept at making judgments and they may become better at deciding how likely it is that their judgments are correct. As another example, when clinicians learn about the limitations and capabilities of computer programs that can be used to make judgments, they will be able to make better use of them.

Judgment research is marked by controversy. For example, in a recent book, *House of Cards: Psychology and Psychotherapy Built on Myth* (Dawes, 1994), the clinical practice of psychology and psychiatry was strongly criticized. Judgment research was cited along with other areas of research to support the criticisms. That is, studies in which mental health professionals made unreliable and invalid judgments were cited to support criticisms of psychology and psychiatry.

A goal of this book is to provide a balanced review of the empirical research on judgment and decision making. Because Dawes (1994) wrote his book for the general public, he cited a relatively small number of studies. He referred readers to a three-volume publication by Ziskin and Faust (1988) for documentation of many of his criticisms of mental health practice (Dawes, 1994, p. 153). However, the Ziskin and Faust volumes have been criticized for being one sided (e.g., Brodsky, 1989). That is, they have been criticized for describing studies in which clinicians did poorly, but not studies in which they did well. Ziskin and Faust (1991, p. 881) have agreed that their three-volume work is one sided, but they noted that their intent was to provide instruction for attorneys on how to criticize testimony provided by mental health professionals.

Since judgment research is important, one might expect that an increasing amount of research is being done in the area. However, interest in judgment research is not as great in the mental health professions as it is in other fields. For example, physicians treating physical conditions have a journal, *Journal of Medical Decision Making,* and a society, the Society for Medical Decision Making, devoted entirely to research on judgment and decision making. Similarly, scientists from a range of fields (e.g., psychology, economics, political science) belong to the Society for Judgment and Decision-Making, but the focus of their meetings is decidedly not clinical. In many areas of science, the number of investigators and scholarly publications seems to double in size at regular intervals, but this is not true of judgment research in the areas of psychodiagnosis, personality assessment, and neuropsychological assessment. Although research continues at a steady but slow rate on some issues (e.g., gender bias, race bias), practically no research is being done on other important issues (e.g., the validity of clinicians' ratings of personality traits, the validity of diagnoses made by clinicians when test results are made available in addition to interview and history information).

This book is organized into two sections: (I) Validity of Judgments and (II) Methods and Recommendations for Making Judgments. Validity is broadly defined to include reliability and bias. Validity results are described for the assessment of personality and psychopathology, psychodiagnosis, case formulation, behavioral prediction, treatment planning, and neuropsychological assessment. When the task of a study was to make diagnoses, predictions, or treatment plans for patients with neurological impairment, the studies were included in the chapter on neuropsychological assessment, not in the chapters on diagnosis, prediction, and treatment planning. Because judgments can be made by clinicians or by computers, I describe research both on the cognitive processes of clinicians and on computer use in making judgments. In the final chapter, strategies for improving clinical assessment are described.

In other books and articles describing cognitive processes, research on validity frequently has not been reviewed (e.g., Arkes, 1981; Dawes, 1986; Dumont & Lecomte, 1987; Kayne & Alloy, 1988; Leary & Miller, 1986, pp. 121–146; Turk & Salovey, 1986, 1988). When only research on cognitive processes is described and shows that cognitive processes can lead to errors in judgment, there is a temptation to conclude that the validity of clinical judgments is, or is likely to be, poor. However, when describing validity, one should directly evaluate validity rather than simply describe how cognitive processes can lead to errors in judgment (Funder, 1987). For example, when studying how the eye works, experimental psychologists have described how people can be tricked by optical illusions. However, these experimenters have not concluded that visual perception in the everyday world is poor. Thus, the distinction between cognitive processes and the validity of judgments is crucial.

Throughout this book, an effort was made to exclude studies with poor ecological validity. For example, articles are not cited if only lay judges (e.g., undergraduate students) made judgments, if clinicians were given atypical information, or if the judgment task was atypical of the types of judgments made in clinical practice.

Results on judgment research are neither all positive nor all negative. To the extent that clinicians can acknowledge, but not be complacent with, our shortcomings, we can become better clinicians. Uncertainty and criticism can cause discomfort, but clinicians should try to accept uncertainty and examine criticisms. Clinicians should be embarrassed not if we learn we have shortcomings and limitations, but if we choose to ignore empirical research because it describes those shortcomings and limitations.

I

VALIDITY OF JUDGMENTS

1

ASSESSMENT OF PERSONALITY AND PSYCHOPATHOLOGY

In his classic book *Personality and Prediction: Principles of Personality Assessment*, Jerry Wiggins (1973) reviewed research on a range of topics, including clinical judgment and statistical prediction. Although he described results from many studies, he emphasized the difficulty of determining if a judgment is valid or invalid:

> Criterion analysis has proved to be the most recondite and vexing issue confronting personality assessment today. In fact, criterion assessment is typically referred to as "the criterion problem" in much the same manner as we speak of "the racial problem" or other complex issues defying easy solution. (p. 39)

Twenty-five years after the publication of his book, one may wonder how much progress has been made on the criterion problem.

Though progress has been made in personality assessment, little progress has been made in solving the criterion problem. Dramatic advances have been made in psychometric theory with the growth of modern test theory, and new tests have been developed while older tests have been revised. Just as important, during the past 25 years, research, including research from behavioral genetics, has supported the use of personality-trait terms to describe people (e.g., Kenrick & Funder, 1988; Rowe, 1987). Also, advances have been made in modeling the structure of personality; for instance, the five-factor model and the interpersonal circumplex model have grown in importance (e.g., Costa & Widiger, 1994; Wiggins & Trobst, 1997; though also see Block, 1995). With regard to judgment research and the description of personality traits and psychopathology, progress has occurred in several areas, for example, in understanding the effects of race and gender bias. However, at least with respect to judgment studies, little progress has been made in solving the criterion problem in personality assessment. Thus, when clinicians are given all of the information that they usually have available in clinical practice and when they make ratings of personality traits and psychopathology, it is not always clear how the validity of their ratings can be evaluated.

Even though little ground has been gained in solving the criterion problem in personality assessment, research on the reliability and validity of judgments has yielded important results. Topics reviewed in this chapter include (a) reliability; (b) comparison of clinical judgments to indicators of a construct; (c) illusory correlations; and (d) biases and errors, such as race bias, gender bias, labeling effects, and overperception of psychopathology. In addition to describing results from empirical research, the current status of the criterion problem in personality assessment is described.

RELIABILITY

One does not need to solve the criterion problem to study reliability. To study reliability, one can give two or more clinicians the same information about a client and have them make judgments (*interrater reliability*), have a clinician evaluate a client on two or more occasions (*reliability across time*), or have different clinicians use different assessment instruments to make ratings for the same clients (*reliability across assessment instruments*).

Reliability is frequently evaluated by calculating kappa or an intraclass correlation. Reliability is generally thought to be poor if values for an intraclass-correlation coefficient or kappa coefficient are below .40, fair if values are between .40 and .59, good if values are between .60 and .74, and excellent if values are .75 or greater (Cicchetti & Sparrow, 1981; Fleiss, 1981, p. 218).

In many older studies, intraclass-correlation coefficients and kappa coefficients were not calculated. Results from these studies are described, but they are more difficult to interpret. While intraclass-correlation coefficients and kappa coefficients correct for chance level of agreement, other statistics do not. *Chance level of agreement* refers to the amount of agreement that will occur if two clinicians make diagnoses in a random manner. For example, if two clinicians make diagnoses for a group of patients on a geropsychiatry ward, a majority of the patients have dementia, and both clinicians make a large number of diagnoses of dementia, but their diagnoses are randomly distributed across the patients, then the clinicians may agree on the diagnoses for a large number of patients. If one calculates the percentage of times the diagnoses made by the two clinicians are in agreement, then one might conclude that interrater reliability is good. However, if one calculates a kappa coefficient, one would conclude that interrater reliability is poor.

Little research has been conducted on the interrater reliability of ratings of personality traits. For example, according to the the five-factor model of personality, the major features of personality can be described by the following five factors: Extroversion, Agreeableness, Conscientiousness, Emotional Stability, and Openness to Experience (Costa & Widiger, 1994). Though the five-factor model of personality has grown in importance, there have been no studies on whether interrater reliability is good when clinicians use this model to describe the personalities of their clients.

Results of research on the interrater reliability of ratings of personality traits have varied widely. For example, in an old but classic study (Little & Shneidman, 1959), clinical psychologists completed Q sorts to describe behavioral patterns (they ranked items from least characteristic to most characteristic of a patient). Q sorts based on Thematic Apperception Test (TAT) results were compared with other Q sorts based on TAT results, and similarly Q sorts based on Rorschach or Minnesota Multiphasic Personality Inventory (MMPI) results were compared to other Q sorts based on Rorschach (or MMPI) results. The average interrater-reliability correlations were .27 for clinicians using the TAT, .31 for clinicians using the Rorschach, and .39 for clinicians using the MMPI. All of the clinicians in this study were considered to be experts. MMPI judges were selected in consultation with Robert Harris and Starke Hathaway, and Rorschach and TAT judges were selected in consultation with the editors of the *Journal of Projective Techniques*. In another study (Nystedt, Magnusson, & Aronowitsch, 1975), the results were quite different. Each psychologist interpreted the results from a test battery comprised of the Rorschach, TAT, and Sentence Completion Test protocols. Intraclass-correlation coefficients for interrater reliability were .87 for rating intelligence, .83 for rating ability to relate to others, and .73 for rating ability to control affect and impulses.

In another study on the interrater reliability of personality ratings (Heumann & Morey, 1990), interrater reliability was described for rating the dominance–submission dimension of the interpersonal circumplex model of personality (Leary, 1957) and Cloninger's novelty-seeking and reward dependent-personality dimensions (Cloninger, 1987). Five clinicians made ratings after reading 10 case histories that were selected from textbooks. All of the cases described patients with features of borderline personality disorder. Interrater reliability ranged from poor to good. Treating clinicians as a random effect, values for the intraclass-correlation coefficients ranged from .28 for the reward-dependent dimension to .35 for the novelty-seeking dimension to .63 for the dominant–submissive dimension.

As with ratings of personality traits, little research has been done on the reliability of mental-status ratings. Describing a patient's mental status involves describing the person's speech, affect, mood, thoughts (e.g., delusions, thoughts about suicide or homicide), perceptual experiences (e.g., hallucinations), and cognitive functioning (e.g., concentration, memory, insight, judgment). In early studies, interrater reliability was reported to be good, but results were not described by calculating kappa or intraclass correlation coefficients (Geertsma & Stoller, 1960; Jones & Kahn, 1966; Rosenzweig, Vandenberg, Moore, & Dukay, 1961). For example, when psychiatrists and psychiatry residents made mental-status ratings on a 4-point scale (e.g., *none*, *slight*, *moderate*, or *extensive preoccupation with somatic symptoms*), 95% of the ratings were in perfect agreement or were within one point of agreement (Jones & Kahn, 1966).

Interrater reliability may be good for clinicians who all work at the same hospital, but not for clinicians who work at different hospitals or in different geographical locations. Empirical research indicates that intercenter and national differences are related to how clinicians perceive psychopathology. For example, after viewing videotapes of clinical interviews, American psychiatrists made more severe ratings for different psychiatric symptoms than did British psychiatrists (Kendell et al., 1971; Sharpe et al., 1974). The severity of ratings also differed significantly across hospitals in the British Isles (Copeland, Cooper, Kendell, & Gourlay, 1971).

Most studies on the reliability of mental-status ratings from the 1980s and 1990s have described whether clinicians can make reliable ratings when they use a structured interview or rating scale. Satisfactory reliability has often been reported (e.g., Widiger, Frances, Warner, & Bluhm, 1986), but a description of the hundreds of studies that have been done on this topic is beyond the scope of this book.

While many studies have been conducted to establish reliability for a rating scale or a structured interview, other studies have been conducted to learn about interrater reliability for tasks that seem especially difficult. In several studies, psychiatrists and psychiatry residents read case vignettes and rated whether bizarre or nonbizarre delusions were present. The task is important because the diagnosis of schizophrenia requires clinicians to be able to rate whether bizarre delusions are present (American Psychiatric Association, 1994). Interrater reliability was poor (kappa < .40) in two of three studies (Flaum, Arndt, & Andreasen, 1991; Mojtabai & Nicholson, 1995; Spitzer, First, Kendler, & Stein, 1993).

In addition to describing an individual's personality traits and mental status, clinicians sometimes describe a person's defense mechanisms. Interrater reliability for assessing defense mechanisms has been problematic, even when considerable efforts have been made to define the various defense mechanisms (for a review, see Endler & Parker, 1995, pp. 332–334). For example, the mean intraclass correlation coefficient for raters using the Defense Mechanism Rating Scales was only .37, even though these rating scales provide definitions of the defense mechanisms (Perry & Cooper, 1989).

Besides describing interrater reliability, one can also describe the stability of ratings (reliability across time). In the few clinical judgment studies that have been done, stability has been described as being fair or good for a range of tasks, depending on the information given to the clinicians (e.g., Goldberg & Werts, 1966; Little & Shneidman, 1959; Nystedt, Magnusson, & Aronowitsch, 1975). In these studies, the same protocols were presented to clinicians on more than one occasion, for example, 2 months apart. The stability of clinicians' ratings is an important problem and deserves more attention than it has received. For example, it would be interesting to learn how and if clinicians describe personality traits when clients are depressed. Empirical research indicates that clients' reports about their patterns of behavior are distorted when they are depressed. Investigators have recommended that personality traits not be evaluated until acute depression has been successfully treated (e.g., Stuart, Simons, Thase, & Pilkonis, 1992). Thus, trait ratings made when a patient is depressed may be quite different from ratings made later when the patient is no longer depressed. It would also be interesting to learn if stability is likely to be poor under other conditions.

Finally, *convergence* (reliability across assessment instruments) has frequently been poor (e.g., Goldberg & Werts, 1966; Howard, 1962, 1963; Little & Shneidman, 1959; Nystedt et al., 1975). For example, in three studies ratings were made by clinical psychologists using (a) the Rorschach alone, (b) the Sentence Completion Test alone, or (c) the TAT alone. Howard (1962) reported that correlations between the three different sets of ratings ranged from $-.11$ to $.30$ for ratings of personality traits (e.g., abasement, emotionality, dominance, isolation). Howard (1963) reported that correlations between the three different sets of ratings ranged from an average of $.06$ for rating psychotherapy prognosis and $.07$ for rating adjustment to $.22$ for rating intelligence. Finally, Nystedt et al. (1975) reported that the correlations between the three different sets of ratings ranged from $.25$ to $.28$ for rating intelligence, $.13$ to $.24$ for rating ability to relate to others, and $.06$ to $.15$ for rating ability to control affect and impulses.

Convergence was also poor when clinical psychologists made ratings by using either (a) MMPI protocols, (b) Rorschach protocols, (c) Wechsler-Bellevue Intelligence Scale protocols, or (d) vocational histories (Goldberg & Werts, 1966). For example, intercorrelations among the four sets of ratings ranged from $-.31$ to $.23$ when clinicians rated ego strength and $-.14$ to $.15$ when they rated dependency.

It is not surprising that convergence was poor when psychologists made ratings by using either MMPI protocols or Rorschach protocols. When scores from the Rorschach and scores from the MMPI are compared, there is usually little or no relation between the scores, even when the scores purportedly measure the same constructs (for reviews, see Archer & Krishnamurthy, 1993a, 1993b). In these studies, clinicians did not make judgments;

instead scores from the tests were directly compared. As observed by Archer (1996)

> An extensive literature, spanning 50 years and 45 published investigations, leads to the conclusion that the Rorschach and the MMPI bear little or no meaningful relationship to each other. (p. 504)

COMPARISON OF JUDGMENTS TO INDICATORS OF A CONSTRUCT

To evaluate the validity of clinical ratings of personality and psychopathology, one can compare these ratings to indicator ratings, which are made by other clinicians using separate information. For example, clinical ratings may be made by psychologists using test results, whereas indicator ratings may be made by clinicians using history and interview data. Historically, the clinicians making the indicator ratings have been called *criterion judges* and their ratings have been called *criterion ratings*, but these terms are inaccurate because the ratings are fallible. Even though indicator ratings are fallible, the comparison of clinical ratings to indicator ratings can be valuable because the results provide evidence about the construct validity of both the clinical judgments and the indicators (Cronbach & Meehl, 1955).

In the following sections, results from empirical studies on the following topics are described: (a) presumed expertise, experience, training, and validity; (b) confidence and validity; (c) incremental validity; and (d) the overall validity of clinical judgments. Afterward, methodological comments about the criterion problem and the use of indicators of a construct to evaluate validity are made.

Presumed Expertise, Experience, Training, and Validity

Among the most provocative results reported in the area of clinical judgment are those that indicate that presumed-expert clinicians are no more accurate than other clinicians. These results were obtained in two studies in which clinicians were given projective-test protocols and one in which clinicians were given MMPI protocols. Turner (1966) gave Rorschach protocols to 25 fellows of the Society for Projective Techniques and 25 recently graduated PhD psychologists. Clinicians were to describe the patients' symptoms, past behaviors and likely future behaviors, motivations, conflicts, and emotions. Indicator judgments were agreed on by hospital staff members working with the patients. In the other study on the use of projective test protocols (Silverman, 1959), judges were 10 psychologists who were renowned "for their high competence in dealing with projective test material" (p. 6) and who had 10 or more years of experience in projective testing; 10 psychologists with 5 to 8 years of experience in projective testing; and 10 psychologists with 3 or fewer years of experience in using projective tests. Judges were given Rorschach, TAT, and House–Tree–Person drawing protocols. Clinicians were to describe defense mechanisms, motivations, personality traits, symptoms, interpersonal behaviors, and infancy and childhood as perceived by each patient. Indicator ratings were made by psychiatrists who had seen patients in at least 35 therapy sessions. In neither the Turner (1966) nor the Silverman (1959) study was level of presumed expertise significantly related to validity. In a third study (Graham, 1967), clinicians were given MMPI protocols. They performed Q sorts to describe the personality characteristics of patients. The items varied, and were described as "symptomatic, diagnostic, inferential, dynamic, historical" (Graham, 1967, p. 298). Indicator Q sorts were based on interviews with the patients and the patients' relatives. PhD clinical psychologists who had used the MMPI extensively for more than 5 years and who were thought to have a thorough knowledge of the research literature concerning the MMPI were no more accurate than PhD clinical psychologists who had used the MMPI routinely for about 5 years.

Findings obtained when clinicians are compared to graduate students in mental health fields are equally striking. Clinicians consistently failed to make more valid ratings of personality and psychopathology than did graduate students (Garb, 1989). This was true when clinicians were given interview data (Anthony, 1968; Grigg, 1958; Schinka & Sines, 1974), observation data (Garner & Smith, 1976), biographical information (Oskamp, 1965; Soskin, 1954), Rorschach protocols (Gadol, 1969; Turner, 1966), and MMPI protocols (Chandler, 1970; Graham, 1967). In only one study did clinicians achieve better validity than graduate students. When judges were given Rorschach data and were to predict IQ scores, clinical psychologists were more accurate than graduate students who had just completed a course on the Rorschach, but they were not more accurate than graduate students who had already started their practica training (Grebstein, 1963; data reanalyzed by Hammond, Hursch, & Todd, 1964). However, results from Todd's (1954) study undermined these results. Todd (1954; cited in Hammond, 1955) reported that clinical psychologists who used Rorschach data to predict IQ scores were not significantly more accurate than undergraduate students. Thus, even for this task, clinicians have not been consistently more valid than inexperienced judges. Finally, it is worth noting that though clinicians in most of the studies were clinical or counseling psychologists, some of the studies included judges from other professions, including special education teachers, medical personnel, physical therapists, occupational therapists (Garner & Smith, 1976), and social workers (Anthony, 1968). These judges from other professions did not out-perform graduate students either.

Results have been more gratifying when advanced graduate students have been compared to beginning graduate students. Advanced psychology graduate students made significantly more valid ratings than beginning psychology graduate students, in three studies. In one study, already described (Grebstein's 1963 data reanalyzed by Hammond, Hursch, & Todd, 1964), graduate students who had already begun their training practica were more accurate than graduate students who had just completed a course on the Rorschach when the task was to use the Rorschach to predict IQ scores. A second study (Aronson & Akamatsu, 1981) is a rare example of a longitudinal clinical-judgment study in which clinical judges were studied over a period of a year. In it, 12 psychology graduate students performed Q sorts to describe personality characteristics before they took a course on the use and interpretation of the MMPI, after they completed the course, and again after they completed a year-long assessment and therapy practicum. The validity of Q sorts improved after the graduate students completed the MMPI course (mean validity coefficients increased from .20 to .42), but not after they completed their year-long practicum (mean validity coefficient of .44). In the third study (Sines, 1959), the task again was to perform Q sorts to describe personality characteristics. Five psychology graduate students were given biographical data alone or biographical data and one or more of the following types of assessment data: (a) a chance to interview each patient, (b) MMPI protocols, and (c) Rorschach protocols. Mean validity coefficients were .39 for a second-year graduate student; .46, .48, and .54 for third-year students; and .53 for a fourth-year student. The overall differences in validity were statistically significant.

Psychologists and psychology graduate students are sometimes more accurate than lay judges, depending on the type of information judges are given, the task, and the sophistication of the lay judges (Garb, 1989). With regard to judgments based on interview data, clinicians (psychiatrists, clinical psychologists, social workers) and psychology graduate students were more accurate than undergraduate students (Grigg, 1958; Waxer, 1976), but not more accurate than physical scientists (Luft, 1950), presumably because of differences in intelligence and maturity between undergraduate students and physical scientists. Tasks ranged from rating severity of depression (Waxer, 1976) to predicting clients' responses on personality test items (Grigg, 1958; Luft, 1950). When judges were given biographical data, clinicians were more accurate than undergraduate students when personality and symptom ratings were made for psychiatric patients (Horowitz, 1962; Stelmachers & McHugh, 1964), but not when judges were to describe the personality traits of normal subjects (Griswold & Dana, 1970; Oskamp, 1965; Weiss, 1963). This is an important distinction because clinicians do not usually make ratings for individuals who are not in treatment. When judges were given Rorschach protocols, clinical psychologists were not significantly more accurate than undergraduate students. This was true when the task was to estimate IQ scores (Todd, 1954, cited in Hammond, 1955) and when the task was to perform Q sorts with personality items (Gadol,

1969). Finally, results for the MMPI were mixed. In one study (Aronson & Akamatsu, 1981), clinical psychology graduate students were more accurate than undergraduates. The task was to perform Q sorts to describe the personality characteristics of psychiatric patients. Undergraduate judges had attended two lectures on the MMPI. Indicator Q sorts were based on interviews with the patients and patients' relatives. The mean correlation between judges' Q sorts and indicator Q sorts was about .24 for undergraduates and .44 for graduate students (calculated from Aronson & Akamatsu, 1981, Figure 1). In a second study involving the MMPI, clinical psychologists did not do better than lay judges (Chandler, 1970), but the judgment task was described as being "so idiosyncratic that there is little reason to assume that professional diagnosticians or anyone else might perform very differently" (Chandler, 1967, p. 129). The task was idiosyncratic in part because judges were to base their judgments on abbreviated MMPI profiles in which scores for only 5 of the 10 clinical scales were presented to judges.

Overall, results on presumed expertise, experience, training, and validity are disappointing. Presumed experts were not more accurate than other clinicians, and clinicians were generally no more accurate than graduate students, although clinicians may be more accurate than beginning graduate students. The only positive results were obtained when advanced graduate students were compared to beginning graduate students and when clinicians and graduate students were compared to lay judges. Similar results have been reported for other judgment tasks, and are described in later chapters.

Though the results for mental health professionals are disappointing, they are not dissimilar to results obtained for physicians. In a study on medical care (Shortliffe, Buchanan, & Feigenbaum, 1979), high school graduates selected for intelligence, poise, and warmth of personality were able to provide competent medical care for a circumscribed range of problems after only 4 to 8 weeks of training.

Confidence and Validity

Clinicians should know when their judgments are likely to be correct and when they are likely to be wrong. In some studies, in addition to making personality and psychopathology ratings, clinicians also made confidence ratings describing their level of certainty in each of their judgments.

The relation between confidence and validity was positive in only one study. In this study (Graham, 1967), MMPI protocols were presented and ratings were made for psychiatric patients. Clinical psychologists had greater success performing Q sorts with items that had been rated as being easy to sort than with items that had been described as being difficult to sort.

Confidence ratings were poor in other studies. For example, in one study (Oskamp, 1965), clinicians were given history information. They were to describe the behavior patterns and attitudes of a normal subject. Though they estimated that they would be correct for 53% of the items, they obtained a hit rate of only 28%. In two other studies (Gadol, 1969; Holsopple & Phelan, 1954), confidence ratings were not positively related to validity when clinicians were given Rorschach or TAT protocols. Finally, confidence and validity were not significantly related in one study on the MMPI. However, in this study (Chandler, 1967), as already mentioned, judges were given abbreviated MMPI profiles.

Incremental Validity

Clinicians almost always know something about a client before they conduct an interview or administer and interpret a psychological test, even if it is only information contained in a referral. For this reason, instead of comparing results to the level of accuracy expected by chance, it makes sense to compare them to the level of accuracy achieved by using easily available information (APA, 1985). If the addition of information leads to an increase in validity, then incremental validity is said to be good. In the discussion that follows, incremental validity is described for (a) auditory and visual cues, (b) interviews, (c) history information, and (d) psychological tests.

Surprisingly, the effect of being able to see and hear an interview, as opposed to reading a transcript of the interview, did not result in an increase in accuracy in several studies. These results were obtained when clinicians were to predict how patients responded on self-report personality question-naires such as the Gough Adjective Checklist (Borke & Fiske, 1957; Giedt, 1955; Grigg, 1958; Segel, 1952) and when they were to make ratings of personality traits (Giedt, 1955; Sperber & Adlerstein, 1961). Only Anthony (1968) reported that judgments made after listening to recordings were more accurate than ratings made by reading transcripts. However, in this study, clinicians read the transcripts from a reading pacer (a mechanical device that controls the rate at which text is presented). They were not allowed to re-read any passages.

Though the results on the incremental validity of auditory and visual cues are surprising, similar results were reported in another review. Ambady and Rosenthal (1992), in an article that won the Behavioral Science Prize from the American Association for the Advancement of Science in 1993, reviewed research on the accuracy of judgments based on brief observations. They reviewed studies from the areas of social and clinical psychology. The authors did not include the clinical-judgment studies cited in the preceding paragraph because the interviews in the above studies were relatively long and they wanted to describe the accuracy of judgments based on brief samples of behavior. Ambady and Rosenthal concluded that judgments based on transcripts are generally as accurate as judgments based on observations of "face, body, and speech" (p. 264).

Several investigators have challenged the validity of interview data. For example, according to Dawes, Faust, and Meehl (1989), "clinical judgments based on interviews achieve, at best, negligible accuracy or validity" (p. 1672). Their argument is not supported by the little research that has been done on the incremental validity of interviews. For example, Sines (1959) had psychology graduate students perform Q sorts to describe the personality traits and symptoms of patients. Their Q sorts were compared to those performed by therapists who had seen the patients in 10 or more therapy sessions. Validity increased from .40 to .57 when interviews were added to biographical data sheets, from .37 to .45 when interviews were added to biographical data sheets and Rorschach protocols, and from .38 to .60 when interviews were added to biographical data sheets and MMPI protocols.

A recurring theme in this book is that clinicians have difficulty making valid judgments for normal populations (people they would not normally see in clinical practice). This is true of research on the incremental validity of history data. For normal subjects, personality ratings became less valid or did not change in validity when case history material or interview transcripts containing primarily historical data were added to demographic data (Oskamp, 1965; Weiss, 1963). For example, in one of the studies (Oskamp, 1965), clinical psychologists, psychology graduate students, and undergraduates were given demographic information about an individual, such as that he is a college graduate and works as a business assistant in a floral decorating studio. They were then given information about the person's experiences during childhood, adolescence, and young adulthood. The evaluator's task was to describe the person's behavior patterns, attitudes, and interests, for example, his attitude toward his mother, his conversations with men, and his attitude toward his job. The history information and the task were written to "approximate as closely as possible the situations found in actual psychological practice" (p. 264). Results did not differ significantly for the different groups of judges. Judges became significantly more confident but not significantly more accurate after they were given the history information. They initially expected to be correct for 33% of the items, but after receiving the history information they predicted they would obtain a hit rate of 53%. Accuracy increased from 26% to only 28%.

For psychiatric patients, the results offer tentative support for the incremental validity of history data. When clinicians predicted patients' responses on personality items (e.g., MMPI items), validity increased when demographic data (e.g., age, sex, education, occupation) were added to diagnosis (Stelmachers & McHugh, 1964). In the same study, validity increased when extensive case history data and Sentence Completion protocols were added to demographic data and diagnosis. However, in a second study (Guarendi, 1979), validity did not increase when clinicians were given case history information in addition to minimal data. Validity may not have increased because the case history information was limited: Case history material included developmental, school, and family histories. Incremental validity may have been better if the case history information had included clients' descriptions of their recent behaviors and symptoms. Furthermore, information about psychopathology was presented as part of the minimal data, which consisted of demographic data and a description of the presenting problems. Failure to improve on minimal data occurred partly because clinicians did well with only the minimal data. The correlation between clinical Q sorts and indicator Q sorts was .37, which is a high value for clinicians using only demographic or minimal data.

Incremental validity has been fair for the MMPI, but poor for projective tests. The addition of MMPI test data to demographic data has generally led to increased validity (Aronson & Akamatsu, 1981; Duker, 1959; Golden, 1964; Graham, 1967; Marks, 1961). Validity also increased when MMPI protocols were added to other test results or biographical information (Golden, 1964; Sines, 1959). In contrast, validity did not significantly improve when a test battery that included the Rorschach and Sentence Completion Test was added to demographic data (Cochrane, 1972; Kostlan, 1954) or when the TAT, Rorschach, or House–Tree–Person Test were added to other test results or history information (Barendregt, 1961; Bilett, Jones, & Whitaker, 1982; Golden, 1964; Sines, 1959; Soskin, 1954).

Overall Level of Validity

How valid are descriptions of personality and psychopathology? Mischel (1968), in his famous and provocative book *Personality and Assessment*, reviewed research on clinical and social judgment and concluded that correlations between observed behaviors and ratings of personality traits are seldom larger than .30. He argued that because correlations between observed behaviors and ratings of personality traits are low, clinicians should not use ratings of personality traits to make predictions. Instead, he felt that behaviors can be better predicted by considering a person's life situations.

In subsequent research in social psychology, correlation coefficients between personality ratings and indicator measures of personality traits have usually ranged from .30 to .40 (e.g., Funder, 1987; Kenrick & Funder, 1988). In these studies, lay judges, not clinicians, made ratings. Even larger correlations have been obtained in social psychology when personality ratings have been used to predict aggregates rather than single instances of behavior (e.g., Epstein & O'Brien, 1985). In these studies, a personality rating is correlated with a composite score based on a range of behaviors thought to be related to the personality trait. Composite scores are likely to be more reliable and valid than a score based on a single instance of behavior for the same reason that a test is likely to be more reliable and valid if it is composed of more than one item. These studies are important because when people describe personality traits, they hope they are describing a pattern of behavior, not a single behavior.

Although the accuracy of judgments and the person–situation debate has been a focus of research in social psychology, in the mental health fields there has been little interest in describing the overall validity of personality and symptom ratings. An interesting attempt was made by Ambady and Rosenthal (1992). They wanted to compare the validity of judgments made on the basis of brief samples of behavior (30 seconds to 5 minutes) to the validity of judgments made by using traditional methods of personality assessment. To make the comparison, they needed to describe validity results for judgments made by using traditional methods of assessment. To do this, they presented results from two studies (Holt & Luborsky, 1958; Kelly & Fiske, 1951) that were described by Wiggins (1973) as milestone studies in personality assessment. Correlation coefficients in these studies ranged from .28 to .31. However, though the studies they used are of historical interest, whether they describe the validity of ratings made by clinicians in clinical practice is questionable. In both of the studies, judges made ratings not for clients or patients, but for graduate students in clinical psychology. Their task was to predict the future performance of the graduate students. Many of the predictions were made on the basis of personality tests that had been administered to the graduate students, which is not a common practice for supervisors when they try to predict who will be a competent clinician.

Are validity coefficients for mental health professionals as low as has been estimated by Mischel (1968) and Ambady and Rosenthal (1992), or are they similar to the results obtained for lay judges in the social psychology studies? Kenrick and Funder (1988) argued that judgments made by clinicians may be less valid than judgments made by lay judges when the lay judges are "thoroughly familiar with the person being rated" (p. 31). Kenrick and Funder related that

> One of us underwent clinical training . . . and came across a viewpoint much closer to the "pure trait" position than is remotely tenable on the basis of the data available now. Ten years ago, there were, and probably still are, clinical professionals overconfidently making grand predictions from minute samples of behavior of highly questionable reliability and validity. (p. 31)

One can question whether clinicians, based on relatively few hours of contact, can make more accurate ratings than can people (e.g., family members, roommates) who have known an individual for long periods of time can. Certainly clinicians believe they can, but personality and social psychologists do not necessarily share this belief.

As with results for lay judges in social psychology studies, correlations between clinical ratings and indicator measures frequently range from .30 to .40. For example, in many studies, correlations were calculated between

Q sorts made by clinical judges using assessment data and Q sorts made by clients' therapists or research investigators who interviewed the patients and their families. When Q sorts were made by using the MMPI, correlations obtained were .30 and .36 (Graham, 1967), .36 (Duker, 1959), .36 (Marks, 1961), .38 (Sines, 1959), and .44 (Aronson & Akamatsu, 1981). When Q sorts were made by using projective test data, correlations obtained were .05 to .22 (Gadol, 1969), .35 (Horowitz, 1962), and .37 (Sines, 1959). For interview or case history data, correlations obtained were .35 and .37 (Grigg, 1958), .40 and .40 (Guarendi, 1979), and .57 (Sines, 1959). When clinical judges were given biographical, interview, and test data, a correlation of .48 was obtained when the test data included Rorschach and MMPI results, but a correlation of .60 was obtained when MMPI results were included and Rorschach results were excluded (Sines, 1959). Other tasks yielded even higher correlations. A mean correlation of .70 was obtained when interview data were used to estimate intelligence and IQ tests were used as indicator measures (Sperber & Adlerstein, 1961). Overall, correlations obtained in the clinical studies are as high as correlations reported in the social psychology studies and higher than the estimates for the validity of clinical ratings made by Mischel (1968) and Ambady and Rosenthal (1992).

Given that correlations between clinical ratings and indicator measures frequently range from .30 to .40, how should one interpret these findings? One could argue that the results are disappointing because clinical ratings accounted for only 9% to 16% of the variance (using r^2 as a measure) and that 84% to 91% of the variance was unaccounted for. However, indicator measures in the studies were often of unknown reliability and validity. If indicator measures have low reliability, then one cannot expect clinicians' ratings to be highly correlated with them. Also, small effects can have important implications in practical contexts, and procedures other than calculating r^2 can be used to describe effect size (e.g., see Abelson, 1985; Dunlap, 1994; Ozer, 1985; Prentice & Miller, 1992; Rosenthal, 1995). Thus, understanding the practical implications of a correlation of .2 versus a correlation of .3 or .4 can be difficult. However, as indicator measures improve, it will become easier to understand and interpret results.

Indicator Measures and the Criterion Problem

Having described results on the validity of judgments, in this section I turn to methodological comments about the criterion problem. The indicator measures (or construct measures) that have been used are criticized, and recommendations are made for improving the way clinicians evaluate validity.

Several criticisms can be made of the indicator measures that have been used to evaluate validity. First, the reliability of indicator measures has often been unassessed. For example, when therapists made indicator ratings, it was unknown whether other therapists evaluating the patients would have made similar ratings. Ideally, both interrater and intercenter reliability will be described; reliability should be good even when ratings are made by clinicians at different settings. Second, results will be difficult to interpret as long as the validity of the indicator measures is unknown. Thus, both indicator measures and clinical ratings should be an object of study.

Several alternative methods for making construct-indicator ratings will be described. However, these methods have not yet been used in clinical-judgment studies. First, one can use the act-frequency approach to obtain standardized ratings of a construct (Buss & Craik, 1986; but also see Block, 1989). Using the act-frequency approach, clinicians (not the clinical judges using assessment information, but clinicians who help to develop the indicator measure) are instructed to list behaviors that exemplify a trait, motivation, or need. One can then follow the clients over time (after clinical judges make their ratings using assessment data) and learn whether the clients exhibit behaviors that exemplify those traits, motivations, or needs. One may want to interview family members and peers in addition to clients to learn about clients' behaviors. When using the act-frequency approach, one must consider the effects of situations and settings when relating clients' behaviors to trait constructs (Widiger, Freiman, & Bailey, 1990; also see Funder, 1995).

Other methods can also be used to obtain standardized ratings of constructs. For example, behavior sampling methods can be used. After clinical judges make their ratings, clients can be instructed to write a description of the thoughts and feelings they have at different time intervals, for example, every time a preset timer goes off on their watch. Then construct-indicator ratings could be made using these descriptions. Psychometric methods can also be used. For example, clinicians can construct psychometrically sound questionnaires to obtain measures of attitudes. Still another approach would be to use structured interviews, such as those for evaluating positive and negative symptoms of schizophrenia. The completeness of clinical descriptions of symptomatology can be evaluated by comparing them to descriptions that are based on structured interviews that are thorough and comprehensive.

By using the act-frequency approach, behavior sampling methods, psychometric methods, or structured interviews, clinicians will have a better understanding of how construct-indicator ratings are made. This will make it easier to interpret the results of a study.

ILLUSORY CORRELATIONS

An *illusory correlation* is "the report by observers of a correlation between two classes of events which, in reality, (a) are not correlated, or (b) are correlated to a lesser extent than reported, or (c) are correlated in the opposite direction from that which is reported" (Chapman, 1967, p. 151). Research on illusory correlations indicates that clinicians frequently report correlations between test indicators and personality traits or psychiatric symptoms when in fact no relations exist.

In a pioneering study, Chapman and Chapman (1967) tried to learn why the Draw-a-Person test continues to be used even though research on the interpretation of specific picture characteristics (e.g., head, ears, lips, hair, clothing, mouth, etc.) has not supported clinical observations (Kahill, 1984; Motta, Little, & Tobin, 1993; Swensen, 1957). For example, clinicians who use the Draw-a-Person test often report observing that paranoid patients draw figures with elaborate eyes, but empirical research has failed to support this observation.

As a first step in their study, Chapman and Chapman (1967) gave clinical psychologists a list of personality traits and psychiatric symptoms. The psychologists were instructed to list characteristics of Draw-a-Person protocols that are associated with the different personality traits and psychiatric symptoms. The clinicians generally agreed with one another on what features of drawings are associated with different symptoms and traits. For example, 91% of the clinicians said that a suspicious patient would draw large or atypical eyes. Similarly, 82% said that a person worried about being intelligent would be likely to draw a large or emphasized head.

As the second step of their study, Chapman and Chapman (1967) had undergraduate participants look at Draw-a-Person protocols. Each drawing was paired with a statement that reportedly described a personality characteristic or a psychiatric symptom of the person who drew the picture. Statements were randomly paired with protocols. After the participants examined the drawings and statements, they were asked if they had observed any relations between the drawings and the personality characteristics and psychiatric symptoms of the patients. The relations that the undergraduates said that they had observed corresponded to the types of relations that psychodiagnosticians have reported observing in their clinical work. For example, participants reported that the most frequently associated drawing characteristic of paranoid patients was an atypical rendering of the eyes.

An implication of the Chapman and Chapman (1967) study is that clinicians also discovered these relations on the basis of verbal associative connections rather than on the basis of the co-occurrence of pathological symptoms and features of drawings. Thus, clinicians may continue to use the Draw-a-Person test despite negative research results because they believe that they have observed relations between drawing characteristics and symptoms and traits even though the relations do not actually exist.

The results from Chapman and Chapman (1967) have been replicated using different groups of judges and different types of judgment tasks and assessment information. In all of the studies clinicians have been affected by the verbal associations of test indicators, and they have been relatively unaffected by feedback describing the co-occurrence of the test indicators and traits and symptoms (Chapman & Chapman, 1969; Dowling & Graham, 1976; Golding & Rorer, 1972; Kurtz & Garfield, 1978; Lueger & Petzel, 1979; Mowrey, Doherty, & Keeley, 1979; Rosen, 1975, 1976; Starr & Katkin, 1969; Waller & Keeley, 1978). For example, before homosexuality was removed as a diagnostic category from the *DSM*, Chapman and Chapman (1969) surveyed clinicians on how they use the Rorschach to diagnose homosexuality. Of the 42 clinicians surveyed, 32 reported that they had seen the Rorschach responses of a number of homosexual patients. They also reported that they believe that many Rorschach responses are associated with homosexuality including responses referring to (a) buttocks or anus, (b) genitals, (c) feminine clothing, (d) human figures of indeterminate gender, and (e) human figures with both male and female characteristics. None of these indicators has been supported by empirical research. Chapman and Chapman (1969) then had undergraduates make judgments. Undergraduate judges were given Rorschach protocols paired with statements describing personality features or psychiatric symptoms (e.g., "He has sexual feelings toward other men" and "He believes other people are plotting against him"). The personality and symptom statements were assigned to the cards so that there was no relation between any of the statements and any of the signs. After they had examined all of the cards, students reported that seeing buttocks, genitals, feminine clothing, figures of indeterminate gender, and androgynous figures were indicators of homosexuality.

Illusory correlations may be less of a problem for the interpretation of objective test results. For example, if clinicians refer to interpretations contained in books or computer-based test reports (as they usually do when using objective test results), illusory correlations are unlikely to occur as long as the books and computer programs are empirically based. Illusory correlations could occur if clinicians attend to the names of clinical scales inappropriately. For example, even though clinicians have been widely warned against attaching importance to the names of MMPI scales, a practitioner could still erroneously use the name of Scale 8 of the MMPI—the Schizophrenia scale—to mean that the scale is a measure of schizophrenia (which it is not; Dowling & Graham, 1976). Illusory correlations could also occur if clinicians interpret content scales or critical items inappropriately.

BIASES AND ERRORS

Biases and errors in the description of personality traits and psychopathology include race bias, social class bias, gender bias, labeling effects, and the bias to perceive psychopathology. Research in this area is less well known than research on biases and errors in psychodiagnosis, in part because findings have been better replicated in the area of psychodiagnosis.

Studies to date have been limited to the description of traits and symptoms. Research has not been conducted on biases and errors in the assessment of defense mechanisms and the assessment of the motivations, values, and attitudes of clients.

Studies on biases and errors have been included in the following re-view only if levels of psychopathology were controlled for because otherwise it would be impossible to learn if biases and errors occurred (Garb, 1997). Several methods have been used to control for level of psychopathology. For example, in many of the studies, case histories were presented to different groups of clinicians. The case histories were identical except that the des-ignation of a characteristic of the client (e.g., race, social class, or gender) differed for the different groups of clinicians. Similarly, in other studies, videotapes using actors following scripts verbatim were presented to differ-ent groups of clinicians. The scripts were identical, but the actors portraying a client differed in at least one characteristic (e.g., race, social class, or gender).

In the studies on biases and errors, clinicians typically made ratings by using Likert rating scales. For example, in some studies reviewed in the following sections, they rated impulsivity on a scale from 1 to 7 with 1 indicating *no impulsivity* and 7 indicating *severe impulsivity*. When the differ-ence between average ratings for two groups of clients (e.g., male clients and female clients) is statistically significant, but of tiny magnitude (less than .5), then the magnitude of the difference is described.

Whenever possible, comments are made about individual differences among clinicians. For example, the effect of clinician race on race bias has been noted in a few studies. However, in most of the studies, individual differences among clinicians were not described.

Race Bias

Studies on the assessment of African American, Mexican American, and White clients are described in this section, and are followed by a discussion of studies on the assessment of Asian American and White clients. Most of the studies conducted in this area of research are on the assessment of Black and White clients.

African American, Mexican American, and White Clients

When White and Black mental health professionals have described their attitudes and thoughts about African American people, Whites have made less favorable ratings than Blacks, for example, when they described the impulse control, child-rearing practices, and sexual values and behaviors of African Americans (Wyatt, Powell, & Bass, 1982). Ratings reported in the Wyatt et al. study were made for African Americans as a group; that is, clinicians were supposed to indicate whether they believe "Afro-American parents subject their children to harsh and conservative upbringing which restricts development of free and open personalities" (p. 22). Given that White and Black therapists differ in their attitudes toward African Americans (and presumably toward White people), one can reasonably wonder if race bias occurs when clinicians describe the personality traits and psychiatric symptoms of individual clients or patients.

In several studies of White, African American, and Mexican American children, results were not biased in favor of White children. When ratings were made by school psychologists, a child's race (White, African American, Mexican American) did not have a significant effect on ratings of hyperactive behavior (impulsive, fidgety, distractible, confused, insensitive, frustrated, tense, wild, and extroverted; Stevens, 1981) or ratings of intelligence, classroom behavior, personality, and social relationships (Frame, Clarizio, Porter, & Vinsonhaler, 1982). In the Stevens study, clinicians read brief history information and watched films of children in a classroom setting. In the Frame et al. study, clinicians were given case history information and test results. In two other studies (Nalven, Hofmann, & Bierbryer, 1969; Sattler & Kuncik, 1976), school psychologists and clinical psychologists reviewed results on the Wechsler Intelligence Scale for Children (WISC). They were instructed to estimate "a S's 'true IQ' score, i.e., the score which best reflects the S's 'effective intelligence.' " Even though the children of different races were described by the same WISC profiles, estimates of 'effective intelligence' were higher for Black children and Mexican American children than for White children.

As with the assessment of children, when ratings were made for adult clients, ratings of personality traits and psychiatric symptoms were not more disparaging for Black clients than for White clients. For example, after clinicians read case histories, client race did not have a significant effect on ratings of emotional maturity, adequacy of sexual functioning, sexual aggressiveness, and social appropriateness of sexual behavior (Benefee, Abramowitz, Weitz, & Armstrong, 1976; Bloch, Weitz, & Abramowitz, 1980). For ratings of social maturity, client race did not affect White clinicians, but Black clinicians rated Black clients as being more socially mature than White clients (Benefee et al., 1976; Bloch et al., 1980). In a related study (Franklin, 1985), White clinicians, but not Black clinicians, judged a Black client as being more mature than a White client (even though they were described by the same case history). In this same study, client race did not significantly affect clinicians' ratings of degree of insight, anxiety level, and expected amount of acting out behavior. Similarly, Umbenhauer and DeWitte (1978) reported that client race was not significantly related to ratings of impulse control.

Similar to the results obtained when clinicians read case histories, when different groups of clinicians watched videotapes of African American and White actors portraying clients, ratings were not consistently more disparaging for Black clients than for White clients. In these studies, Black and White actors followed identical scripts. In the first study (Strickland, Jenkins, Myers, & Adams, 1988), actors portrayed clients who were normal, neurotic, or psychotic. The actors were trained for about 2 hours every week for 2 months on verbatim scripts to ensure that the psychopathology depicted across White and Black vignettes was equivalent. Black "normals" and Black "neurotic clients" were given lower ratings of verbal facility than their White counterparts, but Black "psychotic clients" were given higher ratings of verbal facility than White "psychotics."

In a second study (Ridley, 1986), the effect of race was not significant when clinicians made ratings of schizoid features, confusion, tension–anxiety, anger–hostility, or vigor–activity. Black clinicians rated White clients as being less friendly than Black clients, but race of client did not affect ratings of friendliness made by White clinicians. Finally, Black clinicians rated Black clients as being significantly less depressed than White clients, while White clinicians rated White clients as being significantly less depressed than Black clients.

In a third study (Jenkins-Hall & Sacco, 1991), depressed and nondepressed female clients complained of communication problems with their husbands. Scripts were written so that depressed confederates expressed pessimism and helplessness and nondepressed confederates expressed optimism or a matter-of-fact attitude. However, all of the clients complained of problems and they were all dissatisfied. Client race did not have a significant effect on ratings of hostility, anxiety, or fearfulness. However, in the nondepressed condition (but not the depressed condition), Blacks were rated as being significantly more depressed than Whites. Clinicians also made ratings on an adjective checklist and the Interpersonal Rating Scale. No significant differences were found for the nondepressed clients. However, in the depressed condition, Black clients were given more negative evaluations and were described as having poorer interpersonal skills. The statistical significance test was performed on composite scores not individual items. Though statistically significant, the size of the difference was small: The difference between the average composite score on the 17-item Adjective Checklist for Blacks (a score of 55) was significantly different from the average composite score for Whites (a score of 62). Ratings for the 17 individual items were made on 6-point rating scales.

In summary, the evidence indicates that the effect of client race is not statistically significant in the description of many personality traits and psychiatric symptoms. The effect of client race has been statistically significant for some tasks, but the ratings have not been consistently more disparaging for Black clients than White clients. Unfortunately, studies with statistically significant findings have not been replicated. Finally, when the effect of client race has been statistically significant, it has not been clear if the ratings have been less valid for the White clients or the Black clients. For example, in the Jenkins-Hall and Sacco (1991) study, Black clients in the nondepressed condition were described as being more depressed than White clients in the nondepressed condition, but it is not clear if the ratings were less valid for Blacks or Whites. After all, clients in the nondepressed condition still reported having some problems and dissatisfactions.

Asian American, White American, and Japanese Clients

Bias in the assessment of White American, Asian American, and Japanese clients has also been investigated. White American therapists may believe Asian American and Japanese clients are emotionally inhibited, and Asian American and Japanese therapists may believe White American clients are emotionally labile.

In two studies, White American clinicians and Japanese or Asian American clinicians made ratings after viewing videotapes of actual clients. Because clients were not actors following scripts, level of psychopathology was not equated across the different ethnic groups. Because all clinicians saw videotapes of all of the clients, conclusions can be drawn about the effect of clinician race on the judgments. In one of the studies (Tseng, McDermott, Ogino, & Ebata, 1982), Japanese and American psychiatrists viewed videotapes of Japanese and American families. American psychiatrists were more likely than Japanese psychiatrists to describe Japanese fathers as "not participating" and as "passive" in family interactions. In the other study (Li-Repac, 1980), five Chinese American and five White American psychologists viewed videotapes of interviews with five Chinese American and five White American clients. Two of the Chinese American psychologists and all five of the Chinese American clients were born in Hong Kong or China. White therapists were more likely than Chinese American therapists to rate the Chinese American clients as being depressed and inhibited (withdrawn, introverted, rigid in thought, flat in affect, and lacking energy). Also, White therapists were more likely than Chinese American therapists to describe Chinese American clients as being less socially poised (less likely to be socially perceptive, less likely to have satisfying interpersonal relationships). Chinese American therapists were more likely than White therapists to describe the White clients as being disturbed (more likely to have unusual thought associations, bizarre behavior, inappropriate affect, and poor reality testing). Statistically significant differences were not found for ratings of submissiveness–dependence, expressive ability, or anxiety.

Social Class Bias

If social class bias exists, one might expect clinicians to make more negative ratings of personality and psychopathology for lower-class children and adults than for middle- or upper-class children and adults. However, in most studies, as discussed below, the effect of social class was not statistically significant.

When ratings were made for children, social class effects were generally not statistically significant. Children's social class did not have a significant effect on ratings of hyperactive behavior (Stevens, 1981); ratings of intelligence, classroom behavior, personality, and social relationships (Frame, Clarizio, Porter, & Visonhaler, 1982); or ratings of "true IQs" and "effective intelligence" (Sattler & Kuncik, 1976; though also see Nalven et al., 1969).

When clinicians were given case history information and ratings were made for adult clients, the effect of social class was sometimes statistically significant when personality traits were rated, but was never statistically significant when psychiatric symptoms were rated. For example, social class effects were not significant when clinicians made ratings of (a) impulse control (Umbenhauer & DeWitte, 1978); (b) 6 personality traits including warmth, activity, and strength and 12 psychiatric symptoms including impaired judgment, suspiciousness, and thought disorder (Settin, 1982); (c) degree of insight, level of maturity, anxiety level, and expected amount of acting out behavior (Franklin, 1985); and (d) motivation for change and capacity for insight (Hardy & Johnson, 1992). Social class was significant when clinicians made ratings of self-concept (e.g., an unemployed welfare recipient was rated as having lower self-esteem than a commercial artist; Sutton & Kessler, 1986). Similarly, lower class clients were less often described as being self-confident, independent, permissive, and democratic than were middle-class clients (Briar, 1961).

Results were more confusing when clinicians used Rorschach results to make their judgments. Results ranged from bias against lower class clients (Levy & Kahn, 1970) to bias against middle-class clients (Koscherak & Masling, 1972) to reports of no bias (Trachtman, 1971). Clinicians made similar, and at times identical, ratings in the different studies, for example, ratings of personality traits and defense mechanisms.

The occurrence of social class bias may depend not only on the rating task and the information given to the clinicians, but also on individual differences among the clinicians. Social class bias has been found to be a function of the clinician's authoritarianism (Kurtz, Kurtz, & Hoffnung, 1970). In the Kurtz et al. study, 16 first-year graduate students in social work and 24 residents in psychiatry made ratings using three evaluative scales of the semantic differential (good–bad, awkward–graceful, beautiful–ugly). Clinicians high on authoritarianism judged the lower class protocols more negatively than the middle-class protocols. The results were statistically significant for the psychiatric residents and were of borderline statistical significance for the student social workers.

Gender Bias

The effect of client gender on ratings of personality traits and psychiatric symptoms has been negligible. In all but one of the studies reviewed, groups of clinicians read case histories that were identical except for the designation of gender.[1] In most of the studies, the effects of client gender were nonsignificant when ratings were made for a range of personality traits and psychiatric symptoms (Adams & Betz, 1993; Agell & Rothblum, 1991; Garfinkle & Morin, 1978; Hardy & Johnson, 1992; Hecker, Trepper, Wetchler, & Fontaine, 1995; López, Smith, Wolkenstein, & Charlin, 1993; Nalven et al., 1969). In another study (Stearns, Penner, & Kimmel, 1980), the effect of client gender was significant for only 2 of 22 ratings of personality traits: Men were rated as being more masculine and less competent. Similarly, in another study (Fischer, Dulaney, Fazio, Hudak, & Zivotofsky, 1976), female clients were rated as being more emotionally mature and intelligent. However, in a replication of this study (Dailey, 1980), the effect of client gender on ratings of emotional maturity was nonsignificant and female clients were rated as being less intelligent. Also, in another study (Settin & Bramel, 1981), female participants were rated as being less competent than males. Finally, just as significant findings for ratings of intelligence, maturity, and competency were not replicated in later studies, significant findings for ratings of aggressiveness, ambition, and independence (Hayes & Wolleat, 1978) were not replicated in later studies (Agell & Rothblum, 1991; Garfinkle & Morin, 1978; Settin & Bramel, 1981). Thus, the effect of client gender has usually not been significant, and the few significant findings that have been reported have not been replicated.

Additional Biases

There are other patient variables—client age, physical attractiveness, obesity, physical disability, sexual orientation, and gender role—that researchers have explored for rater bias. In over half of the studies reviewed in these areas, groups of clinicians were given case history information or test results that were identical except for the designation of the patient variable that was manipulated by the experimenters. In the other studies, groups of clinicians viewed videotapes of intake interviews with actors portraying clients.

The effect of client age on ratings was generally nonsignificant. Further-

---

[1]In the study by Hayes & Wolleat, 1978, clinicians listened to audiotapes of actors portraying clients.

more, the few significant findings that have been reported have not been replicated. In one study (Nalven et al., 1969), clinicians were given results from the Wechsler Intelligence Scale for Children (scaled scores and Full Scale IQ score) and were told either that the child was 8 or 14 years old. The effect of client age on ratings of true IQs and effective intelligence was not statistically significant. Apparently, clinicians do not believe that the validity of the Wechsler Intelligence Scale for Children varies with the age of the child. In a second study (James & Haley, 1995), psychologists read a case history that described a depressed client and were told that the client was 35 years old or 70 years old. The effect of age was not significant when the psychologists made ratings of 14 personality traits. In a third study (Settin, 1982), the effect of client age was not statistically significant for ratings of 13 of 16 personality traits and psychiatric symptoms. With regard to the effects that were statistically significant, a client was rated as being (psychologically) stronger, but more disoriented and more likely to have a thought disorder, when described as being elderly (72 years old) than when described as being middle aged (46 years old).

There has long been speculation that there is a halo effect for physcial attractiveness—that an attractive client will be judged to have more positive personality traits than will a less attractive client. However, the effect of physical attractiveness has not been statistically significant when clinicians have made ratings of personality traits (Schwartz & Abramowitz, 1978; but also see Hobfoll & Penner, 1978). In the study conducted by Schwartz and Abramowitz (1978), the level of personality traits was controlled by having an actress portray both the attractive and unattractive clients. In this study, clinical and counseling psychology graduate students viewed one of four videotapes of an actress portraying a client. In two of the videotapes, the actress was made-up (glasses, blemishes added) to mask her natural attractiveness. In the other videotapes, she followed the same script, but was not made-up to appear unattractive. Severity of psychiatric symptoms was also manipulated: The actress portrayed clients having mild or severe test anxiety. Regardless of whether test anxiety was mild or severe, the effect of attractiveness was not statistically significant when the clinicians made ratings for the following 16 personality traits: truthful, intelligent, warm, mature, interesting, kind, thoughtful, trustworthy, unforgiving, ill tempered, hostile, selfish, annoying, greedy, narrow minded, and spiteful.

The effect of obesity was statistically significant for a number of ratings, particularly when clients were described as being severely depressed. When clients were described as being moderately depressed and having problems at school or work, obese clients were rated as more often experiencing embarrassment and more often being self-conscious, but they were also rated as being kinder and they were not rated as being more sad, tense, depressed, lazy or weak willed, dull or bored, dependent, or angry (Agell & Rothblum, 1991). When clients were described as being severely depressed and having suicidal ideation, obese clients were rated more severely than overweight clients on the following symptoms: agitation, emotional behavior, impaired judgment, inadequate hygiene, inappropriate behavior, obsessive–compulsive behavior, self-injurious behavior, and stereotyped behavior (Young & Powell, 1985). The results occurred even though in both studies the clients were described by the same case histories except for being designated as being obese, overweight, or of average weight. Interestingly, female, young, and average-weight therapists were significantly more likely to be biased in their ratings.

The effect of a client having a physical disability was not statistically significant when clinical and counseling psychology graduate students made ratings of symptoms of depression (Elliott, Frank, & Brownlee-Duffeck, 1988). In this study, videotapes of an actor portraying a client differed with respect to the presence or absence of cues revealing a spinal cord injury. When ratings were made for 21 symptoms of depression (e.g., crying spells, feeling guilty, libido loss), the effect of physical disability was statistically significant for only one symptom: disturbed body image.

The effect of the health of a client had a statistically significant, but tiny, effect on ratings of personality traits (James & Haley, 1995). In the James and Haley study, psychologists read a case history that described a depressed client. When 371 psychologists made ratings of 14 personality traits, the health of the client (good health vs. congenital heart disease) had a very small effect on ratings, with healthy clients being given slightly more favorable personality ratings than unhealthy clients: Mean ratings for healthy and unhealthy clients differed by less than .5 (ratings were made using a 7-point rating scale).

Although the effect of client gender on ratings of traits and symptoms was negligible, the effect of sex-role behavior and the effect of sexual orientation seem to be important. Sex-role behavior refers to whether a client conforms to a traditional sex role. In a study on the effect of sex-role behavior (Robertson & Fitzgerald, 1990), licensed marriage and family therapists watched one of two videotapes. The same actor portrayed a client in both videotapes. The two videotapes were "virtually identical" (p. 4), but in one videotape the client was portrayed as being primarily responsible for taking care of the home and children while his wife was employed as an engineer, and in the second videotape the client was portrayed as being an engineer while his wife took care of the home and children. In both videotapes, the client explicitly stated that his marriage was satisfactory. He said, "My wife's not the problem. My kids . . . they aren't the problem either. I'm the problem" (p. 4). When clinicians made ratings of personality traits, the nontraditional client was rated as being less masculine (e.g., less independent, assertive, forceful, ambitious) than the traditional client, but was not rated as being more feminine.

In a second study on sex-role behavior (Dailey, 1983), clients who were described as having both aggressive and passive personality characteristics were judged to be significantly more mature and intelligent than clients who were described as having only passive personality characteristics or only aggressive personality characteristics. This occurred even though clinicians read identical case histories except for the designation of sex-role behavior.

In a study on sexual orientation (Garfinkle & Morin, 1978), lesbian and gay male clients were rated less favorably than heterosexual male and female clients. This occurred even though all of the clients were described by the same case histories except for the designation of gender and sexual orientation. The lesbian and gay male clients were rated by psychologists as having less favorable values than the heterosexual clients on the following four adjective pairs: *gentle–rough*, *quiet–loud*, *easily experiences tender feelings–does not easily express tender feelings*, and *strong need for security–little need for security*. Lesbian and gay male clients were not rated more or less favorably than female and male heterosexual clients on seven other factors including a factor reflecting psychological health, which was defined as evidenced by intelligence, contact with reality, and personality integration.

Labeling Effects

Labeling effects occur when clinicians are influenced by the diagnoses that have been made for a client or patient. According to Rosenhan (1973), "Once a person is designated abnormal, all of his other behaviors and characteristics are colored by that label" (p. 253).

Anecdotal evidence has been presented to support the argument that labeling effects occur when clinicians describe personality traits and psychopathology. For example, in one study (Temerlin & Trousdale, 1969), clinical psychologists and psychiatrists listened to a tape recording of an interview with an actor who was instructed to portray a "relaxed, confident, and productive man" (p. 24). Before listening to the interview, clinicians were told that an expert clinician believes that the client "looked neurotic but actually was quite psychotic" (p. 25). The clinicians were harsh in how they described the client. For example, one psychiatrist wrote the following narrative: "This individual appears like a boastful, self-reassured [sic], outspoken person, striving to conceal deep concern for shortcomings which he seems to be partially aware of" (p. 26). In another study (Rosenhan, 1973), "normal" people (confederates of the experimenter) went to psychiatric hospitals and complained of hearing voices. They were admitted to the hospitals, and on occasion staff viewed their behavior as inappropriate or abnormal even though the subjects were not trying to act abnormally. Unfortunately, in both studies, the experimenters reported anecdotal, but not quantitative, data when reporting results for clinicians' descriptions of personality traits and psychopathology (though they did code and analyze data on diagnosis; those results will be described in the next chapter).

Empirical data on labeling bias have been collected and analyzed in subsequent studies. Though results on the occurrence of labeling effects are mixed, overall the results do not support Rosenhan's assertion that "once a person is designated abnormal, all of his other behaviors and characteristics are colored by that label" (p. 253). For example, in one study (O'Connor & Smith, 1987), undergraduate students and trainee social workers watched videotapes of interviews. Before watching videotapes, they were told that all of the clients had been seen at a mental health center and were given the clients' diagnoses (schizophrenia, normal, or no diagnosis assigned). In reality, none of the interviewees had attended a mental health center and the labels were randomly assigned. Undergraduate students rated the pseudo-clients with diagnoses of schizophrenia as more deviant on measures of social skill. Trainee social workers did not.

Similarly, in three other studies (Herbert, Nelson, & Herbert, 1988; Lee, Barak, Uhlemann, & Patsula, 1995; Lee, Richer, & Uhlemann, 1992), labeling effects did not occur when clinical and counseling psychologists and trainees described whether a client is depressed or described behaviors that are related to depression. The psychologists had been randomly assigned to either a label condition (e.g., "client diagnosed with Dysthymic Disorder by a referral source in the community") or a no-label condition.

In a final study (Lewis & Appleby, 1988), a labeling effect was found. Psychiatrists read case histories that were deliberately restricted in amount of information so that the clinicians would be forced to make inferences. Different versions of the case described the client as having been diagnosed as having a personality disorder, diagnosed as having a depressive disorder, or not previously being given a diagnosis. Clients who had been diagnosed as having a personality disorder were rated as being more manipulative, attention seeking, difficult to manage, and annoying. This labeling effect had a more powerful effect on clinical ratings than did sex and social class, which had also been manipulated by the experimenters.

Bias to Perceive Psychopathology

Clinicians' judgments are consistently less favorable than laypersons' judgments, irrespective of whether judgments are made for normal or psychologically impaired populations (for a review, see Wills, 1978). Of course, if psychopathology is present, a bias to perceive psychopathology can lead clinicians to make accurate judgments. However, bias for perceiving psychopathology has not been positively related to the validity of judgments.

In one study (Garner & Smith, 1976), judges watched 1-minute videotape segments of 10 children, 5 of whom were intellectually normal and 5 of whom were developmentally disabled. Judges estimated each child's level of intellectual functioning. Clinicians and trainees in a professional program made lower estimates than undergraduate students, irrespective of whether the child was normal or developmentally disabled. Undergraduates were more accurate for ratings of normal children, but the professionals were more accurate for ratings of the developmentally disabled children.

The addition of psychological test data may cause clinicians to make more negative ratings of personality traits and psychopathology. This occurred in two studies when clinicians were to describe the interests, attitudes, and behavior patterns of a normal individual (Soskin, 1954, 1959). In these studies, the addition of Rorschach and TAT results led clinicians to pick more alternatives that were suggestive of maladjustment than adjustment. Validity did not increase with the addition of the Rorschach or TAT.

Clinicians may see both normal and psychologically impaired clients as being more impaired than they really are. For example, Graham (1967) reported that in his study accuracy was low for severely disturbed patients, possibly because when clinicians believed a patient was psychotic they thought the patient would have many psychotic symptoms, but in reality a psychotic patient may have few psychotic symptoms. The issue of whether clinicians make more accurate ratings for normal or psychiatric patients would seem to depend in part on the items clinicians make ratings for. For example, if items describe a range of psychotic symptoms, clinicians may make more valid ratings for normal than for psychiatric patients.

SUMMARY AND DISCUSSION

Working toward good reliability remains a goal for clinicians. Interrater reliability is poor for describing defense mechanisms, varies widely for describing personality traits, and may often be good for describing psychiatric symptoms. Intercenter and international differences in describing personality traits and psychiatric symptoms probably exist, though research on this topic is over 20 years old. Stability of ratings (reliability across time) has been reported to be fair or good for a range of tasks. However, stability of ratings has not been studied for some key tasks, such as the description of personality traits for depressed clients. Finally, convergence (e.g., reliability across psychological tests) has frequently been poor.

Training, but not experience, was related to the validity of judgments. For some tasks, but not for other tasks, judgments made by psychologists and advanced graduate students were more valid than those made by lay judges and beginning graduate students. Psychologists who were thought to be experts did not make more valid judgments than other psychologists. Finally, judgments made by psychologists were generally not more valid than those made by graduate students.

Confidence ratings were often not appropriate. Clinicians were over-confident when they made ratings for normal subjects, and confidence was not positively related to validity when clinicians made ratings using projective test results. Confidence ratings were appropriate when clinicians were given MMPI protocols, but only for some tasks.

Results on incremental validity varied widely. Clinicians who were able to see and hear interviews were not more accurate than clinicians who read transcripts of interviews. The incremental validity of interview data, when added to brief biographical information and test protocols, was positive. The incremental validity of history data was better when ratings were made for psychiatric patients than when ratings were made for normal participants. Finally, incremental validity has been fair when ratings were made by using the MMPI, but not when they were made by using projective test data.

Correlations between clinical judgments and indicator measures frequently range from .30 to .40. The development of better indicator measures will make it easier to understand and interpret results on the validity of clinical judgments.

Many of the studies on the comparison of clinical judgments and indicator ratings are from the 1950s and 1960s. New methods can be used to evaluate the validity of clinical judgments. For example, the act-frequency approach, behavior sampling and psychometric methods, and structured interviews can be used to make construct indicator ratings.

In many instances, clinicians do not attend to empirical research. Research on illusory correlations indicates that clinicians may believe that they are basing their judgments on their clinical experiences, but instead they may be responding to the verbal associations of test indicators. This has been demonstrated for clinicians using the Rorschach and Draw-a-Person tests.

Empirical research indicates that the effects of gender, age, physical attractiveness, and physical disability are typically not significant when clinicians describe personality traits and psychiatric symptoms. The effect of race is generally not significant when ratings are made for African American, Mexican American, and White clients, but at times may be important when ratings are made for White and Asian American or Japanese clients. The effect of social class is typically not significant when ratings are made for psychiatric symptoms, but is sometimes significant when ratings are made for personality traits. Finally, the effect of sexual orientation and the effect of sex-role behavior seem to be important when ratings are made for personality traits, and the effect of obesity may be important when ratings are made for psychiatric symptoms.

A labeling effect was significant when psychiatrists read case histories that were deliberately restricted in amount of information so that the clinicians would be forced to make inferences. Labeling effects were not statistically significant when judgments were more closely tied to the behaviors that clinicians were allowed to observe, for example, when clinicians were to rate whether depressive symptoms were reported during an interview.

Clinicians may make overly negative ratings of personality traits and psychiatric symptoms. When clinicians and lay judges describe normal or psychologically impaired individuals, clinicians perceive more psychopathology than do lay judges. Also, the addition of psychological test data to interview information can cause clinicians to make negative ratings of personality traits and psychopathology. When this has occurred, the addition of the test data did not lead to an increase in the validity of judgments.

In evaluating these results, it is important to recognize that clinicians can make reliable and valid judgments—if they guard against overperceiving psychopathology and if they are careful about the information they use and the types of judgments they make. For example, reliability and validity are likely to be fair when clinicians make ratings of psychiatric symptoms, at least when the ratings are based on interviews or objective test results. The results also support the value of training but, surprisingly, not the value of clinical experience.

2

PSYCHODIAGNOSIS

The most commonly used diagnostic classification system in the United States is the American Psychiatric Association's *Diagnostic and Statistical Manual of Mental Disorders*, Fourth Edition (1994; commonly referred to as *DSM–IV*). Using *DSM–IV*, clinicians make ratings on the following five axes: Axis I—mental disorders and conditions other than personality disorders and mental retardation; Axis II—personality disorders, mental retardation, and maladaptive personality features and defense mechanisms; Axis III—general medical conditions; Axis IV—psychosocial and environmental problems; and Axis V—global assessment of functioning (level of adjustment). Diagnoses of personality disorders and mental retardation are made on a separate axis "to ensure that consideration will be given to the possible presence of Personality Disorders and Mental Retardation that might otherwise be overlooked when attention is directed to the usually more florid Axis I disorders" (American Psychiatric Association, 1994, p. 26).

To improve interrater reliability, criteria for Axis I and Axis II disorders are written to be specific and explicit. For example, Criterion A for the diagnosis of schizophrenia specifies that the diagnosis should be made only if the following symptoms are present for a significant amount of time during a 1-month period (or less if successfully treated): (a) bizarre delusions; (b) auditory hallucinations of a voice keeping up a running commentary on the person's thoughts or behavior; (c) auditory hallucinations of two or more voices conversing with each other; or (d) two or more of the following symptoms: delusions, hallucinations, disorganized speech, grossly disorganized or catatonic behavior, or negative symptoms, such as, flat affect (American Psychiatric Association, 1994, p. 285). In addition to satisfying Criterion A, a diagnosis of schizophrenia should not be assigned unless the person also meets criteria related to social or occupational dysfunction, duration of signs of the disturbance, and the exclusion of the following disorders as a cause of the disturbance: schizoaffective disorder, mood disorder with psychotic features, a substance abuse disorder, and a general medical condition. An additional criterion must be satisfied when diagnosing schizophrenia for an individual with autistic disorder or another pervasive developmental disorder.

The focus of this chapter is on how well clinicians make diagnoses. Topics that relate to the reliability and validity of clinicians' diagnoses, but not to the validity of diagnostic criteria, include: (a) interrater reliability in using diagnostic criteria; (b) the extent of adherence to criteria when making diagnoses; (c) the relation between presumed expertise, experience, training, and the validity of diagnoses; (d) the relation between the confidence of clinicians and the validity of judgments; (e) the effects of patient variable biases including race, gender, and age biases on the use of diagnostic criteria; and (f) the occurrence of errors including context and labeling effects, the overperception of psychopathology, diagnostic overshadowing, and the overdiagnosis and underdiagnosis of different disorders.

RELIABILITY AND ADHERENCE TO CRITERIA

Reliability

For most purposes, reliability is most appropriately evaluated by calculating kappa or an intraclass correlation (e.g., Langenbucher, Labouvie, & Morgenstern, 1996). Reliability is generally thought to be poor if values for an intraclass correlation coefficient or kappa coefficient are below .40, fair if values are between .40 and .59, good if values are between .60 and .74, and excellent if values are .75 or greater (Cicchetti & Sparrow, 1981; Fleiss, 1981, p. 218).

Results for psychodiagnoses (Axes I and II) and for ratings of level of adustment (Axis V) are described in this section. Reliability for ratings of psychosocial stressors (Axis IV) will be discussed in the chapter on case formulation. Reliability is not described for diagnoses of medical conditions (Axis III).

Psychodiagnoses

The reliability of psychodiagnoses made for research projects dramatically improved during the 1970s. Three reasons for this improvement have been noted (Grove, Andreasen, McDonald-Scott, Keller, & Shapiro, 1981). First, training improved for raters who make diagnoses in large-scale research projects. Second, diagnostic criteria were made more specific and explicit.

Third, structured interviews for making diagnoses were developed. However, though there is a general consensus that the reliability of research diagnoses has improved, criteria may not be applied in exactly the same way at different research centers (Zimmerman, Coryell, & Black, 1993). For example, research teams at the University of Pittsburgh and the University of Iowa have used different cutoff scores on the Schedule for Affective Disorders and Schizophrenia (SADS; Endicott & Spitzer, 1978) and on the Hamilton Rating Scale for Depression (Hamilton, 1967) when rating symptoms of *DSM–III* melancholia (Kupfer & Frank, 1984; Zimmerman, Coryell, Pfohl, & Stangl, 1985).

One may wonder if clinicians in everyday practice are able to make reliable psychodiagnoses. On the one hand, structured and semistructured interviews are not normally used in everyday clinical practice. Also, many practicing clinicians have not had intensive training in psychodiagnosis. On the other hand, since the publication of *DSM–III* (*Diagnostic and Statistical Manual of Mental Disorders*, 3rd edition; American Psychiatric Association, 1980), specific and explicit diagnostic criteria have been widely available.

With the publication of *DSM–III* in 1980, acceptable levels of reliability have been obtained for many, but not all, diagnostic categories (e.g., Grove, 1987; Matarazzo, 1983; but see Kutchins & Kirk, 1986, for an opposing point of view). Overall unweighted kappa coefficients for phase one ($n = 339$) and phase two ($n = 331$) of the *DSM–III* field trials were .68 and .72 for Axis I diagnostic classes for adults, .56 and .64 for Axis II diagnostic classes for adults, .68 and .52 for Axis I diagnostic classes for children, and .66 and .55 for Axis II diagnostic classes for children (American Psychiatric Association, 1980, pp. 470–471; also see Spitzer, Forman, & Nee, 1979). However, these kappa coefficients describe interrater reliability for general diagnostic categories (e.g., schizophrenia), rather than for many specific diagnostic categories (e.g., subtypes of schizophrenia).

In a subsequent study on the use of *DSM–III* (Mellsop, Varghese, Joshua, & Hicks, 1982), lower kappa coefficients were obtained for the diagnosis of personality disorders in adults. When clinicians judged if a personality disorder was present or absent, the kappa coefficient for interrater agreement was reported to be only .41. Interrater reliability was even lower when clinicians made diagnoses for specific personality disorders. For example, the kappa coefficient for the diagnosis of borderline personality disorder was only .29.

More recently, two large-scale international field trials (both of which were sponsored by the Division of Mental Health of the World Health Organization) have been conducted on the interrater reliability of diagnoses made by clinicians using the 10th revision of the *International Classification of Diseases (ICD–10)*. Different versions of the *ICD–10* have been prepared, including one designed for use in clinical settings and one for use in research settings. The versions differ in degree of detail and ease of use, but are compatible with one another.

The field trial for the clinical version of the *ICD–10* was conducted in 39 countries at 112 clinical centers with 711 clinicians who performed 15,302 assessments (Sartorius et al., 1993). Results were presented for specific diagnoses as well as for general diagnostic categories. Kappa coefficients were calculated for 10 two-character diagnoses (e.g., organic mental disorders), 31 three-character diagnoses (e.g., dementia in Alzheimer's disease), and 55 four-character diagnoses (e.g., dementia in Alzheimer's disease, senile onset). Overall kappa coefficients were .81 for the two-character diagnoses, .71 for the three-character diagnoses, and .59 for the four-character diagnoses. Though overall interrater reliability was excellent for the two-character diagnoses, good for the three-character diagnoses, and fair for the four-character diagnoses, interrater reliability was poor ($\kappa < .40$) for many of the four-character diagnoses. The lowest kappa coefficients were obtained for the diagnosis of histrionic personality disorder ($\kappa = .12$), impulsive personality disorder ($\kappa = .21$), and mixed anxiety and depressive disorder ($\kappa = .23$). Historically, it has been hard to obtain good interrater reliability for diagnoses of personality disorders and diagnoses of childhood mental disorders. In the *ICD–10* clinical field trial, kappa coefficients were .47 for personality disorder and .74 for disorders of childhood onset.

The field trial for the research version of the *ICD–10* was conducted in 32 countries at 151 clinical centers with 942 clinicians and researchers who performed 11,491 assessments (Sartorius, Üstün, Korten, Cooper, & van Drimmelen, 1995). Interrater reliability was even better for the research version of the *ICD–10* than for the clinical version of the *ICD–10*. For example, kappa coefficients were .61 for personality disorder and .94 for disorders of childhood onset. Furthermore, interrater reliability was excellent or good for the 10 two-character diagnoses; generally excellent or good for the three-character diagnoses, and generally good or fair for the four-character diagnoses. Diagnostic categories with poor interrater reliability were (a) recurrent depressive disorder, current episode mild ($\kappa = .30$), (b) mixed anxiety and depressive disorder ($\kappa = .09$), (c) histrionic personality disorder ($\kappa = .25$), and (d) anxious personality disorder ($\kappa = .33$). The criteria for these diagnostic categories were modified in the final version of the *ICD–10 Diagnostic Criteria for Research* as a result of the field trial.

Ratings of Level of Adjustment

Questions have been raised about the interrater reliability of ratings of level of adjustment. In the *DSM–III* field trials, ratings of level of adaptive functioning were made on Axis V by using a 6-point scale (the final published version of *DSM–III* had a 7-point rating scale). Intraclass correlation coefficients for phase-one and phase-two studies were .75 ($n = 321$) and .80

(n = 316) for adults and .77 (n = 67) and .52 (n = 53) for children. Though interrater reliability in the field trials was excellent for ratings made for adults, in a later study on the use of *DSM–III* with adults (Fernando, Mellsop, Nelson, Peace, & Wilson, 1986), an intraclass correlation coefficient of only .49 was obtained for Axis V ratings.

When using *DSM–IV*, one is supposed to use the Global Assessment of Functioning (GAF) Scale to make ratings of level of functioning on Axis V. Using this scale, one makes a rating from 1 to 100, with a rating of 1 indicating "Persistent danger of severely hurting self or others (e.g., recurrent violence) Or persistent inability to maintain minimal personal hygiene Or serious suicidal act with clear expression of death" and a rating of 100 indicating "Superior functioning in a wide range of activities, life's problems never seem to get out of hand, is sought out by others because of his or her many positive qualities. No symptoms" (American Psychiatric Association, 1994, p. 32). Other points on the scale are also defined.

In a recent study on Axis V ratings made by using *DSM–IV* (Loevdahl & Friis, 1996), interrater reliability was described as being unsatisfactory. In this study, 104 clinicians made ratings after reading five clinical case vignettes. The difference between the highest score and the lowest score for each case vignette, averaged across all five, was 43 points. The average difference between the scores at the 10th and 90th percentiles was 22 points (thus the highest 10% of the ratings differed from the lowest 10% of the ratings by an average of at least 22 points). Unfortunately, intraclass correlation coefficients were not calculated to describe the overall level of reliability.

Adherence to Criteria

A reason why interrater reliability was good for clinicians who participated in the *DSM–III* and *ICD–10* field trials is that these clinicians were familiar with, and presumably adhered to, the diagnostic criteria. For example, in the *ICD–10* field trials, practice assessments were conducted to help the clinicians and clinician–researchers become familiar with the criteria.

One would expect reliability to be relatively low when clinicians adhere to diagnostic criteria in an idiosyncratic or excessively flexible manner. Thus, it is significant that empirical research indicates that clinicians frequently do not attend to criteria when they make diagnoses (Blashfield & Herkov, 1996; Davis, Blashfield, & McElroy, 1993; Jampala, Sierles, & Taylor, 1988; Lipkowitz & Idupuganti, 1985; Morey & Ochoa, 1989; Rubinson, Asnis, & Friedman, 1988). For example, in one of the studies (Davis et al., 1993), 42 psychologists and 17 psychiatrists read case histories and made diagnoses. Case histories contained varying numbers of the *DSM–III–R* criteria (American Psychiatric Association, 1987) for narcissistic personality disorder. A clinician adhering to the *DSM–III–R* criteria will make a diagnosis of narcissistic personality disorder if and only if five or more of the criteria are satisfied.

Davis et al. reported that diagnoses of narcissistic personality disorder were made by 22% of the clinicians when two criteria were satisfied, 72% of the clinicians when four criteria were satisfied, and 78% of the clinicians when six criteria were satisfied.

In perhaps the best-known study on adherence to diagnostic criteria, Morey and Ochoa (1989) sent questionnaires to a national sample of psychologists and psychiatrists. Each clinician was to describe a client who (a) had been diagnosed as having a personality disorder and (b) had been seen by the clinician in at least 10 hours of contact during the past year. The 291 clinicians who participated in the study were instructed to make diagnoses that were consistent with *DSM–III*. They were then asked to complete symptom checklists. The experimenters made criterion-based *DSM–III* diagnoses using the 166-item checklists, which contained (verbatim) every criterion listed in the *DSM–III* personality disorders section. Clinical diagnoses were compared to criterion-based diagnoses. More than one diagnostic error per patient was possible. For example, if a clinician diagnosed a client as having a narcissistic personality disorder while the criterion-based diagnosis was histrionic personality disorder, then the clinician would have made two errors: (a) overdiagnosis of narcissistic personality disorder and (b) underdiagnosis of histrionic personality disorder. The results indicate that clinical diagnoses of personality disorders often diverge from the rules designated in *DSM–III*. For example, the mean number of diagnostic errors per case was 1.4. In only 28% of the cases were no diagnostic inconsistencies found. Kappa coefficients, measuring the amount of agreement between clinicians' diagnoses and criterion-based *DSM–III* diagnoses for different diagnostic categories, ranged from .09 to .59.

Other results also indicate that clinicians do not adhere closely to diagnostic criteria. For example, studies described later in this chapter on race, gender, age, and other biases show that at least some clinicians do not attend closely to criteria. If they did, these biases would not occur.

To improve adherence with criteria, diagnostic criteria have been simplified. For *DSM–IV*, efforts were made to reduce the number of criteria listed for different disorders (e.g., Widiger et al., 1996). However, because many clinicians did not adhere to criteria when they used *DSM–III* and *DSM–III–R*, it may be wishful thinking to believe that they will adhere to *DSM–IV* criteria.

VALIDITY

Conceptual and Methodological Issues

How do we know when a diagnosis is correct or incorrect? If we cannot tell if diagnoses are correct or incorrect, then how can the validity of the diagnoses be evaluated? The issues are complex. For example, many research investigators believe that different people who have been diagnosed as having schizophrenia actually have distinct disorders that as yet are unidentified (e.g., Chapman, 1990; for a dissenting view see Meehl, 1990). The basis for this view is that in empirical studies (e.g., in studies on the course of the disorder and in studies on performance on neuropsychological tests), results for people with diagnoses of schizophrenia are frequently widely divergent. Also, many different organic disorders can cause patients to have symptoms that mimic schizophrenia and there may be additional disorders that have not yet been discovered that have the same effect (Davison & Bagley, 1969; Propping, 1983). If what is now thought of as schizophrenia is not a unitary disorder, then in what sense is a diagnosis of schizophrenia valid?

A second question will also illustrate the difficulty of evaluating the validity of diagnoses. If a diagnosis is made using test results and an interview, how can the validity of the diagnosis be evaluated? If a structured interview is used to make a criterion diagnosis, how can the validity of this criterion diagnosis be evaluated?

Open Concepts

When evaluating the validity of a diagnosis, it is helpful to recognize that mental disorders are *open concepts* (Meehl, 1986b): As more is learned about a mental disorder, one can expect the working definition of the disorder to change. A term (e.g., *schizophrenia*) can be useful even when we are aware that the meaning of the term will change as more empirical data are collected. Similarly, a term can be useful even though it cannot be defined precisely, except in an arbitrary way. Thus, though Carson (1990) noted that "there does not appear to be a single recognized diagnosis with either a precise core of meaning or clear boundaries that is not imposed by arbitrary decision rules" (p. 12), the validity of diagnoses is not necessarily poor. For example, according to Widiger and Trull (1985), "we cannot define absolutely or precisely what we mean by mental illness, but . . . there are enough indirect (convergent and discriminant) indicators to support the construct's validity" (p. 469).

It is unlikely that a mental disorder can be precisely and nonarbitrarily defined until there is a clear understanding of its nature and etiology (Meehl, 1986b). At the same time, a diagnosis can be moderately valid and useful even if only partial information about the nature, etiology, course, and treatment of the disorder exists.

Methods for Evaluating Validity

Five methods for studying the validity of a set of diagnoses are described in the following sections. The methods involve the use of (a) structured interviews, (b) the LEAD standard, (c) the Robins and Guze criteria, (d) construct validation procedures, and (e) latent class analysis.

Structured Interview Approach. One approach to evaluating the validity of a diagnosis is to compare it to a diagnosis made by using a structured interview. According to Wetzler and van Praag (1989)

> The structured interview represents the gold standard of psychiatric diagnosis . . . and all other assessment methods and vantage points must be evaluated against this criterion. While other assessment methods may approach this standard, the most that can possibly be said is that they are interchangeable with a structured interview diagnosis. (p. 73)

Thus, one could compare diagnoses made in clinical practice with those made by a structured interview. The results could be important because if there was a large discrepancy, one might want to recommend that clinicians use structured interviews in their clinical work.

If one believes that structured interviews represent "the gold standard of psychiatric diagnosis," then the value of using psychological tests to make diagnoses can be questioned. As argued by Goldstein and Hersen (1984)

> Those advocating the use of structured interviews point to the fact that in psychiatry, at least, tests must be ultimately validated against judgments made by psychiatrists. And these judgments are generally based on interviews and observation, since there really are no biological or objective markers of most forms of psychopathology. If that is indeed the case, there seems little point in administering elaborate and often lengthy tests when one can just as well use the criterion measure itself, the interview, rather than the test. (p. 5)

The premise of this argument is that one can only validate diagnoses made by using psychological tests by comparing them to diagnoses made by psychiatrists. This premise is false. Other methods for validating diagnoses can also be used.

Before describing other methods for validating diagnoses, problems with using structured interviews to validate diagnoses will be described. First, using a structured interview, one may not know if clients are malingering or "faking good." For example, in one study (Alterman et al., 1996), a group of methadone-maintenance patients were interviewed using a semistructured interview (the Addiction Severity Index; McLellan et al., 1985) and a structured interview (the NIMH Diagnostic Interview Schedule; Robins, Helzer, Croughan, & Ratcliff, 1981). All of the patients also completed a psychological test (the Personality Assessment Inventory; Morey, 1991b). The Personality Assessment Inventory has both a "fake good" and a "fake bad" validity scale. An interviewer reported that only 1 of the 229 patients did not seem to answer questions honestly. However, when the results of the psychological test and structured interviews are viewed together, they suggest that many of the patients were faking good or faking bad. Patients who scored high on the "fake bad" scale of the Personality Assessment Inventory reported having the severest levels of psychopathology during the interviews, and patients who scored high on the fake good scale reported having the lowest levels of psychopathology during the interviews.

There are other problems with using structured interviews to validate diagnoses. For many structured interviews, diagnoses are made by using only the interview data (e.g., the Diagnostic Interview Schedule [DIS]; Robins et al., 1981). These interviews have been criticized because their use leads to other sources of information being ignored (Brockington & Meltzer, 1982; Carpenter, Sacks, Strauss, Bartko, & Rayner, 1976; Spitzer, 1983). Research has demonstrated that diagnoses made by using structured interviews with patients often differ from diagnoses made by clinicians using information from medical records and interviews with patients and family members (Kosten & Rounsaville, 1992). Research has also demonstrated that participant reports in interviews are often inaccurate or incomplete. For example, in a longitudinal study (Henry, Moffitt, Caspi, Langley, & Silva, 1994), a large sample of 18-year-old youth were studied prospectively since birth. The retrospective reports of participants showed poor agreement with data that were collected prospectively.

For other structured or semistructured interviews, clinicians are instructed to base their diagnoses on information contained in medical records and information obtained from an interview (e.g., the Structured Clinical Interview for DSM–III–R [SCID–R]; Spitzer, Williams, Gibbon, & First, 1990). However, these interviews are also fallible. As noted by Rubinson and Asnis (1989)

> They require the use of considerable clinical judgment on the part of the interviewer. Not only must conflicting sources of information be evaluated, but questions can be open-ended so that a coding of criteria must be assessed and extrapolated from the subject's responses. (p. 61)

Thus, structured interviews do not represent an ultimate criterion for validating diagnoses.

Problems will occur if structured interviews are regarded as an ultimate criterion. For example, if structured interviews are used as an ultimate criterion, it will be impossible to tell if one structured interview is more valid than another. Also, it would be valuable if we could evaluate whether diagnoses are more valid when psychological test results are made available along with history and interview information. Unfortunately, if test results are added to history information and unstructured interview results and if criterion diagnoses are made by using structured interviews, then the incremental validity of test results may be underestimated because judgments made by using history and interview data alone will share methodological variance as well as substantive variance with the criterion diagnoses. For example, if interviewers share a bias (e.g., a race bias), then diagnoses based on structured interviews and diagnoses based on unstructured interviews may be in agreement in part because of this shared bias. This will make it more difficult for the addition of a psychological test to result in a meaningful increase in validity.

LEAD Procedure

Recognizing that there is no gold standard for validating psychodiagnoses, Spitzer (1983) proposed the LEAD standard for assessing the validity of diagnostic assessment instruments. LEAD is an acronym for *longitudinal, expert,* and *all data.* Using this admittedly imperfect approach, longitudinal data are collected (patients or clients are followed for a period of time), expert clinicians make judgments, and all data that are available are given to clinicians.

Compared to using structured interviews to make criterion diagnoses, the LEAD approach has several advantages. For example, one can learn about the validity of a structured interview with this approach. To do this, one could first administer a structured interview and make structured-interview diagnoses, then follow the patient for a period of time, and then make LEAD diagnoses. Another advantage of the LEAD approach is that it can be determined if the addition of psychological test results to structured-interview data leads to increased validity. To do this, one would make diagnoses based on structured interviews and structured interviews and test results, follow the patients over a period of time, and then make LEAD diagnoses.

Perhaps the most important feature of the LEAD approach is that longitudinal data are used to validate diagnoses. As already noted, clients' retrospective reports in interviews have frequently been in conflict with information that is collected prospectively. For example, a large number of studies have demonstrated that the assessment of personality traits and personality disorders is affected substantially by the mood of the participants (for references, see Widiger, 1993b, p. 78). People who are depressed tend to describe themselves as being dependent, self-conscious, introverted, pessimistic, and self-critical, but before their depressive episode they may not have had these traits. Stuart et al. (1992) have recommended that clinicians "defer definitive assessment of Axis II until an acute depressive disorder has been optimally treated" (p. 281). Thus, prospective data can be more accurate than data collected in a single interview.

Other aspects of the LEAD approach may not be as advantageous as one might presume. The use of expert clinicians can be valuable if by *expert* one means that clinicians are knowledgeable about diagnostic criteria and that they have demonstrated good interrater reliability. However, one should be aware that in at least some empirical studies, allegedly expert clinicians have not been more accurate than other clinicians (Garb, 1989). Also, interrater reliability for LEAD diagnoses has typically not been described (Widiger, 1993a, 1993c). One should also be aware that validity does not always increase as clinicians are given more information, even when clinicians believe that the additional information has helped them become more accurate (Garb, 1984).

The validity of LEAD diagnoses has not been studied. Results on the validity of expert, all-data diagnoses are available from one study (Pilkonis, Heape, Ruddy, & Serrao, 1991), but though the authors called these diagnoses LEAD diagnoses, they are not true LEAD diagnoses because information was not collected over time. At the time of the study, all of the patients were being treated for major depressive disorder. Diagnoses were made when participants first entered the study. Expert, all-data diagnoses were made on the basis of structured interviews with patients, interviews with the patients' significant others, and the results of psychological tests. It is widely believed that patients with personality disorders are less likely to do well in treatment for major depression. Patients with personality disorders identified by the expert, all-data procedure had worse outcomes at a 6-month follow-up assessment than patients who were not identified as having a personality disorder. Results were more pronounced when diagnoses were made by using the expert, all-data approach than when they were made by using structured interviews.

In the next two sections, methods for evaluating the validity of LEAD diagnoses are described. These methods are (a) the use of the Robins and Guze criteria and (b) the use of broader methods for evaluating construct validity.

Robins and Guze Criteria

In one of the most widely cited articles in the history of psychiatry, Robins and Guze (1970) described five phases of research involved in formulating and evaluating diagnostic criteria. The five phases of research are (a) describing the clinical picture, (b) delimiting the disorder from other disorders (specifying exclusion criteria), (c) conducting follow-up studies, (d) conducting family studies, and (e) conducting laboratory studies.

To validate diagnoses, one can conduct follow-up studies, family studies, and laboratory studies. By conducting follow-up studies, the longitudinal consistency of diagnoses can be evaluated, and treatment response and course of psychopathology can be related to diagnosis. A diagnosis can be considered to be valid if it does not change over time as more information is collected about a patient, and if it can be related to treatment response and course of psychopathology. The longitudinal consistency of diagnoses has been described in several studies (e.g., Beiser, Iacono, & Erickson, 1989; Kovacs & Gatsonis, 1989; Pilkonis et al., 1991). For example, according to Beiser et al. (1989), about one in five patients originally diagnosed as having major depression are later reclassified as having bipolar affective disorder. If clinicians could use a psychological test to identify persons with bipolar affective disorder who initially present with depression rather than mania, then this would support the validity of the psychological test. The validity of diagnoses has also been evaluated by looking at treatment response and course of psychopathology (e.g., Grove et al., 1987; Kovacs & Gatsonis, 1989; Pilkonis et al., 1991). If treatment response and course of psychopathology are related more strongly to diagnoses when diagnoses are made by psychologists using psychological tests and structured interviews rather than structured interviews alone, then the incremental validity of psychological tests will be supported.

One can also conduct family studies to validate diagnoses (e.g., Grove et al., 1987, 1991; Haier, Rosenthal, & Wender, 1978; Moldin, Gottesman, Erlenmeyer-Kimling, & Cornblatt, 1990; Moldin, Rice, Gottesman, & Erlenmeyer-Kimling, 1990a, 1990b). For example, Grove et al. (1991) sought to identify individuals who have a genetic predisposition for schizophrenia. On several tests (e.g., tests of smooth-pursuit eye movement and attention), first degree relatives of schizophrenics differed from medically and psychiatrically screened normal control subjects. Thus, the assessment instruments used to diagnose the schizophrenics were validated by conducting a family study.

Another method for validating diagnoses is to show that diagnoses are related to performance on laboratory tasks and results from biological measures. Many examples from the field of experimental psychopathology could be described to show that patients assigned to different diagnostic categories differ in how they perform on laboratory tasks and biological measures (e.g., see Iacono, 1991). McNally et al. (1987), using an auditory recognition task, found that when presented with target words related to Vietnam stressors (e.g., *firefight*), Vietnam combat veterans with posttraumatic stress disorder (PTSD) exhibited larger skin-conductance responses than control participants. In another study (Gerardi, Keane, Calhoon, & Klauminzer, 1994), participants were veterans who were waiting in the admissions area of a V.A. Medical Center. Cardiovascular arousal was higher for Vietnam veterans with combat-related PTSD than for Vietnam-era veterans with no combat experience. These results help to support the validity of the diagnoses of PTSD and the validity of the assessment instruments used to make the diagnoses. Additional studies on the use of biological measures to validate diagnoses have been reviewed by Kupfer and Thase (1989) and Carroll (1989).

A difference and a similarity between the Robins and Guze approach and the LEAD approach will be described. Using the LEAD approach, one generates criterion diagnoses. Investigators typically do not generate criterion diagnoses when using the Robins and Guze criteria. That is, one would not have an expert clinician make criterion diagnoses after looking at treatment response, prevalence of mental disorders among family members, performance on laboratory tasks and biological measures, and other information. The approaches do share one important similarity, though. Using both the LEAD approach and the Robins and Guze approach, one collects longitudinal data to evaluate the validity of diagnoses. A study that evaluates the validity of diagnoses by collecting data on the longitudinal consistency of diagnoses would be highly similar to a study using the LEAD procedure.

Construct Validity

Though the Robins and Guze criteria have had a substantial impact on research in psychodiagnosis, theoretical work on construct validation provides an even broader framework for evaluating the validity of diagnoses (e.g., Cronbach & Meehl, 1955; Hogan & Nicholson, 1988; Morey, 1991a; Skinner, 1981; Widiger, 1993a, 1993c). Using the construct validation approach, one places diagnoses in a theoretical context and then tests the theory. That is, construct validation involves the validation of a theory. Using this approach, one can go beyond relating diagnoses to follow-up data, family data, laboratory data, and biological data. For example, using a broader theoretical model, one can argue that diagnoses are not likely to be valid if large context effects and labeling biases occur or if diagnoses are strongly related to race, gender, or age bias.

Latent Class Analysis

One more method for validating diagnoses—latent class analysis—involves the use of statistical procedures to determine if data are dimensional or categorical. For example, latent class analysis can be used to try to determine if it is appropriate to say that individuals lie along a continuum or can be sorted into categories. Furthermore, if the results of a latent class analysis are valid, the probability that a person has a mental disorder (not how well a persons meets a set of criteria, but the probability of the person having the disorder) can be determined (Faraone & Tsuang, 1994). Put another way, given that a person has a particular constellation of symptoms and behaviors, a diagnostic manual of the future may be able to tell clinicians the probability that a diagnosis is correct. Using latent class analysis in this way is done by performing an analysis on the assessment information, not by analyzing the relation between assessment and criterion information. This is important because criterion information in the area of psychodiagnosis is fallible and will not allow calculation of the probability that a person really has a particular disorder.

To support their argument that latent class analysis can be used to estimate the accuracy of diagnoses, Faraone and Tsuang (1994) described studies on medical decision making. In these studies, latent class analyses were performed on assessment data (e.g., magnetic resonance imaging, computed tomography, and radionuclide scintigraphy data). The analyses yielded estimates for different diagnoses. These results were compared to results using a gold standard, such as diagnoses based on clinical follow-up, disease progression, and histopathology. The estimates were virtually identical to results obtained using the gold standard.

Several researchers have described problems with using the latent class analysis approach (Garb, 1996a; Grove & Andreasen, 1986, 1989; Miller, 1996; though also see Meehl, 1995, 1996). For example, some latent class detection and estimation methods depend on an assumption (assumption of local independence) that is not always tenable. Also, as Faraone and Tsuang (1994) acknowledged, one needs to have a strong justification for believing that the latent structure specified for the analysis actually exists. Otherwise accuracy estimates may be incorrect. This may be a minor problem in medicine when the etiology and nature of medical diseases is well understood, but it is a major problem in the area of psychodiagnosis. As previously mentioned, most mental disorders are open concepts and the latent structures for an area of psychopathology are frequently unknown. For example, according to Frances and Widiger (1986), there is no theoretical model to tell us how many categorical personality disorders exist: the number could range from none to 4,000.

Though latent class analyses have been validated in medicine (Faraone & Tsuang, 1994), they have received only mixed support in psychodiagnosis. For example, Golden and Meehl (1979) used taxometric analyses to construct a scale to identify individuals who are predisposed to having schizophrenia. This scale has not received empirical support (Chapman, Chapman, & Miller, 1982; Grove et al., 1991; Miller, Streiner, & Kahgee, 1982; Nichols & Jones, 1985; Van den Bosch, Rozendaal, & Mol, 1987; though see Asarnow, Nuechterlein, & Marder, 1983). On the other hand, Grove et al. (1987) used latent class analysis to investigate the nosology of endogenous depression. They isolated and characterized a nuclear depressive syndrome, and they described empirical research that supports the use of this diagnostic category.

Conclusions

Several methods can be used to study the validity of diagnoses. For example, studies comparing unstructured interviews or psychological tests to structured interviews can provide information about concurrent validity. The LEAD approach can be valuable if interrater reliability has been demonstrated to be good for the so-called expert clinicians, if longitudinal data are collected, and if the process of making diagnoses is well described. Also, one can expect clinicians making LEAD diagnoses to use structured interviews. The reliability and validity of LEAD diagnoses need to be described when they are used to evaluate the validity of diagnoses. The Robins and Guze criteria can be used to evaluate the validity of structured interview and LEAD diagnoses. Although the Robins and Guze criteria are valuable, the construct validation approach can provide greater flexibility for studying the validity of diagnoses. Finally, though the use of latent class analyses may gain in importance as further analytical work and Monte Carlo (computer simulation) investigations are completed, at the current time one should be cautious when using them to validate diagnoses.

Validity of Diagnoses

The following sections describe the validity of diagnoses made by clinicians. The use of interviews and history data and the use of psychological tests are discussed separately. Also, specific errors in diagnosis will be described including race bias, gender bias, age bias, context effects, labeling bias, and overlooked secondary diagnoses.

Validity, Interviews, and History Data

To evaluate the validity of diagnoses made by clinicians using interview and history data, several methods have been used. In older studies conducted prior to the advent of structured interviews, validity was evaluated by comparing clinicians' diagnoses to criterion diagnoses made by judges using all of the interview and history data usually available in clinical practice. However, if both clinicians and criterion judges are given extensive interview and history data, results will inform us about reliability rather than validity. Thus in the studies on validity, clinicians were given less interview and history data than was given to the criterion judges. For example, in one study (Kendell, 1973), psychiatrists made diagnoses after reading transcripts, listening to tape recordings, and viewing and listening to videotapes of interviews. The interviews were brief; they lasted only 2 to 5 minutes. The interview diagnoses were compared to patients' final hospital diagnoses, which were based on extensive information. Hit rates were not significantly different for the transcript diagnoses ($n = 218$), videotape diagnoses ($n = 252$), and tape recording diagnoses ($n = 263$; for related results in a study using a much smaller sample size, $N = 32$, see Rock & Bransford, 1992). These results are interesting, in part, because in studies on the description of personality and psychopathology, the addition of audio and visual cues to transcripts has also led to no increase in accuracy except when clinicians are not allowed to reread the transcripts (see chapter 1).

Validity has also been evaluated by comparing clinicians' diagnoses to diagnoses made by judges using structured interviews. When structured interview diagnoses have been compared to diagnoses made in clinical practice, agreement has been poor (e.g., Brockington, Kendell, & Leff, 1978; Molinari, Ames, & Essa, 1994; Steiner, Tebes, Sledge, & Walker, 1995).

For example, in the Steiner et al. (1995) study, clinical diagnoses made for 100 patients were compared to diagnoses made by research investigators using the SCID. A kappa coefficient was calculated for a diagnostic category only if the diagnosis was made $2k^2$ (eight) times, in accordance with a formula for the valid use of kappa (Cicchetti & Sparrow, 1981). Kappa coefficients were fair for schizophrenia (.55) and bipolar disorder (.47), but poor for dysthymia (.22), major depression (.34), obsessive–compulsive disorder (.38), panic disorder (0), schizoaffective disorder (.04), and adjustment disorder (.10). An overall weighted kappa, which took into account the base rates and kappa coefficients for all of the diagnoses, also indicated that agreement was poor (.25).

The validity of diagnoses was also disappointing when validity was evaluated by using the LEAD procedure (Skodol, Oldham, Rosnick, Kellman, & Hyler, 1991; Vitiello, Malone, Buschle, Delaney, & Behar, 1990). For example, in one of the studies (Vitiello et al., 1990), clinical diagnoses and structured-interview diagnoses made for 46 hospitalized children were compared to diagnoses made using the LEAD procedure. Clinical diagnoses and structured-interview diagnoses were made during the first week of hospitalization. LEAD diagnoses were made after the patients were discharged. The LEAD judges used all of the information that had been collected during the hospitalizations including the structured interview results. Unfortunately, a kappa coefficient was not calculated to describe interrater reliability for the two LEAD judges. For the clinical diagnoses and LEAD diagnoses, kappa coefficients indicated poor agreement for three categories (conduct disorder, adjustment disorder, encopresis), fair agreement for three categories (enuresis, oppositional disorder, and attention-deficit/hyperactivity disorder), and good agreement for one category (major affective disorder). For LEAD diagnoses and diagnoses from two structured interviews, kappa coefficients indicated poor agreement for six categories, fair agreement for five categories, good agreement for one category, and excellent agreement for two categories.

One can also learn about the validity of clinical diagnoses from studies on the validity of diagnostic classification systems. If a clinician faithfully adheres to diagnostic criteria when making a diagnosis, then we can learn about the validity of that clinician's diagnoses by learning about the validity of the classification system the clinician uses. Diagnostic criteria are useful to the extent that they allow clinicians to make valid inferences about the nature, etiology, course, and treatment of a mental disorder. Construct validity for diagnoses is sometimes good and sometimes poor (Robins & Barrett, 1989). For example, fundamental questions about the nature and etiology of schizophrenia remain unanswered. Meehl (1990) has argued that most cases of schizophrenia are caused by a single pathophysiological mechanism, but most other research investigators, as Meehl acknowledges, believe that what is called *schizophrenia* is actually a heterogeneous group of disorders that share some clinical features, but are etiologically diverse (e.g., Andreasen et al., 1988; Chapman, 1990). On the positive side, the etiology of schizophrenia is at least partially understood. Empirical evidence suggests that there are genetic causes for some mental disorders, including schizophrenia (e.g., Gottesman, McGuffin, & Farmer, 1987). But because outcome varies widely for individuals who are diagnosed as having schizophrenia, the criteria are limited in their usefulness (Wyatt, Alexander, Egan, & Kirch, 1988). On the other hand, if one considers all patients seen by a mental health professional, it becomes clear that a diagnosis of schizophrenia has considerable power for predicting differences in outcome. Finally, with regard to the treatment of schizophrenia, psychopharmacological and family education programs are helpful, but certainly clinicians are struggling to find more effective treatments (e.g., Falloon et al., 1985; Hogarty et al., 1986).

Can clinicians make valid diagnoses? That is, given a diagnosis made by a clinician who has conducted an interview and collected history information, can valid inferences be made about the etiology, nature, course, and treatment of the patient's disorder? The answer seems to be yes. A diagnosis can be useful even if there is limited knowledge about the disorder. A term such as *schizophrenia* can be used in a productive way even when clinicians are aware that the meaning of the term will change as more empirical data are collected (Meehl, 1986b; Rorer & Widiger, 1983).

Validity and Psychological Tests

Diagnoses made by psychologists using psychological test results have been compared to diagnoses made by criterion judges using (unstructured) interview and history data. Structured interviews, the LEAD approach, and the Robins and Guze criteria have not been used to evaluate the validity of diagnoses made by psychologists using test results. Despite the methodological limitations of the studies, several interesting results have been obtained and deserve to be described. The following topics are reviewed in subsequent sections: (a) the relation between presumed expertise, experience, training, and validity; (b) the relation between confidence and validity; and (c) incremental validity. As will become clear, the results for psychodiagnosis are similar to the results that were obtained for the description of personality and psychopathology.

Presumed Expertise, Experience, Training, and Validity. For the task of psychodiagnosis, presumed expert clinicians were no more accurate than other clinicians, regardless of the type of psychological test information that was given to the clinicians (Garb, 1989). For example, Levenberg (1975) had psychologists classify children as normal or disturbed on the basis of Kinetic Family Drawing protocols. A group of PhD psychologists were correct for 72% of the cases, whereas an alleged expert, the author of two books on the Kinetic Family Drawing Test, achieved only 47% accuracy. Presumed expertise was also unrelated to validity when Draw-a-Person protocols were used to make psychodiagnoses (Wanderer, 1969; Watson, 1967) and when MMPI protocols were used to detect malingering (Walters, White, & Greene, 1988). For example, in the Walters et al. (1988) study, clinicians used MMPI test results and demographic data to decide if prison inmates were pretending to have a serious emotional disorder. One group of judges was made up of 24 experts who had published research on the MMPI and had displayed expertise in the theory, research, teaching, and practical application of the test. A second group of judges was composed of 16 staff psychologists working for the Federal Bureau of Prisons. Criterion ratings were made by two psychologists who were involved in the assessment and treatment of the inmates and who received information from staff members familiar with the inmates' daily behavior (e.g., work supervisor, cell house officer). The expert clinicians were not more accurate than the staff psychologists.

Similar results were obtained when psychologists and graduate students in psychology were compared. Diagnoses made by psychologists were not more valid than diagnoses made by psychology graduate students (Garb, 1989). This was true when clinicians were given sentence completion test protocols (Walker & Linden, 1967), projective drawing protocols (Levenberg, 1975; Schaeffer, 1964; Stricker, 1967), and MMPI data (Danet, 1965; Goldberg, 1965, 1968; Graham, 1971; Walters et al., 1988). For example, in the Walters et al. (1988) study described in the preceding paragraph, in which judges tried to detect malingering in a prison population, a group of psychology graduate student judges were just as accurate as the staff and expert psychologists.

The importance of training was supported in some studies. Psychologists sometimes made more valid diagnoses than lay judges (e.g., undergraduates, secretaries, college graduates), depending on the task and the type of information (Garb, 1989). When given Wechsler Adult Intelligence Scale (WAIS) subtest results, clinical psychologists made significantly more valid ratings of the severity of schizophrenic pathology than did undergraduate judges (Jones, 1959). In several studies, psychologists made more valid diagnoses than lay judges when judges were given MMPI results (Goldberg & Rorer, 1965, and Rorer & Slovic, 1966, described in Goldberg, 1968; Karson & Freud, 1956; Oskamp, 1962). For example, when judges were to use MMPI protocols to make differential diagnoses of psychosis versus neurosis, PhD clinical psychologists, psychology graduate students, and nonpsychologists were correct for 65%, 65%, and 52% of the cases, respectively (Goldberg & Rorer, 1965, and Rorer & Slovic, 1966, described in Goldberg, 1968). After all of the judges received a large number of training trials (for a separate sample of protocols, they could look at protocols and criterion diagnoses), the psychologists, graduate students, and lay judges were correct for 65%, 65%, and 58% of the cases, respectively.[1]

The importance of training was not supported for the interpretation of projective test protocols. Ratings made by PhD psychologists and psychology trainees were not significantly more valid than those made by lay judges when judges were given projective drawing protocols or sentence completion test data (Cressen, 1975; Hiler & Nesvig, 1965; Levenberg, 1975; Schaeffer, 1964; Schmidt & McGowan, 1959; Walker & Linden, 1967). A common task in these studies was to indicate if a test protocol belonged to a normal subject or a psychiatric inpatient.

Confidence and Validity. With regard to whether clinicians are more confident when their diagnoses are correct, the relation between confidence and validity is generally stronger when the validity of judgments is good (Gambara & Leon, 1996). Confidence was not positively related to validity when clinicians were to use Rorschach protocols to detect malingering (Albert, Fox, & Kahn, 1980). Validity in this study was also disappointing: Presumed experts in the use of the Rorschach were unable to detect faking of psychosis by normal participants even though the normal participants had little knowledge about psychosis and no previous experience with the Rorschach. With regard to the MMPI, confidence was positively related to validity, but only when validity was relatively good. For example, confidence was positively related to validity when the tasks were to (a) differentiate medical from psychiatric patients (Oskamp, 1962) and (b) differentiate neurotic from psychotic patients (Goldberg, 1965). When the task required an "uncommonly difficult discrimination" (Young, 1972, p. 459), confidence and validity were not significantly related. In this study, MMPI profiles were not randomly sampled, but instead MMPI profiles for neurotic and psychotic patients were matched for psychotic tendency by using the Goldberg (1965) index, which made the differential diagnosis of neurosis versus psychosis using the MMPI a much more difficult task. Finally, clinicians who used MMPI profiles to decide if prison inmates were feigning a serious mental disorder made ratings of marginal validity, and the correlation between their confidence ratings and the validity of their judgments was positive but not statistically significant (Walters et al., 1988).

Incremental Validity. The incremental validity of psychological tests was studied by adding the results from one test to the results from another.

---

[1]The importance of training for psychodiagnosis was also supported, at least in part, when judges were given information from interviews and therapy sessions. In one study (Rock & Bransford, 1992), training in the use of *DSM–III* was related to the validity of diagnoses. In this study, clinical psychology graduate students made diagnoses after being given transcripts, tape recordings, or videotapes of interviews and therapy sessions. Validity was not related to year in graduate school, number of practicum hours completed, or number of different patients seen for assessment and therapy. Validity was positively related to (a) number of hours of classroom and clinical experience with *DSM–III* and (b) current use of *DSM–III* to diagnose patients.

Wildman and Wildman (1975) had clinicians sort test protocols according to whether they believed the protocols were those of a psychiatric patient or a nurse. The addition of projective test data led to decreases in validity. When the House–Tree–Person was added to the Bender Visual Motor Gestalt Test, accuracy dropped from 62% to 53%. Accuracy dropped from 88% to 80% when TAT protocols were added to MMPI protocols. Addition of the MMPI to the TAT led to an increment in accuracy from 57% to 80%. In another study (Bilett et al., 1982), the addition of projective data also did not lead to an increase in validity. The addition of Rorschach data to Wechsler Adult Intelligence Scale data actually led to a decrease in the validity of judgments when the task was to diagnose schizophrenia.

It would be beneficial to be able to describe the incremental validity of psychological tests when test results are made available along with other information that clinicians usually have available in clinical practice (e.g., history and interview data). To evaluate the validity of diagnoses based on test results and interview and history data, one would have to evaluate the validity of diagnoses by using structured interviews, the LEAD approach, the Robins and Guze criteria, or another construct-validation procedure.

Discussion of Results on Test Validity and Diagnosis. Would the results on presumed expertise, experience, training, confidence ratings, and incremental validity be different if structured interviews, the LEAD approach, the Robins and Guze criteria, or another construct-validation approach had been used to evaluate the validity of judgments? One can speculate that the results would probably be similar even if more sophisticated methods had been used. It could be argued that it would be easier to detect significant differences among predictors of a criterion if there were more powerful measures of that criterion. But it should be noted that results were often in a direction opposite of desirable results, for example, expert judges were at times less accurate than other clinicians or graduate students (Levenberg, 1975; Walters et al., 1988) and the addition of projective tests made it more difficult to differentiate psychiatric patients from normal participants (Wildman & Wildman, 1975). Thus, while the use of a more powerful criterion measure would make it easier to detect significant differences, results could still be disappointing. Also, in the majority of the studies, the task was to judge whether a person had a mental disorder. Status as a psychiatric patient or a normal participant is a powerful measure of the construct of mental illness, and it is unlikely that different results would have been obtained if the LEAD approach, the Robins and Guze criteria, or another method had been used to evaluate validity.

If the use of more sophisticated validation methods would not have led to different results being obtained, one might wonder why investigators should use them. First, by using sophisticated validation methods, psychologists will be able to obtain interesting measures of constructs, such as, for example, better indicators of schizophrenia. Second, if more sophisticated validation methods are used, psychologists can learn about the incremental validity of psychological tests when test information is made available along with history and interview information.

The goal of this section has been to describe the validity of diagnoses made by clinicians using psychological tests, not the validity of test scores used to predict diagnoses (e.g., the MMPI Post Traumatic Stress Disorder subscale or the Rorschach Schizophrenia Index). However, it could be argued that if research supports the use of test scores for making diagnoses, then clinicians' diagnoses will be valid if they use the test scores in a way supported by the research. However, the incremental validity of test scores added to interview and history data has rarely been studied, especially for the task of diagnosis. Thus, it would be largely unfounded to argue, on the basis of research on the validity of test scores, that the validity of diagnoses made by clinicians is likely to be more accurate when clinicians attend to test results as well as history and interview data.

Biases and Errors

Rather than comparing diagnoses made by clinicians to diagnoses made by using structured interviews or the LEAD approach, one can evaluate diagnoses by studying biases and errors. This falls under the construct validity approach to evaluating validity. Biases and errors that have been studied in relation to diagnosis include race, social class, gender, and age bias; context and labeling effects; the overperception of psychopathology; diagnostic overshadowing; and the overdiagnosis and underdiagnosis of different disorders.

Both experimental and quasiexperimental methods have been used to study biases and errors. In experimental studies, different groups of clinical judges are given the same assessment information (usually case histories) except that a patient variable is manipulated. For example, some judges may be told that the patient is female and another group may be told that the patient is male. In quasiexperimental studies, sometimes referred to as *archival studies* or *field studies*, investigators review medical charts and use diagnoses made in clinical practice as a dependent variable. Quasiexperimental studies are reviewed in this discussion only if investigators sought to determine if patient variables (e.g., race, gender) could be used to predict diagnoses after psychopathology was controlled for by the investigators.

Diagnoses can be biased for several reasons. First, data collection can be biased. For example, a clinician may quickly form an impression or hypothesis (e.g., a tentative diagnosis) based in part on the race, gender, or age of a patient, and the clinician may then ask questions that support the hypothesis rather than questions that could disconfirm the hypothesis or support an alternative diagnosis. Second, even if identical information is collected for different clients, bias can occur if a clinician's judgment processes are biased. Finally, diagnoses can also be biased because a set of diagnostic criteria are biased (Widiger & Spitzer, 1991, pp. 16–17). For example, with the publication of the *DSM–III*, the ratio of male to female patients with schizophrenia increased (Lewine, Burbach, & Meltzer, 1984). Earlier onset, worse premorbid functioning, chronic course, and flat affect were more characteristic of male patients who had been diagnosed as having schizophrenia using the *DSM–II* (American Psychiatric Association, 1968) criteria than females who had been diagnosed using the *DSM–II* criteria. These features received greater emphasis in the *DSM* schizophrenia criteria beginning with the publication of *DSM–III*. One can argue that the *DSM–III* criteria were less sex biased than the *DSM–II* criteria, even though more males than females were diagnosed as having schizophrenia when the *DSM–III* criteria were adopted, because empirical research suggests that the *DSM–III* criteria were more valid than the *DSM–II* criteria.

The research described in this book addresses judgment bias and bias in data collection, but not biases that may be inherent in diagnostic criteria. The quasiexperimental studies address both judgment bias and bias in data collection, but the experimental studies address only judgment bias. In the experimental studies, clinicians were given case histories, test results, or videotapes of interviews. To learn how bias affects data collection, clinicians would need to collect information themselves. In the quasiexperimental studies, clinicians collected information and made judgments.

Because the studies described in this book do not allow for making inferences about diagnostic criterion bias, it cannot be concluded that diagnoses were unbiased, even when judgment bias and bias in data collection were reported to be absent. It can only be concluded that the cognitive processes of clinicians or the way data were collected was unbiased.

Significant progress has been made during the past 20 years in describing the biases and errors that are associated with diagnosis. Though research from the 1960s and 1970s dramatically illustrated the potential seriousness of context and labeling effects (e.g., Rosenhan, 1973), research from the same era suggested that, except for social class, the effects of patient variables (e.g., race, gender) are not significantly related to diagnosis (e.g., Abramowitz & Dokecki, 1977; Sattler, 1977; Smith, 1980; Stricker, 1977; Whitley, 1979). Subsequent research has documented that the effects of many patient variables are statistically significant (e.g., race, gender, and age bias; bias against the mentally retarded), but, surprisingly, recent research has not shown that the effect of client social class is statistically significant (Garb, 1997; López, 1989).

Race Bias. The most widely replicated example of race bias involves the differential diagnosis of schizophrenia and psychotic affective disorders. African Americans and Hispanics (Puerto Ricans) are more likely than Whites to be diagnosed as having schizophrenia, and they are less likely to be diagnosed as having an affective disorder. This has been found in several well-designed studies.

Simon, Fleiss, Gurland, Stiller, and Sharpe (1973) compared diagnoses made in clinical practice to those made by using a structured interview. Data were obtained for 188 hospitalized mental patients. Socioeconomic class was similar for Black patients and White patients. Of 55 Black patients, 80% were given a hospital diagnosis of schizophrenia, and 0% were diagnosed by the treating clinicians as having an affective disorder. Of 133 White patients, 55% were diagnosed as having schizophrenia, while 10% were diagnosed as having an affective disorder. Using the structured interview, 29% of the White patients and 42% of the Black patients were given an affective disorder diagnosis, and 31% of the White patients and 27% of the Black patients were diagnosed as having schizophrenia. White and Black depressive patients were similar in their complaints about depressed mood and psychomotor retardation, but the Black depressive patients complained more frequently about tension, anxiety, autonomic symptoms, and irritability.

Data from a second study (Mukherjee, Shukla, Woodle, Rosen, & Olarte, 1983) indicate that Blacks and Puerto Rican Hispanics with bipolar affective disorder are more likely than Whites with bipolar affective disorder to have been misdiagnosed as having schizophrenia. All patients with a diagnosis of bipolar affective disorder at the outpatient department of an inner-city hospital were included in the study. None of the patients had a history of nonaffective psychotic episodes. The sample consisted of 37 Whites, 21 Blacks, and 18 Hispanics. Of the 76 patients, 68% had a previous misdiagnosis of schizophrenia (51% of Whites, 86% of Blacks, and 83% of Hispanics). For the patients who had had persecutory delusions, 39% of Whites, 40% of Hispanics, and 100% of Blacks were misdiagnosed as having paranoid schizophrenia. Thus, even when both White and Black patients had persecutory delusions, White patients were less likely than Black patients to be misdiagnosed.

In another study (Pavkov, Lewis, & Lyons, 1989), data were collected on 313 severely mentally ill individuals. Almost all of the individuals were poor; only 21 of the 313 had incomes of more than $1,000 per month. Structured interviews were conducted by the experimenters. Being Black was predictive of a diagnosis of schizophrenia even after the variance attributable to psychiatric symptoms was partialed out (even after stuctured interview diagnoses were used to predict hospital diagnoses). Finally, results from other studies also suggest that African American patients are more likely than White patients to be diagnosed as having schizophrenia (Blake, 1973; Coleman & Baker, 1994; Loring & Powell, 1988; also see Garb, 1996b).

When a differential diagnosis is to be made between schizophrenia and an affective disorder, African Americans are more likely than Whites to be diagnosed as having schizophrenia. However, when a differential diagnosis is to be made between schizophrenia and drug-induced psychosis, they are more likely than Whites to be given a diagnosis of drug-induced psychosis. This result was obtained when 139 United Kingdom psychiatrists made diagnoses after reading a case history for a psychotic patient (Lewis, Croft-Jeffreys, & David, 1990).

For other diagnostic tasks, there is no strong, and certainly no replicated, evidence that race is related to diagnosis. When mental health professionals made diagnoses after reading case history information or after watching videotapes of interviews, the effect of client race was not significant when clinicians made diagnoses of the following: drug dependence; alcoholism; hysterical, antisocial, and paranoid personality disorders; anxiety neurosis; and schizophrenia, simple and paranoid types (Warner, 1979); psychosis; alcoholism; personality disorder; neurosis; and situational disturbance (Bamgbose, Edwards, & Johnson, 1980); educable mental retardation or mild mental handicaps (Huebner & Cummings, 1986); normality, neurosis, and psychosis (Strickland et al., 1988). Race was also not significant when clients were most often diagnosed as having a personality disorder, paranoid psychosis, or neurotic stress reaction and only infrequently diagnosed as having schizophrenia, manic-depressive psychosis, or major depressive disorder (Littlewood, 1992).

Similarly, the effect of client race has generally not been significant when clinicians have been instructed to rate level of adjustment or the severity of mental disturbance (Amira, Abramowitz, & Gomes-Schwartz, 1977; Bamgbose et al., 1980; Benefee et al., 1976; Bloch, Weitz, & Abramowitz, 1980; Franklin, 1985; McLaughlin & Balch, 1980; Schwartz & Abramowitz, 1975; Seligman, 1968; Umbenhauer & DeWitte, 1978; also see Merluzzi & Merluzzi, 1978). These results were obtained when ratings were made for African American, Mexican American, and White patients. In a typical study, the same case history was given to different groups of clinicians except clinicians in one group were told the patient was Black or Mexican American and clinicians in a second group were told that the case described a White patient. Though ratings of severity of mental disorder were generally not influenced by race, in one study (Strickland et al., 1988), ratings of mental disturbance were more severe for White patients than for Black patients. In this study, White actors and Black actors followed the same scripts when portraying neurotic and psychotic patients. Clinicians (psychology graduate students) made their ratings after viewing one of the videotapes.

Social Class Bias. The prevalence of mental disorders varies as a function of socioeconomic status. Though poverty may have a causal effect on the occurrence of mental disorders, and though the occurrence of mental illness may lead to a decline in socioeconomic status, Hollingshead and Redlich (1958) speculated that the covariance between diagnoses and social class may also be due in part to a bias to diagnose lower social class individuals as having a mental disorder.

Though a review of early research on diagnosis concluded that the effect of social class is statistically significant (Abramowitz & Dokecki, 1977), subsequent research has not supported this claim. For example, with regard to results for children, Neer, Foster, Jones, and Reynolds (1973) reported that a child with an IQ score within the mild range of mental retardation was more likely to be diagnosed as being mentally retarded if the child was described as being of low, rather than middle or high, socioeconomic status. Their results were not replicated in a later study (Amira et al., 1977). The sample size was larger in the later study (217 psychologists versus 31 psychologists).

Similarly, with regard to results for adults, in early studies (DiNardo, 1975; Haase, 1964; Lee & Temerlin, 1970; Trachtman, 1971), diagnoses and ratings were consistently more severe for lower class clients than for middle-class or upper class clients. For example, lower class clients were more often diagnosed as being mentally ill rather than as normal, and they were more often diagnosed as having a character disorder rather than as neurotic. In these studies, prior to listening to a recording of an interview or reviewing Rorschach protocols, clinicians were told that a client was of low, middle, or upper socioeconomic status.

In most of the more recent studies, when clinicians made diagnoses and rated the severity of disturbance, lower class participants were not seen as having more severe mental disorders (Amira et al., 1977; Bamgbose et al., 1980; Franklin, 1985; Hardy & Johnson, 1992; Settin, 1982; Sutton & Kessler, 1986; Umbenhauer & DeWitte, 1978; but also see Luepnitz, Randolph, & Gutsch, 1982). Thus, the colloquial saying, "If you're poor you're called crazy, if you're rich you're called eccentric" does not seem to be true. For example, in one study (Sutton & Kessler, 1986), three groups of clinical psychologists were each given a 600-word case history describing a client with a personality disorder. The client was described as being a commercial artist with 3 years of college, a bulldozer operator with a high school education, or an unemployed welfare recipient with a seventh grade education. Otherwise the same case history information was given to each of the three groups of clinicians. Lower social class was associated with less severe ratings of illness. It is also important to note that clinician sample sizes were small for the studies that reported that ratings were more severe for lower class clients than for middle-class or upper class clients (an average clinician sample size of 49 compared to an average clinician sample size of 279 for the other studies).

Gender Bias. An early and influential study on gender bias led many clinicians and research investigators to conclude that gender bias does occur when mental health professionals evaluate clients. Broverman, Broverman,

Clarkson, Rosenkrantz, and Vogel (1970) concluded that "clinicians are significantly less likely to attribute traits which characterize healthy adults to a woman than they are likely to attribute these traits to a healthy man" (p. 5). In the study, participants described their concepts of "normal adult men," "normal adult women," and "normal adults." Descriptions of normal adult men were highly similar to descriptions of normal adults, but descriptions of normal adult women were not. These results have been interpreted to mean that a woman cannot be considered to be both a healthy normal adult woman and a healthy normal adult. As put by Kaplan (1983), "The implications of the stereotyping described by Broverman et al. (1970) . . . are that to be considered an unhealthy adult, women must act as women are supposed to act" (p. 788).

The Broverman et al. (1970) study has been criticized because the inventory that clinicians used to describe their conceptions of healthy adults, healthy females, and healthy males contained more items that describe socially desirable, stereotypically male characteristics than items that describe socially desirable, stereotypically female characteristics (Stricker, 1977). If the inventory had contained more positive "female" characteristics and fewer positive "male" characteristics, then the descriptions of normal adult women would have been closer than the descriptions of normal adult men to the descriptions of normal adults. This has been demonstrated empirically by Widiger and Settle (1987). Thus, one cannot reasonably conclude that women cannot be seen as being both healthy adult females and healthy adults; the results obtained will depend on the questionnaire used.

When clinicians have rated severity of disturbance or level of adjustment, the effect of client gender has usually not been statistically significant, though there are exceptions. For example, the effect of client gender was not statistically significant when clients were described as being depressed (Hardy & Johnson, 1992); being nonassertive, having no friends, being uncertain about choosing a career, being promiscuous, or having frequent diarrhea (Murray & Abramson, 1983); feeling mildly anxious and depressed due to a divorce (Schover, 1981); being clinically depressed, having marital conflict, or being active, aggressive, independent, ambitious, and interested in business as opposed to staying at home and being family oriented (Austad & Aronson, 1987); being depressed with symptoms of reactive depression (López et al., 1993); being perfectionistic and depressed with somatic complaints and sexual conflicts (Schwartz & Abramowitz, 1975); being either psychotic–explosive or phobic (Billingsley, 1977); behaving either passively or aggressively (Dailey, 1980; Fischer et al., 1976); being dependent–passive or hostile–aggressive (Teri, 1982); being an adolescent with either internalizing (e.g., depression) or externalizing (acting-out behavior) symptoms (Prout & Frederickson, 1991); or parenting a mildly defiant teenager (McCollum & Russell, 1992).

The effect of gender was significant in six studies when clinicians rated level of adjustment or severity of problems. A politically active, liberal client with significant emotional problems was rated more severely by conservative clinicians when the client was described as being female (Abramowitz, Abramowitz, Jackson, & Gomes, 1973). Ratings of severity made by liberal clinicians, and ratings of severity made for conservative, politically active clients, were not related to client gender. In three studies (Hansen & Reekie, 1990; Miller, 1974; Oyster-Nelson & Cohen, 1981), male clients described by the same case histories as female clients were rated as being more severely disturbed than the female clients. In a fourth study (Lowery & Higgins, 1979), this same effect of client gender was also statistically significant, but only for the clinicians (psychologists, psychiatrists, social workers) with 7 or more years of experience. In these four studies, the clients were described as having problems with depression and anxiety, alcohol, antisocial behaviors, or schizophrenia. In a final study (Feinblatt & Gold, 1976), children exhibiting behavior inappropriate to their sex were seen as being more severely disturbed. For example, male children were described as being more disturbed than female children when the problem behaviors involved passivity, whereas female children were described as being more disturbed than male children when the problem behaviors involved aggression. However, the sample size for this study was small (27 psychology graduate students), and other studies have subsequently reported that (a) females are not given more severe ratings when a client is described as being aggressive and (b) males are not given more severe ratings when a client is described as being dependent or passive (Austad & Aronson, 1987; Dailey, 1980; Fischer et al., 1976; Prout & Frederickson, 1991; Teri, 1982; also see Oyster-Nelson & Cohen, 1981).

With regard to diagnoses (rather than ratings of level of adjustment), personality disorders have been underdiagnosed more often for female patients than for male patients. In one study (Molinari et al., 1994), clinical diagnoses were compared to structured interview diagnoses for 100 male patients on a V.A. geropsychiatric inpatient unit and 100 female patients on a private hospital geropsychiatric inpatient unit. Using the Structured Interview for Disorders of Personality–Revised (SIDP–R; Pfohl, Blum, Zimmerman, & Stangl, 1989), personality disorder diagnoses were made for 52 of the female patients and 61 of the male patients. However, psychiatrists diagnosed only 4 of the female patients and 27 of the male patients as having a personality disorder.

The results presented thus far indicate that clinicians are not less likely to attribute traits that characterize healthy adults to a woman than a man, female clients are not generally described as being less well adjusted than male clients, and female clients are not more likely than male clients to be given an incorrect diagnosis of a personality disorder. In the discussion of the remaining studies, results for specific diagnostic categories are presented.

The effect of client gender has been statistically significant for the differential diagnosis of histrionic personality disorder and antisocial personality disorder. In studies on the prevalence rates of personality disorders, when diagnoses have been made by using unstructured clinical interviews and self-report measures, 81% of the patients given a diagnosis of histrionic personality disorder have been female. When semistructured interviews have been used, 69% of the patients given a diagnosis of histrionic personality disorder have been female (for a review of the studies, see Corbitt & Widiger, 1995).

In studies using a different experimental design, when different groups of clinicians have been given identical case histories except for the designation of gender, clinicians have been more likely to diagnose women as having a histrionic personality disorder (Adler, Drake, & Teague, 1990; Becker & Lamb, 1994; Ford & Widiger, 1989; Hamilton, Rothbart, & Dawes, 1986; Loring & Powell, 1988; Warner, 1978, 1979; though also see Blashfield & Herkov, 1996; Morey & Ochoa, 1989) and have been more likely to diagnose men as having an antisocial personality disorder (Becker & Lamb, 1994; Fernbach, Winstead, & Derlega, 1989; Ford & Widiger, 1989; Warner, 1978, 1979; also see Hamilton et al., 1986). These effects have been found for both male and female clinicians (Adler et al., 1990; Ford & Widiger, 1989; Warner, 1978), though in one study (Loring & Powell, 1988) the effect of client gender for diagnosing histrionic personality disorder was found for male psychiatrists and Black female psychiatrists, but not for White female psychiatrists.

The effect of client gender was not statistically significant when clinicians made separate ratings for each of the histrionic personality disorder and antisocial personality disorder criteria (Ford & Widiger, 1989). For example, when clinicians read a case history and were told that the patient is female, they were not more likely to rate histrionic criteria as being satisfied and antisocial personality disorder criteria as not being satisfied. Gender bias in the diagnosis of histrionic and antisocial personality disorders might not occur if clinicians made diagnoses by (a) evaluating whether individual criteria are satisfied and (b) referring to *DSM–IV* to decide whether enough criteria are satisfied to assign a diagnosis.

Results from studies on the prevalence rates of dependent personality disorder are surprising (for a review, see Corbitt & Widiger, 1995). When diagnoses were made by using semistructured interviews, 74% of the patients diagnosed as having a dependent personality disorder were female. When diagnoses were made by using unstructured clinical interviews, 59% of the patients diagnosed as having a dependent personality disorder were female. The results would be easier to interpret if semistructured and unstructured interviews had been conducted in the same studies with the same sample of patients. However, the results do suggest that when clinicians conduct unstructured interviews, dependent personality disorder may be underdiagnosed among female clients or overdiagnosed among male clients.

For the diagnosis of borderline personality disorder, when case histories have been presented to clinicians and gender has been experimentally manipulated, findings of gender bias have not been replicated. Becker and Lamb (1994) reported that gender bias occurs in the diagnosis of borderline personality disorder. In their study, clinicians made ratings on a 7-point Likert scale, with a rating of 1 indicating that the disorder is not present and a rating of 7 indicating that the client meets all of the criteria for the disorder. Though they obtained a statistically significant difference, the difference was of small magnitude: The male version of a case was given a mean rating of 5.2, whereas the female version of the case was given a mean rating of 5.6. Furthermore, the effect of gender in the diagnosis of borderline personality disorder has not been statistically significant in other studies (Adler et al., 1990; Henry & Cohen, 1983; Ford & Widiger, 1989).

Client gender has not been statistically significant for other Axis II disorders including dependent personality disorder (Adler et al., 1990; Becker & Lamb, 1994), masochistic or self-defeating personality disorder (Fuller & Blashfield, 1989; Becker & Lamb, 1994), and passive–aggressive personality disorder (Ford & Widiger, 1989). Adler et al. (1990) found that men were more likely to be diagnosed as having a narcissistic personality disorder, but Becker and Lamb (1994) and Ford and Widiger (1989) reported that gender was unrelated to the diagnosis of narcissistic personality disorder.

Despite speculation that clinicians may overdetect depression in female clients (Potts, Burnam, & Wells, 1991), the effect of client gender has rarely been statistically significant for the diagnosis of Axis I disorders. This is true both for the diagnosis of affective disorders and for other Axis I disorders.

The effect of gender was significant in one study on the diagnosis of Axis I disorders (Wrobel, 1993). In this study, 209 psychologists read a vignette describing a patient with cognitive and affective symptoms. Symptoms and behaviors included sleep disturbance, forgetfulness, loss of appetite, feelings of hopelessness, crying spells, poor hygiene, and confusion. When a group of 103 of the psychologists were told that the patient was male, 77% of them made a diagnosis of depression and 8% made a diagnosis of organic disorder. When a separate group of 106 clinicians were told that the patient was female, 84% of them made a diagnosis of depression and only 1% made a diagnosis of organic personality disorder.

When clients did not have as striking a combination of affective and cognitive symptoms, the effect of client gender on the diagnosis of Axis I disorders was not usually statistically significant. This was true when clinicians made diagnoses of learning disability (Clarizio & Phillips, 1986); schizophrenia (Pavkov et al., 1989); schizophrenia, substance induced psychosis, and acute reactive psychosis (Lewis et al., 1990); adjustment disorder (Wrobel, 1993); adjustment disorder, dysthymic disorder, and anxiety disorder (Agell & Rothblum, 1991; Garfinkle & Morin, 1978); adjustment disorder, dysthymic disorder, intermittent explosive disorder, posttraumatic stress disorder, schizophrenia, generalized anxiety disorder, and delusional disorder (Becker & Lamb, 1994); adjustment reaction and depressive neurosis (Settin, 1982); and adjustment disorder, dysthymic disorder, cyclothymic disorder, and alcohol abuse (Ford & Widiger, 1989).

Sex-Role Bias. Unlike the effect of client gender, the effect of sex-role behavior has frequently been statistically significant. Female clients were not judged to be more maladjusted if they were thinking of majoring in engineering instead of social work (Hill, Tanney, Leonard, & Reiss, 1977), but they were given more severe diagnoses if they were described as being a lesbian, as having a job that men usually hold (a TV repairperson), and if they expressed a wish to move in with a lover (Rosenthal, 1982). When male clients were described by the same case history except for a statement about whether they have a job outside of the home or have primary responsibility for the home and children, ratings of pathology were more severe when they were portrayed as having primary responsibility for the home and children (Robertson & Fitzgerald, 1990). Another study suggested that clinicians may judge androgynous clients to be better adjusted than clients with masculine or feminine personality traits, even when they are all described as having the same symptoms (Dailey, 1983). Finally, when clinicians watched one of two videotapes of actors portraying a matriarchical or patriarchical style of family interaction, ratings of global family functioning were more favorable for the patriarchical family (Ivey, 1995).

Age Bias. Compared to young and middle-aged clients, old clients are more likely to be diagnosed as having organic impairment and they are less likely to be seen as having a depressive disorder, even when all of the clients are described by the same case histories except for the designation of age (Meeks, 1990; Pat-Horenczyk, 1988; Perlick & Atkins, 1984; Settin, 1982; Wrobel, 1993; also see Garb & Florio, 1997; James & Haley, 1995; Nadler, Mittenberg, DePiano, & Schneider, 1994). For example, in one study (Wrobel, 1993), 209 clinical psychologists read a case history that described a patient with cognitive and affective symptoms. Different groups of clinicians were told that the client is 45-, 55-, 65-, 75-, or 85-years-old. None of the clients described as being 45 or 55 were diagnosed as having an organic disorder, but 12% of the 75- and 85-year-old clients were.

For the diagnosis of other mental disorders (e.g., personality disorders, schizophrenia), the effect of age was rarely statistically significant (Blashfield & Herkov, 1996; Hill et al., 1977; Hillman, Stricker, & Zweig, 1997; Morey & Ochoa, 1989; Pavkov et al., 1989). For example, when structured interviews were conducted by experimenters and the structured interview diagnoses were used to predict the diagnoses that were made by the clinicians treating the patients, the addition of age as a predictor did not lead to the enhanced prediction of hospital diagnoses of schizophrenia (Pavkov et al., 1989).

Additional Biases. For other patient variables, effects either have not been statistically significant or have not been replicated. Obesity and attractiveness have not been related to diagnoses or ratings of level of adjustment (Agell & Rothblum, 1991; Murray & Abramson, 1983; Schwartz & Abramowitz, 1978). Student background (rural versus suburban) was not related to the diagnosis of learning disability (Huebner & Cummings, 1985; also see Huebner, 1985). Skin tone of African American clients (light, medium, dark) was not significantly related to the diagnoses that psychologists made for clients (Atkinson et al., 1996). Health of client (good health versus congenital heart disease) was not significantly related to differential diagnoses of major depression, adjustment disorder, uncomplicated bereavement, and dysthymia (James & Haley, 1995). In a single study (Mazer, 1979), a politically radical client was rated as less disturbed than a politically moderate client, even though the case history for the clients was identical except for the designation of political beliefs. In two studies (Lewis & Lewis, 1985; Wadsworth & Checketts, 1980), the religious beliefs of clinicians and patients were not related to diagnosis.

Illusory Correlations. Instead of adhering to criteria, clinicians may make diagnoses based on their own beliefs about how symptoms and behaviors co-occur. Their categorizations are likely to have poor validity if illusory correlations dominate their thinking about the co-occurrence of symptoms and behaviors.

When clinicians are given a list of symptoms and problem behaviors and are asked to cluster the symptoms and behaviors into groups that reflect how the symptoms and behaviors naturally co-occur, the clusters produced by clinicians differ markedly from clusters that are obtained by objectively measuring the co-occurrence of the symptoms and behaviors. In one study (Krol, De Bruyn, & Van Den Bercken, 1995), the symptoms and behaviors that clinical child psychologists were instructed to cluster were taken from the Child Behavior Checklist (Achenbach, Conners, Quay, Verhulst, & Howell, 1989). Multivariate analyses of the Child Behavior Checklist have produced nine clusters that have been found for different age and gender groups (Achenbach et al., 1989; Achenbach, Verhulst, Baron, & Akkerhuis, 1987). The nine core syndromes have been given the following labels: (1) *aggressive,* (2) *delinquent,* (3), *attention problems,* (4) *schizoid,* (5) *somatic complaints,* (6) *anxious–depressed,* (7) *withdrawn,* (8) *socially inept* (boys only), and (9) *cruel* (girls only). Correspondence between clinicians' clusters and the empirically derived clusters was said to be fair if at least half of the items of a clinician's cluster overlapped with the items of one of the nine empirically derived clusters. Correspondence was fair for only 18% of the clinicians' clusters.

Context Effects. Context effects occur when the environment of the clinician influences what diagnoses are made. That is, diagnoses can vary as a function of setting or circumstances. For example, if a client is using insurance to pay for treatment, the clinician may be careful to make a diagnosis that will lead the insurance company to approve payment for the treatment. Also, a clinician may diagnose a patient as having a severe mental disorder to justify keeping the person longer in the hospital. Conceivably, the person might have received a different diagnosis if instead of being hospitalized, the person had been treated at an outpatient clinic.

In perhaps the best known judgment study ever done, normal people gained admission to psychiatric hospitals by complaining of hearing voices (Rosenhan, 1973). The pseudopatients answered questions in a truthful manner except when asked their name, vocation, and place of employment and when asked why they had come to the hospital and whether they heard voices. All participants were diagnosed as having a mental disorder and were hospitalized. Rosenhan argued that the pseudopatients were given invalid diagnoses. The discharge diagnosis for 11 of the 12 pseudopatients was "Schizophrenia, in remission" while the discharge diagnosis for the other person was "Manic–depressive psychosis, in remission." Length of hospitalization ranged from 7 to 52 days, with an average stay of 19 days.

One can argue that it was appropriate to admit these individuals to the hospital, though it would be difficult to argue that the length of stay was appropriate. If a person is complaining of hearing voices, wants to come into the hospital, and does not seem to be malingering, then admission may be appropriate so that the person can be observed and a complete evaluation can be done. Furthermore, research indicates that clinicians do not routinely hospitalize individuals who complain of auditory hallucinations. For example, in one study (Meyerson, Moss, Belville, & Smith, 1979), only 49% of individuals who complained of hallucinations were admitted. The figure must be even lower now with the wide-spread shift from inpatient care to outpatient care.

Besides being famous, the Rosenhan study is also controversial (for criticisms of the study see the special section that appeared in the *Journal of Abnormal Psychology* in 1975 and also see Davis, 1976, and Spitzer, 1975). The Rosenhan study is controversial because of the conclusions that the author drew from his results. For example, he concluded that a psychiatric diagnosis reveals "little about the patient but much about the environment in which an observer finds him" (1973, p. 251) and "we cannot distinguish the sane from the insane in psychiatric hospitals" (1973, p. 257). He later concluded that, "My own preference runs to omitting diagnoses entirely, for it is far better from a scientific and treatment point of view to acknowledge ignorance than to mystify it with diagnoses" (1975, p. 467).

A different interpretation of the results is offered here. The Rosenhan study was conducted in the 1970s. Explicit and specific criteria did not become widely available until *DSM–III* was published in 1980. If clinicians adhered to the criteria in *DSM–III, DSM–III–R,* or *DSM–IV,* they would not have made a diagnosis of schizophrenia if a person's only presenting symptom was hearing voices. When diagnoses are made by clinicians who are adhering to explicit diagnostic criteria, the effects of context on diagnoses will be minimal. Instead of arguing that diagnoses should be omitted, it is more credible to argue that clinicians adhere to criteria when making diagnoses. At the same time, it is important to remember that research indicates that many clinicians frequently do not attend to criteria when they make diagnoses.

In their book on coping with psychological and psychiatric testimony, Ziskin and Faust (1988) devoted an entire chapter to the Rosenhan study. They recommended that when an attorney wants to deprecate the testimony of a psychologist or psychiatrist in a legal proceeding, she or he should refer to the Rosenhan study and argue that diagnoses can be influenced by context and are thus of questionable validity. Clinicians can respond by noting that clinicians in the Rosenhan study did not use explicit diagnostic criteria, and that for the present legal hearing they did attend to the criteria and are prepared to say which of the criteria the person in question meets.

Labeling Effects. Labeling effects are said to occur when clinicians are influenced by the diagnoses that other clinicians have made. Clinicians are frequently exposed to diagnoses made by others because they regularly obtain records from previous hospitalizations or outpatient psychotherapy sessions. Labeling effects typically refer to the influence of diagnoses that have previously been made for a client or patient, but they can also refer to the influence of a diagnosis that has been made for a patient's family member.

Several studies conducted prior to the publication of *DSM–III* demonstrated that labeling effects can dramatically affect diagnoses (DiNardo, 1975; Dixon, LeLieuvre, & Walker, 1981; Langer & Abelson, 1974; Reade & Wertheimer, 1976; Temerlin, 1968; Temerlin & Trousdale, 1969). For example, Temerlin (1968) had psychologists and psychiatrists make diagnoses after listening to a tape recording of an interview with a nonpsychotic outpatient. Before listening to the interview, one group of clinical judges heard a highly respected clinician, acting as a confederate of the experimenter, say that the individual to be diagnosed was "a very interesting man because he looked neurotic but actually was quite psychotic" (p. 350). A control group listened to the interview without first hearing the remarks made by the prestigious clinician. No control judge made a diagnosis of psychosis (they did make diagnoses of neurosis and character disorder). In the experimental group, diagnoses of psychosis were made by 60% of the psychiatrists and 28% of the psychologists. In two of the other studies (Dixon et al., 1981; Reade & Wertheimer, 1976), ratings of the likelihood of schizophrenia were higher when clinicians were told that a family member has schizophrenia.

If clinicians make diagnoses by adhering to diagnostic criteria, then labeling bias will be minimized. However, because research indicates that many clinicians frequently do not adhere to diagnostic criteria, there is reason for concern about the occurrence of labeling effects. A research study from the 1980s has helped to clarify the conditions when labeling effects occur. Herbert, Nelson, and Herbert (1988) had 36 PhD clinical and counseling psychologists make diagnoses after watching three 12-minute videotapes. The psychologists were told that they were watching videotapes of intake interviews with clients at a university psychology clinic. Actually, three advanced drama students served as hypothetical clients in the study. Nine videotapes were produced, with each of the three actresses portraying three different levels of depression (normal behavior, dysthymic disorder, and major depression). The scripts for the two disorders were carefully devised in accordance with *DSM–III* criteria. The script for the normal tape was characterized by a lack of significant abnormal behavior. Each clinician saw three videotapes. They saw a portrayal of each level of depression and a portrayal by each actress. Judges were randomly assigned to either a label or a no-label condition. The 18 psychologists in the label condition were told that each of the three videotaped clients had been diagnosed with dysthymic disorder by a referral source in the community. A label effect was found for the clients portrayed as being normal. That is, for the normal tapes, 16 of the 18 judges who did not receive the label made diagnoses of normal, whereas only 11 of the 18 judges in the label condition made accurate diagnoses. On the other hand, label effects were not found for clients portrayed as having dysthymic disorder or major depression. One can conclude that a label effect is likely to occur when psychopathology is absent but clinicians have been told, or believe a priori, that there is reason to believe a mental disorder exists. A label effect is unlikely to occur when clinicians observe severe psychopathology, but are told that it is likely that only a moderately severe mental disorder is present.

False Positives: Overperception of Psychopathology. Mental health professionals tend to overperceive psychopathology. Results are presented for the use of psychological tests and for the use of case history information.

The overperception of psychopathology has been more pronounced when psychologists have used projective tests than when they have used the MMPI. One of the most interesting and one of the oldest studies is a longitudinal study by Grant, Ives, & Ranzoni (1952). Participants in the study had been sampled from the birth registry in Berkeley, California, and thus they were considered a "normal" population. Detailed information about participants was collected from them, their parents, and their teachers over a period of 18 years. Clinicians, using Rorschach data, found it difficult to approximate a normal distribution when they used a 4-point scale to describe adjustment even though they had been asked to do so. In fact, across clinicians, 61 to 71% of the cases were rated as maladjusted. Ratings made by Rorschach clinicians were not significantly related to the ratings of adjustment made on the basis of the longitudinal data.

In a second study (Little & Shneidman, 1959), misperceptions of psychopathology were more pronounced for psychologists interpreting projective test protocols than for (a) psychologists interpreting MMPI protocols and (b) psychiatrists making inferences from case histories. When psychologists made ratings for three normal participants on a 9-point rating scale, ratings of maladjustment were higher when they were based on the Rorschach ($X = 4.5$), Thematic Apperception Test ($X = 4.8$), and the Make a Picture Story Test ($X = 4.8$) than when ratings were based on the MMPI ($X = 3.3$) or a case history ($X = 1.6$).

In another study (Wallach & Schooff, 1965), psychologists interpreted MMPI protocols and psychiatric residents conducted interviews. Ratings were made for 48 college applicants who were required to have a psychiatric and psychological evaluation because they had previously been under psychiatric care. Ratings of adjustment were made by the psychiatric residents and by the psychologists (who based their ratings solely on the MMPI results) on a 7-point scale. With lower ratings indicating poorer adjustment, psychiatric residents made an average rating of 3.4 and psychologists made an average rating of 2.9 (using this rating scale, a rating of 4 was to indicate mild maladjustment, a rating of 3 was to indicate moderate maladjustment, and a rating of 2 was to indicate considerable maladjustment).

In a field study by Loro and Woodward (1975), the medical records of 500 psychiatric inpatients were reviewed. Diagnoses made by psychiatrists were compared to diagnoses made by psychologists based on psychological testing. The diagnoses made by psychologists were based on test batteries that usually included WAIS, Rorschach, MMPI, and Draw-a-Person protocols. Psychologists, compared to psychiatrists, overperceived psychopathology in moderately impaired patients. Most of the disagreements in diagnosis occurred when psychiatrists made diagnoses of "lesser psychopathology" or depression and psychologists made diagnoses of hysterical personality, personality disorder, or schizophrenia (p. 638).

Clinicians can falsely perceive psychopathology not only when they are given test results, but also when they are given case history information. For example, in one study (Kullgren, Jacobsson, Lynöe, Kohn, & Levav, 1996), 184 psychiatrists in Sweden made judgments after reading three case histories. One of the case histories was written to describe a person who may not have a mental disorder. According to the case history

A 40-year-old male economist is brought to the psychiatrist. Over the last 2 months he has been making speeches against government policy, claiming that the country must become racially and ethnically pure. The patient is enraged, talking loudly, without evidence of pressured speech. He is uncooperative during the examination, stating that he is not insane, and that he is being harassed without any justification by being brought to the psychiatrist against his will. His family had difficulty in calming him down in the psychiatrist's office, and reported that they had never seen him this upset previously. They stated that he has held these views all his life. The family denied any previous history of mental disorder or any current change in mood or behavior at home. (pp. 390–391)

Surprisingly, "65% [of the psychiatrists] suggested various diagnoses ranging from manic–depressive psychosis and paranoid psychosis to personality disorder. Less than half were confident about their diagnosis" (p. 392). Unfortunately, the exact number of psychiatrists who were confident about their diagnosis was not reported.

Diagnostic Overshadowing. A patient may have more than one mental disorder. Once an initial diagnosis is made, a clinician may not attend to diagnostic criteria and make additional diagnoses. Overshadowing bias is said to occur when a clinical problem is so salient it inhibits a clinician's processing of information related to a second clinical problem.

Clinicians tend to underdiagnose mental disorders in the mentally retarded even though retarded individuals are probably more susceptible to emotional disturbance (Alford & Locke, 1984; Hurley & Sovner, 1995; Reiss, Levitan, & Szyszko, 1982; Reiss & Szyszko, 1983; Spengler & Strohmer, 1994; Spengler, Strohmer, & Prout, 1990; Tranebjærg & Ørum, 1991). This occurs even when clients are described by the same case histories except for the designation of level of intelligence. According to Spengler and Strohmer (1994), this bias is common among psychologists with low cognitive complexity. *Cognitive complexity* is a construct used to describe how individuals process information and will be described in chapter 7.

Diagnostic overshadowing also occurs when judgments are made for terminally ill patients. Specifically, terminally ill patients are unlikely to be diagnosed as having a major depressive disorder even when they meet the diagnostic criteria for this disorder and might be able to benefit from treatment. Perry and Tross (1984) reviewed the medical records of 52 AIDS patients. Of the 52 patients, 43 suffered from an affective disorder and nine met the criteria for major depression. However, none of the patients were diagnosed as being depressed. Similarly, Walker and Spengler (1995) had clinical and counseling psychologists read a case history. The person was described as being severely depressed. Different groups of clinicians were told that the person had AIDS, cancer, or no medical condition. Diagnoses of major depression were most likely for the person described as having no medical condition.

Clinicians may underdiagnose the co-occurrence of anxiety and affective disorders. Two thirds of patients with panic disorder may at sometime also have major depression, and 20 to 30% of depressed patients have anxiety attacks (Clayton, 1990). Patients with a diagnosis of panic disorder or generalized anxiety disorder almost always meet diagnostic criteria for additional disorders (Barlow, DiNardo, Vermilyea, Vermilyea, & Blanchard, 1986). The most common additional diagnoses are simple phobia and social phobia. Similarly, patients with obsessive–compulsive disorder often meet the criteria for a depressive disorder. Treatment planning should be based on a recognition of the full-range of a person's problems.

Personality disorders are frequently underdiagnosed by mental health professionals, presumably because Axis I disorders are so salient they inhibit the processing of information related to the diagnosis of personality disorders (Casey, Dillon, & Tyrer, 1984; Molinari et al., 1994). For example, in one study (Molinari et al., 1994), diagnoses made by psychiatrists were compared to structured interview diagnoses made by research investigators. To obtain the diagnoses made by psychiatrists, medical records were reviewed for 200 patients on two geropsychiatric inpatient wards. The research investigators made their diagnoses by using the SIDP–R (Pfohl et al., 1989). Psychiatrists diagnosed 31 of the patients as having a personality disorder, but research investigators made diagnoses of personality disorder for 113 of the patients.

When psychiatric residents and psychology interns received intensive training in psychodiagnosis (a didactic course on *DSM–III* and a focus on diagnosis during the course of their residency and internship), personality disorders were not underdiagnosed (Skodol, Williams, Spitzer, Gibbon, & Kass, 1984). However, the trainees rarely listed maladaptive personality features on Axis II (Skodol, 1989, pp. 385–386). Trainees made diagnoses for 200 outpatients. Personality disorder diagnoses were made for approximately 50% of the outpatients, and maladaptive personality traits were listed on Axis II for an additional 5% of the outpatients. When the charts were reviewed by the research investigator, personality disorder diagnoses were made for approximately 50% of the outpatients and maladaptive personality traits were identified for an additional 35% of the outpatients. By listing maladaptive personality traits (e.g., histrionic features), one can clarify the problems that need to be addressed in treatment.

Even when a clinician makes an Axis II diagnosis, diagnostic overshadowing is likely to occur. Empirical evidence indicates that most clinicians will diagnose a patient as having only one or two personality disorders even when the patient satisfies the criteria for as many as four personality disorders. Adler et al. (1990) gave psychiatrists, psychiatric residents, PhD psychologists, social workers, and masters-level psychiatric nurses a 950-word case history. The person described by the case history met the *DSM–III* criteria for the histrionic, narcissistic, borderline, and dependent personality disorders, and the case history was written to reflect this. Clinicians were told that they could refer to the *DSM–III* manual while they made their diagnoses. Most clinicians assigned just one Axis II diagnosis; 65% diagnosed a single personality disorder, 28% diagnosed two personality disorders, 7% diagnosed three personality disorders, and 0% diagnosed four personality disorders.

When clients meet the criteria for more than one personality disorder including borderline personality disorder, clinicians are more likely to make a diagnosis of borderline personality disorder than a diagnosis of the other personality disorders (Adler et al., 1990; Herkov & Blashfield, 1995). For example, in one of the studies (Herkov & Blashfield, 1995), a national sample of 320 clinicians (primarily psychologists and psychiatrists) described clients whom they had evaluated and treated. Each clinician described a client who they had diagnosed as having a personality disorder. Clinicians listed the diagnoses they had made and completed symptom questionnaires. Using the symptom questionnaires, the research investigators were able to determine if clients met the DSM–III–R criteria for different personality disorders. When clients met the criteria for borderline personality disorder and another personality disorder, diagnoses of borderline personality disorder were made significantly more often than diagnoses for the other personality disorders, except for diagnoses of narcissistic personality disorder. For example, 31 clients met the criteria for borderline personality disorder and dependent personality disorder. Diagnoses of borderline and dependent personality disorders were assigned to 84% and 32% of the clients, respectively.

The tendency for clinicians to diagnose only one or two personality disorders is of concern because several studies have demonstrated that patients frequently meet the criteria for more than two personality disorders (Clarkin, Widiger, Frances, Hurt, & Gilmore, 1983; Dolan, Evans, & Norton, 1995; Widiger, Frances et al., 1986; Widiger, Sanderson, & Warner, 1986). For example, Widiger, Frances et al. (1986) had lay interviewers use a structured interview to rate the presence of symptoms. Lay interviewers were used because they had no expectations about the covariation of symptoms. The experimenters made diagnoses using the symptom ratings and the DSM–III criteria. In the study, 55% of the borderlines also met the criteria for schizotypal personality disorder, 47% met the criteria for antisocial personality disorder, and 57% met the criteria for histrionic personality disorder.

Overlooking diagnoses of personality disorders can be important for both researchers and clinicians. For example, if one conducts a research study on borderline personality disorder, but does not diagnose co-occurring personality disorders, then it will be hard to generalize the results. Results may be due to a co-occurring personality disorder that one has not described. Similarly, for clinicians, if treatment differs markedly for different personality disorders (e.g., borderline personality disorder and antisocial personality disorder), then treatment may be less effective if one of the diagnoses is overlooked.

Another example of a frequently overlooked diagnosis involves the diagnosis of substance abuse and substance dependence in psychiatric patients. Ananth et al. (1989) reported that psychiatrists on the inpatient units of a state hospital made 29 diagnoses of substance abuse and substance dependence for a sample of 75 psychiatric patients. A week after the clinical staff made their diagnoses, a research team made 187 diagnoses of drug abuse or dependence (many of the patients received more than one diagnosis of drug abuse). The research team found that about 75% of the patients met the criteria for drug abuse or drug addiction even after excluding occasional use. The study suggests that substance abuse and substance dependence are underdiagnosed among psychiatric patients. Drake et al. (1990) also found that substance abuse and substance dependence are underdiagnosed on a psychiatric inpatient unit. Hospital discharge summaries for a sample of 75 patients with diagnoses of schizophrenia or schizoaffective disorder were examined. For 29% of the patients, the discharge summaries contained diagnoses of alcohol abuse or alcohol dependence. When a research team made diagnoses after conducting structured interviews and collecting longitudinal data, 51% of the patients were given a diagnosis of alcohol abuse or alcohol dependence. Similar results on the underdiagnosis of substance abuse and substance dependence have subsequently been reported by Goethe and Ahmadi (1991) and Wilkins, Shaner, Patterson, Setoda, and Gorelick (1991).

Diagnostic overshadowing may also occur for individuals admitted to a substance abuse treatment program. In one study (Kranzler et al., 1995), clinical diagnoses and diagnoses based on the SCID structured interview were obtained for a sample of 100 substance abuse patients. Clinicians diagnosed a greater number of patients as having major depression (clinicians 21%, research technicians 9%) while research technicians diagnosed a greater number of patients as having an anxiety disorder (clinicians 9%, research technicians 31%). Thus, overshadowing may not occur for the diagnosis of major depression, but may occur for the diagnosis of anxiety disorders.

Other studies of diagnostic overshadowing in substance abuse treatment programs have also reported that overshadowing occurs for the diagnosis of anxiety disorders. Riemann, McNally, and Cox (1992) reported that 12% of the patients in an alcohol inpatient program were found to meet the DSM–III–R criteria for obsessive–compulsive disorder when assessed by the research investigators with the SCID–R structured interview. Clinicians had missed the diagnoses of obsessive–compulsive disorder (R. J. McNally, personal communication, December 10, 1992). Similarly, in a second study (Fals-Stewart & Angarano, 1994), research staff conducted sturctured interviews with 217 patients in two community-based substance abuse outpatient treatment programs. Using the structured interviews, 24 of the patients (11%) met the diagnostic criteria for obsessive–compulsive disorder. Only 8 of these patients had been given this diagnosis by their primary counselors.

Overdiagnosis and Underdiagnosis. Controversies exist over whether some mental disorders are overdiagnosed and others underdiagnosed. In this section, comments are made about dissociative identity disorder (called *multiple personality disorder* in DSM–III–R), attention-deficit/hyperactivity disorder, and schizophrenia.

Many clinicians are reluctant to diagnose dissociative identity disorder, but other clinicians believe it is underdiagnosed. Spanos (1994) reported that the number of diagnoses of multiple personality disorder in the United States increased astronomically since 1970 whereas in other countries, including France, Great Britain, Russia, India, and Japan, the diagnosis has rarely been made. In the United States, some clinicians have diagnosed the disorder at high rates (e.g., 16% of the patients on one acute psychiatry unit) while many others report they have never made the diagnosis (Spanos, 1994). According to Ofshe and Watters (1994)

> As late as 1979 there were only two hundred cases of Multiple Personality Disorder in all recorded medical history. . . . Since 1980, thousands of recovered memory clients have been told that they harbor multiple personalities. Dr. Colin Ross, one of the most prominent promoters of the Multiple Personality Disorder diagnosis, believes that "One percent of the population fits the criteria for being a multiple personality." (p. 205–206)

Clearly, either dissociative identity disorder is underdiagnosed by some clinicians or overdiagnosed by others.

Attempts have been made to describe clinicians who are more or less likely to diagnose dissociative identity disorder. Hayes and Mitchell (1994) reported that psychiatrists were significantly more skeptical about multiple personality disorder than were social workers. Psychologists were more skeptical than social workers, but less skeptical than psychiatrists. A humanistic theoretical orientation was positively related to belief in multiple personality disorder. In another survey (McMinn & Wade, 1995), therapists were sampled from (a) the American Association of Christian Counselors and (b) the American Psychological Association. No differences were observed between members of the American Association of Christian Counselors and psychologists belonging to the American Psychological Association. Also, when considering only members of the American Association of Christian Counselors, differences among psychologists, nonpsychology licensed therapists (e.g., social workers, marriage and family counselors), and nonpsychology nonlicensed therapists (e.g., social workers, marriage and family counselors, lay counselors) were not statistically significant.

Just as there is a controversy over the diagnosis of dissociative identity disorder, there is also a controversy over the treatment of the disorder (e.g., Gleaves, 1996; Ofshe & Watters, 1994; Spanos, 1994). Ofshe and Watters (1994) have argued that by purporting to treat dissociative identity disorder, some clinicians may be harming clients:

> One of the most troubling and telling facts of the disorder is that patients develop their most dramatic and debilitating symptoms only in the course of treatment. Therapists readily admit that at the beginning of treatment patients do not switch between child and adult personali-

ties in front of them. Nor do they howl, growl, scream uncontrollably, talk in the persona of the Devil, or speak in strange voices that tell of a desire to kill the host personalities. (p. 207)

Thus, misdiagnosis of dissociative identity disorder can be harmful to clients.

Another controversy involves the diagnosis of attention-deficit/hyperactivity (ADHD) disorder. There have been recent reports showing a doubling in the number of visits to physicians for the evaluation and treatment of this disorder. Psychologists disagree on whether the disorder is being overdiagnosed (Edwards, 1995). At the present time, there is little empirical evidence that can resolve this issue, but ADHD may be a critical area for future investigation.

Historically, schizophrenia has been overdiagnosed in many areas of the United States, but major affective disorders have been underdiagnosed (Cooper et al., 1972; Garvey & Tuason, 1980; Joyce, 1984; Katz, Cole, & Lowery, 1969; Weller, Weller, Tucker, & Fristad, 1986). In the classic "U.S.–U.K." study performed in the early 1970s (Cooper et al., 1972), psychiatric patients were interviewed at hospitals in the United States and the United Kingdom. Research teams using structured interviews assigned diagnoses of (a) schizophrenia and (b) depressive psychosis or manic–depressive illness to approximately equal numbers of patients. With regard to the diagnoses made by the clinicians who were treating the patients, the ratio of diagnosis of schizophrenia to depressive psychosis and manic–depressive illness was approximately 1:1 at the London hospitals but 12:1 at the New York hospitals.

As a consequence of research findings on the overdiagnosis of schizophrenia, diagnostic criteria for schizophrenia have been made more stringent. The American Psychiatric Association's DSM–II (1968) implied that a diagnosis of schizophrenia should be made if Bleulerian symptoms (Bleuler's four As are looseness of associations, flatness of affect, ambivalence, and autism) or Schneiderian symptoms (e.g., thought broadcasting, thought insertion) were present. With the advent of DSM–III in 1980, the criteria for schizophrenia were made more stringent so that fewer diagnoses of the disorder would be made. For example, one can adhere to the criteria of DSM–III (or DSM–III–R or DSM–IV) and make a diagnosis of a major affective disorder for a patient with Bleulerian or Schneiderian symptoms.

With the adoption of DSM–III, fewer diagnoses of schizophrenia and more diagnoses of affective disorder are being made in the United States (Grace & Stiers, 1989). However, there is evidence that, depending on the hospital, schizophrenia is still overdiagnosed and major affective disorders (and even organic disorders) are underdiagnosed (Fennig, Craig, Tanenberg-Karant, & Bromet, 1994; Lipton & Simon, 1985; Lyketsos, Aritzi, & Lyketsos, 1994; Pulver, Carpenter, Adler, & McGrath, 1988).

For example, in one of the studies (Lipton & Simon, 1985), research clinicians reviewed the charts of 131 psychiatric inpatients at a state hospital. They formed diagnostic impressions based solely on the information provided in the charts. Treating clinicians made diagnoses of schizophrenia for 89 of the 131 patients. Research clinicians confirmed only 16 of these diagnoses. Treating clinicians made only 15 diagnoses of affective disorder while research clinicians assigned diagnoses of affective disorder to 50 patients. Similarly, treating clinicians made seven diagnoses of organic disorder while research clinicians made the diagnosis for 26 of the patients.

Different results were reported by Pulver et al. (1988). They compared discharge diagnoses at five state hospitals to research diagnoses based on a structured interview, medical records, and subsequent interviews with patients or their relatives 6 months after discharge. Results did not confirm the overdiagnosis of schizophrenia: Clinicians' diagnoses of schizophrenia were usually confirmed by the research team. The authors speculated that schizophrenia may not have been overdiagnosed because the state hospitals participating in the study were able to recruit psychiatrists from training programs that stress adherence to diagnostic criteria (Weintraub et al., 1984).

Results from a final study (Fennig et al., 1994) help to clarify when to expect to find the overdiagnosis of schizophrenia and the underdiagnosis of affective disorders. When discharge diagnoses were compared to SCID structured interview diagnoses, schizophrenia was overdiagnosed (42 clinical diagnoses of schizophrenia, 35 research diagnoses) in two state hospitals and a Department of Veterans Affairs medical center. Schizophrenia was underdiagnosed at a university hospital (11 clinical diagnoses, 17 research diagnoses), and it was neither overdiagnosed nor underdiagnosed at six community hospital inpatient units (12 clinical diagnoses, 13 research diagnoses). There was a tendency to underdiagnose affective disorders at the state hospitals and Veterans Affairs medical center (20 clinical diagnoses, 24 research diagnoses), the university hospital (23 clinical diagnoses, 27 research diagnoses), and the community hospital inpatient units (28 clinical diagnoses, 33 research diagnoses).

Biases, Errors, and Base Rates. Critics of mental health professionals often argue that a major shortcoming of clinical practice is that clinicians disregard or underuse information about base rates (e.g., Arkes, 1981; Dawes, 1986; Faust & Ziskin, 1988; Finn, 1982, 1983; Hsu, 1988; but also see Grove, 1985; Meehl, 1986b; Widiger, 1983). One could argue that if the base rates for a mental disorder vary as a function of patient variables like race, social class, gender, or age or as a function of other variables like context or diagnoses given by other clinicians, then these variables should have an effect on diagnosis (see Davis, 1976, 1979; Tsujimoto & Berger, 1986). For example, if organic disorders are more common among older people than younger people, then perhaps one should be more willing to make the diagnosis when evaluating an older person.

For the task of psychodiagnosis, it is often inappropriate to attend to base rates. If a client or patient clearly meets or does not meet the DSM–IV criteria for a mental disorder, then it would be inappropriate to attend to base rates (Morey & McNamara, 1987; Widiger & Frances, 1987). When it is unclear if a client or patient meets the criteria for a mental disorder, then the best course of action is for a clinician to gather more information. Thus, if a person seems to meet the criteria for an organic disorder, but one is not really sure, one should make a referral for neuropsychological testing, a neurological exam, or a brain imaging procedure rather than make the diagnosis because the client is elderly.

After attempting to collect all of the relevant information, if it is still unclear whether a person meets the criteria for a mental disorder, then clinicians will have to use their clinical judgment. *According to DSM–IV* (American Psychiatric Association, 1994)

> The specific diagnostic criteria included in DSM–IV are meant to serve as guidelines to be informed by clinical judgment and are not meant to be used in a cookbook fashion. For example, the exercise of clinical judgment may justify giving a certain diagnosis to an individual even though the clinical presentation falls just short of meeting the full criteria for the diagnosis as long as the symptoms that are present are persistent and severe. (p. xxiii)

Thus, one could make a diagnosis even if the full criteria are not satisfied. Alternatively, one could make a provisional diagnosis: A provisional diagnosis indicates that "enough information is available to make a 'working diagnosis,' but the clinician wishes to indicate a significant degree of diagnostic uncertainty" (American Psychiatric Association, 1994, p. 5). Also, instead of diagnosing a specific mental disorder, one could make diagnoses of, for instance, unspecified mental disorder (nonpsychotic) or psychotic disorder not otherwise specified. A final choice would be to specify only the class of the disorder, such as, for instance, depressive disorder not otherwise specified.

It is important to point out that clinicians frequently do not act in accordance with true base rates. For example, mentally retarded individuals are susceptible to emotional disorders, but clinicians are less likely to diagnose emotional disorders for this group than for an intellectually average group. Similarly, African American patients are more likely than White patients to be diagnosed as having schizophrenia even though in many settings the base rates for schizophrenia are similar for White and Black patients. Clinicians may not act in accordance with true base rates because they do not accurately perceive base rates or because, as will be argued in chapter 7, they attend to stereotypes, not base rates, when they make diagnoses.

Biases should not be excused by saying that clinicians are appropriately attending to base rates, not only because they frequently do not act in accordance with true base rates, but also for another reason. Base rates are most appropriately considered when case history information is ambiguous and when base rates are very high or very low. When case history information is clear and when base rates are near .5, base rates are much less valuable. Ford and Widiger (1989) manipulated client gender and amount of ambiguity of case history information. Contrary to the appropriate use of base rates, they found that the diagnoses for the least ambiguous case histories were those most affected by client gender.

SUMMARY AND DISCUSSION

Clinicians can make reliable diagnoses. Reliability was good for many diagnostic categories in the *DSM–III* and *ICD–10* field trials. However, in the field trials, clinicians probably attended closely to criteria. Reliability will not be as good when clinicians do not adhere to criteria. There is evidence that clinicians frequently do not adhere to criteria.

For diagnoses to be valid, they must inform a clinician about the nature, etiology, course, and treatment of mental disorders. A diagnosis can be moderately valid even if we have only limited knowledge about the nature, etiology, course, and treatment of a disorder.

The validity of clinicians' diagnoses has been disappointing when they have been compared to (a) diagnoses based on structured interviews and (b) diagnoses made by using the LEAD procedure. However, these results are preliminary and are in need of further replication. The Robins and Guze criteria have not been used to evaluate the validity of diagnoses made in clinical practice.

Structured interviews are fallible. Clients can fake good or fake bad on a structured interview. Also, when using a structured interview, clinicians must either use clinical judgment to integrate results of the structured interview with other information or they must base a diagnosis solely on the results of the structured interview.

Psychological testing can help to clarify diagnoses. If interview and history information clearly indicate that a person meets or does not meet the criteria for a particular disorder, then psychological testing is not needed to clarify the person's diagnosis. However, if the diagnosis is unclear, testing can help to clarify whether a person satisfies a particular criterion. Because clients who share similar test results may be likely to have the same mental disorders, testing can also indicate diagnoses that may be correct. Finally, psychological testing can be done to clarify if a person is malingering or minimizing symptoms.

Biases in diagnosis have been described. A widely replicated example of race bias involves the differential diagnosis of schizophrenia and psychotic affective disorders, especially bipolar affective disorder. Findings of gender bias in the diagnosis of antisocial personality disorder and histrionic personality disorder have also been replicated. In addition, significant findings for the effect of age have been replicated: Elderly clients are more likely to be diagnosed as having an organic disorder and middle-age clients are more likely to be diagnosed as having an affective disorder, even when clients are described by case histories that are identical except for the designation of age.

Much of the research on context effects and labeling effects predates the publication of *DSM–III*. If clinicians closely adhere to current diagnostic criteria, context effects and labeling effects will be minimized. However, research indicates that many clinicians do not adhere closely to diagnostic criteria.

With regard to other types of errors, clinicians consistently overlook secondary diagnoses (e.g., substance abuse among psychiatric patients). Also, some disorders are overdiagnosed or underdiagnosed by large numbers of clinicians (e.g., dissociative identity disorder, attention-deficit/hyperactivity disorder, and schizophrenia).

In conclusion, many clinicians make poor diagnoses. Unless clinicians adhere closely to diagnostic criteria,

- interrater reliability is likely to be poor,
- agreement between clinicians' diagnoses and diagnoses made by using structured interviews or the LEAD procedure is likely to be poor,
- biases are likely to be present (e.g., race, gender, and age biases), and
- some mental disorders may be underdiagnosed (e.g., personality disorders) while others may be overdiagnosed (e.g., schizophrenia).

Of course, diagnoses will be imperfect even when clinicians conduct structured interviews and adhere to diagnostic criteria, but at least these diagnoses can be expected to be moderately reliable and valid.

3

CASE FORMULATION

In addition to making diagnoses and describing personality traits and psychiatric symptoms, clinicians also collect case history data and try to understand the causes of their clients' behaviors and symptoms. Two broad areas of research will be reviewed in this chapter: (a) the collection and evaluation of history data and (b) judgments about the causes of behaviors and symptoms.

CASE HISTORY DATA

To evaluate the validity of case history data, one can try to determine (a) if clients' accounts of past events are accurate, (b) if case history data are biased, and (c) if case history data are comprehensive. Clients' accounts of past events can be inaccurate for different reasons. Memories may be distorted to fit a person's implicit theories of the causes of their problems, or because a person may be motivated to give an inaccurate account, for example, a child may be afraid to report having been abused. Case history data are biased if their collection is influenced by extraneous factors, such as the race or gender of a client. Furthermore, important areas of clients' histories may be neglected. *Comprehensiveness* refers to the thoroughness with which a client's history is explored.

Accuracy of Clients' Statements

If a client inaccurately describes past events, then it will be difficult, if not impossible, for the clinician to describe causal relations. History information can be inaccurate because a client's memories are distorted or because a client is motivated to give inaccurate information.

Implicit Theories and Memory

When clients try to understand why they have behaved maladaptively or why they are distressed, their memories may be affected by their implicit theories about the causes of behaviors and feelings (Ross, 1989). For example, if an individual believes that stress can cause maladaptive behavior or distress, and if the person behaves maladaptively or experiences distress, then the person's memories may become distorted and the person may be inclined to recall that stressful events occurred. Dawes (1994) gave several examples of how this may occur. Three of the examples will be described.

In one study (Lewinsohn & Rosenbaum, 1987), 998 participants living in the community were followed over a period of 12 months. Participants were asked how they were feeling (e.g., depressed versus nondepressed), and they were asked about their childhood experiences and how they were raised. Depressed participants were more likely than those who were not depressed to recall their parents as having been rejecting and unloving. Because they were followed over time, during the course of the study some of the nondepressed participants became depressed. Memories of how they were raised were related to whether they were currently depressed. Before they became depressed, their reports about their childhood experiences and the way they were raised did not differ from the reports of participants who never became depressed during the course of the study. After they became depressed, they described their parents as having been rejecting and unloving. Similarly, individuals who had a depressive episode before the study began, but who were not depressed during the 12-month period of the study, did not differ from those who had never been depressed.

In another study (Stott, 1958), women who had Down's syndrome children were retrospectively asked to describe their pregnancies. The women reported a high incidence of "shocks" during early pregnancy. The investigator concluded that the syndrome might be caused by stress in pregnancy. Of course, it is now known that Down's syndrome is caused by the presence of a third 21st chromosome, and thus is determined at conception. Perhaps the women's memories were distorted because they believed stress during pregnancy to be related to the occurrence of Down's syndrome.

In the third study (McFarland et al., 1989), participants were female university students and women recruited from the community. They were asked to keep a record of their menstrual cycle and to make daily ratings on several measures of physical and affective symptoms. Later, they were asked to recall the ratings they had made on different days. They also completed a questionnaire designed to assess their theories of how their emotions are affected by menstruation. The results indicated that memories

Memory distortion

were distorted to fit their implicit theories. Memories of having experienced affective distress were more likely to be distorted if the women believed that affective distress is strongly related to the menstrual cycle.

Motivation and Accuracy of Clients' Reports

Clients and their family members can be dishonest when asked about past events. Determining whether a past event has occurred can be difficult to ascertain as demonstrated by research on judging whether a child has been sexually abused.

Interrater reliability has been poor when clinicians have judged whether a child has been sexually abused (Boat & Everson, 1988; Horner, Guyer, & Kalter, 1992; Kendall-Tackett, 1992; Realmuto & Wescoe, 1992). For example, in one study (Horner et al., 1992), four clinicians watched an interview with a child, an interview of the child with her mother, and an interview of the child with her father. Allegations had been made that the child had been sexually abused by her father. The clinicians' probability ratings ranged from .05 to .75 that she had been abused.

Biases

Little research has been conducted on the influence of extraneous factors on the collection of case history data. For example, little is known about the influence of context effects and race, social class, gender, age, and labeling bias on the collection of case history data.

There is reason to suspect that case history data is biased, though the degree of bias is unknown. To understand why case history data may be biased, one needs to be aware of research on confirmatory hypothesis testing. Confirmatory hypothesis testing describes a cognitive strategy of clinicians. To be exact, confirmatory hypothesis testing describes a tendency to confirm, rather than refute, hypotheses. If the confirmatory hypothesis testing strategy is descriptive, then once clinicians entertain a hypothesis, they are unlikely to entertain alternative hypotheses. For example, if a clinician believes that a patient may have a cyclothymic disorder, then the clinician may ask many questions that relate to cyclothymic disorder; for example, the clinician may ask about the occurrence of mood swings and hypomanic episodes. If the clinician does not believe that it is likely that the client has a cyclothymic disorder and if the confirmatory bias is descriptive of the clinician's cognitive strategy, few questions will be asked that relate to cyclothymic disorder. Overall, research indicates that the confirmatory bias is descriptive of clinicians, though the research is not conclusive (see chapter 7).

If extraneous factors influence how clinicians generate hypotheses and if the confirmatory hypothesis testing strategy is descriptive of clinicians

Hypothesis Confirmation Bias

when they collect history data, then case histories will be biased. For example, if upon review of a client's medical records a clinician learns that a client was previously diagnosed as having cyclothymic disorder, the clinician may not ask for information that could rule out cyclothymic disorder or support alternative diagnoses. To be more specific, the clinician may ask about the occurrence of mood swings, but not about a history of head trauma. In this example, labeling bias is said to be present. The case history is biased because the collection of information was influenced by an extraneous factor: the client's previous diagnosis.

Comprehensiveness

Undoubtedly, many case histories are not comprehensive. For example, in the previous chapter, studies on the underdiagnosis of mental disorders (e.g., substance abuse) were reviewed. When results from a study indicate that a mental disorder is underdiagnosed, one can surmise that case histories are probably incomplete (e.g., they may not include a good history of substance abuse). Research that does not relate to underdiagnosis, but does indicate that histories are incomplete, is described in this section.

Research indicates that clinicians do not regularly ask clients if they have been sexually or physically abused. For example, in one study (Pruitt & Kappius, 1992), a survey was completed by 105 psychologists who were all members of the Division of Independent Practice of the APA. When asked how often they inquire about sexual abuse, the psychologists' responses were variable: 17% indicated that they always ask, 33% indicated that they ask most clients, 31% indicated that they ask some clients, 15% indicated that they ask few clients, and 4% indicated that they never ask directly. Responses did not differ as a function of the psychologists' gender or the psychologists' orientation (psychodynamic, cognitive–behavioral, eclectic), but younger psychologists were more likely to ask about sexual abuse.

Since many clinicians do not routinely ask clients if they have been sexually or physically abused, one can wonder whether they are adept at knowing when to ask about abuse. Unfortunately, many studies indicate that clinicians are frequently unaware of which of their clients have been, or are being, abused. For example, in one study (Jacobson, Koehler, & Jones-Brown, 1987), structured interviews were conducted by research assistants to learn if patients had ever been physically or sexually assaulted. In this study, 100 adult psychiatric inpatients were interviewed. They described a total of 151 assaults. The following year, the medical records for the same 100 patients were reviewed. Only 9% (14) of the assault histories obtained from the structured interviews were mentioned in the patients' charts.

In a second study (Briere & Zaidi, 1989), participants were nonpsychotic women at a psychiatric emergency room. Two samples of charts were compared: 50 charts were randomly sampled from the emergency room files and 50 charts had notes written by clinicians who had been asked by the research investigators to ask about a history of child sexual abuse. A higher rate of sexual abuse was found when clinicians were instructed to ask about sexual abuse history (70% compared to 6%).

In a third study (Jacobson & Herald, 1990), for a sample of adult psychiatric inpatients, 56% of the patients who reported to the research interviewers that they had experienced severe sexual abuse during childhood (abuse involving genital contact) also reported that they had been in psychotherapy and had not told their therapists about the abuse. Thus, clinicians need to directly ask clients if they have been abused.

In a fourth study (O'Leary, Vivian, & Malone, 1992), participants were husbands and wives attending a university marital therapy clinic. The occurrence of physical aggression or abuse was evaluated in three ways: (a) each husband and each wife listed the most important problems in their marriage, (b) in separate interviews, each spouse was directly asked about physical aggression or abuse, and (c) each spouse completed a questionnaire that evaluated the occurrence of physical aggression in the marriage. When asked about the most important problems in their marriage, only 15% of the spouses listed physical aggression or anger control as a problem. When asked about the occurrence of physical aggression or abuse in an interview, 46% of the husbands and 44% of the wives acknowledged that violence occurred. When they completed the questionnaire, 53% of the husbands and 53% of the wives reported that aggression occurred and 17% of the men and 21% of the women reported that severe aggression occurred.

In a final study (Cascardi, Mueser, DeGiralomo, & Murrin, 1996), 69 psychiatric inpatients met with a trained research assistant and completed self-report instruments. Of 26 patients who reported that they were the victims of severe physical abuse by family members or partners during the past year (hitting, punching, choking, beating up, threatening with or using a knife or gun), abuse was documented in the medical charts of only 9 of the patients, even though 16 had been injured.

CAUSAL INFERENCES

Little research has been conducted on how well clinicians make causal inferences. For example, few studies have been done on patient variable biases, the labeling bias, or context effects. The studies that have been done raise questions about how well clinicians make causal judgments.

Reliability

Ratings of Psychosocial Stressors

When using DSM–IV (American Psychiatric Association, 1994), one is supposed to list on Axis IV the problems and stressors that (a) may have been involved in the etiology of a mental disorder, (b) may affect the prognosis for an individual, and (c) should be considered when planning treatment. Case formulations are likely to be unreliable if clinicians cannot agree on the problems and stressors in a client's life.

Types of problems that can be listed on Axis IV are described in the *DSM–IV* (pp. 29–30). They include (a) problems with primary support group, for example, death of a family member; (b) problems related to the social environment, for example, death or loss of a friend; (c) educational problems, such as illiteracy; (d) occupational problems, for example, unemployment; (e) housing problems, for example, homelessness; (f) economic problems, for example, extreme poverty; (g) problems related to interaction with the legal system/crime, such as arrest; (h) problems with access to health care services; and (i) other psychosocial and environmental problems, for example, exposure to disasters.

An important change in the use of Axis IV occurred with the adoption of *DSM–IV*. With *DSM–IV*, one lists problems and stressors on Axis IV. With *DSM–III* and *DSM–III–R*, clinicians were instructed to list stressors and rate the severity of stressors, for instance, on a 6-point scale.

Results on the interrater reliability of ratings of severity of psychosocial stressors, made by clinicians using *DSM–III* and *DSM–III–R*, ranged from poor to good. Intraclass correlation coefficients ranged from .25 for ratings of children (Mezzich, Mezzich, & Coffman, 1985) to .44 for ratings of adolescents (Rey, Stewart, Plapp, Bashir, & Richards, 1988) to .58 and .62 for ratings made as part of the *DSM–III* field trials (Spitzer & Forman, 1979).

Psychodynamic Formulations

The interrater reliability of psychodynamic formulations has been described in several studies. The results suggest that interrater reliability is poor except under special circumstances.

Interrater reliability has not been good when clinicians have been asked to make open-ended descriptions of clients' neurotic conflicts (DeWitt, Kaltreider, Weiss, & Horowitz, 1983; Seitz, 1966; also see Stoller & Geertsma, 1963). For example, in one of the studies (DeWitt et al., 1983), two teams of psychodynamically trained clinicians formulated descriptions after viewing videotapes of intake evaluations that lasted from 60 to 90 minutes. Each team was composed of three clinicians, and descriptions were made by consensus. Participating clinicians were psychiatrists, social workers, and a psychologist. Each team was instructed to, "Define the basic neurotic conflict(s) that lie at the core of the patients' difficulties. Include the kind of stress to which the patient is vulnerable" (p. 1124). Formulations were written by both teams for 18 adults who sought psychotherapy for pathological grief reactions after the death of a parent. Agreement between formulations was evaluated by two psychodynamically trained clinicians with 5 or more years of postdegree experience. The raters followed a structured rating process. Formulations written by the two teams of clinicians were given an average rating of "definite nonoverlap with some distinct areas of agreement or similarity in inclusion" (p. 1125). Typically, the two teams of clinicians mentioned different symptoms, emphasized different conflictual areas, and formulated different cause–effect explanations. The authors concluded that the formulations made by one treatment team are not interchangeable with the formulations made by other treatment teams.

Interrater reliability has also been poor when the judgment task has been structured but clinicians did not share the same psychodynamic orientation. In one study (Collins & Messer, 1991), psychodynamic formulations were made by teams of clinicians who practice therapy using either Weiss's cognitive–psychoanalytic theory or Fairbairnian object relations theory. The clinicians used the Plan Formulation Method (Curtis & Silberschatz, 1989) to make ratings. The task was to describe (a) clients' goals for therapy, (b) pathogenic beliefs that might prevent attainment of the goals, (c) the means by which clients could work in therapy to disconfirm their pathogenic beliefs, and (d) insights that would be helpful to the clients. There were highly significant differences in the dynamic content of plans formulated by the two teams of clinicians. As noted by Collins and Messer (1991), "uniformly negative Pearson coefficients demonstrate that by consistently rating their own Plans differently from the other panel's Plans, both judging panels indicated that they viewed the two Plans as unlike in content" (p. 80). Thus, when clinicians did not share the same psychodynamic orientation, reliability was poor even when the judgment task was structured.

The reliability of psychodynamic formulations has been better when the judgment task has been tailored separately for each client, as long as clinicians share the same psychoanalytic orientation (e.g., Crits-Christoph et al., 1988; Rosenberg, Silberschatz, Curtis, Sampson, & Weiss, 1986). For example, in one of the studies (Rosenberg et al., 1986), different questionnaires were written for each patient. To write these questionnaires, a team of experienced clinicians, who shared the same psychoanalytic orientation, read transcripts of intake interviews and therapy sessions. Using the Plan Formulation Method (Curtis & Silberschatz, 1989), a series of concise statements were written for each patient. Four psychodynamic clinicians, all sharing the same cognitive psychoanalytic approach described by Weiss, Sampson, and the Mount Zion Psychotherapy Group (1986), made ratings for these statements and for other statements that are frequently included in case formulations, but were not descriptive of these particular patients. Clinicians were to rate the degree to which each statement was pertinent for the particular client. To make their ratings, the clinicians read the transcripts of the intake interviews and therapy sessions. Though several different analyses were performed, reliability generally ranged from fair to excellent. The authors noted that interrater reliability may not be as good when case formulations are made by clinicians with diverse psychodynamic viewpoints.

In conclusion, the interrater reliability of psychodynamic formulations has only been good when clinicians have shared the same psychoanalytic orientation and when the task has been to make ratings for statements that have been tailored for different clients. In one of these studies (Crits-Christoph et al., 1988), the authors noted that by structuring the clinical task, "good reliability is obtained by keeping the level of clinical inference to a moderate or low amount" (p. 1004). Thus, good reliability has been obtained by restricting the range of inference. Of course, in clinical practice, case formulation is open ended, the range of inference is not restricted, and clinicians do not make ratings for statements that have been tailored for each client.

Distinguishing Primary Versus Secondary Negative Symptoms of Schizophrenia

Negative symptoms of schizophrenia include affective flattening or blunting, impoverished thinking, avolition or apathy, anhedonia or asociality, and inattentiveness. Negative symptoms may be due to a primary neural abnormality or a variety of secondary negative factors including neuroleptic side effects, depression, social withdrawal as a consequence of positive symptoms of schizophrenia (e.g., hallucinations, delusions), and apathy resulting from environmental understimulation.

Reliability has been disappointing when clinicians have rated whether negative symptoms of schizophrenia are due to primary or secondary factors. In one study (Flaum & Andreasen, 1995), ratings were made for 462 patients at nine sites. To assess interrater reliability, pairs of clinicians interviewed patients together, but made independent ratings. To assess test–retest reliability, independent interviews were conducted one day apart by different clinicians. The median kappa coefficient for interrater reliability was .50, and the median kappa coefficient for test–retest reliability was .38.

Validity

To explain why a person is experiencing emotional distress or is behaviorally dysfunctional, clinicians may conclude that past events were harmful enough to have caused the symptoms or behavioral problems. According to Meehl (1973), many of these causal inferences may be invalid:

> We find ourselves in possession of two sorts of facts [about a client]. The first kind of fact, present by virtue of his being a patient, is that he has mental or physical symptoms, or characterological traits, that are pathological. . . . The second kind of fact about the person is not true of him by virtue of his being a "patient," but is true of him simply because he is a human being—namely, he has conflicts and frustrations;

there are areas of life in which he is less than optimally satisfied, aspects of reality he tends to distort. . . . The seductive fallacy consists in assuming, in the absence of a respectable showing of causal connection, that this first set of facts . . . *flows from* the second set. . . . [Among clinicians] the tradition is to take almost any kind of unpleasant fact about the person's concerns or deprivations, present or historical, as *of course* playing an etiological role. (pp. 244–247)

Because all of us have conflicts and frustrations and not all of us have mental disorders, one should be careful about making causal inferences. Put another way, just because a hypothesis about a causal relation seems sensible does not mean that it is valid. Most hypotheses that scientists test seem to make sense and may have a theoretical basis, but scientists are often surprised by results when they test their hypotheses.

Research on the validity of causal judgments will be reviewed. Topics include: (a) the validity of psychoanalytic formulations, (b) the validity of behavioral formulations, (c) the validity of clinicians' theories about the relation between child sexual abuse and the etiology of adult psychopathology, (d) patient variable biases, such as gender bias, (e) context effects, and (f) attribution theory and relating a client's maladaptive behaviors to personality traits or environmental variables. The results suggest that clinicians' causal inferences may often be invalid.

Psychoanalytic Formulations

When clinicians describe a client using psychoanalytic theory, it is difficult to know whether their judgments are valid. However, two examples of poor validity will be described.

Stress can be a cause of physical disorders. However, it is now known that three of the seven classic psychosomatic disorders formulated by Alexander (1950) are physical disorders with no special psychological causative factors (North, Clouse, Spitznagel, & Alpers, 1990). These disorders are thyrotoxicosis, rheumatoid arthritis, and ulcerative colitis.

For example, research indicates that ulcerative colitis is not caused by psychological factors like stress. Early research indicated that there is a connection between psychological factors and ulcerative colitis, but when flaws in experimental designs were corrected (e.g., by using control participants), a connection between psychological factors and ulcerative colitis was not observed (North et al., 1990). It is now known that most ulcers are caused by a bacterium that burrows into the lining of the stomach and duodenum ("New cure," 1996).[1] Thus, it appears that many clinicians were wrong when they sought to explain the etiology of ulcerative colitis.

With regard to the etiology of schizophrenia, a number of psychoana-

---

[1]To publicize his findings, the discoverer of the bacterium infected himself with the bacterium, developed ulcers, and then used antibiotics to kill the bacterium and cure his ulcers.

lytic writers concluded that "the mother is the main dynamic factor in the genesis of the child's future psychiatric condition" (Arieti, 1974, p. 76). For example, Fromm-Reichmann (1948) even referred to _schizophrenogenic mothers._ Schizophrenogenic mothers were described as being overanxious, cold, overprotective, and hostile.

Currently, the concept of the schizophrenogenic mother has been largely abandoned, at least by scientifically minded mental health professionals. Not only was the concept not based on research (e.g., observations of families of patients with schizophrenia and observations of control-group families), but even the quality of the clinical observations was flawed since the psychoanalysts worked with the families only after a family member had already developed schizophrenia. When empirical research has been done, it has not supported the concept of the schizophrenogenic mother. For example, Schofield and Balian (1959) compared patients with schizophrenia to a matched group of patients who were in the same hospital for nonpsychiatric reasons and who did not have a history of mental illness. Based on clinical interviews, relationships with parents were thought to be good for both groups, and relationships between parents were described as being hostile, indifferent, and ambivalent more often for the parents of the normal participants than for the parents of the patients with schizophrenia. Thus, it seems unfair to blame mothers for the onset of schizophrenia.

Behavioral Assessment

Behavior therapists often conduct functional analyses to understand the relations that exist between causal variables and behavior problems. Estimates of the covariation between causal variables and behavior problems are typically made on the basis of clinical judgment. Research suggests that clinicians' estimates of the size of these relations may often be inaccurate.

In one study (O'Brien, 1995), eight clinical psychology graduate students were given the self-monitoring data for a client who complained of headaches. For example, for day one, the client made the following ratings: a stress level of 3 (on a 0–9 scale), 7 arguments, 8 hours of sleep, 4 headaches, headache severity of 9 (on a 0–9 scale), duration of headaches of 1 hour, and 8 pain killers taken. The client made ratings for 14 days. The clinical psychology graduate students were to estimate "the magnitude of functional relationships that existed between pairs of target behaviors and controlling factors by generating a subjective correlation" (p. 352). Remarkably, the graduate students identified the controlling variables that were most strongly correlated with each headache symptom only 51% of the time.

Misinterpretation of Sexual Abuse as a Cause of Mental Disorders

Some authors of popular books have argued that many survivors of incest do not remember being abused, but that they can be identified by the nature of their symptoms. For example, according to one therapist in private practice

> So few incest survivors in my experience have identified themselves as abused in the beginning of therapy that I have concluded that perhaps half of all incest survivors do not remember that the abuse occurred. (Blume, 1990, p. 81)

In a similar vein, according to Bass and Davis (1988):

> Often the knowledge that you were abused starts with a tiny feeling, an intuition. . . . Assume your feelings are valid. So far, no one we've talked to thought she might have been abused, and then later discovered that she hadn't been. The progression always goes the other way, from suspicion to confirmation. If you think you were abused and your life shows the symptoms, then you were. (p. 22)

Symptoms that have been listed as indicators of sexual abuse include low self-esteem, depression, sexual dysfunction, and self-destructive or suicidal thoughts.

In a survey of clinical and counseling psychologists (Polusny & Follette, 1996), 20% of the respondents indicated that "they believe there is a constellation of symptoms that almost always indicates a history of child sexual abuse in adults" (p. 43). When asked to list indicators of child sexual abuse, these psychologists tended to list different symptoms, even though they all believed that there is a constellation of symptoms that almost always indicates a history of child sexual abuse in adults. No symptom was listed by more than 20% of these psychologists as an indicator of child sexual abuse.

Though some clinicians believe that sexual abuse during childhood causes low self-esteem, depression, sexual dysfunction, and self-destructive or suicidal thoughts, empirical research indicates that there is no well-defined postchild-sexual-abuse syndrome (for a review, see Beitchman et al., 1992). Thus, not only is it inappropriate to infer from a set of symptoms that a person was sexually abused as a child, but it is simplistic to infer that if symptoms are present and a person was sexually abused, then the abuse caused the symptoms.

Patient Variable Biases

Case formulations have been biased. For example, writings on psychoanalytic theory leave no doubt that gender bias has been embarrassingly present when clinicians have made case formulations. According to Freud (1933), girls "fall victim to 'envy for the penis,' which will leave ineradicable traces on their development and the formation of their character" (p. 125). Additional examples of sexism in psychoanalytic theory have been described in a number of feminist articles and books (e.g., Chesler, 1972). In addition, one can reasonably assume that psychoanalytic case formulations for gay men and lesbians were biased in the past.

One can wonder whether case formulations are still biased. Unfortunately, only a few studies have been conducted on patient-variable biases and case formulations. Results have been reported for gender, race, sex-roles, age, and religion.

The influence of client gender on causal reasoning was statistically significant, but of slight or unknown magnitude (Abramowitz, 1977; Berman, 1979). For example, in one study (Abramowitz, 1977), family therapists read case histories describing children, and they were asked to assume that the parents were to blame for the child's behavioral and emotional problems. They were then asked to rate how much each parent was to blame (for each case vignette, the ratings were supposed to add up to 100%). In each case history, a boy or a girl was described as being athletically incompetent or obese and unattractive. Gender biases were statistically significant but of slight magnitude. For example, mothers were assigned 52% of the blame for the obese–unattractive girls and 53% of the blame for athletic incompetence in girls, but only 48% of the blame for obesity–unattractiveness in boys and 50% of the blame for athletic incompetence in boys. Overall, there is no strong evidence that gender bias occurs when clinicians make causal judgments.

The interaction between client race and clinician race was significant in one study (Berman, 1979). In this study, judges were graduate students in a mental health profession. They viewed videotapes of Black, White, and Spanish-speaking clients, and the task was to describe clients' problems. All of the clients described problems related to obtaining employment. Black graduate students more often mentioned societal factors for the Black clients and Spanish-speaking clients, while White graduate students more often mentioned societal factors for the White clients.

Case formulations differ for men who are gender traditional versus gender nontraditional (Fitzgerald & Cherpas, 1985; Robertson & Fitzgerald, 1990). For example, in one study (Robertson & Fitzgerald, 1990), 47 licensed marriage and family therapists watched a videotape that purportedly showed segments of therapy sessions that occurred over a span of 6 weeks. The client was portrayed by a professional actor. He reported having symptoms of depression including poor appetite, boredom, sleeplessness, and guilt. Two versions of the videotape were produced, with the same actor in both versions. In the gender-nontraditional version, the client was portrayed as bearing the primary responsibility for domestic matters, including child care. His wife was described as being the main wage earner and as being employed as an engineer. In the gender traditional version, the client was described as being an engineer and his wife was described as being a homemaker. In each version of the videotape, the client reported that the marital arrangement was satisfactory: "My wife's not the problem. My kids . . . they aren't the problem either. I'm the problem" (p. 4). After viewing the videotape, the therapists were asked to rate factors that might be contributing to the client's problem. The factors were his marriage, his children, his financial situation, his physical health, intrapsychic factors (e.g., conflict, self-image, identity issues, ego integrity, etc.), poor coping skills, and biological factors. The effect of sex role was significant; therapists were more likely to attribute the client's depression to his marriage and his children when the client was portrayed as the homemaker. Differences for the other factors were not statistically significant.

The effect of age is sometimes statistically significant. Hansen and Reekie (1990) had different groups of social workers read case vignettes that were identical except for the designation of age. Female therapists rated intrapsychic conflicts and interpersonal issues as more important for young clients than for old clients. There are a number of reasons why a therapist may not weigh intrapsychic conflicts and interpersonal issues as heavily for elderly clients. For example, when trying to understand the causes of an elderly person's mental disorder, therapists may weigh life stressors or organic impairment more heavily. As was noted in the chapter on diagnosis, several studies have indicated that elderly clients are more likely than middle-aged clients to be diagnosed as having an organic mental disorder, even when they are described as having the same psychopathology.

The effect of religion was also statistically significant. Houts and Graham (1986) had clinical and counseling psychologists view videotapes of an actor portraying a client who was experiencing depression and guilt related to his girlfriend becoming pregnant and having an abortion. Different groups of clinicians viewed videotapes that were identical except that the client was portrayed as being moderately religious or very religious. Clinicians rated whether they believed that the client's problems could be attributed to external, circumstantial factors or internal, dispositional factors. Religious clinicians attributed the problems more to the client when the client was portrayed as having few religious beliefs, whereas the nonreligious clinicians attributed the problems more to the client when the client was portrayed as having stongly held religious beliefs.

Context Effects

Context effects can occur when clinicians make causal judgments. This was illustrated in the Rosenhan (1973) study discussed in the previous chapter. In this study, normal individuals went to different psychiatric hospitals, complained of hearing voices, were hospitalized, and then correctly answered questions about their mental status and their backgrounds except that they continued to say that they heard voices prior to hospitalization and they did not report their true vocations (they were all psychologists or psychology graduate students). Thus, the significant events of confederates' life histories and their relationships with parents, siblings, spouses, children, employers, and coworkers were presented as they had actually occurred.

One of the confederates had reported that during early childhood he had a close relationship with his mother but a remote relationship with his father. During adolescence and beyond, he became close to his father, but his relationship with his mother cooled. This individual also reported having a good relationship with his wife, except for occasional arguments, and a good relationship with his children, except for occasional spanking. However, the case summary for this person was distorted, evidently to account for his hospitalization and presumed mental disorder:

> This white 39-year-old male . . . manifests a long history of considerable ambivalence in close relationships, which begins in early childhood. A warm relationship with his mother cools during his adolescence. A distant relationship to his father is described as becoming very intense. Affective stability is absent. His attempts to control emotionality with his wife and children are punctuated by angry outbursts and, in the case of the children, spankings. And while he says that he has several good friends, one senses considerable ambivalence embedded in those relationships also. . . . (p. 253)

Thus, events in this person's past were misinterpreted as having been stressful and harmful. Furthermore, more psychopathology was observed in the person's current behavior than was justified by his actual behavior.

Attribution Theory

According to attribution theory, individuals often believe they act a particular way because of their setting or environment while observers often believe that the individuals act a particular way because of their predisposing traits (for a recent review, see Gilbert & Malone, 1995). *Attribution bias* is said to be present when a situation provides an adequate explanation for an individual's behavior, but a dispositional attribution is made.

Attribution theory has often been descriptive when clinicians have rated whether internal or external factors are responsible for a client's problems (Batson, 1975; Batson & Marz, 1979; Compas & Adelman, 1981; Harari & Hosey, 1981; Houts & Graham, 1986; Shenkel, Snyder, Batson, & Clark, 1979; Snyder, 1977; for reviews, see Jordan, Harvey, & Weary, 1988; López & Wolkenstein, 1990). In several studies (Batson, 1975; Batson & Marz, 1979; Plous & Zimbardo, 1986), clinicians were more likely than nonprofessional judges to attribute the cause of clients' problems to the clients' dispositions. Attribution theory was not descriptive of clinicians in only one study. In this study (Worthington & Atkinson, 1993), a large number of clinicians believed that external factors were responsible for a client's problems. When psychologists read a case history describing a person suffering from an adjustment disorder, 83% of the psychologists believed that responsibility for the cause of the disorder was not attributable to the client.

It is difficult to know whether the tendency of clinicians to focus on internal causes rather than external causes is inappropriate (e.g., Davis, 1979; Langer & Abelson, 1981; Tsujimoto & Berger, 1986). The issue is not so much whether clients should be responsible for the solution of their problems (psychotherapy can involve helping clients become more responsible), but whether clinicians are correct for believing that internal factors are oftentimes causes of problem behaviors.

Individual differences among clinicians have been found when the task has been to rate whether a client's problems are due to internal or external causes. The presence of individual differences implies that not all clinicians make highly valid ratings.

Psychodynamic clinicians tend to make dispositional attributions while behavioral, cognitive–behavioral, family, and eclectic therapists tend to make situational attributions or a combination of dispositional and situational attributions (Langer & Abelson, 1974; McGovern, Newman, & Kopta, 1986; Plous & Zimbardo, 1986; Snyder, 1977). For example, when data collected by Langer and Abelson (1974) were reanalyzed by Snyder (1977), psychodynamic clinicians perceived a problem to be more person-based than did behaviorally trained clinicians. All of the clinicians had watched a videotape of an actor portraying a client who had conflicts with an employer and who had had a failed business enterprise. The psychodynamic clinicians had also made more severe ratings of psychopathology than had the behavior therapists.

Individual differences among clinicians were also reported in two other studies. In one study (Houts & Graham, 1986), described in the previous section, religious psychologists attributed the problems more to the client when the client denied being strongly religious, but nonreligious psychologists made more internal attributions when the clients were described as being strongly religious. In the other study (Berman, 1979), graduate students in a mental health profession viewed videotapes and responded in writing to the question, "What do you think is the problem?" Societal factors were more often mentioned by Black graduate students than by White graduate students. White graduate students more often mentioned societal factors when they made ratings for White clients, but Black graduate students more often mentioned societal factors when they made ratings for Black or Spanish-speaking clients.

Empirical Methods for Deriving Causal Inferences

Case formulations are frequently made on the basis of clinical experience, clinical intuition, common sense, and theories of psychopathology that are based largely on clinical experience. An alternative approach for making causal judgments is to use the scientific method.

Haynes, Spain, and Oliveira (1993) have described several methods for empirically deriving causal inferences. First, one can read empirical studies that have related causal variables—or marked variables that are highly correlated with causal variables—to problem behaviors or mental disorders. For example, empirical research indicates that there is no well-defined postchild-sexual-abuse syndrome (e.g., Beitchman et al., 1992). Thus, clinicians should not infer from a set of symptoms that a client was sexually abused. The obvious weakness of this method for deriving causal judgments is that knowledge of cause and effect relations based on empirical study is limited. However, progress continues to be made (e.g., in understanding the psychological antecedents of panic attacks; see Schmidt, Lerew, & Jackson, 1997).

Haynes et al. (1993) also described other empirical methods for deriving causal judgments. They are (a) observing the effect of varying a hypothesized causal variable, as is most often done in applied behavior analyses using ABAB interrupted time series research designs (Kazdin, 1992); (b) collecting data (e.g., behavioral observations, questionnaire or self-monitoring data) for a single client on several occasions and performing a time-series analysis; and (c) asking clients about their perceptions of cause-and-effect relations, either by developing new self-report measures or new structured interviews.

CONCLUSION

Relatively little research has been conducted to evaluate the reliability and validity of case formulations. The research that has been conducted suggests that the validity of case formulations is often poor.

One reason case formulations may have poor validity is that the accuracy of clients' memories may be poor. History information obtained from clients may be distorted to fit clients' implicit theories about the etiology of emotional distress and behavioral dysfunctioning.

Case formulations may also have poor validity because the collection of history data can be biased and because case history information may not be comprehensive. For example, many clinicians do not regularly ask clients if they have been sexually or physically abused.

The reliability of causal judgments is often disappointing. Estimates of the interrater reliability of ratings of psychosocial stressors vary widely. Interrater reliability for psychodynamic formulations was typically poor unless the judgment tasks were tailored individually for each patient and clinicians shared the same psychoanalytic theoretical framework. Interrater reliability was fair, but test–retest reliability was poor, for judging whether negative symptoms are caused by schizophrenia or by secondary factors (e.g., neuroleptic side effects or depression).

A review of the validity of causal judgments did not reveal any task for which validity was good or excellent. This was true for psychoanalytic formulations of the etiology of schizophrenia and the etiology of several alleged psychosomatic disorders, descriptions of the functional relations between controlling variables and behavioral problems, and theories about the relation between childhood sexual abuse and the etiology of adult psychopathology. For other tasks, context effects and the effects of patient variables (e.g., sex-role compliance, age, religious beliefs) were frequently significant. Individual differences among clinicians were frequently found when clinicians attributed clients' emotional distress and behavioral difficulties to dispositional or environmental factors.

In conclusion, the reliability and validity of case formulations have been disappointing. For this reason, clinicians should be very careful about making causal judgments. Because case formulations are frequently made on the basis of clinical experience and clinical intuition, and because reliability and validity have often been poor for case formulations, clinicians may frequently want to defer from making judgments about the causes of a client's problems or they may want to try to use empirical methods to derive causal inferences.

4

BEHAVIORAL PREDICTION

Clinicians often make behavioral predictions. For example, they need to be able to judge whether a patient is likely to commit suicide or homicide. Also, clinicians are interested in prognosis and would like to be able to predict the course of a disorder and response to treatment.

Historically, some clinicians have argued that they can make valid predictions on the basis of their assessment of an individual's personality structure and dynamics. Meehl (1959b) argued that clinicians are poor at making predictions that are mediated by dynamic constructs. He also argued that when predicting the course of an illness or response to therapy, predictions based on knowledge of a person's diagnosis and crude life-history statistics will be as accurate as predictions based on an evaluation of the person's personality structure and dynamics. The issue continues to be of interest. Though the phrase *structure and dynamics* may sound antiquated to some psychologists, it would be interesting to learn if predictions based on a knowledge of a person's personality traits, motivations, values, interests, and attitudes are more accurate than predictions based on a knowledge of a person's diagnosis and demographic data or other "crude life-history statistics."

Another issue of interest is whether clinicians can make valid predictions when they learn about a person, but not the person's environment. Based on research in personality psychology, Kenrick and Funder (1988) concluded that "Systematic effects of situations, and systematic interactions between persons and situations, must be explicitly dealt with before we can predict from trait measures" (p. 31). Do clinicians systematically evaluate situations and consider interactions between persons and situations when they make predictions? If not, can their predictions be valid?

In this chapter, research on the reliability and validity of predictions is reviewed along with research on biases. In a departure from the first three chapters of this book, some results will be described for statistical prediction rules though the focus of this chapter is on clinical judgment.

RELIABILITY

Interrater reliability has been studied for the prediction of suicide and the prediction of violence. For the prediction of suicide, when clinicians were allowed to interview the patients, interrater reliability ranged from good to excellent. Intraclass correlation coefficients were .66 for ratings of "currently suicidal" (Lidz, Mulvey, Appelbaum, & Cleveland, 1989) and .90 for predicting suicidal behavior "in the next seven days" (Janofsky, Spears, & Neubauer, 1988). However, in a different study (Stelmachers & Sherman, 1990), the information presented to clinicians "was often rather scant" (p. 69). In this study, intraclass correlation coefficients were .22 for the long-term prediction of suicide and .49 for the short-term prediction of suicide.

For the prediction of violence, interrater reliability has ranged from fair to excellent. Intraclass correlation coefficients ranged from .46 when rating the likelihood of a patient attacking someone during the first week of hospitalization (McNiel & Binder, 1991) to .67 when making ratings of "currently dangerous" (Lidz et al., 1989) to .72 when rating the likelihood of threatening behavior for patients for their first week on an inpatient unit and 1.0 when predicting if patients would commit battery during the first week of their hospitalizations (Janofsky et al., 1988). The correlations of .46 and .67 were obtained when ratings were made by psychiatrists and nurses. The correlations of .72 and 1.0 were obtained when ratings were made by medical interns and their psychiatrist supervisors. The correlation of 1.0 was obtained when the interns and the psychiatrists agreed that none of the 29 patients would commit battery.

CRITERION VALIDITY

The validity of predictions will be described in this section. The bulk of the research is on the prediction of suicide and the prediction of violence. In addition, the relation between experience, training, reliability, and validity will be described. Finally, results on validity will be related to (a) the comparison of idiographic and nomothetic approaches to prediction and (b) the importance of evaluating a person's setting when making predictions.

Prediction of Suicide

Predictions of suicide were valid in one study. In this study (Shneidman, 1971), an expert clinician used unusually extensive information to make predictions. The clinician, Dr. Shneidman, is well known for his research on suicide. Predictions were made for 30 subjects, 5 of whom had committed suicide, and all of whom were participants in the longitudinal study of gifted people initiated by Lewis Terman in 1921 (see Terman, 1940). Information had been collected from the subjects, family members, and teachers over a period of 50 years. Shneidman made valid predictions for 4 of the 5 subjects who had committed suicide and 24 of the 25 subjects who had not committed suicide. The predictions may have been valid because the clinician was an expert, because the quantity and quality of the assessment information was superior to information that clinicians can reasonably hope to collect in their clinical practices, or because many of the subjects had always been emotionally stable. Presumably it is more difficult to predict suicide when all of the participants are seeking, or have been referred for, psychological treatment. Furthermore, validity may have been good because Shneidman knew that five of the people had committed suicide (he knew the local base rate) and because the base rate was relatively high (5/30 compared to 13/100,000 per year for the general population; Kaplan, Sadock, & Grebb, 1994).

In other studies, predictions of suicide have not been valid. In one of the studies (Janofsky et al., 1988), psychiatrists and medical interns on an acute psychiatry inpatient unit interviewed patients and then rated the likelihood of suicidal behavior in the next 7 days. Their predictions did not exceed a chance level of validity. In another study (Lemerond, 1977), the subject population consisted of 6,500 current or former patients who had been referred for psychological assessment at a community mental health center. Of the patients in the sample, 75 later killed themselves. The test reports of these 75 patients and the test reports of 75 other patients who served as controls were examined for predictions of suicide. A clinical prediction of suicide consisted of a statement in a patient's psychological test report indicating that the psychologist believed the patient was a suicide risk. The test reports contained warnings about suicide risk for 38% of the patients who later killed themselves and 32% of the patients who did not later kill themselves.

Results from a recent study clarify one reason why validity has been poor for clinical predictions of suicide. In this study (Malone, Szanto, Corbitt, & Mann, 1995), a research team interviewed inpatients, and they used scales and forms to evaluate history of suicidal behavior. The medical records for these patients were then reviewed. Admissions clinicians failed to document a history of suicidal behavior for 12 of 50 patients who had a history of suicidal behavior. This is significant because past suicidal behavior has often been found to be the best predictor of suicide (e.g., Pokorny, 1983). One can expect validity to be poor when clinicians are not even aware that patients have made past suicide attempts.

Impressive studies on the statistical prediction of suicidal behavior have been conducted, and a description of these studies will make clear how difficult it is to predict suicide. The studies have been impressive not for the validity of the predictions, but for the effort that went into the development of the prediction rules and into testing the validity of the predictions. The statistical rules were unsuccessful because the base rates for the occurrence of suicide were extremely low. Many years ago, Meehl and Rosen (1955) demonstrated algebraically that even when assessment information is valid, predictions may be more accurate if one ignores the assessment information and instead makes predictions using only base-rate information.

Pokorny (1983) followed 4,800 V.A. psychiatric inpatients for 5 years. Assessment data were collected using structured interviews and rating scales. During the 5-year follow-up period, 67 of the 4,800 subjects committed suicide. Patient characteristics that were strongly associated with suicide included history of suicide attempt, having been placed on suicide precautions, overt evidence of depression, diagnoses of affective disorders or schizophrenia, complaints of insomnia, and presence of guilt feelings. When a discriminant function analysis was used to make predictions, 74% of the predictions were correct. However, this procedure correctly identified only 35 of the 63 patients who committed suicide at the cost of making 1,206 false-positive predictions. Put another way, of the 1,241 predictions of suicide, only 3% were correct. On the other hand, of the 3,463 predictions of no suicide, 3,435 were correct. When base-rate information was used to set the cutoff score for the discriminant analysis function rule, 99% of the predictions were correct. However, using this approach, only one prediction of suicide was made and this prediction was incorrect. Simply predicting that no one would commit suicide would have led to a higher percentage of accuracy.

In a second study (Goldstein, Black, Nasrallah, & Winokur, 1991), 1,906 patients with affective disorders were followed for several years. The investigators also identified several risk factors for suicide (e.g., history of suicide attempts, suicidal ideation on index admission, and gender). They were also unable to predict suicide at the individual level. For example, if one predicted suicide when the statistical rule indicated that the probability of suicide is greater than .5, then no predictions of suicide would have been made even though 46 of the 1,906 patients did kill themselves. If one decided to predict suicide when the statistical-prediction rule yielded a probability value of .15 or greater, then five predictions of suicide would have been made, but only one of them would have been valid and predictions of no suicide would have been made for 45 of the 46 patients who did kill themselves.

Prediction of Violence

In a review of studies on the prediction of violence, Mossman (1994) concluded that short-term predictions of violence made by clinicians are valid. This conclusion was based on a meta-analysis of data from six studies. The meta-analysis was sophisticated because receiver operating characteristic (ROC) analysis was used to evaluate the validity of the predictions from each of the studies. Using ROC methods, measures of validity (measures of area under the ROC curve) are unaffected by base rates or by clinicians' biases for or against Type I or Type II errors (Rice & Harris, 1995). For the six studies, the average area under the ROC curve (AUC) was .69. The AUC is equal to the probability of a randomly selected violent patient being predicted to be violent more often than a randomly selected nonviolent patient. Of course, the higher the AUC, the greater the accuracy of predictions. A value of .5 would represent the chance level of prediction. AUC values were even higher when clinicians were given information that was representative of the information they obtain in clinical practice. That is, validity was highest when clinicians were allowed to interview the patients, review medical records, and in some cases interview family members or other significant others. AUC values for these four studies were .68, .71, .74, and .75 (see Mossman, 1994, Table 3).

In one of the studies reviewed by Mossman, a study by McNiel and Binder (1987), involuntary commitments to a hospital because of perceived dangerousness were considered to be implicit predictions of violence. Twenty-eight percent of the patients committed as a danger to others were physically assaultive within the first 72 hours of hospitalization compared with 7% of the patients who were committed to the hospital for other reasons (e.g., because they were a threat to hurt themselves or because they could not care for themselves). The patients judged to be dangerous might have been even more violent if they had been returned to the community instead of being committed to the hospital. At least when they are in the hospital they are likely to receive medicine.

Long-term prediction of violence is widely believed to be a more difficult task than short-term prediction of violence. Early research on the long-term prediction of violence indicated that clinicians were twice as likely to be wrong as right (for a review, see Monahan, 1981). However, these early studies were flawed. First, as noted by Lidz, Mulvey, and Gardner (1993), clinicians did not directly predict whether they thought a patient would become violent. Instead, a patient's status as being in a hospital voluntarily or on a commitment was used as an implicit prediction of whether the patient would become violent. This is not a "fatal" flaw, but one should recognize that when clinicians have been asked to directly predict the likelihood of violence, their ratings have been more valid than predictions made by using commitment status as a predictor (Apperson, Mulvey, &

Lidz, 1993). One reason this is true is because a clinician may believe a patient is violent, but may not seek a commitment because the patient is willing to enter the hospital voluntarily. Another reason some early studies on the prediction of violence were flawed is that they did not use good measures to determine if patients later became violent. To obtain criterion scores, investigators often used records of police arrests, commitment hearing reports, and clinical records. They did not routinely interview patients or their families after the patients were discharged from the hospital.

In his review of studies on the prediction of violence, Mossman (1994) concluded that long-term predictions of violence made by clinicians are as accurate as short-term and medium-term predictions of violence. This particular conclusion was based on a meta-analysis of data from 17 studies. In one of these studies (Lidz et al., 1993), clinicians directly predicted whether they thought patients would become violent in the next 6 months. Individuals coming to the psychiatric emergency department at Western Psychiatric Institute and Clinic at the University of Pittsburgh were asked to participate in a research study. Of 2,452 patients asked to participate, 1,948 consented. Clinicians predicted that 564 of these patients would become violent. Of these 564 patients, 131 dropped out of the study. Another 76 patients were dropped from the study because they could not be matched with comparison patients on the following variables: sex, race, age (within 10 years), and admission status (hospitalized or not hospitalized). Outcome scores were obtained for the remaining 357 patients and a sample of 357 matched comparison patients who served as controls. To evaluate the validity of the predictions, patients and informants (people whom the patients identified as knowing the most about them) were interviewed over the following 6 months. Also, commitment, hospital, and police records were searched for reports of violent incidents. Patients were judged to be violent if they had "laid hands on another person with violent intent or threatened someone with a weapon" (Lidz et al., 1993, p. 1008). During the next 6 months, 45% of the patients became violent. Of their violent incidents, 80% were more serious than "a push, shove, or kick" and 24% of the incidents "involved weapons, rape, attempted homicide, or assaults requiring medical treatment" (p. 1008). Predictions were significantly better than chance. Clinicians made valid predictions for 60% of the patients who became violent and 58% of the patients who did not become violent. The AUC value for this study, reported by Mossman (1994), was .66.

Though clinicians can make modestly valid long-term predictions of violence, better results have been obtained with statistical prediction rules. In the meta-analysis performed by Mossman (1994), results on clinical prediction were obtained from 17 studies and results on statistical prediction were obtained from 14 studies. The average area under the ROC curve for cross-validated statistical prediction rules was .71, but the average area under the ROC curve for clinical predictions was .67. Further analysis revealed that validity was about the same for clinicians and statistical prediction rules for short-term predictions, but statistical prediction rules were significantly more valid than clinicians for long-term predictions.

In the ongoing study at the Western Psychiatric Institute and Clinic at the University of Pittsburgh, the superiority of statistical prediction is illustrated. In this study, predictions made by using statistical rules have been significantly more accurate than predictions made by clinicians (Gardner, Lidz, Mulvey, & Shaw, 1996). The sample in this study overlapped with, but was larger than, the sample in the Lidz et al. (1993) study. Sample size in this study was 784 cases (sample size in the Lidz et al. study was 714 cases). Sample size was larger because the investigators included cases that could not be matched for age, gender, race, and admission status. The best statistical prediction rule weighed the following information: age, drug use, hostility, prior incidents of violence, seriousness of prior incidents, and presence of a thought-disorder. Individuals were most likely to become violent if they were young, were heavy drug abusers, reported recent urges to harm others, had extensive histories of violence, had past violent behavior that was serious, and did not have a thought-disorder. The statistical prediction rule was derived and validated using the same sample, but researchers used a statistical correction procedure intended to eliminate the effects of capitalization on chance (Efron, 1983). The AUC for the statistical prediction rule was .74. For this same sample, the AUC for clinical prediction was only .62.

Instead of deriving a complex statistical prediction rule, one can simply use past behavior to predict future behavior. In the meta-analysis conducted by Mossman (1994), the average accuracy of predictions based on past behavior was significantly higher than the average accuracy for clinical judgments and also significantly higher than the average for cross-validated discriminant functions. In more recent results, Gardner et al. (1996) reported that violence is predictable from prior history (AUC = .71) and that the addition of other information to prior violence did not significantly improve the accuracy of predictions (AUC = .74). However, it was also true that violence could be predicted by actuarial rules that did not include information about prior violent behavior (AUC = .70).

Additional Prediction Tasks

In most of the studies on the validity of predictions made by clinicians, the task was to predict suicide or violence. Other prediction tasks are also of great importance, but they have generally not been the subject of clinical-judgment studies. For example, clinicians would like to be able to make statements about prognosis. However, the validity of their prognostic statements has rarely been studied.

The validity of clinicians' prognostic ratings for schizophrenia may be poor (Harding, Zubin, & Strauss, 1987). Longitudinal studies indicate that many formerly chronic patients with schizophrenia significantly improve and about 25% recover. However, until appropriate longitudinal studies were conducted, many authorities on schizophrenia believed that outcome is poor for most people with schizophrenia. One reason clinicians have believed that outcome is poor for schizophrenia is because they tend to see only individuals who continue to do poorly and not individuals who improve. Practicing clinicians may not be familiar with the longitudinal studies on schizophrenia, and therefore the validity of their prognoses may be poor.

Experience, Training, Reliability, and Validity

Clinical experience has generally not been related to validity, both when experienced clinicians have been compared to inexperienced clinicians and when clinicians have been compared to graduate students (Garb, 1989). This is true for the prediction of behavior as well as for other clinical tasks (e.g., diagnosis, the description of personality and psychopathology). Specifically, clinical experience was not related to validity when graduate students and clinicians were to rate (a) risk for mental illness (Danet, 1965), (b) risk for schizophrenia (Walker & Lewine, 1990), (c) the likelihood of assaultive behavior (Werner, 1992; Werner, Rose, & Yesavage, 1983), or (d) length of stay in a psychiatric hospital (Johnston & McNeal, 1967).

Little research has been conducted on the relation between training, reliability, and validity. In one study (Quinsey & Ambtman, 1979), interrater reliability was poor for both forensic psychiatrists and high school teachers when the task was to predict the likelihood of a patient, released from a maximum-security mental hospital, committing a property offense within 12 months or an assaultive offense against persons within 12 months. Interrater reliability was also poor for both groups when the task was to rate how serious an assault would be should one occur.

A second study evaluated whether mental health professionals are more knowledgeable than lay judges. In this study by Holmes and Howard (1980), judges completed a brief multiple-choice test on factors that are related to suicide lethality. For example, the first item in their test was, "Persons who are most likely to succeed in committing suicide are (a) female and under 50 years of age, (b) female and over 50 years of age, (c) male and under 50 years of age, or (d) male and over 50 years of age" (the correct answer is male and over 50 years of age; Holmes & Howard, 1980, pp. 384–385). Physicians and psychiatrists were significantly more knowledgeable than psychologists, psychologists were significantly more knowledgeable than social workers, and social workers were significantly more knowledgeable than ministers and college students.

Idiographic and Nomothetic Approaches to Prediction

Are predictions based on an understanding of a person's traits, motivations, values, interests, and attitudes more accurate than predictions based on a knowledge of a few key pieces of information about a person? Advocates of the *idiographic* approach argue that the more one knows about a person and the more one knows about what makes a person unique, the better one will be able to predict the person's behavior. Those who espouse a *nomothetic* approach argue that general laws are applicable to all people and that an individual may be able to make predictions using only a few key pieces of information.

The empirical results support the nomothetic approach. Predictions made by using single items of information have been more valid than predictions made by clinicians who interviewed patients and reviewed medical records. For example, as already discussed, for the task of predicting violence, clinicians have been outpredicted by the single cue: past behavior of violence. (For a review, see Mossman, 1994; also see Gardner et al., 1996.)

Evaluating the Person and Setting

Prediction might be more accurate if clinicians could better evaluate the living environments of their clients and patients. For example, to predict when a patient is likely to become physically violent and when the patient is likely to be only verbally abusive and threatening, it may help to know about the patient's setting. Patients who are on a psychiatric unit with a skilled or intimidating staff may be unlikely to escalate in their behavior. Similarly, patients may be more likely to act out when a unit is crowded or other patients are intrusive.

Advances in evaluating settings have already helped to improve prediction. Most notably, many studies have demonstrated that the likelihood of relapse of schizophrenia is related to the presence of high expressed-emotion (EE) behaviors at home (e.g., parents being hostile, critical, and/or emotionally overinvolved; Bellack & Mueser, 1993). More recent research indicates that the relation between EE and relapse is even stronger for individuals with mood disorders than for individuals with schizophrenia (Coiro & Gottesman, 1996; Hooley, Rosen, & Richters, 1995).

BIASES

As in the previous chapters, studies on bias are included in the following discussion only if level of psychopathology is controlled for. For example, in the studies on prognosis, case histories presented to different groups of clinicians were identical except for the designation of a patient variable, such as the race or social class of the patient. By controlling for level of psychopathology, the effect of a patient variable, in this case race, can be tested for statistical significance. However, to learn if race bias is present in this example, research investigators need to collect criterion scores. For example, in studies on the prediction of violence, patients were sometimes followed over time to learn if they became violent. The investigators could then learn whether patient variables were related to the overprediction or underprediction of violence; that is, they could learn if predictions were less valid for female patients than male patients.

Race

In most of the studies on race bias, clients were adults and were either Black or White. It does seem that race bias is present when clinicians make predictions, but only for some tasks.

Predictions were made for children in only one study. In this study (Huebner & Cummings, 1986), ratings were made for children who were purportedly referred by their classroom teachers for a psychoeducational assessment. School psychologists were given information about classroom behavior, background information, and test results. Race of the child (Black or White) and test results (mildly mentally handicapped, borderline–ambiguous, or normal) were manipulated by the experimenters when they constructed the protocols. The school psychologists made predictions of academic, social, adaptive, and vocational behavior. The effect of client race was not statistically significant.

In a number of studies, prognoses were more favorable, or equally favorable, for Black clients than for White clients. In three studies (Lewis et al., 1990; Schwartz & Abramowitz, 1975; Strickland et al., 1988), clinicians made more favorable prognostic ratings for Black clients than for White clients. In a fourth study (Rabinowitz & Lukoff, 1995), ratings were equally favorable for Black clients and White clients.

Individual differences among clinicians have been described in several studies. For example, in one study (Franklin, 1985), the effect of client race was not statistically significant for ratings made by White therapists, but Black clients were given more favorable prognoses by Black therapists. In another study (Benefee et al., 1976), a group of Black clinicians that scored low on a measure of adherence to traditional social beliefs and values made marginally ($p < .09$) more favorable prognostic ratings for Black clients than White clients. The effect of client race was not statistically significant when a group of White clinicians made prognostic ratings after being given the same case history protocols—even when analyses were performed on ratings made by a subset of clinicians who had all scored low on the measure of adherence to traditional social beliefs and values (Bloch et al., 1980). In a final study (Atkinson et al., 1996), when psychologists predicted whether African American clients were likely to benefit from psychotherapy, there was little difference between ratings made by White clinicians (mean rating of 5.46) and ratings made by African American clinicians (mean rating of 5.71). Ratings were made on a 7-point scale.

Research on race bias and prognosis has not addressed whether prognostic ratings are worse for African American patients than for White patients when the patients have symptoms of a psychotic affective disorder. Research on diagnosis has indicated that patients with a psychotic affective disorder are more likely to be misdiagnosed as having schizophrenia if they are Black or Hispanic than if they are White (e.g., Mukherjee et al., 1983; Pavkov et al., 1989; Simon et al., 1973). Prognostic ratings are typically less favorable for patients who are believed to have schizophrenia than for patients who are believed to have major depression or bipolar affective disorder.

Predicting rehospitalization differs from the task of making prognostic ratings. When making *prognostic* ratings, one forecasts the probable course of a disorder. When predicting *rehospitalization*, one can consider a patient's prognosis, but it is also worthwhile to consider other factors (e.g., whether a patient is homeless and will seek shelter at a hospital; dependency needs that are satisfied when a patient is in the hospital; secondary gains achieved by family members when a patient is hospitalized, including not having to care for the patient). For the task of predicting rehospitalization, there was a bias to predict that Black psychiatric inpatients are more likely to be rehospitalized (Stack, Lannon, & Miley, 1983). In their study, at the time patients were discharged, primary therapists were asked to predict whether a patient would be rehospitalized during the following 2 years. To obtain criterion scores, the patients were followed for 2 years. Criterion scores were obtained for 269 patients. White patients were more often readmitted than minority patients (45% vs. 42%). Therapists had predicted that 81% of the minority patients and 63% of the White patients would be readmitted.

Race bias was reported for the prediction of violence in psychiatric hospitals and in prisons, but not for the prediction of violence in the community. For the prediction of violence on a psychiatric ward, Black psychiatric inpatients were thought to be more dangerous than White patients (Lewis et al., 1990; McNiel & Binder, 1995). In one of these studies (McNiel & Binder, 1995), the patients were observed for violence after they were admitted to a ward. The investigators were able to conclude that the risk of violence was overestimated for the Black patients, but not for the White patients. For the prediction of violence in a federal correctional institution, Black inmates and American Indian inmates were predicted to be more violent than White inmates (Cooper & Werner, 1990). Predictions were made by psychologists and case managers who were employed at federal correctional institutions. To obtain criterion scores, violent incidents were recorded for a period of 6 months. Race was not significantly related to the occurrence of violence.

For predicting violence in the community (e.g., violence against family members) race bias was not present (Lewis et al., 1990; Lidz et al., 1993). For example, in a longitudinal study on the prediction of violence (Lidz et al., 1993), the validity of predictions made by clinicians was affected only slightly by the race of the patients. Of the predictions of violence, 61% of the predictions for the White patients and 58% of the predictions for the Black patients were accurate. Of the predictions of no violence, 59% of the predictions for the White patients and 56% of the predictions for the Black patients were accurate. The difference in accuracy for White and Black patients was not statistically significant.

The effect of race was not significant for the prediction of suicide or for the prediction of compliance with treatment. These results were obtained when British psychiatrists read case histories that were identical except for the designation of race of patient (Lewis et al., 1990).

Social Class

The effect of social class has been statistically significant when clinicians have made prognostic ratings. In several studies, prognostic ratings have been worse for lower-class clients than for middle-class and upper-class clients. This has occurred when clinicians have based their judgments on case history information or recordings of an interview (Franklin, 1985; Lee & Temerlin, 1970; Rabinowitz & Lukoff, 1995; Sutton & Kessler, 1986) and when they have based their judgments on Rorschach protocols (Haase, 1964; Levy & Kahn, 1970; Trachtman, 1971). In other studies, the effect of social class was not statistically significant (Foon, 1989; Hardy & Johnson, 1992; Koscherak & Masling, 1972; Settin, 1982; Settin & Bramel, 1981; Wright & Hutton, 1977). Prognostic ratings were never more favorable for lower-class patients than for middle-class or upper-class patients.

In one study, Sutton and Kessler (1986) had clinicians (242 clinical psychologists) read one of three case histories. The case histories were identical except for the designation of social class. The client was described as having a personality disorder. The clinicians were to rate the client's prognosis on a 10-point Likert scale. Prognosis was rated as being less favorable when the client was described as being an unemployed welfare recipient with a seventh-grade education (Class V on the Two-Factor Index; Hollingshead & Redlich, 1958) compared to when the client was described as being a commercial artist with 3 years of college (Class III) or a bulldozer operator with a high school education (Class IV). Prognostic ratings for members of Class III and Class IV were not significantly different.

Gender

Though the effect of gender was typically not significant when clinicians made prognostic ratings, when it was significant ratings were less favorable for male clients than female clients. In most of the studies, prognoses for male and female clients were not significantly different (Adams & Betz, 1993; Bernstein & LeComte, 1982; Billingsley, 1977; Dailey, 1980; Elovitz & Salvia, 1982; Fischer et al., 1976; Foon, 1989; Hardy & Johnson, 1992; Lewis et al., 1990; López et al., 1993; Rabinowitz & Lukoff, 1995; Schwartz & Abramowitz, 1975; Settin, 1982; Stearns et al., 1980; Wrobel, 1993; Zygmond & Denton, 1988). In other studies, female clients were given more favorable prognoses than male clients even though both the female and male clients were described by the same case histories (Agell & Rothblum, 1991; Fernbach et al., 1989; Hansen & Reekie, 1990; Teri, 1982).

For several other prediction tasks, the effect of gender was not statistically significant. These tasks were the prediction of suicide risk (Lewis et al., 1990), of compliance with treatment (Lewis et al., 1990), and of being readmitted to a psychiatric hospital within 2 years (Stack et al., 1983).

Finally, gender bias was present when clinicians predicted the occurrence of violence. Male clients were more often predicted to be violent than were female clients (Lewis et al., 1990), and violence was overpredicted for male clients and underpredicted for female clients (Lidz et al., 1993; McNiel & Binder, 1995). For example, in the Lidz et al. study, patients were followed for 6 months after clinicians made predictions of violence. Surprisingly, more women than men became violent (49% versus 42%). However, clinicians predicted violence for men more often than for women (45% versus 22%).

Age

When ratings were made for elderly patients and young or middle-aged patients, the elderly patients were described as having a poorer prognosis than the young and middle-aged patients, even when the young and middle-aged patients and the elderly patients were described by the same case histories (Ford & Sbordone, 1980; James & Haley, 1995; Meeks, 1990; Ray, McKinney, & Ford, 1987; Ray, Raciti, & Ford, 1985; Settin, 1982; Wrobel, 1993; but also see Hansen & Reekie, 1990; Hillman et al., 1997). For example, this occurred when the clients were described as having a history of alcohol abuse or symptoms of depression or mania. Even when prognostic ratings did not vary by age (Hillman et al., 1977), risk of suicide and likelihood of hospitalization were thought to be greater for elderly patients than for middle-aged patients.

In another study when clinicians predicted the course of a client's mental disorder (Hill et al., 1977), the effect of age was not significant when clinicians viewed videotapes of 20-year-old and 35-year-old females portraying clients. The 20-year-old and 35-year-old actresses followed identical scripts.

Age bias occurred when psychologists and case managers predicted the occurrence of violence at a federal correctional institution (Cooper & Werner, 1990). The mean age of prisoners was 21.9, with a range of 18 to 30 years. Age of prisoner was not significantly correlated with the psychologists' predictions or the case managers' predictions. Four other cues were significantly correlated with the psychologists' predictions: current offense, history of violence, severity of current offense, and race of prisoner. Contrary to the predictions of the psychologists, none of these four cues were significantly correlated with the occurrence of violence during a 6-month period. However, a correlation of $-.42$ was obtained between age and the occurrence of violence during a 6-month period, with younger prisoners more often acting violently.

Sex Role

A sex-role effect is significant if clinicians predict that clients will respond better to treatment when male clients have stereotypically masculine traits and female clients have stereotypically feminine traits. Results on sex-role effects are mixed. Hill et al. (1977) reported that predictions of how much a female client would profit from counseling did not vary if the client said she was planning on going into social work or engineering. Dailey (1983) reported that ratings of prognosis in treatment were significantly more favorable for androgynous clients (clients with masculine and feminine traits) than for clients with either feminine or masculine clients. In a final study, the effect of sex-role behavior was significant. Rosenthal (1982) reported that clinicians believed a lesbian client would make less progress in treatment than other clients.

Additional Client and Clinician Characteristics

Results for other client and clinician characteristics are mixed. First, knowledge of a child's sociocultural background (rural versus suburban) was not significantly related to ratings of prognosis when school psychologists evaluated children referred because of learning problems (Huebner & Cummings, 1985). Second, ratings of the likelihood of suicide were higher and ratings of prognosis were worse when a client was described as having congenital heart disease rather than being in good health (James & Haley, 1995). Third, obesity has not been significantly related to ratings of prognosis (e.g., when clients are described as being depressed; Agell & Rothblum, 1991; Young & Powell, 1985). Fourth, prognostic ratings have been worse for unattractive clients than attractive clients (e.g., when an actress portraying a client was made-up to be relatively attractive or relatively unattractive; Elovitz & Salvia, 1982; Schwartz & Abramowitz, 1978). Finally, when Christian clinicians and nonreligious clinicians watched videotapes or listened to audiotapes of actors portraying a Christian client or a nonreligious client, the religiousness of the clients was related to ratings of prognoses in one study (Houts & Graham, 1986), but not another (Lewis & Lewis, 1985). In the study conducted by Houts and Graham (1986), both the religious and nonreligious clinicians rated a moderately religious client as having a less favorable prognosis than a nonreligious client and a strongly religious client. It is hard to understand why this result occurred and given the small sample of clinicians ($N = 48$) and clients (only 1 client in each of the three conditions), these results should be treated skeptically until they are replicated.

SUMMARY AND DISCUSSION

When clinicians were given all of the information they usually have available in clinical practice, interrater reliability for the prediction of suicide and the prediction of violence ranged from fair to excellent.

For individuals receiving treatment from a mental health professional, clinical and statistical predictions of suicide were of low validity. Also, clinicians often failed to document a history of previous suicide attempts.

In contrast to the prediction of suicide, predictions of violence have often been more accurate than chance. Though clinicians often make moderately valid short-term and long-term predictions of violence, better results have been obtained with statistical-prediction rules. Surprisingly, if predictions are based only on past behavior of violence, these predictions will often be more accurate than clinical predictions and more accurate than, or as accurate as, predictions made by cross-validated discriminant-function rules.

The validity of clinicians' prognostic ratings has rarely been studied, except indirectly in studies on patient variable bias. Clinicians' prognostic ratings for patients with schizophrenia may frequently be too pessimistic, but this has not been studied directly.

Predictions of behavior made by clinicians were not more valid than predictions of behavior made by graduate students. For ratings of dangerousness, interrater reliability was not better for psychiatrists than for teachers. With regard to identifying factors that are related to suicide, mental health professionals are more knowledgeable than ministers and college students.

Predictions made by using single items of information (e.g., past behavior of violence) have often been more valid than predictions made by clinicians who interviewed patients and reviewed medical records. There is no evidence that predictions based on an evaluation of an individual's personality structure and dynamics are more accurate than predictions based on a limited set of information (e.g., a diagnosis or information about a person's past behavior).

Predictions may become more accurate with the improved evaluation of settings. For example, relapse of schizophrenia has been related to characteristics of patients' families.

Race bias has been documented. First, when bias occurred in describing patients' prognoses, Black clients were frequently given more favorable ratings than White clients though prognoses may be less favorable for Black patients when White and Black patients have symptoms of a psychotic affective disorder. Second, when predicting which patients were likely to be rehospitalized within 2 years, there was a tendency to predict that Black psychiatric inpatients are more likely to be rehospitalized even though, after all of the patients were followed for 2 years, it turned out that White patients were more often readmitted than minority patients. Finally, race bias occurred for the prediction of violence on psychiatric wards and in prisons, but not for the prediction of violence in the community.

The effect of social class is frequently significant. Clients with a lower-class background were often given less favorable ratings of prognosis than clients with a middle-class or upper-class background.

When the effect of gender was significant, ratings for male clients were more negative than ratings for female clients. For example, in some studies, female clients were given more favorable prognoses than male clients. Also, violence was overpredicted for males and underpredicted for females. The effect of gender was not significant for the prediction of suicide risk or compliance with treatment.

The effect of age has been significant. Most notably, prognoses have been less favorable for elderly clients than for young or middle-aged clients.

Results for other client characteristics have been mixed. Sexual preference, physical attractiveness, and physical health may be related to prognostic ratings, but evidence either does not exist or findings have not been replicated for biases related to obesity, area of residence (suburban versus rural), and religious beliefs.

In conclusion, clinicians have been able to make reliable and moderately valid predictions, at least for some tasks (e.g., the short-term and long-term prediction of violence). Efforts to improve behavioral prediction are likely to involve the use of statistical prediction rules and the formal assessment of clients' settings.

5

TREATMENT DECISIONS

Research on treatment decisions can be differentiated from research on therapeutic processes. Treatment decisions are often based on assessment information such as interviews, medical records, and test results. In therapy-process research, clinicians listen to clients' statements during therapy sessions and then describe their perceptions and or responses.

The utility of treatment decisions is described in this chapter. Research on the following topics is reviewed: (a) the reliability of decisions, (b) the relation between training and the reliability and validity of treatment decisions, (c) biases that affect the decision-making process, (d) the agreement or lack of agreement between decisions and legal or ethical standards, and (e) the relation between decisions and treatment outcomes.

RELIABILITY

For many important types of treatment decisions, reliability has been poor. This has even been true when clinicians have used powerful treatment interventions. For example, interrater reliability has been low when behavior therapists have identified problem behaviors and when psychiatrists have made decisions about the use of antidepressant medicine, psychotherapy, and electroconvulsive therapy. Results on reliability, including positive results from a few studies, are described in the sections that follow.

Behavioral Assessment

Interrater reliability has been poor for behavioral assessment (Felton & Nelson, 1984; Hay, Hay, Angle, & Nelson, 1979; Persons, Mooney, &

Padesky, 1995; Wilson & Evans, 1983). In one study (Hay et al., 1979), four graduate students trained in behavioral assessment interviewed four clients who were in therapy. Each graduate student interviewed each client. Only clients who indicated that they had "very many difficulties" in at least three different problem areas were included in the study. After the interviews, the graduate students were to dictate a report with the goal of identifying a client's problems. The interviews, which had been recorded, and the dictated reports were then coded by research psychologists for problem areas that the graduate students had asked about or identified. Graduate students' ratings of problem areas were in agreement only 55% of the time; their ratings for specific problem behaviors were in agreement only 40% of the time.

Similarly, in another study (Wilson & Evans, 1983), 118 doctoral psychologists, all members of the American Association of Behavior Therapy, formulated treatment goals after reading three case history descriptions. The case histories described children with the following behavioral problems: fearfulness, conduct disorder, and social withdrawal. When the psychologists described a single primary target behavior for each case, they agreed with each other only 39% of the time. When they were asked to specify and rank-order treatment targets, agreement was again low.

Finally, in a third study (Felton & Nelson, 1984), six clinical psychologists, all trained in behavioral assessment, interviewed three students who portrayed clients. The students were given extensive information about the clients they were to portray, and they participated in three 1-hour practice sessions with the experimenter to ensure that they would be consistent when interviewed by the different psychologists. The psychologists were told that the purpose of the study was to learn about interrater reliability in behavioral assessment. They were asked to formulate specific treatment plans and describe controlling variables that produced or maintained the problem behaviors. Controlling variables could include environmental antecedents; organism variables, including physiological variables and learning history; and consequences, including short-term consequences that positively reinforce the behaviors and long-term consequences that make the behaviors problematic. Three of the six psychologists were also allowed to have the "clients" complete questionnaires and role-play how they would respond in different situations. For the three psychologists who only conducted interviews, ratings were in agreement only 38% of the time for stimulus variables, 24% of the time for organism variables, 42% of the time for consequence variables, and 59% of the time for treatment proposals. For the three psychologists who conducted interviews and also used questionnaires and role-playing sessions to collect assessment information, ratings were in agreement only 32% of the time for stimulus variables, 21% of the time for organism variables, 43% of the time for consequence variables, and 62% of the time for treatment proposals.

Somatotherapy and Psychotherapy

Interrater reliability has also been poor when psychiatrists have made decisions about the use of psychotropic medicine, electroconvulsive therapy (ECT), and psychotherapy (Goldberg et al., 1988; Hermann, Dorwart, Hoover, & Brody, 1995; Keller et al., 1986; Mayou, 1977; Nierenberg, 1991). For example, Keller et al. (1986) described the treatment received by 338 patients at five university medical centers. All of the patients had nonbipolar major depressive disorders. Differences in the amount and type of treatment (medicine, ECT, psychotherapy) provided at the five medical centers were described as being very large. In fact, the best predictor of treatment was medical center. This finding was not explained by variation in the clinical characteristics of the patients at the five hospital settings. Measures of the severity of depression could not be used to predict dosage levels of medicine, number of ECT sessions, or frequency of psychotherapy sessions. Patients who received less medicine and less ECT did not receive more psychotherapy than patients who received relatively more medicine and ECT.

Similarly, in another study (Nierenberg, 1991), interrater reliability was low for a group of 118 psychiatrists who were asked if they would choose ECT, lithium augmentation, or a different antidepressant to treat a patient who had failed to respond to an antidepressant. The psychiatrists were given a vignette describing a patient with major depression who failed to respond to 4 weeks of nortriptyline treatment at adequate blood levels. Of these psychiatrists, 34% chose lithium augmentation, 18% decided to continue nortriptyline for another 2 weeks, 16% switched to fluoxetine, 11% chose ECT, and 7% switched to a monamine oxidase inhibitor. The remaining 14% of the psychiatrists chose a number of other treatment alternatives.

In a third study (Hermann et al., 1995), the use of ECT was shown to vary widely across the United States. In this study, a survey was completed by 17,729 psychiatrists. Respondents reported the number of patients to whom they had administered ECT in the past month. The average response was 4.0. Of 320 metropolitan areas across the country (areas containing 50,000 or more people), 115 reported no ECT use, and the remaining areas reported ranges from .4 per 10,000 people to 81.2 per 10,000. The proportion of patients with affective disorders in psychiatrists' caseloads was not significantly related to the use of electroconvulsive therapy. One would expect that the variability in the use of ECT cannot be attributed to different rates of depression in different metropolitan areas because the prevalence of depression among the five sites of the Epidemiologic Catchment Area study evidenced little variation; rates ranged from 1.7% to 3.4% (Robins & Regier, 1991). State regulations regarding the use of electroconvulsive therapy were significantly and negatively related to the frequency with which patients received electroconvulsive therapy. For example, at the time of the study, California had stringent regulations regarding ECT. Of the 24 metropolitan areas in California, 50% of the areas studied reported zero cases of ECT and an additional 42% of the metropolitan areas reported low rates of use. Number of psychiatrists per capita and number of primary-care physicians per capita were also significantly related to the use of ECT. Primary-care physicians may have influenced ECT rates by detecting cases of mental disorder and referring patients for treatment. In conclusion, whether one receives medication, ECT, or psychotherapy for the treatment of depression often depends on the geographical area, setting, and personal bias of the clinician rather than empirical evidence about what type of treatment works best for what type of patient.

Level of Care

Interrater reliability has also been poor when clinicians have made recommendations for referral to one of five levels of treatment: (a) outpatient therapy, (b) intermediate nonresidential care, (c) intermediate residential care, (d) residential treatment center, and (e) inpatient care. In one study (Bickman, Karver, & Schut, 1997), 18 clinicians at a mental health clinic made ratings for 47 child and adolescent clinical profiles. They were to use written standards to make their level-of-care assignments. For the cases when clinicians agreed that they had adequate information, the kappa coefficient for interrater reliability was only .03. The results indicate that children may not receive the level of services that are best matched to their needs.

Psychodynamic Psychotherapy

Several of the studies on psychodynamic case formulation also presented results on the reliability of treatment plans. For example, using the Plan Formulation Method (Curtis & Silberschatz, 1989), the task was to describe clients' goals for therapy, pathogenic beliefs that might prevent attainment of the goals, the means by which clients could work in therapy to disconfirm their pathogenic beliefs, and insights that would be helpful to the clients. In these studies, reliability was poor when clinicians did not share the same psychodynamic orientation (Collins & Messer, 1991), but good when clinicians shared the same psychodynamic orientation and the judgment task was tailored separately for each client (Rosenberg et al., 1986). By tailoring the judgment task for each client, the task was made easier for clinicians. Of course, in clinical practice, clinicians do not make ratings for statements that have been tailor written for each client.

Techniques for Recovering Memories of Child Sexual Abuse

Consensus has also been poor when psychologists have been asked about techniques they use to help clients recover memories of child sexual

Recovering memories of sexual abuse

Hypnosis.
Dream interpretation
Guided imagery
Interpreting Physical symptoms

abuse (Polusny & Follette, 1996; Poole, Lindsay, Memon, & Bull, 1995). For example, in two surveys of psychologists working in the United States (Poole et al., 1995), 29% and 34% of the psychologists reported using hypnosis to recover memories. However, 27% and 33% of the psychologists disapproved of using hypnosis for this purpose. Similarly, 44% and 37% of the psychologists reported using dream interpretation to recover memories, but 26% and 28% of the psychologists disapproved of using dream interpretation for this purpose. In another example, 26% and 32% of the psychologists reported using guided imagery related to abuse situations, and 34% and 31% of the psychologists disapproved of its use for this purpose. Also, 36% and 36% of the psychologists reported interpreting physical symptoms, whereas 25% and 24% disapproved of interpreting physical symptoms to help clients recover memories of sexual abuse.

Breaking Confidentiality

When clinicians decide if they should break confidentiality, interrater reliability varies depending on the case. For example, in one study (Haas, Malouf, & Mayerson, 1986), the following vignette was presented:

> The mother of a 12-year-old boy comes to pick him up after his initial appointment with you. She asks you if he is taking drugs. He has in fact revealed to you that he has been sniffing glue. (p. 318)

Although 72% of the psychologists would maintain confidentiality, 24% responded that they would tell the mother about the substance abuse.

Interrater reliability was good when psychologists had to make a decision about mandatory reporting of threatened violence. In two studies (Haas et al., 1986; Tymchuk et al., 1982), psychologists read a vignette and decided if they had a duty to warn. For example, the following vignette was presented in one of the studies (Haas et al., 1986):

> You are treating a Vietnam veteran with a history of impulsive antisocial actions. You and he have established a good therapeutic relationship (his first after three previous attempts in therapy). At the end of the session, he disclosed that he is planning to kill his current girlfriend, because she has been dating another man. (p. 318)

Of the psychologists surveyed, 87% reported that they would tell the client they must warn the girlfriend or the police, 8% reported that they would contact the girlfriend or the police without telling the client, and 5% reported that they would simply plan to talk about the client's violent impulses at the next therapy session.

Civil Commitment

Interrater reliability was also good for deciding whether a person should be committed to a hospital. In one study (Lidz et al., 1989), ratings were made by 96 different clinicians for 411 individuals. Ratings were made by clinical staff at the emergency room of a large urban psychiatric hospital. For each individual, ratings were made by two clinicians, usually a psychiatrist and nurse. An intraclass correlation coefficient of .68 was obtained.

TRAINING, RELIABILITY, AND VALIDITY

Are psychologists, psychiatrists, and social workers able to make better treatment decisions than lay people, paraprofessionals, graduate students, and individuals who call themselves marital and family therapists, but either do not have a degree or have only a bachelor's degree? In several empirical studies, training was unrelated to reliability, but positively related to validity. In the first study on training and reliability (Quinsey & Ambtman, 1979), nine high school teachers and four forensic psychiatrists made decisions about whether to release patients from a maximum-security mental hospital. The patients were 9 child molesters, 10 property offenders, and 11 individuals who had committed a nonsexual assault against an adult (in most cases a murder). Information presented to judges included a description of the crimes, biographical information including information about previous offenses, and assessment data including psychological test data (when available), information from interviews, and progress notes describing ward behavior and medications. Kappa coefficients were among the lowest reported in any judgment study: .06 for psychiatrists and .11 for teachers. Kappa coefficients may have been low because base rates were high: Psychiatrists and teachers were generally unwilling to say that they would recommend that a patient be released. Psychiatrists and teachers frequently agreed on whether to release a patient (76% agreement for psychiatrists, 83% agreement for teachers), but agreement would be nearly as high if one compared a judge's ratings to judgments made by following the base rate (always saying that a patient not be released).

In a second study (Clavelle & Turner, 1980), 32 paraprofessionals, 11 social workers, and 13 clinical psychologists made decisions about whether a client should be referred to a psychiatrist for medication and whether the client should be hospitalized. Paraprofessionals had completed an 8-week, Army-sponsored training course for psychology or social work assistants or the equivalent of this course. Case histories described two individuals who had been seen at a community mental health center on an Army post. The two clients met the criteria for borderline personality disorder. Reliability coefficients were not reported, but the authors did report that (a) interrater reliability was low for all groups and (b) interrater reliability for the psychologists and for the social workers was not better than the interrater reliability for the paraprofessionals.

In a study on training and validity (Falvey & Hebert, 1992), 62 graduate students in master's degree programs and 137 certified clinical mental health counselors read case histories and wrote treatment plans. About half of the students had not completed even one semester of course work related to diagnosis and treatment planning. To obtain criterion scores, clinicians with special expertise in the treatment of anxiety and affective disorders were asked to read the case histories and formulate treatment plans. Different treatment plans and interventions were assigned different criterion scores depending on the percentage of expert clinicians who endorsed a particular goal or intervention. The validity of these criterion scores stems as much from the fact that they represent average ratings for a group of clinicians as from the fact that the clinicians were thought to be experts: Having a group of clinicians make ratings and averaging their ratings is one way to improve the reliability and validity of ratings (e.g., Horowitz, Inouye, & Siegelman, 1979). Treatment plans written by the mental health counselors were more valid than those written by the graduate students. These results are similar to results that have been obtained for other judgment tasks: Clinicians are frequently more accurate than beginning graduate students.

In a final study on training and validity, 869 psychotherapists in clinical practice in the United States were surveyed regarding their beliefs about memory and hypnosis (Yapko, 1994). Most of the clinicians were sampled at the annual meeting of the American Association of Marriage and Family Therapists, the Family Therapy Networker Symposium, a regional meeting of the American Society of Clinical Hypnosis, and the Fifth International Congress on Ericksonian Approaches to Hypnosis and Psychotherapy. PhD-level mental health professionals were less likely than other mental health professionals to endorse statements that have not been supported by empirical research. For example, when asked if "Hypnosis can be used to recover memories of actual events as far back as birth" (p. 168), affirmative responses were made by 70% of clinicians with a BA, 59% of clinicians with an MA, 64% of clinicians with an MD, 48% of clinicians with a PhD, and 80% of all other clinicians (individuals can call themselves marital and family therapists even if they do not have a degree). In another example, when asked whether "People cannot lie when in hypnosis" (p. 167), affirmative responses were made by 36% of clinicians with a BA, 20% of clinicians with an MA, 16% of clinicians with an MD, 13% of clinicians with a PhD, and 33% of all other clinicians. This is the only study cited in this book that indicates that PhD-level clinicians are more accurate than other mental health professionals. However, one should not assume that the results can be generalized to mental health professionals who are not members of the organizations that were sampled for this study.

Race Bias

Adults

Black adults are more likely than White adults to be hospitalized in, and committed to, public mental institutions (Lindsey & Paul, 1989). Many explanations for why African Americans are overrepresented have been proposed (e.g., that they are more vulnerable to mental illness because of the stresses associated with poverty and inner-city life), but one disturbing explanation that has been proposed is that clinicians are biased against Blacks.

Race bias and the decision to hospitalize or seek a commitment have been investigated in several studies. In three studies, clinicians read a case history and decided whether the person should be hospitalized. In two of the studies (Bamgbose et al., 1980; Lewis et al., 1990), clinicians who were told that the person is White and those told that the person is Black made similar ratings. In the third study (Schwartz & Abramowitz, 1975), ratings for hospitalization were higher when the person was described as being White than when the person was described as being Black, even though the case histories were identical except for the designation of race.

In one of the best clinical judgment studies ever conducted, researchers used a different methodological approach to determine whether race bias influences decisions to admit patients to the hospital or decisions to involuntarily commit patients. Lindsey, Paul, and Mariotto (1989) had 17 trained observers code the behaviors of staff and patients on 12 inpatient treatment units in the Chicago area using direct observational coding instruments. The data were originally collected as part of a larger study on observational assessment in residential treatment settings. The raters were blind to the purpose of the judgment study (to search for the presence of race bias). They did not talk with staff about the patients or review the patients' records: They were simply to make behavioral ratings. The raters were unaware of whether patients were voluntary or committed. As is typical of public mental institutions, Blacks were overrepresented among all admissions, including involuntary admissions. On measures of level of functioning, White and Black voluntary patients received similar scores. Also, White and Black involuntary patients did not differ significantly in their level of functioning. Furthermore, White and Black involuntary patients did not differ in their level of dangerous behavior. Black voluntary patients did exhibit significantly higher levels of dangerous behavior than White voluntary patients. All of these results indicate that Black patients were hospitalized more frequently than White patients, and were more often hospitalized involuntarily, because of their level of functioning and level of dangerous behavior, not because of racial prejudice.

There is evidence of race bias in the prescription of psychotropic medicine. Studies are reviewed here only if symptomatology was controlled for, either by presenting the same case history except for the designation of race to different groups of clinicians or by evaluating symptomatology using structured interviews.

The results on the prescription of psychotropic medicine mirror the results on diagnosis. Bias in prescription tends to occur when there is bias in diagnosis. For example, race bias in rating level of functioning and prescribing medicine did not occur when 102 psychiatrists were given a case history describing a patient who was depressed, had somatic complaints and sexual conflicts, and was perfectionistic (Schwartz & Abramowitz, 1975). Race bias in diagnosis and the prescription of medicine did occur when patients had symptoms of both major depression and schizophrenia (Elk, Dickman, & Teggin, 1986; Mukherjee et al., 1983). For example, White patients were more likely than Black patients to be diagnosed correctly and given lithium (Mukherjee et al., 1983). Similarly, when White patients and Black patients were thought to have schizophrenia (using a broader definition than that found in *DSM–IV*), the presence of depression in Black patients was underdetected and undertreated (Elk et al., 1986). In this study, which was conducted in South Africa, 82% of the depressed White patients were treated for depression in addition to schizophrenia (they received antidepressant medicine or ECT in addition to the medicine they were receiving for the treatment of schizophrenia) whereas only 17% of the depressed Black patients received treatment for their depression.

When clinicians read a case history describing a patient with psychotic symptoms and a history of smoking cannabis, client race was significantly related to diagnoses and recommendations for the use of neuroleptic medication (Lewis et al., 1990). Cannabis psychosis was rarely listed as a primary diagnosis for either the White or Black patients, but it was listed significantly more often as a secondary or tertiary diagnosis when the patient was described as being Black. Neuroleptic treatment was recommended significantly more often when the patient was described as being White.

In a recent study (Segal, Bola, & Watson, 1996), race bias in the prescription of neuroleptic medicine was documented. Data were collected on 442 patients at the psychiatric emergency rooms of four general hospitals. Specifically, data were collected for 107 African American patients, 256 White patients, 47 Hispanic patients, 10 Asian patients, and 22 patients from other racial or ethnic groups. Investigators controlled for (a) level of functioning (using the Global Assessment Scale), (b) presence of a psychotic disorder, (c) danger to self or others or gravely disabled, (d) history of mental disorder, and (e) whether physical restraints were used. African American patients, compared to other patients, received a significantly larger number of injections of antipsychotic medication, a significantly larger number of doses of antipsychotic medicine, and a significantly larger number of psychotropic medications. Furthermore, the clinicians spent significantly less time evaluating the African American patients than they spent evaluating the other patients. When clinicians spent more time evaluating the African American patients, the dosage of antipsychotic medication decreased.

Race bias was frequently not present when clinicians made decisions about psychotherapy. When client race effects were present, the treatment decisions made for the Black and Hispanic clients were not consistently less favorable than the treatment decisions made for the White clients. For example, client race generally had no effect when clinicians judged whether clients were likely to benefit from psychotherapy (Benefee et al., 1976; Blake, 1973; Franklin, 1985; Seligman, 1968; Vail, 1970). However, Strickland et al. (1988) reported that Black clients were given higher ratings of likelihood of successful therapy than were White clients.

With regard to formulating whether a client should be seen for brief-term, short-term, or long-term psychotherapy, client race did not have a significant effect in four studies (Bloch et al., 1980; McLaughlin & Balch, 1980; Rabinowitz & Lukoff, 1995; Tomlinson-Clarke & Cheatham, 1993). However, clinicians who scored low on a scale of traditional social values believed that the White clients should be seen for fewer sessions than the Black clients (no race effect was observed for the clinicians who scored higher on the traditional social values scale; Benefee et al., 1976). Also, in another study (Franklin, 1985), Black therapists said they would keep Black clients significantly longer than White clients. Client race was not significant in this study for the White therapists.

Finally, with regard to the type of therapy recommended (e.g., individual, couple, group, family, behavioral, nondirective, insight-oriented), no client race effect was observed in a number of studies (Lewis et al., 1990; McLaughlin & Balch, 1980; Schwartz & Abramowitz, 1975; Vail, 1970). When client race effects were observed, one cannot say that less desirable treatments were recommended for Black clients. For example, in one study (Seligman, 1968), family therapy was more often chosen for Whites and individual therapy was more often chosen for Blacks. In another study (Benefee et al., 1976), clinicians who scored high on a scale of traditional social beliefs recommended insight-oriented or nondirective therapy rather than behavior therapy more often for Black clients than for White clients. In a final study (Franklin, 1985), there were no significant client race effects for the following interventions: (a) active (making frequent interventions) versus passive (making few interventions), (b) amount of support and warmth needed, (c) emphasizing historical versus current materials, (d) emphasizing intrapsychic conflicts or interpersonal issues, and (e) being strict or permissive. However, in this same study, for the Black clients, Black therapists indicated that they would be significantly more nondirective than would the White therapists.

Children and Adolescents

In five of six analogue studies, the effect of client race was not significant when treatment decisions were made for children and adolescents. For example, race bias did not occur when school psychologists were to rate the desirability of different remedial programs for children with behavioral and academic difficulties (Amira et al., 1977; Hannaford, Simon, & Ellis, 1975; Huebner & Cummings, 1986; Matuszek & Oakland, 1979). However, when mental health professionals, physicians, and, in some cases, school principals were to make judgments and decisions regarding child abuse, the effect of the race of the child was nonsignificant in one study (Zellman, 1992) but significant in another (Jackson & Nuttall, 1993). In the study by Jackson and Nuttall (1993), clinicians were more likely to believe that child abuse had occurred with a minority child than a White child, even though the children were described by case histories that were identical except for the designation of race.

In field studies, treatment decisions were not biased against African American children, but they were sometimes biased against White children. Decisions regarding placement in a classroom for the learning disabled were more appropriate for African American children than for White children in one study (Leinhardt, Seewald, & Zigmond, 1982), but equally appropriate for African American children and White children in a second study (Payette & Clarizio, 1994). When the task was to decide whether to report child abuse, the decisions were more appropriate for African American children than for White children (Hampton & Newberger, 1985). In this study, data were collected at hospitals and child protection services in 26 counties in 10 states. The research investigators asked hospital personnel to inform them when they were treating children who had been abused. At the same time, lists of cases that had been reported for possible child abuse were obtained from local child protection services. Hospital personnel informed the research investigators about over 77,000 cases of child abuse. However, about half of the cases of child abuse described by the hospital personnel were never reported to the child protection services. Cases of child abuse were more likely to be reported when they were African American than when they were White, even when the following factors were controlled for: nature of emotional abuse, family income, and role of mother.

Social Class Bias

Children

When school psychologists have made treatment recommendations, lower social class children have not been more likely than middle-class or upper-class children to be referred to a special education program. In two studies (Amira et al., 1977; Matuszek & Oakland, 1979), school psychologists recommended more special services (e.g., custodial placement at a separate school) for middle-class children than for lower-class children. In three other studies (Bernard & Clarizio, 1981; Frame et al., 1982; Ysseldyke, Algozzine, Regan, & McGue, 1981), the effect of social class was not significant for placement decisions. The results are surprising because many people had believed that if bias occurred, recommendations would have been made for the lower-class children to be referred for special services.

Child abuse is more likely to be reported for lower social class children than for middle-class children. In one study (Zellman, 1992), a total of 1,196 psychologists, child psychiatrists, social workers, school principals, pediatricians, child care providers, and general and family practitioners read case histories and indicated if they would report child abuse. Case histories presented to different groups of clinicians were identical except for statements describing social class. For three of six cases, the effect of social class was not statistically significant. However, for the other three cases, child abuse was more likely to be reported for the children described as having a lower class background. These results have been replicated in a field study (Hampton & Newberger, 1985). In this study, child abuse was more likely to be reported for lower social class children than for middle-class and upper-class children.

Adults

The effect of social class was not significant for decisions related to hospitalization. This result was obtained (a) when different groups of mental health professionals made decisions after reading case histories that were identical except for the description of social class (Bamgbose et al., 1980; Hardy & Johnson, 1992) and (b) when field studies were conducted and the decisions made by mental health professionals in the course of their work were analyzed (Lindsey et al., 1989; Rabinowitz, Massad, & Fennig, 1995). For example, in one of the studies (Rabinowitz et al., 1995), clinicians were psychiatrists and psychiatric residents working in Israel. When level of psychopathology was controlled for, the level of education of the patients was not significantly related to decisions to hospitalize, admit to an unlocked unit, or discharge from the hospital.

Though the effect of social class was not statistically significant for decisions related to hospitalization, it was significant for decisions related to psychotherapy. Individuals were thought to be in greater need of professional help when they were described as being middle-class rather than lower-class, especially when a vignette described them as having relatively few problems or as having problems that are related to neurosis rather than psychosis (Routh & King, 1972). Lower-class clients were judged to be less likely to benefit from psychotherapy, they were less likely than middle-class clients to receive psychotherapy, and when they were seen in psychotherapy, they were relatively more likely to be seen for supportive counseling than insight-oriented therapy (Franklin, 1985; Levy & Kahn, 1970; Neumann, Salganik, Rabinowitz, Bauer, & Kastner, 1990; Rabinowitz & Lukoff, 1995; Rowden, Michel, Dillehay, & Martin, 1970; Sutton & Kessler, 1986; Umbenhauer & DeWitte, 1978; though in one study, Settin & Bramel, 1981, the difference was not statistically significant). For example, at an outpatient mental health clinic in Israel, clients were more likely to receive psychotherapy if they had a higher level of education, even though no correlation was found between educational status and diagnosis (Neumann et al., 1990). As another example, when treating lower-class clients, psychodynamic clinicians reported that they would focus on interpersonal and current conflicts rather than intrapsychic conflicts (Franklin, 1985).

There may be several reasons why the effect of social class was significant when clinicians made decisions regarding psychotherapy. For example, there is evidence that cognitive variables vary with social class (Herrnstein & Murray, 1994) and that many clinicians believe these cognitive variables are positively related to psychotherapy outcome (Dowds, Fontana, Russakoff, & Harris, 1977). If clinicians attend to the cognitive variables of clients and not to social class when they decide if psychotherapy is appropriate, then it will be important for research investigators to ascertain if these referrals are appropriate and if new treatments can be developed for lower-class clients. On the other hand, referrals for psychotherapy may be made less often for lower-class clients than for middle-class clients because most clinicians have middle-class backgrounds and are better able to empathize with clients who share a similar background. If this is the case, then it will be important to train more clinicians with lower-class backgrounds.

Gender Bias

Adults

The effect of client gender has not been statistically significant when clinicians have made decisions about hospitalization after reading case histories (Fernbach et al., 1989; Hansen & Reekie, 1990; Lewis et al., 1990; Lowery & Higgins, 1979; Murray & Abramson, 1983; Schwartz & Abramowitz, 1975; Wrobel, 1993). However, gender bias has been described when archival data have been collected. Results from the field studies are described below.

In one study (Rosenfield, 1982), data were collected at a large hospital in New York City. For 666 individuals who had been brought to the psychiatric emergency room at the hospital in September and October of 1979, clinicians recorded each person's gender, diagnosis, and disposition (hospitalization or nonhospitalization). Of this sample, 49% of males and 50% of females were hospitalized. If one grouped individuals by severity of disorders, one would conclude that gender bias did not occur. For psychotic individuals, 63% of the males and 58% of the females were hospitalized. The difference is not statistically significant. For individuals with diagnoses of personality disorder or neurosis, 25% of the males and 32% of the females were hospitalized. The difference was again not significant. However, significant differences did occur when psychopathology was inconsistent with traditional sex-role norms. For example, women more often have been diagnosed as having depression and neurosis, but men more often have exhibited aggressive or antisocial behavior and have been diagnosed as having substance abuse and personality disorders. For individuals with diagnoses of personality disorders and substance abuse, 50% of the female clients and only 18% of the male clients were hospitalized. For individuals with diagnoses of neurosis or psychotic depression, 66% of the men and 43% of the women were hospitalized.

In a related study (Baskin, Sommers, Tessler, & Steadman, 1989), gender bias was observed when prison inmates were placed in mental health facilities. Data were obtained on 3,637 inmates, of whom 142 (4%) were female and 3,495 (96%) were male. Female inmates were significantly more likely to be placed in a mental health facility even when psychiatric need was controlled for. Psychiatric need was controlled for by having correctional case managers rate whether, during the 90 days prior to the survey, an inmate had bizarre habits or strange ideas, depression, or suicidal behavior. Results also indicated that gender bias was more likely to occur when inmates evidenced behaviors or symptoms that were incongruent with traditional sex-role norms. For example, the likelihood of mental health placement increased for female inmates but not for male inmates when the inmates were violent. Male inmates were more likely than female inmates to be placed in a mental health facility when both the male and female inmates were depressed.

In another field study on client gender and hospitalization (Rabinowitz et al., 1995), the effect of client gender on decisions of whether to hospitalize individuals was not statistically significant. Unlike the other two studies discussed in this section, an analysis was not performed to learn if the effect of client gender was related to whether a patient's behaviors were sex-role congruent or incongruent. The effect of client gender was significant for a related decision: Once a clinician decided hospitalization was appropriate, a decision had to be made about whether the person should be on an open or locked unit. Male clients were more likely than female clients to be sent to a locked ward.

Generally, gender effects were not significant for referrals for clients to be seen for psychiatric treatment (Farmer & Griffiths, 1992), for referrals for clients to receive electroconvulsive treatment (Lowery & Higgins, 1979; Schwartz & Abramowitz, 1975), or for the prescription of psychotropic medicine (Del Gaudio, Carpenter, & Morrow, 1978; Fernbach et al., 1989;

Hansen & Reekie, 1990; Lowery & Higgins, 1979; Murray & Abramson, 1983; Oyster-Nelson & Cohen, 1981; Schwartz & Abramowitz, 1975; Stearns et al., 1980; Wrobel, 1993). When gender bias was found, results were never replicated. Stein, Del Gaudio, and Ansley (1976) described the occurrence of gender bias for a sample of men and women who were all diagnosed as having neurotic depression. Descriptions of the men and women did not differ with regard to symptoms, mood, or interpersonal behavior. They were all assigned to either individual or group therapy. Significant differences were present in the prescription of medicine though the number of patients in the study was small: Psychotropic medicine was prescribed for 18 of 30 women and only 5 of 13 men. Gender bias was also reported by Lewis et al. (1990). For a case history that typically elicited diagnoses of schizophrenia or affective disorder, neuroleptic medicine was more often recommended when the patient was described as being male rather than female. A gender effect for antidepressant medicine was not significant.

Referrals for psychotherapy were also usually not influenced by gender. This was true when clinicians were to decide if they should refer clients to insight-oriented therapy (Schwartz & Abramowitz, 1975); individual therapy or a partial hospitalization program (Lowery & Higgins, 1979); individual therapy or group therapy (Murray & Abramson, 1983); psychotherapy, supportive therapy, or group therapy (Stearns et al., 1980); insight-oriented therapy, humanistic–experiential therapy, group therapy, systematic desensitization, social skills training, or cognitive–behavior therapy (Oyster-Nelson & Cohen, 1981); bereavement counseling, family counseling, community self-help group, genetic counseling, or day hospital (Lewis et al., 1990); insight-oriented therapy, cognitive–behavioral therapy, supportive therapy, social skills training, or day hospital (Wrobel, 1993); and no therapy, supportive–educative therapy, short-term therapy, or long-term therapy (Hecker et al., 1995).

Referrals for type of therapy were influenced by client gender. In one study (Bowman, 1982), couple therapy was recommended more often for male clients than for female clients, while individual insight-oriented psychotherapy was recommended more often for female clients than for male clients—even though male and female clients were described by the same case history except for the designation of gender. In a second study (Fernbach et al., 1989), group therapy was more often recommended for men, and there was a trend for insight-oriented individual therapy to be recommended more often for women, but gender effects were not significant for referral to marital or family therapy or behavioral medicine. In this study, men were more often diagnosed as having an antisocial personality disorder even though men and women were described by the same case histories except for the designation of gender.

A related issue is whether clinicians are more directive (or nondirective) with male or female clients. In one study (Fischer et al., 1976), social workers said they would be more nondirective with female clients, but in a replication of this study (using the same experimental design but a larger number of clinicians), the gender effect for being directive versus nondirective was not significant (Dailey, 1980). Similarly, in another study (Bernstein & LeComte, 1982), client gender was not significantly related to mental health professionals' expectations of whether they would be directive or nondirective. In a final study (Fernbach et al., 1989) clinicians indicated they would be more nondirective with female clients. In this study, clinicians had more often diagnosed the male clients as having an antisocial personality disorder even though the male and female clients had been described by the same case histories.

The effect of gender was significant when clients were assigned to therapists. When data were collected at a university counseling center, 103 of 142 clients (73%) were referred to counselors of the same sex (Shullman & Betz, 1979). Similarly, in another study (Schover, 1981), all of the therapists felt it would be easier to establish a good therapeutic relationship with a same-sex client.

In a number of analogue studies, clinicians made judgments about whether clients are likely to benefit from psychotherapy. Client gender was unrelated to judged need for therapy (Murray & Abramson, 1983) and unrelated to ratings of appropriateness for psychotherapy (Adams & Betz, 1993). Gender was found to be related to need for therapy but unrelated to judgments of whether clients were good candidates for therapy (male clients were judged as being in greater need; Oyster-Nelson & Cohen, 1981). Client gender was found to be unrelated to willingness to accept clients into therapy or expectations of clients completing therapy (Stearns et al., 1980); need for therapy, expectancies for client outcomes, or anticipated use of interpretation (Bernstein & LeComte, 1982); expected usefulness of treatment or interest in treating a client (Settin, 1982); and interest in providing treatment, encouraging a client to seek treatment, and treatment expectations (Agell & Rothblum, 1991). However, gender was related to judgment of motivations to change (female clients were judged as more motivated; Agell & Rothblum, 1991).

Client gender was generally not significant when clinicians made decisions about how long a client should remain in therapy. For example, client gender was not significant for this decision when clinicians read case histories (Agell & Rothblum, 1991; Hecker et al., 1995; Murray & Abramson, 1983; Oyster-Nelson & Cohen, 1981; Stearns et al., 1980) except in one study (Fernbach et al., 1989). In this study, men were diagnosed more often than women as having an antisocial personality disorder, women were more often recommended for insight-oriented therapy, and clinicians recommended that women remain in therapy longer.

Client gender frequently did not have a significant effect on the formulation of treatment goals (Austad & Aronson, 1987; Billingsley, 1977; Dailey,

1980; Fischer et al., 1976; Garfinkle & Morin, 1978; McCollum & Russell, 1992; though see Bowman, 1982; Miller, 1974). For example, in one of the studies (Billingsley, 1977), clinicians read case histories and then chose six initial therapy goals from a checklist of 18 items. Nine of the items were thought to be male-valued (e.g., increase in self-confidence, ability to think logically, assertiveness), and nine of the items were thought to be female-valued (e.g., increase in ability to express emotion, ability to communicate, awareness of feelings of others). Client gender was not significantly related to the choice of treatment goals.

Though client gender was frequently not a significant predictor when the task was to set treatment goals, exceptions did occur. Significant effects were reported in two analogue studies. In one study (Miller, 1974), male and female clients were described as being passive. A goal for the male clients, which was less often a goal for the female clients, was to become less passive. In a second study (Bowman, 1982), achieving a satisfactory balance between home and career responsibilities was more often set as a goal for female clients than for male clients. In this same study, the effect of client gender was not significant for the following goals: (a) improve communication, (b) improve sex life, and (c) develop insight.

Results on making referrals to vocational counseling were mixed. Female clients were neither more nor less often referred to vocational counseling than male clients (Buczek, 1981; Fernbach et al., 1989). However, psychologists were more likely to refer same-sex clients than opposite-sex clients to vocational counseling (Lowery & Higgins, 1979). That is, female psychologists were more likely to refer female clients and male psychologists were more likely to refer male clients.

Children and Adolescents

The effect of client gender was frequently not statistically significant when clinicians made treatment decisions for children and adolescents. When the effect of gender was statistically significant, the results were not replicated. Results for several tasks are described in this section.

Decisions to hospitalize adolescents were unrelated to client gender (Morrissey et al., 1995). In this study, different groups of psychiatrists, psychologists, social workers, and nurse clinicians read case histories that were identical except for the designation of gender.

School psychologists were relatively unaffected by the gender of clients when the task was (a) to advise high school students on choosing a career (Smith, 1974) or (b) to plan an intervention for a behavioral problem (e.g., make no intervention, see in counseling, or develop a behavior modification plan; Prout & Frederickson, 1991). In both studies, the male and female students were described by identical case histories except for the designation of gender.

Psychologists and other groups of health professionals have been unaffected by the gender of a child when reporting suspected child abuse. In several studies (Jackson & Nuttall, 1993; Kalichman, Craig, & Follingstad, 1989; Kennel & Agresti, 1995; Zellman, 1992), when clinicians read vignettes that differed only in the designation of the child's gender, the effect of child's gender was not statistically significant. In a fourth analogue study (Howe, Herzberger, & Tennen, 1988), the effect of child gender was statistically significant, but the magnitude of the effect was tiny. Clinicians rated the severity of abuse on a 7-point scale. Ratings were 5.8 for sons and 5.7 for daughters.

Though a child's gender may have little impact on the reporting of child abuse, the gender of the perpetrator does seem to determine, in part, whether child abuse will be reported. In a field study (Hampton & Newberger, 1985), one of the two most powerful predictors of whether child abuse would be reported was the role of the child's mother in the abuse. Child abuse was less likely to be reported when the child's mother was the alleged perpetrator than when the father was the alleged perpetrator.

For the task of placement of children in special education programs for the treatment of learning diabilities, results on gender bias are mixed. In analogue studies, the effect of child gender was not statistically significant (Elovitz & Salvia, 1982; Hannaford et al., 1975; Ysseldyke et al., 1981). When data were collected in field studies, results ranged from indicating no bias (Clarizio & Phillips, 1986) to indicating bias against male students (Leinhardt et al., 1982) to indicating bias against female students (Payette & Clarizio, 1994). In all of the field studies, expected achievement was calculated by using the Wechsler Intelligence Scale for Children–Revised (WISC–R). Full-scale IQ, and actual achievement was measured using the Wide Range Achievement Test (WRAT). In the Leinhardt et al. (1982) study, female students in a learning disability class were more likely than male students to have a severe discrepancy between actual and expected achievement (i.e., placement was more appropriate for females). In the Payette and Clarizio (1994) study, when students did not have a severe discrepancy between actual and expected achievement, female students were more likely than male students to be placed in learning disability programs (placement was less appropriate for females).

Sex-Role Bias

Sex-role bias occurs if clinicians try to persuade clients to conform to sex roles. For example, they may want male adolescents to choose careers that have traditionally been chosen by men, or they may be biased against gay men or lesbians. All of the studies conducted on sex-role bias and treatment planning have been analogue studies.

The difference between gender bias and sex-role bias is subtle but can be easily explained. To study sex-role bias, one does not manipulate client gender, but instead one manipulates behaviors that are related to sex-roles. A study on sex-role bias can be designed to have clinicians make judgments for only female clients or for only male clients.

In two studies, school counselors advised high school students on vocational plans. Female students who chose male-dominated fields rather than female-dominated fields (e.g., engineering rather than social work) were rated as having inappropriate goals in one study (Thomas & Stewart, 1971), but their choice was accepted by the counselors in a second study (Hill et al., 1977).

In several analogue studies, treatment decisions were not biased against gay men or lesbians. For example, in one study (Garfinkle & Morin, 1978), different groups of psychologists read case histories that were identical except for the designation of client gender and client sexual orientation. Psychologists were to describe the major problems that should be addressed in therapy, write a specific treatment plan, and describe a strategy for therapeutic intervention. The only difference in treatment goals, plans, and interventions for the homosexual and heterosexual clients was that accepting greater responsibility was more often a goal for the heterosexual clients. In a second study (McGuire, Nieri, Abbott, Sheridan, & Fisher, 1995), psychologists read a case history, indicated if they would break confidentiality because the client has AIDS and could be considered to be a danger to others, and completed a measure of homophobia. The likelihood of breaking confidentiality did not differ if clients were described as being a homosexual man, a male hemophiliac, or a female prostitute. McGuire et al. (1995) also observed that the psychologists had "low overall homophobia scores" (p. 610). Finally, in a third study (Fliszar & Clopton, 1995), sexual orientation was not significantly related to decisions about the appropriateness of psychotherapy.

Age Bias

The effect of client age was not statistically significant when decisions were made about admission or commitment to a hospital (Hansen & Reekie, 1990; Lindsey et al., 1989; Rabinowitz et al., 1995), but it was statistically significant when patients were assigned to open or locked wards and when decisions were made about discharging patients from the hospital (Rabinowitz et al., 1995). The Lindsey et al. (1989) and Rabinowitz et al. (1995) studies were field studies. Lindsey et al. reported that the addition of patient age to measures of level of functioning and level of dangerous behavior did not allow the investigators to better predict the clinicians' decisions regarding commitment to the hospital. Rabinowitz et al. reported that though patient age was not related to admission to the hospital, patients who were 20 to 30 years old were more likely to be sent to a locked ward (even after controlling for psychopathology) and patients who were 50 to 60 years old were likely to be discharged sooner (even after controlling for psychopathology).

The effect of age was significant when clinicians made recommendations for psychotherapy or treatment with psychotropic medicine. In general, psychotherapy was recommended more often for young clients than elderly clients, and when there was a tendency to diagnose organic disorders more in the elderly, the elderly were less likely to be prescribed antidepressant medications (Ford & Sbordone, 1980; Hansen & Reekie, 1990; James & Haley, 1995; Pat-Horenczyk, 1988; Perlick & Atkins, 1984; Ray et al., 1985, 1987; Settin, 1982; Wrobel, 1993; but also see Hillman et al., 1997). In all of the studies, different groups of clinicians made recomendations after reading vignettes that were identical except for the designation of age. Results from several of the studies are described below.

In one study (Ford & Sbordone, 1980), no significant differences were found for the type of treatment recommended for young and old clients with problems of agoraphobia, alcohol abuse, or mania. However, treatment recommendations were significantly different when clients were described as having a neurotic depression. For a 32-year-old client, psychotherapy alone, psychotherapy and pharmacotherapy, and pharmacotherapy alone were recommended by 32%, 67%, and 1% of the psychiatrists, respectively. For a 72-year-old client described by the same vignette, psychotherapy alone, psychotherapy and pharmacotherapy, and pharmacotherapy alone were recommended by 8%, 81%, and 11% of the psychiatrists, respectively.

In another study (Settin, 1982), clients were described as having a reactive depression. Ratings made by clinical psychologists were more negative for a 72-year-old client than a 46-year-old client. The psychologists rated (a) usefulness of psychotherapy, (b) interest in providing psychotherapy, and (c) comfort (of the therapist) on initial contact.

In a third study (Perlick & Atkins, 1984), a case description was based on the case of a 64-year-old man with a diagnosis of severe endogenous depression and impairment of recent memory, abstract thinking, and attention–concentration. Clinical psychologists were significantly less likely to recommend treatment with antidepressant medicine when the client was described as being 75 years old compared with when the client was described as being 55 years old. Clinicians made more diagnoses of organic disorder and fewer diagnoses of depression for the 75-year-old client. Thus, clinicians may underdiagnose and fail to treat depression in the elderly.

In a fourth study (Pat-Horenczyk, 1988), ratings were made for clients who were described as having depressive episodes. Pharmacotherapy or electroconvulsive treatment were recommended for 97% of the 34-year-old patients and 87% of the 69-year-old patients. Supportive therapy was recommended for 45% of the 34-year-old patients and 84% of the 69-year-old patients, but dynamic therapy was recommended for 45% of the 34-year-old patients and 6% of the 69-year-old patients.

In a final study (Wrobel, 1993), clinical psychologists made ratings for clients described as having cognitive and affective symptoms of depression. Cognitive–behavioral therapy and chemotherapy were more often recommended for 45-year-old, 55-year-old, and 65-year-old clients but supportive therapy was more often recommended for 75-year-old and 85-year-old clients.

Age bias also occurs when psychologists report suspected child abuse (Jackson & Nuttall, 1993; Kalichman & Craig, 1991; Kennel & Agresti, 1995; Zellman, 1992; but also see Kalichman & Brosig, 1992). Psychologists have been more likely to report suspected child abuse when a victim has been described as being young (e.g., age 7 versus 16). This bias has occurred when groups of psychologists read vignettes that were identical except for the designation of age.

Treatment Decisions Made for Mentally Retarded Clients

In several analogue studies, different groups of psychologists were given case histories that were identical except that some of the clients were described as being mentally retarded and some were described as having average intelligence. For example, in one study (Reiss et al., 1982), the mentally retarded client was described as having an IQ of 58 and a history of: (a) having slow motor and intellectual development since first grade, (b) attending special education during his school years, and (c) attending vocational training for handicapped people following graduation from high school. The client with average intelligence was described as having an IQ of 108 and being a high school graduate.

Treatment was offered less often to mentally retarded clients than to average-intelligence clients. For example, when clients were described as having a phobia, systematic desensitization was recommended less often for the mentally retarded client than for the average-intelligence client (Reiss et al., 1982). Similarly, when clients were described as having schizophrenia, psychotherapy and drug therapy were recommended less often for the mentally retarded client than for the average-intelligence client (Reiss et al., 1982; Reiss & Szyszko, 1983; Spengler & Strohmer, 1994).

Spengler and Strohmer (1994) reported that treatment recommendations were most likely to differ for mentally retarded and average-intelligence clients when ratings were made by psychologists who were described as having low cognitive complexity. *Cognitive complexity* refers to how well individuals can use incongruent or contradictory information, or, put another way, how well they can integrate large amounts of information.

Treatment Decisions Made for AIDS Patients

Results on the effect of having AIDS are mixed. For example, when a client was described as having a major depressive disorder and either cancer, AIDS, or no medical condition, tricyclic antidepressants were more often recommended for the cancer patient and the patient with no medical condition than the AIDS patient, even though all of the patients were described by the same case history except for the medical designation (Walker & Spengler, 1995). In another study (Fliszar & Clopton, 1995), when clients were described by the same case history except for being described as having AIDS or leukemia and being heterosexual or homosexual, type of illness and sexual orientation were not significantly related to decisions about the appropriateness of psychotherapy.

Additional Client Variable Biases

There are several other client variables, such as client attractiveness, obesity, area of client origin, and religious or political affiliation, that may bias clinicians' treatment decisions. The effects of these client variables on treatment decisions were generally nonsignificant. The few effects that were statistically significant were never replicated in follow-up studies.

Results are contradictory on whether the attractiveness of clients is related to treatment recommendations. To vary the level of attractiveness, photographs were included with case history information. When clinicians made decisions about special class placement for children, the effect of attractiveness was statistically significant in one study (attractive children were less likely to be referred to a program for the mentally retarded; Elovitz & Salvia, 1982) but not another study (Ysseldyke et al., 1981). Similarly, when clinicians recommended an optimal number of therapy sessions for adult clients, the effect of attractiveness was statistically significant in one study (attractive clients were recommended to have more frequent sessions; Murray & Abramson, 1983) but not in another study (Schwartz & Abramowitz, 1978).

The obesity of clients was unrelated to ratings of usefulness of therapeutic intervention, interest in providing therapeutic intervention, encouragement to seek therapy, and expected duration of therapy (Agell & Rothblum, 1991; Young & Powell, 1985). In one of the studies, a client's weight and height were listed in the case history. In the other study, clinicians were given a photograph of the client. Attractiveness was controlled by using a special photographic process. A single photograph was modified by a photographer so that the person appearing in prints made from the photograph seemed to vary in weight.

The effect of a child's area of origin—whether the child is from a rural, suburban, or inner-city area—has not been statistically significant when school psychologists have made decisions about educational placement (e.g., recommendations for placement in a regular class or in a full-time special class; Hannaford et al., 1975; Huebner, 1985; Huebner & Cummings, 1985). All of these studies were analogue studies: Recommendations were made by different groups of school psychologists after they reviewed a brief case history and test results that were identical except for the designation of area of habitation. In one of these studies (Huebner, 1985), the school psychologists were told that a White boy in the second grade had recently moved to a new school and was having academic difficulties. The type of setting that the boy had purportedly moved from was also experimentally manipulated by the investigator (the boy was described as being from a rural, suburban, or inner-city area). The effect of this setting was also not significantly related to the placement recommendations made by the school psychologists.

Religious bias and political bias have also been investigated. In one study (Lewis & Lewis, 1985), a nonreligious patient was rated as needing more therapy sessions than a religious patient, but the effect of client religion was nonsignificant for ratings of appropriateness for therapy, likelihood of making progress in therapy, and need for psychiatric hospitalization. In a second study (Mazer, 1979), ratings of the feasibility of therapy did not vary as a function of whether the political views of the therapists and clients were similar or dissimilar.

Labeling Bias

In the context of treatment planning, labeling bias is said to occur when treatment recommendations are affected by being told how a person has been diagnosed by another clinician. Being influenced by diagnoses that have been made by another clinician can be appropriate. However, labeling bias can lead to two problems. First, diagnoses made by another clinician may be wrong, in which case they are obviously a poor basis for treatment decisions. Second, even if the diagnoses are correct, clinicians may make inappropriate inferences from the diagnoses, and again their treatment recommendations may have poor utility.

In several studies (Algozzine & Ysseldyke, 1981; Burns, 1992; Cummings, Huebner, & McLeskey, 1986; Huebner, 1987a, 1987b, 1990; Huebner & Cummings, 1985), professionals at schools (e.g., school psychologists, special education teachers) were to decide if children were eligible for special education classes. They were given test scores and test observations for normal children. However, they were also given referral statements that falsely stated that the children were having behavior or academic problems. Results from the studies were contradictory, but it appears that labeling bias will sometimes occur when the referral statements are strongly biased toward a diagnosis of learning disability.

It is not clear if clinicians make inappropriate inferences from diagnoses. In one study (Lewis & Appleby, 1988), when psychiatrists were told that an adult client was previously diagnosed as having a personality disorder, they were not less likely to recommend psychiatric hospitalization or psychotherapy, but they were slightly less likely to recommend antidepressant medicine, even though the client complained of depression and crying spells. Since this was an analogue study and the psychiatrists were given little information about the client, future investigations will have to determine (a) if clients with diagnoses of personality disorder are undermedicated when they complain of feeling depressed and (b) if the labeling bias leads to the underutilization of antidepressants for clients who have previously been diagnosed as having a personality disorder.

Context Effects

Treatment decisions should be based on a person's problems and needs, not on characteristics of the treatment setting. For example, the length of time a patient is hospitalized should not depend on how long other patients are usually hospitalized, patients should not be mistreated to increase profits from insurance claims, and admission to a hospital should not be influenced by whether a person was brought to an emergency room by a police officer.

Harmful consequences of context effects have been described. In the Rosenhan (1973) study, eight sane individuals (a psychology graduate student, three psychologists, a pediatrician, a psychiatrist, a painter, and a housewife) went to a psychiatric hospital and complained of hearing voices. They answered questions truthfully except when asked their name, vocation, and place of employment; why they had come to the hospital; and whether they heard voices. Once they were admitted to the hospital, they no longer complained of hearing voices and they denied having any psychiatric symptoms. Treatment decisions regarding length of stay were inappropriate: Length of hospitalization ranged from 7 to 52 days, with an average stay of 19 days. Because clinicians were not influenced by the pseudopatients' behavior once the pseudopatients came into the hospital, one can conclude that they were influenced by context.

Journalists have also described the harmful consequences of context effects. Employees at private psychiatric hospitals have been criticized for systematically misdiagnosing and mistreating patients to increase profits from insurance claims (Sharkey, 1994). In his book, *Bedlam*, Sharkey describes the dramatic growth of the private psychiatric industry (e.g., the number of for-profit psychiatric hospitals grew from 220 in 1984 to 444 in 1988), and he describes instances when individuals were unnecessarily hospitalized and were then kept until their insurance ran out. In some cases, workers in the community (e.g., social workers, school counselors, probation officers, crisis hot-line workers, ministers) were allegedly paid to refer individuals to the hospitals. Thus, someone might talk to a trusted individual and enter a hospital based on that person's recommendation without realizing that the person received a financial reward for having referred her or him to the hospital. Now that questions have been raised about some for-profit psychiatric hospitals, clinicians and researchers need to go beyond relating anecdotes and instead conduct empirical research to describe how often patients at for-profit psychiatric hospitals are unnecessarily hospitalized and inappropriately treated.

A context effect was also described in a study (Kullgren et al., 1996) in which Swedish psychiatrists read three case reports. The psychiatrists were significantly more likely to recommend involuntary psychiatric hospitalization when family members demanded that the person be hospitalized. For example, in one of the case histories, a person was described as being extremely depressed. She was unwilling to see a psychiatrist, and she was not able to contract for safety. Sixty-five percent of the psychiatrists indicated that they would have her committed to a hospital. When the case history indicated that a family member insisted that she be hospitalized, 77% of the psychiatrists recommended commitment to a hospital.

In one study in which the effect of police officers bringing patients into emergency rooms was evaluated (Watson, Segal, & Newhill, 1993), the effect of context was not statistically significant. Police officers frequently bring patients to psychiatric hospitals, and clinicians may be more likely to hospitalize someone if they have been brought in by a police officer. In the study, data were gathered on 772 cases over a 6-year period at nine state and county facilities in California. Patients were evaluated by staff clinicians and research clinicians. Interrater reliability for the research clinicians was demonstrated to be good. The results do not indicate that clinicians arbitrarily admitted people because they were brought in by the police. The researchers found that 75% of police-referred patients and 61% of other patients were hospitalized. Of the patients who were hospitalized, the patients who were referred by the police were rated by the research clinicians as scoring higher on measures of overall perceived dangerousness; disability; severity of formal thought disorder; and presence of disorders of thought content, judgment, behavior, and affect. They were also described as being significantly more irritable, expansive, and impulsive. These results suggest that this particular type of context effect did not exert undue influence on decisions to hospitalize patients.

LEGAL AND ETHICAL STANDARDS AND DECISION MAKING

One way to evaluate treatment decisions is to see if they are in agreement with legal and ethical principles. The appropriateness of decisions to seek a commitment for involuntary hospitalization, of decisions to break confidentiality and report suspected child abuse, and of treatment decisions for cases of domestic abuse are all areas of critical importance, and are discussed in the sections that follow.

Civil Commitment

During the 1960s and 1970s, civil rights activists successfully lobbied legislators to revise the criteria for civil commitment. Their intent was to prevent deprivations of liberty by unnecessarily committing individuals to a hospital. In general, necessary criteria for civil commitment are the presence of a mental disorder and inability to care for self or imminent danger to self or others. Paradoxically, though the legislation was intended to decrease the use of civil commitment, there has been an increase in the rate of involuntary hospitalizations (for references, see Bagby, Thompson, Dickens, & Nohara, 1991). Also, studies have shown that commitment certificates filed by psychiatrists are often incomplete; they frequently do not address all of the criteria that are supposed to be necessary for a civil commitment (for references, see Bagby et al., 1991).

Bagby et al. (1991) reported estimates of how often psychiatrists make appropriate and inappropriate judgments about seeking a civil commitment. In their study, 495 psychiatrists read vignettes and rated whether they would seek a civil commitment. Each psychiatrist read three case vignettes. When writing the vignettes, four factors were systematically varied: legal standard, clinical treatability, alternative resources, and psychotic symptoms. Levels for the legal standard factor were high and low dangerousness to others, high and low dangerousness to self, and high and low inability to care for self. Individuals described by the low-dangerousness levels or the low-inability-to-care-for-self level did not meet the legal standards for civil commitment. For example, individuals described by the *low-dangerousness-to-others* level were said to have thought about harming others, but to have no intent or plan to harm them. Similarly, *low inability to care for self* was described as a level of self-care that did not result in serious self-harm. The *clinical-treatability factor* referred to how well an individual had responded to treatment during previous hospitalizations. The *alternative-resources factor* referred to whether a person was married, employed, and had a supportive family or whether the person was single, unemployed, and had an unsupportive family. The *psychotic-characteristics factor* referred to whether a person had psychotic symptoms and no insight about need for treatment or whether the person was described as having no psychotic symptoms and good insight. However, all of the vignettes described the individuals as having a mental disorder. All four of the factors were completely crossed, creating a total of 48 different vignettes (of which any particular judge read only three).

With regard to the results, 26% of the individuals depicted in the vignettes as clearly meeting the criteria for involuntary hospitalization were not recommended for commitment. Furthermore, 20% of those who did not meet the legal standard for commitment were recommended for involuntary hospitalization. Though the legal-standard factor was significantly related to decisions to seek a commitment, the other factors were as well. Likelihood to seek a commitment was greater if individuals were described as having limited alternative resources, being psychotic with little insight, and having a history of responding well to treatment. Nonlegal factors have also been significantly related to decisions about commitment in other studies (Appelbaum & Hamm, 1982; Schwartz, Appelbaum, & Kaplan, 1984; Thompson & Ager, 1988), though in these studies the investigators did not estimate the percentage of appropriate and inappropriate decisions.

Mandated Reporting of Child Abuse

Psychologists are mandated by law to report child abuse. However, a widely replicated finding in clinical judgment research is that large numbers of mental health professionals are not compliant with child abuse reporting laws (for a review, see Brosig & Kalichman, 1992; for additional studies see Beck & Ogloff, 1995; Finlayson & Koocher, 1991; Kennel & Agresti, 1995; Zellman, 1992). In the studies reviewed by Brosig and Kalichman (1992), about 40% of the clinicians failed to report suspected child abuse. These estimates were obtained both when clinicians were given case vignettes and when clinicians were asked about clients they had seen in clinical practice.

In one study (Muehleman & Kimmons, 1981),which illustrates the underreporting of child abuse, psychologists were given the following brief vignette:

> A family presents itself for treatment at an agency. The family consists of four persons at home—mother, father, daughter, and son—plus an older son and daughter who are now out of the home. They are self-referred; the presenting problem is lack of communication and cohesiveness in the family. After four sessions, it is revealed that mental and physical abuse is occurring and, in fact, has occurred in this family since the eldest son was a small child. This has been a closely guarded secret until now and has never been reported due to the family's extreme fear of the father. The family at this point has worked hard in therapy; the members seem motivated to continue the therapy. (p. 632)

When psychologists read this vignette, 49% said they would not report the abuse immediately.

Child abuse is a major health problem in the United States, and a large number of studies have been conducted to understand why clinicians frequently violate state laws and do not report child abuse. The influence of three groups of factors has been investigated: legal factors, individual differences among clinicians, and situational factors (including patient characteristics and type of abuse).

Failure to report may occur because clinicians are unfamiliar with, or do not understand, mandatory reporting laws (Brosig & Kalichman, 1992). Unfortunately, mandatory reporting laws frequently do not clarify the boundary between abuse and nonabuse, and they typically do not specify when a clinician has reasonable grounds to suspect child abuse. Extreme cases will be clear, but in borderline cases clinicians may be unsure of whether they are supposed to report their suspicions of abuse.

Individual differences among clinicians are also important. Though for other judgment tasks it has been hard to identify important individual differences among clinicians, this has not been the case for the task of reporting child abuse.

One important individual difference is that some clinicians will unvaryingly follow laws and others will consider ethical principles along with the laws. In several studies, some clinicians failed to report abuse even when they were aware of the relevant laws (Brosig & Kalichman, 1992). For example, some clinicians have reported that they will not report abuse if they believe the family will withdraw from treatment if abuse is reported (e.g., Finlayson & Koocher, 1991).

Clinicians also differ in their beliefs about whether reporting abuse will be beneficial or harmful. In one study (Kalichman et al., 1989), after reading a vignette, 42% of the psychologists indicated that reporting abuse would have negative consequences for family therapy, but 21% of the respondents predicted that reporting abuse would have positive consequences for therapy. Some of the respondents argued that state investigatory agencies are unable to effectively investigate and intervene when child abuse is reported, and they saw this as a reason for not reporting abuse.

Several demographic characteristics of clinicians have been related to the likelihood of clinicians reporting child abuse. Female clinicians (e.g., psychologists, psychiatrists, social workers) are more likely than male clinicians to report child abuse (Attias & Goodwin, 1985; Finlayson & Koocher, 1991; Jackson & Nuttall, 1994; Zellman & Bell, 1989; also see Snyder & Newberger, 1986). Similarly, young clinicians are more likely than their older colleagues to report child abuse (Finlayson & Koocher, 1991; Jackson & Nuttall, 1994; Zellman & Bell, 1989; but also see Snyder & Newberger, 1986). In addition, clinicians who work in inpatient settings have been less likely than outpatient clinicians to believe that sexual abuse occurred, and clinicians with a history of having been abused themselves have been more likely than other clinicians to believe that sexual abuse occurred (Jackson & Nuttall, 1994). Finally, when clinicians made ratings of "the seriousness of the situation for the child's welfare" (p. 128), the most important individual-difference variable was profession: Social workers and nurses rated the situations as being most serious, psychiatrists and pediatricians rated the situations as being least serious, and psychologists were between these two extremes (Snyder & Newberger, 1986; also see Jackson & Nuttall, 1993).

Research has been conducted on one other individual difference among clinicians. Formal training in ethics has not had an effect on decisions relating to ethical dilemmas (Haas, Malouf, & Mayerson, 1988), and specialized training for working with victims of sexual abuse has not had an effect on decision making related to reporting child abuse (Finlayson & Koocher, 1991).

Situational factors have also been found to influence decisions on whether to report abuse. Several of these factors were described earlier in this chapter. For example, the role of the mother (perpetrator or nonperpetrator) and the social class, race, and age of the victim are related to the likelihood of clinicians reporting child abuse. Research also suggests that sexual abuse is more likely to be reported than emotional or physical abuse (Beck & Ogloff, 1995; Nightingale & Walker, 1986; Wilson & Gettinger, 1989; Zellman, 1990). Similarly, cases of physical abuse are more likely to be reported than cases of emotional abuse and neglect (Hampton & Newberger, 1985). Abuse is more likely to be reported if clinicians believe it is especially severe (Green & Hansen, 1989) or if they believe that it is current and ongoing (Wilson & Gettinger, 1989). Finally, abuse is more likely to be reported if clinicians have clear evidence that it has occurred (see the review by Brosig & Kalichman, 1992).

Protection From Domestic Violence

Protection from domestic violence is a clinical and legal concern that often goes unrecognized. In one study (Hansen, Harway, & Cervantes, 1991), 362 members of the American Association of Marriage and Family Therapy read one of two case histories and described what interventions they would make. The two case histories described husbands with a high risk for domestic violence. In fact, one of the husbands later killed his wife. Both cases explicitly described a history of violence:

> He has repeatedly been physically violent with her and the kids and the day prior, he grabbed her and threw her on the floor in a violent manner and then struck her. (p. 235)

> Recently . . . he punched her in the back and stomach and caused her to miscarry. (p. 235)

Given the high risk for violence, the responses of the clinicians were inappropriate. Only 11% of the respondents recognized the importance of taking steps to ensure the safety of the wife (e.g., developing a safety plan, getting her to a shelter, or helping her get a restraining order). Furthermore, 55% of the clinicians failed to recognize that the family was in a crisis situation. For example, the treatment goal advanced by some clinicians was to improve communication.

TREATMENT DECISIONS AND TREATMENT OUTCOMES

The utility of treatment decisions can be determined by evaluating the outcome of treatment. Several topics will be reviewed: (a) whether clinicians make appropriate referrals, (b) controversies surrounding treatments that are provided by some mental health professionals, (c) the relation between behavioral assessment and treatment outcome, and (d) the appropriateness of decisions regarding the use of psychotropic medications.

Appropriateness of Referrals

A referral is appropriate if it is likely to lead to an improved outcome. Unfortunately, little research has been done on this topic. However, there has been research on referrals to neurologists. In one study (Sbordone & Rudd, 1986), 206 psychologists read four vignettes and made treatment recommendations. All four vignettes described individuals who had symptoms that were indicative of a neurological disease (either Huntington's disease, brain tumor, transient ischemic attack, or Alzheimer's disease). For example, one vignette described an executive with high blood pressure who complained of pressure at work. During the interview session, his speech became hesitant and he complained that his right hand felt numb. These symptoms disappeared after a few minutes, but he could not explain what happened. For this case, 67% of the psychologists said they would refer the client to a neurologist, 12% would refer the client to a nonneurological physician, and 21% would make no referral to a physician but would refer the client for psychotherapy. Across all four cases, 33% of the psychologists did not make a referral to a physician. This result is disturbing because all of the clients may have had a serious neurological disease that was a cause of their distress.

Controversial Treatments

When mental health professionals use treatment interventions that are not empirically supported, the value of their treatment decisions should be questioned. Several controversial treatment interventions, such as facilitated communication, lost-memory recovery, and eye movement desensitization and reprocessing, are described in this section. Efforts to have clinicians use treatment interventions that have been supported by empirical research have been undertaken by the APA's Division of Clinical Psychology. These efforts are also discussed.

Facilitated communication is an intervention for helping people with severe disabilities, typically individuals with autism or moderate to profound mental retardation. As its name implies, the goal of this intervention is to help these individuals communicate. Advocates of facilitated communication claim that many individuals with autism or mental retardation have coherent thoughts and ideas that they are normally unable to express. Using facilitated communication, an individual is given the opportunity to communicate nonverbally, (e.g., by using a typewriter or a computer keyboard). An integral part of facilitated communication is a prompting procedure: A facilitator supports a person's hand to make it feasible for the person to strike the keys. The danger with this procedure is that the facilitator may unwittingly select the letters that spell out the messages. Though the use of facilitated communication has been widespread, empirical research using single- and double-blind procedures indicates that the responses of patients are typically controlled by the facilitators (Jacobson, Mulick, & Schwartz, 1995; though also see Biklen, 1996; Jacobson, Mulick, & Schwartz, 1996).

Another controversy involves the recovery of lost memories. Even when clients have no memory of having been abused, some mental health professionals will still inform them that they believe they were a victim of child abuse or a victim of a satanic cult (Loftus, 1993; Ofshe & Watters, 1994). For example, a mental health professional may believe that a client was abused because the client reports feeling as though abuse had occurred (though the client cannot remember any episodes of abuse) and because the client has a range of symptoms that the therapist believes is indicative of abuse (e.g., low self-esteem, sexual dysfunction, depression, and self-destructive thoughts). Therapists may use a variety of techniques to help clients "remember" having been abused. For example, they may tell the clients that they were abused and repeatedly ask them to remember the events, they may interpret mental images or dreams as signs of memory of abuse, they may use hypnosis to retrieve "buried memories," or they may send clients who have no memory of being abused to incest-survivor groups. Unfortunately, these techniques may help a client "remember" an episode of abuse that never even occurred.

In one study (Hyman, Husband, & Billings, 1995), false memories of childhood were accepted by college students. In this study, the students' parents were contacted by the experimenters. They provided information about real childhood events involving each student. The students were then interviewed several times. They were prompted to remember the real childhood events, and to remember events that had not actually happened (the information given to the students was made up by the experimenters). By the third interview, 25% of the made-up events were remembered by the students as having actually happened. These results do not preclude the possibility that an adult who was abused as a child may not remember having been abused (see Pope & Hudson, 1995; Williams, 1994), but they do indicate that memories can be false and that "memories" may reflect the statements of authority figures rather than the occurrence of actual events.

Eye movement desensitization and reprocessing (EMDR) is a procedure for reducing the stress associated with traumatic memories (Shapiro, 1995). Using EMDR, a therapist moves a finger in front of a client's eyes and the client simultaneously watches the therapist's finger and thinks of a disturbing memory or image, or associated physical sensations. While tracking the therapist's finger as it is moving rapidly from side to side, clients are also instructed to express their beliefs about the traumatic event.

EMDR has been both widely acclaimed and widely criticized. Many clients and therapists have praised EMDR. More than 14,000 mental health professionals have attended training workshops on EMDR. Furthermore, in one study (Wilson, Becker, & Tinker, 1995), clients receiving EMDR reported feeling less anxious than clients placed on a waiting list. After the clients on the waiting list received EMDR, they also reported a decrease in feelings of anxiety. However, EMDR has not been shown to be more powerful than a placebo treatment. Furthermore, a book written by the originator of EMDR (Shapiro, 1995) has been criticized for misrepresenting results from studies that have not supported EMDR (e.g., falsely stating that the clinicians in a study had not received formal training in EMDR; Lohr, 1996; Montgomery, 1996). In addition, Shapiro (1995) recommended that EMDR be used for special populations (e.g., clients with personality disorders, multiple personality disorders) even when no research, or only research published in nonrefereed journals (e.g., the *EMDR Network Newsletter*), could be cited to support her claims (Lohr, 1996; McNally, 1996; Montgomery, 1996). Thus, the use of EMDR remains controversial.

To encourage psychologists to use treatment interventions that have been empirically validated, a number of recommendations have been made by a task force organized by the APA's Division of Clinical Psychology. In the Winter 1995 issue of *The Clinical Psychologist*, the task force listed over 25 treatment interventions that have been empirically validated. Other empirically validated interventions have been described in subsequent issues of the same journal. Though many mental health professionals have used controversial treatment interventions, it is equally clear that many psychologists have been using treatment interventions that have been supported by empirical research.

Behavioral Assessment and Treatment Outcome

An important part of behavioral assessment is the selection of specific behaviors to be increased or decreased. Surprisingly, in a review of studies that described the behavioral treatment of children (Weist, Ollendick, & Finney, 1991), only 1 out of 25 studies used an empirical method to select treatment targets. For example, Bornstein, Bellack, and Hersen (1977) trained unassertive children to improve eye contact and lengthen and increase the loudness of speech. However, Weist and Ollendick (1991) reported that assertive behaviors are not necessarily functional for children. When they compared the behavior of popular boys with the behavior of rejected boys, only two of six behaviors associated with assertiveness were more often displayed by the popular boys.

Another example, also provided by Weist et al. (1991), involved the management of diabetes mellitus. Attempts to instruct diabetic children in dietary management did not result in positive gains (Lorenz, Christensen, & Pichert, 1985). As recommended by Weist et al., to empirically select target behaviors, one could identify diabetic children who successfully manage their diabetes, perform a complete assessment of these children (and also evaluate familial functioning and physician behavior), evaluate the children who have problems managing their diabetes, and then address discrepancies between the two groups of children.

Use and Misuse of Psychotropic Medicine

One example of the inappropriate use of psychotropic medicine has already been described: African American patients are more likely than White patients to be overmedicated with neuroleptic medications, and their depressive symptoms are more likely to be untreated. Unfortunately, there have been other instances of the inappropriate use of psychotropic medicine.

Antidepressant medicine is often prescribed inappropriately (Arpino et al., 1995; Keller et al., 1982, 1986; Uhlenhuth, Balter, Mellinger, Cisin, & Clinthorne, 1983; Wells, Katon, Rogers, & Camp, 1994). A surprisingly low number of depressed clients who are in treatment with a psychiatrist, a physician other than a psychiatrist, or a psychologist are treated with antidepressant medicine, even when the clients have a major depressive disorder. Clients are as likely to be treated with a minor tranquilizer as with an antidepressant. Also, when clients are treated with antidepressants, they are frequently placed on a subtherapeutic dosage level or kept on the medicine for an inappropriately short period of time.

In one study (Wells et al., 1994), clients at HMOs and multispecialty, mixed group practices in Los Angeles, Boston, and Chicago completed screening questionnaires for depression. For clients who exceeded a cutoff score for probable depression and who were receiving ongoing care from a clinician, information about the use of psychotropic medications was obtained. For these same clients, the National Institute of Mental Health Diagnostic Interview Schedule (DIS) was used to make psychodiagnoses (Robins et al., 1981).

Results were obtained for 634 clients. For clients with double-diagnoses of major depression and dysthymic disorder ($N = 133$), only 30% were on antidepressants and 28% were on minor tranquilizers, even though there has been a lack of support for using minor tranquilizers to treat depression with the possible exception of alprazolam. For clients with a diagnosis of major depression only ($N = 161$), only 24% were on antidepressants and 23% were on minor tranquilizers. A further analysis of the data revealed that the frequent use of minor tranquilizers was not due primarily to the use of alprazolam.

For additional analyses, the clients were categorized as having a low or high level of psychological sickness. These ratings were made by using measures of mental health such as the Mental Health Index (Veit & Ware, 1983) and the Hamilton Depression Rating Scale (Potts, Daniels, Burnam, & Wells, 1990). For the clients who were being seen by psychiatrists, 49% who were rated as having a high-severity level of psychological sickness were given antidepressant medicine and 50% were given minor tranquilizers. Clients with a high-severity level of psychological sickness were even less likely to be on antidepressant medications if they were seen by other types of clinicians (e.g., psychologists).

Finally, of the 144 clients on antidepressant medicine, 56 (39%) were on a subtherapeutic daily dose. Clinician's specialty was not significantly related to dosage level. Furthermore, 86% of the non-White clients and 42% of the White clients were on a subtherapeutic dose.

SUMMARY AND DISCUSSION

Reliability has been poor for several tasks, for example, when behavior therapists have set treatment goals and when psychiatrists have made decisions about the use of antidepressant medicine, ECT, and psychotherapy. The most favorable results on reliability have been obtained when clinicians have made decisions about whether a person should be committed to a hospital.

For two tasks, level of training was not related to interrater reliability. However, for two other tasks, level of training was positively related to validity. For example, treatment plans written by mental health professionals appeared to be more valid than treatment plans written by graduate students.

Patient variable biases have been present for some decision tasks. For example, race bias has occured when psychiatrists have prescribed medicine: Black patients have been undertreated for depression, and some evidence indicates that they have been overtreated with antipsychotic medicine. Decisions for reporting child abuse have been more appropriate for Black children than for White children and more appropriate for lower social class children than for middle-class or upper social class children. Referrals for psychotherapy have been made more often for middle-class clients than for lower class clients, even when level of psychopathology has been controlled for. Gender bias may occur when clinicians decide if individuals should be hospitalized at a mental health facility. The effect of age is significant when clinicians make recommendations for psychotherapy or treatment with psychotropic medicine. To give one last example, mentally retarded clients are offered mental health treatment less often than are average-intelligence clients, even when there is reason to believe that the mentally retarded clients can also benefit from treatment.

The implications of results on labeling bias have been unclear, but harmful consequences of context effects have been described. Treatment at for-profit psychiatric hospitals may differ markedly from treatment provided in other settings, and clinicians may be affected by family pressure when they decide if they should hospitalize someone against their will.

For several decision tasks, many clinicians make decisions that are not in agreement with legal and ethical principles. For example, a large number of individuals who meet the legal criteria for involuntary hospitalization are not recommended for commitment, a large number of clinicians fail to report suspected child abuse, and many clinicians do not take steps to protect the safety of a spouse when domestic violence is occurring in the home.

Additional problems have been described. For example, psychologists may not refer clients to a physician even when the client has symptoms of a neurological disorder. Also, many mental health professionals use controversial treatment techniques like facilitated communication, techniques for helping clients recover lost memories, and EMDR. Also, behavior therapists sometimes select inappropriate behaviors to modify, and physicians often prescribe antidepressant medicine inappropriately. On the positive side, many psychologists and psychiatrists use treatment interventions that have been empirically validated.

In conclusion, many problems exist with the treatment decisions made by clinicians. Interrater reliability is sometimes poor; instances of race, social class, gender, and age bias occur; decisions have been biased against the mentally retarded; harmful consequences of context effects occur; many clinicians make decisions that are not in agreement with legal and ethical principles; a significant number of psychologists seem to be reluctant to make referrals to rule out organic factors; and many mental health professionals use controversial treatment techniques. On the other hand, many psychologists and psychiatrists use treatment interventions that have been empirically validated.

6

NEUROPSYCHOLOGICAL ASSESSMENT

Judgment tasks in neuropsychology include (a) detecting neurological impairment; (b) describing the localization of neurological impairment (e.g., left hemisphere of brain or right hemisphere of brain); (c) describing the process of neurological impairment (e.g., static or progressive); (d) describing the etiology of neurological impairment (e.g., Alzheimer's disease, head injury, glioma, seizures); (e) detecting malingering; (f) describing cognitive strengths and weaknesses; and (g) describing and predicting level of adaptive functioning (e.g., predicting whether a client can care for self, predicting whether a client can successfully return to work). Results on reliability and validity for these judgment tasks will be described.

RELIABILITY

Overall, reliability for ratings made by neuropsychologists has ranged from good to excellent (Garb & Schramke, 1996). Results on interrater reliability and intertest reliability are described. Also, comments are made about the limitations of the research.

Interrater Reliability

For the task of detecting impairment, interrater reliability has ranged from good to excellent (Grant, Heaton, McSweeny, Adams, & Timms,

1982; Grant, Mohns, Miller, & Reitan, 1976; Heaton, Grant, Anthony, & Lehman, 1981; Kane, Parsons, Goldstein, & Moses, 1987). For example, in one of the studies (Heaton et al., 1981), two neuropsychologists made independent ratings for 150 patients with neurological impairment and for 100 controls with no history of neurological disease, head trauma, or substance abuse. Ratings were based on results from the Halstead-Reitan Neuropsychological Test Battery (HRB) and the WAIS. Using data presented in the Heaton et al. article (see Table 1 of Heaton et al., 1981), kappa was estimated by Garb and Schramke (1996) to be .86. This falls in the excellent range of reliability.

For the task of describing the localization of brain impairment, interrater reliability has been excellent. Brown, Spicer, Robertson, Baird, and Malik (1989) had two neuropsychologists make ratings on a 5-point scale ranging from -2 (probable left) to $+2$ (probable right). The two neuropsychologists were given results from selected HRB tests, the WAIS or Wechsler Adult Intelligence Scale–Revised (WAIS–R), and the Wechsler Memory Test. They made independent ratings for 24 patients with lateralized ischemic strokes and 24 patients with lateralized arteriovenous malformations. An intraclass correlation coefficient of .84 was obtained.

Finally, for the task of describing cognitive strengths and weaknesses, interrater reliability has ranged from fair to excellent. Brown, Del Dotto, Fisk, Taylor, and Breslau (1993) had three neuropsychologists describe the cognitive strengths and weaknesses of 41 children. The neuropsychologists based their ratings on the results from 14 tests.[1] Intraclass correlation coefficients were .53 for the assessment of attention, .67 for the assessment of global functioning, .72 for the assessment of haptic perceptual functioning, .73 for the assessment of memory, .77 for the assessment of visual-perceptual–visuomotor functioning, .83 for auditory perceptual–language skills, and .88 for ratings of intelligence.

Intertest Reliability

Intertest reliability has also been good. Diamant and Hijmen (1981) had two neuropsychologists make ratings using the Luria-Nebraska Neuropsychological Battery (LNB) and two other neuropsychologists make ratings using the HRB. The neuropsychologists made ratings for 31 psychiatric

---

[1]Tests used in Brown et al., 1993 are the Wechsler Intelligence Scale for Children–Revised (WISC–R), the Beery Test of Visual Motor Integration, Target Test, Verbal Fluency Test, Auditory Analysis Test, Formulated Sentences Test, Judgment of Line Orientation Test, Tactile Finger Recognition Test, Finger Tip–Number Perception Writing Test, Grooved Pegboard Test, Arm and Leg Coordination Tests, Name Writing Test, Underlining Test, and Sentence Memory Test.

inpatients. Kappa coefficients were .64 for rating degree of neurological impairment; .72 for describing lateralization of impairment; and .65 for describing impairment as right frontal, left frontal, right temporal, or left temporal.

Limitations of the Reliability Studies

In most of the reliability studies, the neuropsychologists made judgments by using either the HRB or LNB. However, most neuropsychologists in the United States do not routinely use a single standardized-test battery. According to one survey (Sweet, Moberg, & Westergaard, 1996), only 14% of neuropsychologists consistently administer a standardized battery, whereas 61% use a flexible battery approach and 25% use a flexible approach. In the *flexible battery approach*, neuropsychologists administer different groups of tests to different types of patients. In the *flexible approach*, neuropsychologists choose a group of tests to administer based on the perceived needs of the individual case.

Unfortunately, reliability has not been described for the flexible battery and flexible approaches. Interrater reliability may be lower for these approaches because neuropsychologists following these approaches are likely to administer different combinations of tests.

VALIDITY

Findings on the following topics are reviewed in this section: (a) the validity of ratings of the presence of neurological impairment; (b) the validity of ratings of the localization of impairment; (c) the validity of ratings of the process and etiology of neurological disorders; (d) the validity of ratings of malingering; (e) the validity of ratings of adaptive functioning; (f) the appropriateness of confidence ratings; (g) the relation between the validity of judgments and the training, experience, and presumed expertise of neuropsychologists; and (h) client variable biases (e.g., age bias). The bulk of the research is on detecting, and describing the localization of, brain impairment.

Detection of Impairment

Results will be described separately for clinical psychologists and neuropsychologists. Not surprisingly, ratings made by neuropsychologists using test batteries are more valid than ratings made by clinical psychologists using screening instruments.

The tests most commonly used by clinical psychologists to screen for brain impairment are the Bender Visual Motor Gestalt Test and the WAIS–R (Piotrowski & Zalewski, 1993; Watkins, Campbell, Nieberding, & Hallmark, 1995). A high hit rate was obtained with the Bender in one study (Wagner & Murray, 1969), but the task in this study was criticized for being artificial (Murdock, 1969), and Wagner (1969) later clarified that the purpose of the study was not to describe the validity of judgments but to describe how ratings might differ when made by different clinicians. When the tasks were more representative of clinical practice, hit rates for PhD clinical psychologists ranged from 60% to 73% when ratings were based on results from the Bender (Goldberg, 1959; Lyle & Quast, 1976; Robiner, 1978); 58% to 60% when ratings were based on results from the Wechsler-Bellevue Intelligence Scale (Leli & Filskov, 1981, 1984); and 53% when ratings were based on the WAIS, MMPI, and Bender (Goldstein, Deysach, & Kleinknecht, 1973). In all of these studies, chance level of accuracy was 50% (if one flipped a coin to make diagnoses of impairment or no impairment, then one would be right 50% of the time), and base-rate level of accuracy was 50% (half of the participants were impaired and half were nonimpaired). Hit rates were sometimes higher when expert psychologists made ratings using results from the Bender: Hit rates were 61% (Mehlman & Vatovec, 1956), 69% (Butler, Coursey, & Gatz, 1976), 81% (Kramer & Fenwick, 1966), 83% (Goldberg, 1959), and 90% (Bruhn & Reed, 1975). With these studies, the chance level of accuracy was also 50% and the base-rate level of accuracy was 50%. Hit rates for the expert clinical psychologists may have varied widely because of differences in the brain-impaired participants. The Bender can be a sensitive measure for evaluating some types of brain damage (e.g., right parietal lesions), but not for evaluating other types of brain damage (e.g., left-hemisphere cerebral impairment).

Results for neuropsychologists have been described by a meta-analysis (Garb & Schramke, 1996). Data from 11 studies were analyzed (Boyar & Tsushima, 1975; Faust, Guilmette et al., 1988; Filskov & Goldstein, 1974; Gaudette, 1992; Heaton et al., 1981; Kane, Sweet, Golden, Parsons, & Moses, 1981; Kane et al., 1987; Russell, Neuringer, & Goldstein, 1970; Schreiber, Goldman, Kleinman, Goldfader, & Snow, 1976; Swiercinsky & Leigh, 1979; Wedding, 1983). The neuropsychologists in these studies based their ratings on either HRB and WAIS or WAIS–R results or, less often, on LNB results. Some of the neuropsychologists were also given Wechsler Memory Scale results. Criterion scores were based on neurology reports. The neurology reports were based on history information (e.g., information about head injuries or seizures), neurological exams, in many cases the results of a neuroimaging procedure (e.g., a computerized tomography [CT] scan), and in some cases observations made during neurosurgery. In the 11 studies, the neuropsychologists made a total of 2,383 ratings. The neuropsychologists achieved a hit rate of 84%. This hit rate is significantly more accurate than the chance level of accuracy (50%) and the base-rate level of accuracy (65%). In two of the studies (Gaudette, 1992; Wedding, 1983), the neuropsychologists were given base-rate information. Though one would expect base-rate information to be useful, when the results from these two studies are excluded, the neuropsychologists obtained a hit rate of 86%.

False-positive, correct-negative, false-negative, and correct-positive rates have been calculated for the task of detecting whether neurological impairment is present (Garb & Schramke, 1996). *False positives* occur when neuropsychologists incorrectly say that neurological impairment is present. *Correct negatives* occur when neuropsychologists correctly say that neurological impairment is absent. *False negatives* occur when neuropsychologists incorrectly say that neurological impairment is absent. *Correct positives* occur when neuropsychologists correctly say that neurological impairment is present. In eight studies, hit rates were reported separately for impaired and nonimpaired participants so it was possible to calculate the false-positive, correct-negative, false-negative, and correct-positive rates (Boyar & Tsushima, 1975; Faust, Guilmette et al., 1988; Gaudette, 1992; Heaton et al., 1981; Kane et al., 1981; Russell et al., 1970; Schreiber et al., 1976; Wedding, 1983). In these studies, ratings were made for 1,683 participants. The false-positive rate was 21%, the correct-negative rate was 79%, the false-negative rate was 14%, and the correct-positive rate was 86%. When nonimpaired participants had been referred to a clinic because the person who made the referral believed that they might have neurological impairment, the false-positive rate was 25%. When nonimpaired participants were recruited by the experimenters to have neuropsychological testing for purposes of the study alone, the false-positive rate was 20%.

Knowledge of when false positives and false negatives are likely to occur is limited. For example, little is known about how false-negative rates are related to the etiology, process, and location of impairment. On the other hand, it does appear that false positives are most likely to occur when ratings are made for elderly clients. These results are described in the section on client variable biases.

Localization of Impairment

To describe the validity of the ratings of localization of impairment, the results of another meta-analysis (Garb & Schramke, 1996) are described. Data from 10 studies were analyzed (Boyar & Tsushima, 1975; Brown et al., 1989; Filskov & Goldstein, 1974; Gaudette, 1992; Heaton et al., 1981; Reitan, 1964; Russell et al., 1970; Schreiber et al., 1976; Swiercinsky & Leigh, 1979; Wedding, 1983). Judgment tasks in these studies varied: Sometimes the task was to indicate if left-hemisphere or right-hemisphere impairment is present and sometimes the task was to indicate if neurological impairment is absent or if left-hemisphere, right-hemisphere, or diffuse impairment is present. The neuropsychologists in these studies based their ratings on varying amounts of information from the HRB, results from the WAIS or WAIS–R, and, in four of the studies, results from the Wechsler Memory Scale. A total of 1,749 ratings were made. The neuropsychologists achieved a hit rate of 68%. Base-rate information was reported in eight of the studies. In these studies, the neuropsychologists achieved a hit rate of 67%, and the base-rate level of prediction was 38% (based on results for 1,606 cases).

Further analysis of the data revealed that the validity of the ratings depended in part on two factors. First, validity depended in part on the rating scales used in the different studies. In 2 of the 10 studies (Brown et al. 1989; Reitan, 1964), neuropsychologists rated whether impairment was localized in the left or right cerebral hemisphere. In the other studies, neuropsychologists rated whether impairment was absent, diffuse, localized in the left hemisphere, or localized in the right hemisphere. Making one of two responses is an easier task. Neuropsychologists obtained a hit rate of 89% when they made differential diagnoses of left- versus right-hemisphere impairment (the base-rate level of accuracy was 57%), and obtained a hit rate of 65% when they made differential diagnoses of no impairment, diffuse impairment, left-hemisphere impairment, or right-hemisphere impairment (the base-rate level of accuracy was 40%).

It is also meaningful to sort studies by another factor: reason for neuropsychological testing for the normal participants. Data were included in this analysis only if neuropsychologists rated whether impairment was absent, diffuse, localized in the left hemisphere, or localized in the right hemisphere. When nonimpaired participants were referred to a clinic for testing because of the possibility that impairment was present, clinicians obtained a hit rate of 73%. When neuropsychological testing was conducted because the experimenters needed results from nonimpaired participants for their studies, clinicians had a hit rate of 63%. These results are surprising: It is unclear why hit rates were lower when normal participants were recruited than when they were referred.

Data were also analyzed after excluding ratings of "normal" (Garb & Schramke, 1996). Neuropsychologists made diagnoses of diffuse, left-hemisphere, or right-hemisphere impairment for 1,194 cases. They obtained a hit rate of 70%. The hit rate achieved by the neuropsychologists was significantly higher than the the level of accuracy one could achieve by using only base-rate information (44%).

When neuropsychologists were asked to make more precise localization ratings (e.g., ratings of left-anterior, right-anterior, left-posterior, or right-posterior impairment), estimates of the validity of their ratings varied widely.

Estimates of the validity of ratings ranged from 29% and 56% (Faust, Guilmette et al., 1988) to 79% (Reitan, 1964). The etiology of the neurological disorders was similar for the cases in the two studies, and the neuropsychologists in the two studies received similar information (HRB results). Validity estimates may have varied because the judge in the Reitan study was an expert neuropsychologist, whereas Faust, Guilmette et al. sampled a range of neuropsychologists. Also, the cases in the 1964 study could have been easier to make ratings for because the ability of neurologists to detect subtle forms of impairment improved from the 1960s to the 1980s, and neuropsychologists should have greater success describing the location of gross impairment than the location of subtle impairment. However, it is also possible that hit rates were low in the Faust, Guilmette et al. study because these experimenters chose cases by first examining the neuropsychological test results. These experimenters may have thought that the cases were of only moderate difficulty, but because of hindsight bias the cases may have been more difficult than they thought. According to the *hindsight bias*, when people are told an outcome (e.g., that a neurologist established that impairment exists in the left-anterior region), then people are likely to believe that the outcome was highly likely (e.g., given the neuropsychological test results). In the Reitan study, as in most studies on the validity of judgments made by neuropsychologists, the experimenters did not examine the neuropsychological test results before selecting the cases. Instead, they selected the cases based on the results of neurological summaries.

Process and Etiology

To learn how well neuropsychologists can describe the *process* of neurological impairment (how a client's impairment has been changing over time), experimenters have instructed neuropsychologists to describe disturbances or conditions as being progressive or static (Faust, Guilmette et al., 1988) or as being acute or chronic (Heaton et al., 1981). To make their ratings, neuropsychologists in both studies received HRB and WAIS or WAIS–R results. Neuropsychologists in the Faust, Guilmette et al. study also received Wechsler Memory Scale results. In both studies, patients were tested on only one occasion. Hit rates were 60% for making ratings of static versus progressive and 64% for making ratings of acute versus chronic. However, these hit rates may be deceivingly low. Presumably hit rates would have been higher if testing had been done on more than one occasion or if information describing history of functioning had been made available to the neuropsychologists. For example, if neuropsychological testing is done on one occasion and then the person's neurological impairment becomes progressively worse, one can expect that neuropsychological testing done on a second occasion will reflect the progressive nature of the disorder. It may be unreasonable to have neuropsychologists describe changes over time if they are given information that describes functioning at only one point in time.

When neuropsychologists described the etiology of neurological impairment (e.g., Alzheimer's disease), estimates of the validity of their judgments varied widely. Estimates of the validity of their judgments ranged from 23% (Faust, Guilmette et al., 1988) to 84% (Reitan, 1964) to 85% (Filskov & Goldstein, 1974). In all three studies, the neuropsychologists received similar information (e.g., WAIS or WAIS–R and HRB results). In the Faust, Guilmette et al. study, they also received Wechsler Memory Scale results, but this does not explain why validity was drastically lower in the Faust, Guilmette et al. study. Similarly, it is not clear that differences in the estimates of validity were due to differences in the expertise of the judges. The neuropsychologist in the Reitan study was described as being an expert judge, but the neuropsychologists in the other studies were not. Two other explanations for the differences in the validity of judgments seem more reasonable. First, the validity of judgments made by neuropsychologists may be lower when neurological impairment is subtle rather than gross. In the 1960s and 1970s, neurologists were less adept at describing neurological impairment, for example, because CT scans and other advanced neuroimaging procedures were not yet available. Thus, in studies on neuropsychological testing conducted in the 1960s and 1970s, the patients may have had gross impairment, making it easier for the neuropsychologists to make judgments about etiology. Second, differences in the validity of judgments may have occurred because Faust, Guilmette et al. looked at neuropsychological test results and the neurological exam results when selecting cases to present to judges, but cases presented in the other two studies were selected by determining if neuropsychological testing had been done, and by looking at neurological exam results to determine if the neurologists had identified probable etiology.

Detecting Malingering

Little is known about how well clinicians can detect malingering. The ability of neuropsychologists to detect malingering has been investigated in four studies (Faust, Hart, & Guilmette, 1988; Faust, Hart, Guilmette, & Arkes, 1988; Heaton, Smith, Lehman, & Vogt, 1978; Trueblood & Binder, 1997). In two of these studies (Faust, Hart, & Guilmette, 1988; Faust, Hart, Guilmette, & Arkes, 1988), fabricated histories were presented along with HRB and WISC–R or WAIS–R test results. For example, in one of these studies (Faust, Hart, & Guilmette, 1988), the neuropsychologists were told that the test results were obtained from a child who had been involved in a car accident, had suffered brief loss of consciousness, was disoriented on hospital admission, and whose school grades had dropped since the accident. Actually, the test results were obtained from nonimpaired participants who were told to perform less well than usual, but not so badly that it would be obvious that they were faking. The neuropsychologists in both of these studies achieved hit rates of only 0%. They never made a rating of malingering. However, in responding to criticisms of their articles, Faust and Guilmette (1990) commented that they did not believe the 0% hit rate was indicative of clinical practice: "We did not indicate that the 100% error rate we obtained necessarily generalizes to everyday practice, but rather that our study and those of others raise doubt about clinicians' success in detecting malingering" (p. 248).

The Heaton et al. (1978) study also did not provide a good estimate of how well neuropsychologists are able to detect malingering. The neuropsychologists in this study were given HRB, WAIS, and MMPI test results. No history information was presented. Neuropsychologists made ratings for (a) nonimpaired participants who were instructed to malinger and (b) head trauma patients with neurological impairment. This study did not provide a good estimate of how well neuropsychologists are able to detect malingering in part because the authors reported the range, but not the mean level, of accuracy achieved by the different neuropsychologists. The range of accuracy was 50% to 69%. The level of accuracy one could obtain by chance was 50%.

A better estimate of how well neuropsychologists can detect malingering was reported in a recent study (Trueblood & Binder, 1997). In this study, 60 neuropsychologists made diagnoses for one of four clients who were judged by the research investigators to be malingerers, and 26 neuropsychologists made diagnoses for one of two clients who were judged by the research investigators to have severe neurological impairment. All of the clients had been seen by the research investigators for neuropsychological assessment. Tests administered included the HRB, the WAIS-R, and the Wechsler Memory Scale. All of the malingerers were seeking workers' compensation benefits. Two of the malingerers claimed that they were physically disabled in addition to being cognitively impaired, but while under surveillance they were observed performing vigorous physical work which they had denied being able to perform. All four malingerers did worse than chance on forced-choice memory testing. Also, when brain-imaging procedures were conducted for the malingerers, results were negative. With regard to the results, hit rates of 87% and 88% were obtained for the malingering and neurological impairment cases, respectively. Though these results are impressive, they are in need of replication. Since Trueblood and Binder looked at the neuropsychological test results when selecting the cases, it is possible that they chose cases that are relatively easy to make ratings for.

Level of Adaptive Functioning

Judgment studies have not directly addressed how well neuropsychologists describe level of adaptive functioning and how well they predict behavior. However, there is reason to believe that many psychologists performing neuropsychological evaluations may not be skilled at evaluating a client's level of adaptive functioning.

A survey by Dammers et al. (1995) indicates that many psychologists performing neuropsychological evaluations do not formally evaluate level of adaptive functioning, even though self-report and behaviorally based measures of adaptive functioning exist. Respondents to the survey were licensed clinical psychologists, all of whom reported doing neuropsychological testing. They reported, on average, that 37% of the time they spent on clinical work involved performing neuropsychological evaluations. Some of the clinical psychologists were certified by the American Board of Professional Neuropsychology, but the number was unspecified. Only 44% of the 207 respondents reported that they formally assess level of adaptive functioning. This suggests that many clinicians may be using neuropsychological test results to evaluate level of adaptive functioning, even though results from performance-based measures of adaptive functioning frequently differ from neuropsychological test results.

It is not clear whether neuropsychologists, unlike clinical psychologists, formally evaluate level of adaptive functioning. For example, in a recent survey (Sweet et al., 1996), neuropsychologists were not asked if they formally evaluate level of adaptive functioning by using scales or performance measures, though they were asked about the neuropsychological tests that they use to assess cognitive functioning.

Even if many neuropsychologists do not formally evaluate level of adaptive functioning, the validity of their ratings is not necessarily poor. To demonstrate that the validity of ratings is poor, one has to directly evaluate the validity of their ratings. However, most of the variability in behavioral measures of adaptive functioning cannot be accounted for by neuropsychological test results (e.g., Loewenstein, Rubert, Arguelles, & Duara, 1995).

Appropriateness of Confidence Ratings

Neuropsychologists were sometimes asked to rate how much confidence they have in their judgments. One would hope that neuropsychologists would know when their judgments are likely to be right or wrong. Results in this section specifically address whether validity and confidence are positively related and whether neuropsychologists are overconfident.

Though results have varied widely for different neuropsychologists (Heaton et al., 1978), validity and confidence have generally been positively, but sometimes weakly, related (Brown et al., 1989; Gaudette, 1992; Trueblood & Binder, 1997; Wedding, 1983). For example, in two of the studies (Gaudette, 1992; Wedding, 1983), neuropsychologists were given results from the HRB and the WAIS or WAIS–R. They were to describe participants as nonimpaired or as having diffuse, left-hemisphere, or right-hemisphere neurological impairment. In the Wedding study, they were also to determine if participants had schizophrenia. When the data were pooled and an aggregation analysis was performed (Garb & Schramke, 1996), the correlation between hit rates and confidence ratings was .29, which is of borderline statistical significance, $t(24) = 1.48$, $.05 < p < .10$.

In another study (Heaton et al., 1978), neuropsychologists made judgments of malingering versus neurological impairment. Judgments were based on results from the WAIS, HRB, and MMPI. When a separate correlation was calculated between validity and confidence for each neuropsychologist, the range of the correlations was $-.13$ to .46. Unfortunately, the average correlation was not reported.

In a fourth study (Brown et al., 1989), the judgment task was to rate whether impairment was located in the left or right hemisphere of the brain. Hit rates were higher when the neuropsychologists thought that the likelihood of being correct was probable compared to when they thought the likelihood of being correct was possible (26 of 28 cases correct versus 21 of 28 cases correct; $\chi^2[1, N = 56] = 4.8$, $p < .05$.

In a final study on the relation between validity and confidence (Trueblood & Binder, 1997), neuropsychologists made diagnoses of malingering, neurological impairment, and functional impairment. Judgments were based on results from many tests including the HRB, the WAIS–R, and the Wechsler Memory Scale. Some of the neuropsychologists were also given results from forced-choice tests. *Forced-choice tests* are used to detect malingering: If participants do worse than would be expected by chance, then one can suspect that these participants are malingering. Results on validity and confidence were reported for the ratings that were made for four malingerers. Confidence ratings were made on the following 5-point scale: (1) *very low*, (2) *low*, (3) *moderate*, (4) *high*, and (5) *very high*. Mean ratings of confidence were 3.0 for neuropsychologists who made diagnoses of malingering, but did not receive results from forced-choice tests, 4.1 for neuropsychologists who made diagnoses of malingering and did receive results from forced-choice tests, 2.8 for neuropsychologists who made diagnoses of neurological impairment (some of whom received results from forced-choice tests), and 2.3 for neuropsychologists who made diagnoses of functional impairment (some of whom received results from forced-choice tests). The mean rating for the neuropsychologists who made diagnoses of malingering and did receive results from forced-choice tests was significantly higher than the mean ratings for the other three groups of neuropsychologists.

Validity and confidence can be positively related, and yet neuropsychologists may be overconfident. In judgment research, raters are said to be *well calibrated* if their estimates of being correct are close to the probability of their being correct. For example, if judgments are correct half of the time that a clinician makes a subjective estimate of being correct of .5, then one would conclude that for these judgments the clinician was well calibrated. A positive correlation between confidence and validity, no matter how high, does not ensure good calibration.

Results indicate that neuropsychologists may frequently be overconfident, but these results need to be further replicated, and the conditions when neuropsychologists are most likely to be overconfident need to be clarified. In one study (Kareken & Williams, 1994), neuropsychologists were to estimate premorbid intellectual functioning and set 95% confidence intervals around their estimates. Their estimates of verbal intelligence and performance intelligence were accurate, and they appropriately set confidence intervals around their estimates of verbal intelligence. However, the confidence intervals they set around their estimates of performance intelligence were too narrow, indicating that they were too confident of their estimates of performance intelligence.

In another study (Gaudette, 1992), the task was for neuropsychologists to make diagnoses of no impairment or diffuse, left-hemisphere, or right-hemisphere cerebral impairment. The hit rate for neuropsychologists was 62%. The neuropsychologists thought that they would achieve a hit rate of 77.5%.

Neuropsychologists were underconfident in only one study (Wedding, 1983). The hit rate for neuropsychologists was 55%. The neuropsychologists thought that they would achieve a hit rate of 47%. However, the task in this study was to make differential diagnoses of normal, schizophrenia, left-hemisphere, right-hemisphere, or diffuse brain impairment, and the differential diagnosis of schizophrenia versus brain impairment is no longer considered to be an important task for neuropsychologists.

Training, Experience, and Presumed Expertise

With regard to clinical psychologists using screening instruments, results on training, experience, and presumed expertise are generally disappointing. On the positive side, hit rates for ostensibly expert clinical psychologists were generally higher than hit rates that were obtained by other clinical psychologists (e.g., Bruhn & Reed, 1975; Goldberg, 1959; Kramer & Fenwick, 1966). However, when ratings were based on Bender or Wechsler-Bellevue Intelligence Scale protocols, most clinical psychologists were not more accurate than graduate students, undergraduate students, occupational therapists, or secretaries (Goldberg, 1959; Leli & Filskov, 1981, 1984; Nadler, Fink, Shontz, & Brink, 1959; Robiner, 1978).

With regard to neuropsychologists using test batteries, results on training, experience, and presumed expertise are also disappointing. On the positive side, hit rates for detecting impairment were better for neuropsychologists using test batteries than for clinical psychologists using screening instruments. For example, in one study (Goldstein et al., 1973), to detect the presence of brain impairment, five clinical psychologists interpreted the results from the WAIS, MMPI, and Bender, and five psychology interns and postdoctoral fellows interpreted results from the HRB in addition to these tests. Four of the five clinical psychologists held the American Board of Professional Psychology (ABPP) diploma. They did not want to see the HRB results because they said they would not know how to interpret them. The psychology interns and postdoctoral fellows had attended a seminar on the HRB and had received supervision in its use for 1 year. Psychology interns and postdoctoral fellows with training in the use of the HRB were dramatically more accurate than the clinical psychologists (hit rates of 95% versus 53%).

Beyond attending a seminar on the HRB and receiving supervision for a year, additional training in neuropsychology may not lead to being able to make more accurate judgments (Faust, Guilmette et al., 1988; Nadler et al., 1994). For example, in a study that focused on the relation between training and validity (Faust, Guilmette et al., 1988), neuropsychologists examined HRB, WAIS–R, and Wechsler Memory Scale protocols, and made ratings of the absence or presence, location, and etiology of brain impairment. Level of training (e.g., number of hours of supervision in interpreting neuro-psychological tests) was unrelated to the validity of judgments. To detect positive effects of training, it may by necessary to conduct longitudinal studies and study clinicians before and after a specified training experience.

Experience was frequently unrelated to validity. Ratings made by expe-rienced neuropsychologists were generally no more valid than ratings made by less experienced doctoral-level neuropsychologists (Faust, Guilmette et al., 1988; Gaudette, 1992; Heaton et al., 1978; Nadler et al., 1994; Wedding, 1983).

With regard to presumed expertise, results were mixed. Neuropsycholo-gists with the ABPP diploma were no more accurate than relatively junior doctoral neuropsychologists when the task was to describe the localization of brain impairment (Gaudette, 1992). However, in one study (Wedding, 1983), a presumed expert was more accurate than other doctoral-level neu-ropsychologists (hit rates were 63% and 54%, respectively). The expert judge, who had published extensively on neuropsychology, took only 2 hours to interpret protocols for 30 participants. The other judges required an average of 7 hours to make their ratings.

The appropriateness of confidence ratings was positively, but weakly, related to experience and presumed expertise. In one study (Heaton et al., 1978), a correlation between years of experience and accuracy of confidence ratings was positive but not significant, $r(8) = .24$. In another study (Wed-ding, 1983), when judges were instructed to predict how often their ratings were correct, the average absolute deviation between estimated and actual accuracy was 5% for a presumed expert neuropsychologist and 15% for the other neuropsychologists. In a third study (Gaudette, 1992), average absolute deviations between estimated and actual accuracy ranged from 5% to 25% for ABPP neuropsychologists and 10% to 27% for the other neuropsychologists, depending on the task.

Overperception of Impairment and Client Variable Biases

As already noted, false positives are common for the task of detecting neurological impairment. In fact, averaging across studies, the false-positive rate has been estimated to be 25%. False-positive rates seem to vary as a function of the age of clients. Research has not been done on the influence of other client variables such as race.

False-positive diagnoses of neurological impairment are more likely to be made for elderly clients than for young or middle-aged clients. In one study (Nadler et al., 1994), neuropsychologists based their ratings on identifying information (education, gender, and handedness) and results from the HRB, WAIS–R (scale scores but not Full-Scale IQ), and Wechsler Memory Scale. Each neuropsychologist made ratings for two protocols. They thought that the test results were obtained by testing a 38-year-old adult and a 74-year-old adult, but actually the results for the "38-year-old adult" were obtained from tables of normative data for 38-year-old test participants and the results presented for the "74-year-old adult" were obtained from tables of normative data for 74-year-old participants (Heaton, Grant, & Matthews, 1986; Russell, 1988; Wechsler, 1981). Normative data are obtained by testing "normal" people in the community. Thus, the test results reflected normal functioning. Education, gender, and handedness were held constant across the protocols. When the 77 neuropsychologists who participated in the study made differential diagnoses of normal versus neurological impairment, an overall false-positive rate of 32% was obtained. The false-positive rate was 7% when the neuropsychologists were told that a participant was 38 years old and 58% when they were told that a participant was 74 years old. When the neuropsychologists made differential diagnoses of normal versus dementia, none of the 38 year olds were diagnosed as having dementia. However, 23% of the 74-year-old participants were described as having dementia, even though the participants were described by normal elderly test results. The results of this study have recently been replicated (Garb & Florio, 1997).

CONCLUSIONS

Interrater reliability and intertest reliability are frequently good when neuropsychologists administer a standardized battery, like the HRB or the LNB. However, most neuropsychologists use a flexible battery or flexible approach and do not routinely administer a single standardized-test battery.

Little is known about the reliability of ratings when neuropsychologists use a flexible battery or flexible approach.

When the task is to detect the presence of brain impairment, ratings made by neuropsychologists are moderately valid: A hit rate of 84% was obtained (Garb & Schramke, 1996). Their ratings are more valid than ratings made by clinical psychologists using screening instruments (e.g., the Bender Visual Motor Gestalt Test). However, false positives may be common when neuropsychologists make ratings for elderly clients.

Ratings of the localization of impairment were also moderately valid. When impaired and nonimpaired participants were included, and when the nonimpaired participants were referred for testing because they were suspected of being impaired, the hit rate for ratings of normal, diffuse impairment, left-hemisphere impairment, and right-hemisphere impairment was 73%. The chance level of accuracy was 25%.

Results were less clear for the tasks of describing the process and etiology of impairment. Thus, it is not clear how well neuropsychologists can perform these tasks and whether important individual differences are present among neuropsychologists.

Recent results suggest that neuropsychologists may be able to make accurate differential diagnoses of malingering and neurological impairment. However, these results need to be replicated.

Judgment studies have not directly addressed how well neuropsychologists can describe cognitive strengths and weaknesses. Hopefully this is the task at which neuropsychologists perform best. Neuropsychological testing is usually conducted, not to determine whether neurological impairment is present, but to relate cognitive strengths and weaknesses to the presence of brain impairment (e.g., Benton, 1994).

Judgment studies have not directly addressed how well neuropsychologists describe level of adaptive functioning and how well they predict behavior. It is possible that when neuropsychologists describe level of adaptive functioning, they rely too heavily on results from neuropsychological testing and do not make use of performance-based measures of adaptive functioning.

Results on confidence ratings were disappointing. They indicated that neuropsychologists are at times overconfident. They also indicated that the relation between accuracy and confidence is only slight or modest.

Ratings made by neuropsychologists using the HRB were more accurate than ratings made by clinical psychologists using screening instruments. However, beyond attending a seminar on neuropsychological testing and receiving supervision for 1 year, training and experience may not increase validity. With regard to presumed expertise, ABPP neuropsychologists were not more accurate than other doctoral-level neuropsychologists. However, in one study, a single neuropsychologist who had published extensively in neuropsychology was more accurate than other neuropsychologists. Finally, the accuracy of confidence ratings was positively, but weakly, related to experience and presumed expertise.

In conclusion, neuropsychologists frequently make reliable and moderately valid judgments. However, experimenters have not studied the reliability of ratings when neuropsychologists use a flexible battery or flexible approach, the validity of descriptions of cognitive strengths and weaknesses, and the validity of descriptions of level of adaptive functioning and predictions of behavior. Also, further research needs to be done to clarify how well neuropsychologists can describe the process and etiology of neurological impairment and how well they can make differential diagnoses of malingering and neurological impairment. Finally, the results on the appropriateness of confidence ratings were disappointing and validity was not usually related to experience or presumed expertise, but neuropsychologists were more accurate than clinical psychologists using screening instruments.

II

METHODS AND RECOMMENDATIONS FOR MAKING JUDGMENTS

7

CLINICAL JUDGMENT

Two general approaches for studying how clinicians make judgments are described in this chapter. The first approach involves the use of formal models. A *formal model* of judgment is a statistical equation or a series of if–then rules that can be used to reproduce the judgments made by a clinician. For example, a multiple-regression equation can be derived to predict the judgments made by a clinician. In the second approach, cognitive heuristics, cognitive biases, and knowledge structures are used to describe how clinicians make judgments. *Heuristics* are simple rules that, though they cannot be used to reproduce a set of judgments, can be descriptive of how judgments are made (Kahneman, Slovic, & Tversky, 1982; Nisbett & Ross, 1980; Plous, 1993). *Cognitive biases* describe types of errors that clinicians sometimes make. *Knowledge structures* are beliefs, theories, and information that are stored in memory. Knowledge structures are important for describing clinical judgment because clinicians may frequently make judgments based on their implicit theories of personality and psychopathology.

In addition to evaluating these approaches, this chapter explores issues related to the cognitive processes of clinicians. One issue is whether clinicians are aware of how they make judgments. Some investigators have argued that clinicians have little insight into how they make judgments. For example, they have argued that even when clinicians report that some information is important, the information may have little influence on their judgments. A second issue is whether we can understand why clinicians have trouble learning from experience. Results from the validity studies described previously in this book indicate that clinicians with many years of experience are usually not more accurate than advanced graduate students.

FORMAL MODELS OF CLINICAL JUDGMENT

As already noted, a formal model can be a statistical equation or a series of if–then rules. Process-tracing models, which are discussed later in this section, are an example of a series of if–then rules that have been used to model clinical judgment.

Statistical Models

A wide range of statistical analyses have been used to model clinical judgment. These include multiple-regression analysis (Hammond, 1955; Hammond et al., 1964; Hoffman, 1960), analysis of variance (Hoffman, Slovic, & Rorer, 1968), analyses based on information theory (Bieri et al., 1966), analyses based on signal detection theory (Stenson, Kleinmuntz, & Scott, 1975), three-mode factor analysis (Mills & Tucker, 1966), functional measurement (Anderson, 1972), conjoint measurement (Garb, 1983; Wallsten & Budescu, 1981), multidimensional scaling (Chan & Jackson, 1982), and neural-network simulation (Berrios & Chen, 1993). The most frequently used statistical analysis has been multiple regression.

Several well-known studies on statistical modeling of clinical judgment have made use of a data set collected by Meehl (1959a). In this study, 13 PhD clinical psychologists and 16 clinical psychology graduate students were given MMPI profiles for 861 psychiatric patients. The MMPI profiles were collected at seven different sites in state, federal, and private hospitals and outpatient clinics. Each MMPI profile consisted of 11 MMPI scale scores (Mf and Si were excluded). The clinicians were instructed to sort the profiles on an 11-point forced normal distribution ranging from neurotic to psychotic. Though the clinicians were given less information than they would normally use in clinical practice, the task is generally thought to require complex information processing. Meehl did not describe how well statistical rules can model clinical judgment, though he did describe how well the clinicians and statistical rules could predict the criterion diagnoses (results on clinical versus statistical prediction are described in the next chapter).

Subsequent investigators, using the data collected by Meehl (1959a), have evaluated how well different types of statistical prediction rules can predict judgments made by clinicians. Wiggins and Hoffman (1968) compared three models: the linear-regression model, the quadratic model, and a sign model. Linear models consist of main-effects terms (e.g., x_1, x_2). Interaction terms are not included in these models. The quadratic model includes second-degree nonlinear terms (e.g., x_1^2, x_2^2) and interaction terms (e.g., x_1x_2) in addition to the linear terms that are included in the linear regression model. The third model, the sign model, consisted of a linear combination of 70 clinical signs that many clinicians say are valuable when using the MMPI to discriminate psychosis from neurosis. An example of a simple clinical sign is the Pt (Psychasthenia) scale minus the Sc (Schizophrenia) scale. Other clinical signs are much more complex (e.g., the Meehl–Dahlstrom [1960] sequential rules for discriminating psychotic from neurotic MMPI profiles).

Three of the samples of MMPI profiles collected by Meehl (1959a) were used as derivation samples to calculate regression weights for each of the three types of models. Three linear-regression models, three quadratic models, and three sign models were constructed for each of the 29 clinicians. Each model was then used to predict the judgments the clinicians made for the remaining four samples of MMPI profiles. The average cross-validated multiple-R was calculated for each of the three types of models. This was done separately for each clinician.

Results for each of the 29 clinicians, as reported by Wiggins and Hoffman (1968), are presented in Table 1. For each clinician, the average cross-validated multiple-R is presented for each of the three types of models. Also for each clinician, the model that best predicted a clinician's judgments is listed in the last column. The sign model was the most accurate for 13 of the clinicians, the linear model was the most accurate for 12, the quadratic model for 3, and the sign and linear models were tied for 1.

The results of the study are provocative because the linear-regression rule did well, even though clinicians believed that they used the MMPI results in a very complicated way. As observed by Wiggins and Hoffman (1968), "Though the differences [between the linear model and the other models] appear reliable, their magnitude is not large; the judgments of even the most seemingly configural [nonlinear] clinicians can often be estimated with precision by a linear model" (pp. 76–77). The results were also discussed at length by Goldberg (1968):

> The most overwhelming finding from this study was how much of the variance in clinicians' judgments could be represented by the linear model. For example, if one compares the judgment correlations produced by the linear model with those from each of the two configural models, one finds that (a) the linear model was equal to, or superior to, the quadratic model for 23 of the 29 judges (and at best, for the most configural judge, the quadratic model produced a correlation with his judgments which was only .03 greater than that of the linear model); and (b) the linear model was equal to, or superior to, the sign model for 17 judges (the superiority of the sign model being but .04 for the single most configural judge). (pp. 490–491)

Similar results were obtained by Goldberg (1971) when he also reanalyzed the Meehl (1959a) data. Goldberg compared five models: the linear-regression, conjunctive, disjunctive, logarithmic, and exponential models. The conjunctive and the disjunctive models were designed to capture nonlinearity in the judgment process, whereas the logarithmic model allowed for a logarithmic transformation of the cues and the exponential model allowed

TABLE 1
Average Cross-Validated Multiple Correlations for Linear, Quadratic, and Sign Models

Judge	Linear Model	Quadratic Model	Sign Model	Best-Fit Model
1	.602	.604	.638	Sign
2	.829	.788	.848	Sign
3	.712	.664	.684	Linear
4	.674	.684	.651	Quadratic
5	.763	.749	.763	Sign-Linear
6	.778	.776	.741	Linear
7	.745	.760	.709	Quadratic
8	.815	.808	.833	Sign
9	.837	.830	.858	Sign
10	.698	.706	.731	Sign
11	.863	.843	.872	Sign
12	.744	.698	.720	Linear
13	.730	.688	.563	Linear
14	.543	.561	.533	Quadratic
15	.819	.800	.830	Sign
16	.845	.830	.860	Sign
17	.697	.655	.649	Linear
18	.821	.839	.847	Sign
19	.799	.775	.778	Linear
20	.784	.774	.782	Linear
21	.866	.830	.854	Linear
22	.805	.797	.819	Sign
23	.742	.672	.656	Linmear
24	.656	.602	.672	Sign
25	.871	.875	.891	Sign
26	.794	.763	.784	Linear
27	.715	.658	.597	Linear
28	.755	.781	.787	Sign
29	.752	.734	.738	Linear

Note. Data from "Three models of clinical judgment," by N. Wiggins & P. J. Hoffman, 1968, *Journal of Abnormal Psychology, 73.* Copyright 1968 by the American Psychological Association.

for a logarithmic transformation of the judgments. The linear-regression model was again superior to all of the other models.

The results reported by Wiggins and Hoffman (1968) and Goldberg (1971) raised several important questions. Were clinicians integrating the MMPI results in a simple or complex manner? Is it possible that clinicians think they are doing something complicated when they are actually doing something simple? Is it possible that interactions and complicated relations among variables will rarely be detected when researchers use multiple-regression analysis to analyze data?

During the past 25 years, advances have been made in the ability to detect interactions (e.g., Jaccard & Wan, 1995; McClelland & Judd, 1993;

Rosnow & Rosenthal, 1995). Thus, it should come as no surprise that investigators have continued to try to detect nonlinear relations in the Meehl (1959a) data. In the most recent reanalysis of the data, results indicate that the cognitive processes of the clinicians were nonlinear (Ganzach, 1995). In this reanalysis, the scatter model, first described by Brannick and Brannick (1989), was used to predict judgments made by the clinicians. The scatter model can be used to detect nonlinearity in judgment. Specifically, the scatter model can evaluate whether judgments can be described by a conjunctive or disjunctive strategy. As described by Ganzach (1995):

> Disjunctive and conjunctive strategies are associated with the scatter, or gap, between cue values. To illustrate, consider the evaluation of the severity of the disorder of two mental patients on the basis of two equally important test scores. The two patients have the same mean score, but whereas one has two moderate scores, the other has one high score (a score indicative of severe disorder) and one low score. If decisions follow a linear compensatory strategy, the evaluations of the two patients would be about the same. If decisions follow a disjunctive strategy, the candidate with the higher scatter receives a higher (more severe) evaluation. If decisions follow a conjunctive strategy, the candidate with the higher scatter receives a lower evaluation. (p. 423)

A simple version of the scatter model and a multiple-scatter version model both did better than the linear-regression model. Results for each of the 29 clinicians, as reported by Ganzach (1995), are presented in Table 2. For each clinician, the average cross-validated multiple-R is presented for the linear-regression model, the simple version of the scatter model, and the multiple-scatter version model. Also for each clinician, the model that best predicted a clinician's judgments is listed in the last column. For each clinician, at least one of the two scatter models was more accurate than the linear-regression model. The magnitude of the differences in accuracy was, at least at times, moderate. For example, for Clinician 1, by squaring the multiple correlations, one can see that the multiple-scatter model accounts for moderately more of the variance (54%) than does the linear-regression model (47%).

Process-Tracing Models

Process-tracing models can also be used to study clinical judgment. Process-tracing models are developed by having clinicians talk aloud to describe their thoughts as they make their judgments. Experimenters use these verbal statements to devise computer algorithms that model the cognitive processes of the judges.

In a classic study by Kleinmuntz (1963), MMPI results for 126 college students were given to 10 experienced MMPI interpreters. The clinicians were to order the profiles along a 14-step forced normal distribution ranging

TABLE 2
Average Cross-Validated Multiple Correlations for Linear, Scatter, and Multiple Scatter Models

Judge	Linear Model	Scatter Model	Multiple-Scatter Model	Best-Fit Model
1	.687	.699	.738	Multiple Scatter
2	.819	.819	.835	Multiple Scatter
3	.707	.728	.736	Multiple Scatter
4	.703	.724	.736	Multiple Scatter
5	.756	.761	.786	Multiple Scatter
6	.792	.811	.829	Multiple Scatter
7	.725	.755	.778	Multiple Scatter
8	.795	.816	.807	Scatter
9	.806	.828	.827	Scatter
10	.712	.726	.711	Scatter
11	.836	.841	.840	Scatter
12	.750	.763	.779	Multiple Scatter
13	.717	.724	.731	Multiple Scatter
14	.550	.537	.558	Multiple Scatter
15	.820	.824	.836	Multiple Scatter
16	.830	.836	.861	Multiple Scatter
17	.729	.728	.737	Multiple Scatter
18	.842	.854	.861	Multiple Scatter
19	.772	.786	.800	Multiple Scatter
20	.760	.768	.766	Scatter
21	.836	.845	.836	Scatter
22	.785	.800	.806	Multiple Scatter
23	.729	.728	.742	Multiple Scatter
24	.682	.692	.700	Multiple Scatter
25	.829	.832	.831	Scatter
26	.759	.760	.757	Scatter
27	.719	.723	.724	Multiple Scatter
28	.804	.803	.824	Multiple Scatter
29	.767	.767	.781	Multiple Scatter

Note. Data from "Nonlinear models of clinical judgment: Meehl's data revisited," by Y. Ganzach, 1995, *Psychological Bulletin, 118.* Copyright 1995 by the American Psychological Association.

from *least adjusted* to *most adjusted*. Students were assigned a criterion score of *maladjusted* if their peers or a counseling-center therapist had described them as being maladjusted. Otherwise they were assigned a criterion score of *adjusted*. Of the 126 students, 45 were assigned criterion scores of *maladjusted* and 81 were assigned criterion scores of *adjusted*. The most accurate clinician was able to identify 67% of the adjusted students and 80% of the maladjusted students. After being asked to make ratings a second time for the same MMPI protocols, this clinician obtained a test–retest reliability coefficient of .98.

A process-tracing model was constructed to describe the logic underlying the "expert" clinician's judgments (Kleinmuntz, 1963). The process-tracing model was constructed by giving the clinician some of the profiles again, and having the clinician think aloud into a tape recorder as he sorted the profiles into adjusted and maladjusted categories. The experimenter then constructed a process-tracing model based on the clinician's report of his thoughts. The process-tracing model is presented in Figure 1. The model consists of 16 sequential rules. Once one of the rules is satisfied, then a diagnosis of adjusted or maladjusted is made. When the process-tracing rule was used to predict the judgments of the clinician, the correlation between the predictions of the process-tracing model and the judgments of the clinician was only .46 (reported by Einhorn, Kleinmuntz, & Kleinmuntz, 1979, p. 475). This correlation is lower than the correlations that were obtained when statistical models were used to predict clinicians' judgments of psychosis versus neurosis. It is also a disappointing finding because test–retest reliability for the clinician was described as being very high and, even more importantly, because the process-tracing model was derived and validated on the same profiles.

Comparison of Statistical and Process-Tracing Models

There are limitations to the statistical-prediction rules and process-tracing models. By using a statistical-prediction rule one might be able to predict a clinician's judgments, but this does not necessarily mean that one has described the cognitive processes of the clinician (e.g., Anderson & Shanteau, 1977). For example, a set of numbers can be generated by using a statistical equation that contains nonlinear terms, but one may be able to use a linear model to predict the numbers (e.g., Birnbaum, 1974; Green, 1968; Yntema & Torgerson, 1961). As observed by Goldberg (1968), "judges can process information in a configural fashion but . . . the general linear model is powerful enough to reproduce most of these judgments with very small error" (p. 491).

Similarly, one cannot assume that a process-tracing model will be descriptive of a clinician's cognitive processes. As observed by Simon (1978), "there is very little explicit evidence on the relation of the information contained in the thinking-aloud protocols to the underlying thought processes (p. 291). Furthermore, when a task is routine and familiar, a clinician may make judgments relatively automatically and the clinician's cognitive process may be largely inaccessible (Smith & Miller, 1978). Also, judges' descriptions of their thoughts are likely to be inaccurate if they are verbalized after they made their judgments rather than while they made their judgments (Ericsson & Simon, 1993).

Though it is important to recognize the limitations of the statistical and process-tracing models, it is also important to recognize that they can both be valuable. For example, they can be important for describing clini-

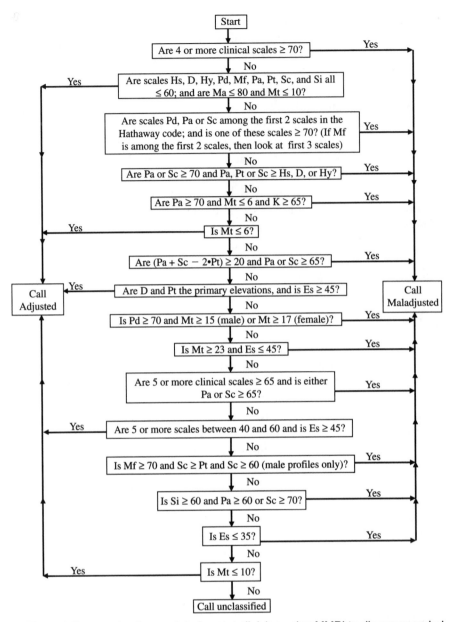

Figure 1. Process-tracing model of expert clinician using MMPI to diagnose maladjustment. Adapted from "MMPI decision rules for the identification of college maladjustment: A digital computer approach," by B. Kleinmuntz, 1963, *Psychological Monographs*, 77 (14, Whole No. 577). Copyright 1963 by the American Psychological Association. Adapted with permission.

cians who are able to make valid judgments (Garb, 1984). In a validity study, when some clinicians are able to make valid ratings but other clinicians are not, it may be misleading to report the average hit rate for all clinicians. Clinicians who made valid judgments for one set of protocols should be given at least one more set of protocols. If they are also able to make valid judgments for these protocols, then one will want to be able to describe how the clinicians formed their judgments. One can use statistical models or process-tracing models to describe these clinicians.

One can wonder if statistical models or process-tracing models are more descriptive of the clinical judgment process. A positive feature of process-tracing models is that "the computer model is a sequential step-by-step set of rules, and since we generally seem to process information sequentially, the model has greater face validity than the regression approach" (Einhorn et al., 1979, p. 470). That is, when people make a judgment, they usually do not believe that the answer suddenly occurs to them, but instead they believe that they arrive at their judgment by thinking about the problem in a series of steps. However, though statistical-prediction rules do not describe the judgment process as consisting of a sequential series of steps, a linear-regression equation can describe the same judgment processes that are described by a process-tracing model (Einhorn et al., 1979). For example, in Table 3, verbal reports made by a clinician are listed, and alongside each of these verbal reports, values have been entered

TABLE 3
Representation of a Clinician's Thoughts by a Linear Rule

Clinician's Statements	Linear Rule
1. I'll look at x_1 first—it's pretty high . . . the x_2 score is also high. This is a maladjusted profile.	$y = .6(7) + .2(6) = 5.4$ call maladjusted.
2. Let's see, x_1 is high but . . . x_2 is low, better check x_3—it's low too. I would say adjusted.	$y = .6(7) + .2(1) + .2(2) = 4.8$ call adjusted.
3. This person's x_1 score is low. Better check both x_2 and x_3 then—both pretty high. Um . . . likely to be maladjusted.	$y = .6(3) + .2(8) + .2(8) = 5.0$ call maladjusted.
4. x_1 is fairly low here . . . x_2 is quite high . . . this is an interesting case . . . x_3 is very low . . . I'd say adjusted.	$y = .6(4) + .2(9) + .2(1) = 4.4$ call adjusted.
5. x_1 is extremely high—this is a maladjusted case.	$y = .6(10) = 6$ call maladjusted.

Note. Additive rule: $y = .6x_1 + .2x_2 + .2x_3$ ($0 \leq x_1, x_2, x_3 \leq 10$). If $y \geq 5$, call maladjusted; if $y < 5$, call adjusted. From "Linear regression and process-tracing models of judgment," by H. J. Einhorn, D. N. Kleinmuntz, and B. Kleinmuntz, 1979, *Psychological Review, 80,* p. 473. Copyright 1979 by the American Psychological Association. Adapted with permission.

into a linear rule to show that the linear rule can make the same ratings as the clinician. The linear rule used in Table 3 is:

$$y = .6x_1 + .2x_2 + .2x_3 \qquad (1)$$

The following decision rule is used to decide if ratings made by the linear rule should be classified as maladjusted or adjusted:

If $y \geq 5$, call *maladjusted*;

If $y < 5$, call *adjusted*. $\qquad (2)$

For example, when the first predictor has a value of 7 and the second predictor has a value of 6 (see first line of Table 3), the clinician's statements indicate that a rating of *maladjusted* is appropriate and use of the linear rule also leads to a diagnosis of maladjusted. Thus, both a process-tracing model and a statistical model can capture the same processes, though the processes are modeled in different ways.

A positive feature of statistical models is that they may be more accurate than process-tracing models. That is, one may be able to better predict a clinician's judgments if one uses a statistical-prediction rule rather than a process-tracing model. This can happen when clinicians are unable to accurately describe their cognitive process or when an experimenter is not able to accurately turn verbal statements into a process-tracing model.

A process-tracing model was compared to a linear-regression equation in one clinical-judgment study (data collected by Kleinmuntz, 1963; additional analyses conducted by Einhorn et al., 1979). The process-tracing model was constructed by Kleinmuntz (1963) and was previously shown in Figure 1. It was derived and validated on the same set of MMPI profiles (i.e., it was not cross-validated), and thus one would expect that the classifications made by using the process-tracing model would be highly correlated with the clinician's actual judgments. The linear-regression rule was cross-validated by randomly splitting the sample of MMPI profiles in half and deriving the model on the first half and cross-validating it on the second half. The phi correlation between the predictions of the models and the judgments of the clinicians was .79 for the linear regression model and .46 for the process-tracing model. The difference between these correlations is statistically significant ($p < .001$).

COGNITIVE HEURISTICS, COGNITIVE BIASES, AND KNOWLEDGE STRUCTURES

Examples of cognitive heuristics are the representativeness heuristic, the availability heuristic, the anchoring and adjustment heuristic, and the past-behavior heuristic. The *representativeness heuristic* is said to be descriptive when a judgment is made by deciding if an object or person is representative of a category. For example, when making a diagnosis of dissociative identity disorder (formerly multiple personality disorder), a clinician may compare a patient to what is understood to be the typical patient with dissociative identity disorder. The *availability heuristic* is said to be descriptive when judgments are influenced by the ease with which objects and events can be remembered. For example, in making a diagnosis, one may be more likely to make a diagnosis of borderline personality disorder than histrionic personality disorder if one can more easily recall patients who have had borderline personality disorder. The *anchoring-and-adjustment heuristic* is said to be descriptive when judgments vary as a function of the order of the presentation of information. The *past-behavior heuristic* is said to be descriptive when predictions of future behavior are based on a person's past behavior.

Examples of biases are confirmatory bias, hindsight bias, the misestimation of covariance, and the ignoring of base rates or norms. *Confirmatory bias* is said to occur when clinicians seek or recall information that can confirm, but not refute, a hypothesis. Confirmatory bias can also occur when clinicians ignore information that does not support their hypotheses, interpret ambiguous information as supporting their hypotheses, or do not consider whether information supports alternative hypotheses. *Hindsight bias* occurs when learning that an outcome has occurred increases the perceived likelihood of the event (e.g., the hindsight bias may occur when a supervisor learns that a client has attempted suicide and the supervisor believes that the supervisee should have been able to see that the client was likely to attempt suicide). Finally, the *misestimation of covariance* occurs when clinicians do not correctly describe the relation between two events. For example, when trying to learn about the relation between a test score and a personality trait, clinicians may remember instances when the test score occurred and the client had a particular personality trait, but may be less likely to remember other instances (e.g., when the test indicator was not present but a client had the personality trait).

Schematic processing involves the use of organized knowledge structures (schemas) to process information. Clinicians' judgments depend on their knowledge of psychopathology and behavior. To understand how clinicians make judgments, it can be important to learn about their knowledge structures. For example, it can be important to learn about their implicit theories of personality and psychopathology, stereotypes and prototypes, and scripts. A stereotype consists of a clinician's beliefs about a typical client (e.g., the typical client with dissociative identity disorder) and a prototype consists of a clinician's beliefs about a prototypical client (e.g., a client with all of the features of dissociative identity disorder). A script is a person's beliefs about events that are likely to unfold (Schank & Abelson, 1977), such as a clinician's expectations about how treatment for a person with schizophrenia is likely to progress.

The concepts of cognitive heuristics, cognitive biases, and schematic processing of knowledge structures are used in the following sections to describe how clinicians collect, integrate, and remember information. In a later section of this chapter, the concepts of cognitive heuristics, cognitive biases, and knowledge structures are related to learning from feedback.

Data Collection

Primacy Effect

Like other people, mental health professionals frequently make judgments quickly, sometimes after collecting relatively little data (Ambady & Rosenthal, 1992; also see Gauron & Dickinson, 1969; Kendell, 1973; Meehl, 1960; Oskamp, 1965; Sandifer, Hordern, & Green, 1970). This has been called the *primacy effect*. An example of the primacy effect was described by Kendell (1973):

> Accurate diagnoses can often be reached very early in an interview, even within the first two minutes, and that after five or ten minutes further expenditure of time is subject to a law of rapidly diminishing returns. Or, looking at the matter from a different angle, in something like 50 per cent of patients the diagnosis is apparent within a few minutes, and in many of the rest it remains a subject of disagreement no matter how much information is accumulated. (p. 444)

A primacy effect has also been observed when the task was to use a Q sort to describe personality traits, needs, conflicts, and defense mechanisms. When psychotherapists completed Q sorts, ratings made after two to four therapy sessions were similar to Q sorts made after the 24th therapy session (Meehl, 1960).

The primacy effect describes the clinical judgment process, but it does not demonstrate that clinicians make invalid judgments. Information obtained toward the end of an interview, or toward the end of psychotherapy, may be in agreement with information collected at the beginning of an interview or at the start of psychotherapy, and thus a revision of judgments may not be warranted.

Anchoring and Adjustment

Unlike the primacy effect, when the anchoring-and-adjustment heuristic is descriptive of cognitive processes, one can infer that validity is less than perfect. Anchoring and adjustment is said to occur when different starting points yield different estimates, which are biased toward the initial values (Tversky & Kahneman, 1974). For example, if a judgment changes depending on whether an item of information is collected early or late in an interview session, or early or late in the course of psychotherapy, then anchoring and adjustment is said to occur. Anchoring and adjustment also occurs when clinicians are influenced by the range of clients they work with. For example, a clinician may be more likely to describe a client as being well adjusted if the clinician works with a population that is relatively more disturbed than that client.

Anchoring and adjustment has occurred when the order of the presentation of information has varied, even when clinicians received identical information by the time they made their final ratings (Ellis, Robbins, Schult, Ladany, & Banker, 1990; Friedlander & Phillips, 1984; Friedlander & Stockman, 1983; Pain & Sharpley, 1989). For example, anchoring and adjustment occurred when 46 psychologists, psychiatrists, and social workers read summaries of five therapy sessions (Friedlander & Phillips, 1984; Friedlander & Stockman, 1983). Each clinician made ratings for two clients. For the two clients, information indicating the presence of suicidal ideation or anorexia was presented in the notes for the first or fourth therapy session. Clients were rated as being more maladjusted and having a worse prognosis when this information was presented in the notes for the first session rather than in the notes for the fourth session.

Anchoring and adjustment has also occurred when the range of cases presented to clinicians has varied (Bieri, Orcutt, & Leaman, 1963; Perrett, 1971; Rich, Paul, & Mariotto, 1988). For example, in one of the studies (Rich et al., 1988), ratings were made by clinical staff for 1,040 clients at 24 treatment units. To make their ratings, clinicians used the Nurses Observational Scale for Inpatient Evaluation (NOSIE-30; Honigfeld, Gillis, & Klett, 1966). The NOSIE-30 consists of 30 items, each of which is rated on a 5-point scale ranging from 0 (*never*) to 4 (*always*). Clinical staffmembers who were most familiar with the clients were asked to make the ratings. The NOSIE-30 ratings were compared to ratings made by using the Time-Sample Behavioral Checklist (TSBC; Paul, 1987). Using the TSBC, trained observers recorded the presence or absence of 72 carefully defined behaviors at regular time intervals. The trained observers were present on the units for 10 consecutive days. With regard to the results, the anchoring and adjustment heuristic was descriptive of the clinicians' NOSIE-30 ratings. Given two patients on different units who were described by the TSBC as having a similar level of adjustment, staff rated the patient on the unit with patients who were functioning at a relatively low level as having a higher level of functioning.

Confirmatory Hypothesis Testing

Confirmatory hypothesis testing describes a tendency to seek, use, and remember information that can confirm, but not refute, a hypothesis. Results have been mixed on whether the confirmatory bias is descriptive of how clinicians seek information. In a number of studies, clinicians read a clinical vignette or watched a videotape of an interview, formulated hypotheses about the client (e.g., a diagnosis they thought might be accurate), and listed questions they would like to ask the client. In many of the studies, the confirmatory bias was not descriptive of how clinicians requested information (Dallas & Baron, 1985; Hayden, 1987; Murdock, 1988; Strohmer & Chiodo, 1984; Strohmer & Newman, 1983). However, it was descriptive in a study that used a more naturalistic design (Haverkamp, 1993). For example, in one of the studies that did not use a naturalistic design (Strohmer & Newman, 1983), clinicians were instructed to "think about the kinds of questions you would like to ask to test the truth or falsity of the hypothesis" (p. 561). The problem with these instructions is that they prompt the clinicians to ask questions that can lead them to refute a hypothesis. In Haverkamp's study, clinical and counseling psychology graduate students watched a videotape of an initial counseling session and listed questions they would like to ask the client. They also described their reasons for wanting to ask the client these questions. Each graduate student's style of hypothesis testing was coded as confirmatory, neutral, or disconfirmatory by an independent panel of psychologists. When the graduate students generated their own hypotheses (rather than have hypotheses suggested to them by the experimenter), their style of hypothesis testing was confirmatory 64% of the time, neutral 21% of the time, and disconfirmatory 15% of the time.

Integrating Information to Make Judgments

Confirmatory Hypothesis Testing

Confirmatory processes can be important for understanding how clinicians integrate information because clinicians may ignore information that does not support their hypotheses, may interpret ambiguous evidence as supporting their hypotheses, and may not consider whether available evidence supports alternative hypotheses. Unfortunately, the issue of whether confirmatory bias occurs when clinicians integrate information has not been studied (though evidence does indicate that confirmatory bias occurs when clinicians search for information and when they remember information).

Representativeness and Knowledge Structures

The *representativeness heuristic* is said to be descriptive when a judgment is made by deciding if an object or person is representative of a category. For example, when making ratings of a trait or symptom, mental health professionals may compare a client to clients who they have worked with who clearly had the trait or symptom (exemplars), to their concept of the "typical" person with the trait or symptom (stereotype), or to a theoretical standard that serves to define the trait or symptom (prototype). Exemplars, stereotypes, and prototypes are all knowledge structures.

In the area of psychological assessment, prototypes have received more attention than exemplars and stereotypes. The concept of a prototype was described by Horowitz, Wright, Lowenstein, and Parad (1981):

> A prototype defines a kind of theoretical ideal, a theoretical standard against which real people can be evaluated. No one person matches the theoretical standard perfectly, but different people approximate it to different degrees. The more closely the person approximates the ideal, the more the person typifies the concept. (p. 568)

Methods for learning about judges' prototypes have been developed in the area of personality psychology (e.g., Buss & Craik, 1983, 1986; Cantor & Mischel, 1979; Horowitz et al., 1981; John, Chaplin, & Goldberg, 1988) and in the area of psychodiagnosis (Cantor, Smith, French, & Mezzich, 1980; Mechelen & De Boeck, 1989). For example, using the act frequency approach, Buss (1991) showed how the trait "narcissism" can be represented as a prototype. Participants were instructed to think of the three most narcissistic people they know. While thinking of these narcissistic people, they were to write down three of the behaviors or acts that exemplify their narcissism. One response that a participant made described a man who talked about himself and did not listen to anyone else. Having obtained a list of acts that exemplify a trait, the investigator then determined which of the acts are central to the trait by having a second sample of participants rate the acts as being central or noncentral to the concept of narcissism. Mean ratings provided a measure of how central each of the acts are for describing narcissism. For example, telling others one is beautiful or great was judged to be a more narcissistic act than looking in the mirror constantly.

Traits and Symptoms. The representativeness heuristic may describe how clinicians make ratings of personality traits and psychiatric symptoms. Empirical studies have not directly investigated whether mental health professionals describe a client's personality traits and psychiatric symptoms by comparing the client to exemplars, stereotypes, or prototypes. However, it seems likely that they do. For example, if a client talks about himself but does not listen to anyone else, tells others he is handsome or great, and looks in the mirror constantly, then it is likely that the comparison of this client to exemplars, stereotypes, or prototypes for narcissism will lead to the client being called narcissistic.

The validity of a clinician's rating may depend in part on the exemplars, stereotypes, or prototypes to which the clinician compares the client. If the exemplars, stereotypes, and prototypes are valid, then the clinician may be able to make accurate judgments. For example, if a client believes that a group of people are planning to take over the world, then most clinicians will probably describe this client as being paranoid. This is likely to be a valid rating and can be made by comparing the client to exemplars, stereotypes, or prototypes. However, when exemplars, stereotypes, and prototypes are invalid, ratings are also likely to be invalid.

A prototype is more likely to be invalid when it is based on a mental health professional's clinical experience than when it is based on empirical research. For example, before homosexuality was removed from the *DSM*, Chapman and Chapman (1969, p. 273) asked psychologists the following questions:

1. Have you seen the Rorschach protocols of a number of men who have problems concerning homosexual impulses, either overt or covert?
2. What kinds of Rorschach content have you observed to be prominent in the Rorschach protocols of men with problems concerning homosexual impulses?

Of the 32 psychologists who reported that they have seen the Rorschach protocols of a number of men who have problems concerning homosexual impulses, all of the psychologists described signs on the Rorschach that they thought were prominent, but only two described a sign that has been supported by research. In a later section in this chapter, reasons why clinicians frequently have difficulty learning from their clinical experiences will be described.

Diagnosis. The representativeness heuristic seems to be descriptive of how many mental health professionals make diagnoses. In one study (Garb, 1996b), 67 psychologists and psychology interns read case histories and then made diagnostic ratings and similarity ratings. The diagnostic ratings were made on a scale with values ranging from 0 to 10, with 0 indicating that the person definitely does not have the disorder, a rating of 5 indicating that the person has a "50–50" chance of having the disorder, and a rating of 10 indicating that the person definitely has the disorder. Similarity ratings were also made on a scale with values ranging from 0 to 10, with 0 indicating that the person is not at all similar to the typical person with the disorder and a rating of 10 indicating that the person exemplifies the disorder. Only 18 of the 67 psychologists and psychology interns made the diagnosis one would make if one adhered strictly to the *DSM–III–R* criteria. Correlations between diagnostic ratings and similarity ratings were very high, indicating that the representativeness heuristic is descriptive of how many clinicians make diagnoses. When clinicians read the case history and made diagnostic ratings and similarity ratings in the same session, a correlation of .92 was obtained. When clinicians made diagnostic ratings and then made similarity ratings after reading the case history again several weeks later, a correlation of .77 was obtained, which is presumably about as high as one would expect for test–retest reliability for the diagnostic ratings.

Empirical evidence indicates that clinicians' prototypes frequently differ from the explicit criteria contained in classification systems, such as that listed in *DSM–IV* (Blashfield & Haymaker, 1988; Livesley, Reiffer, Sheldon, & West, 1987; McFall, Murburg, Smith, & Jensen, 1991; Mechelen &

De Boeck, 1989). For example, in one study (Blashfield & Haymaker, 1988), 20 clinical psychologists and psychiatrists were given the diagnostic criteria for the *DSM–III–R* personality disorders. Each of the 142 criteria was written on a separate card. Clinicians were to assign each criterion to one of the *DSM–III–R* personality disorders. A majority of the clinicians failed to assign 30% of the criteria to the correct personality disorder.

Case Formulation. The representativeness heuristic is at times descriptive of how clinicians make causal judgments. For example, when psychologists were asked to "list the indicators that lead you to suspect childhood sexual abuse," the most frequently listed indicator was "adult sexual dysfunction" (Poole et al., 1995, p. 430). However, many survivors of child sexual abuse report that they do not have sexual dysfunction, and most cases of sexual dysfunction are unrelated to a known or likely history of childhood sexual abuse. The relation between childhood sexual abuse and adult sexual dysfunctioning may be overestimated because of the surface similarity between the two (Poole et al., 1995).

Behavioral Prediction. Results from one study (Garb, 1996b) indicate that the representativeness heuristic is not descriptive of how clinicians predict a patient's behavior. In this study, psychologists read a case history and predicted whether the patient would become violent, would continue to abuse alcohol, and would comply with inpatient treatment (e.g., not refuse medicine). The same psychologists also made similarity ratings for the same patient, for example, they rated how similar the patient is to typical patients who have been violent, who abuse alcohol, and who comply with inpatient treatment. Predictions and similarity ratings were made by the psychologists in the same session. The case history described a patient who was paranoid, delusional, hallucinating, and threatening. He had a history of substance abuse, assaultive behavior, and noncompliance with treatment. The correlation between predictions and similarity ratings was only .42, indicating that the representativeness heuristic is not descriptive of how the psychologists made their predictions. Given that the patient had a history of alcohol abuse, the psychologists thought that it was highly likely that the patient would continue to abuse alcohol. However, the psychologists did not think that he was similar to other patients who abuse alcohol, apparently because most patients who abuse alcohol are not psychotic.

Deterministic Reasoning and the Hindsight Bias

When mental health professionals try to understand the causes of their clients' behaviors and symptoms, their formulations may be overly deterministic. That is, when a clinician has formulated an explanation for why a client acts a particular way or has a particular symptom, one can expect that the clinician will overestimate the likelihood of the explanation being accurate (Brehmer, 1980; Einhorn, 1988). The reason one can expect case formulations to be overly deterministic is not because clinicians' causal explanations are especially bad, but because research in the area of social psychology on the hindsight bias indicates that people are generally over deterministic when they construct causal explanations (Hawkins & Hastie, 1990).

Research on the hindsight bias indicates that "Finding out that an outcome has occurred increases its perceived likelihood. Judges are, however, unaware of the effect that outcome knowledge has on their perceptions. Thus, judges tend to believe that this relative inevitability was largely apparent in foresight" (Fischhoff, 1975, p. 297). When clinicians describe the causes of a behavior or symptom, they already know the outcome (the behavior or symptom), and thus, if hindsight bias is present, the clinicians are likely to overestimate the probability of their causal formulations being correct. The hindsight bias has been observed in the area of neuropsychological assessment (Arkes, Faust, Guilmette, & Hart, 1988), but has not been studied in other areas of psychological assessment.

The Past-Behavior Heuristic, Causal Reasoning, and Prediction

Results have been contradictory on whether the past-behavior heuristic is descriptive of how clinicians make predictions. In two studies, the past-behavior heuristic was descriptive of how clinicians made predictions of violence. In one of the studies (Cocozza & Steadman, 1978), a history of violence was the only significant predictor of predictions of dangerousness made for incompetent patients. In the second study (Quinsey, 1975), when predictions were made for patients in a maximum-security psychiatric institution, the major predictor of judgments of dangerousness was the severity of previous offenses. However, in other studies on the prediction of violence, the past-behavior heuristic was not descriptive (e.g., Dix, 1975; Levinson & York, 1974; Pfohl, 1978; Werner et al., 1983; Yesavage, Werner, Becker, & Mills, 1982). The results from these studies indicate that clinicians also attend to other information and use other strategies to make predictions. In these studies, factors other than a history of violence were significantly related to predictions of violence (e.g., whether a person is hostile, expresses remorse, or possesses dangerous delusions).

One can speculate that clinicians usually attempt to use causal theories to make predictions, but when they are unable to, the past-behavior heuristic may be descriptive. For example, for the prediction of violence, clinicians may try to learn if a person has been violent in the past, and if so, they may construct a causal theory for why the person was threatening or violent (e.g., conflicts with a work supervisor). They may then try to determine if the same causative factors are still present (e.g., the person still works under the same supervisor). If a clinician cannot construct a compelling causal theory to make a prediction, then the past-behavior heuristic may be descriptive of the cognitive processes of the clinician.

An example can be given to illustrate the importance of implicit causal theories. In one study (Schwartz, Friedlander, & Tedeschi, 1986), graduate students in counseling psychology, social work, and educational psychology listened to one of four audiotapes of the first few minutes of an initial counseling session. In two of the tapes an actor said that he came because he wanted a letter to the dean saying that he had talked to a counselor about having gotten into a fight in a dormitory. In the two other tapes an actor said that he came to counseling because he thought that, for his own sake, he needed to talk about having gotten into a fight in a dormitory. Clinicians made more favorable prognostic ratings when the reason for seeking help was intrinsic (self-improvement) rather than extrinsic (non-therapeutic). Apparently the graduate students believed that clients are more likely to improve when their reasons for coming for counseling are intrinsic rather than extrinsic, and they apparently based their prognostic ratings on this implicit causal theory.

Case Formulation and Treatment Planning

To understand how clinicians make treatment decisions, one needs to understand how they formulate case histories. After all, the interventions of different therapeutic schools (e.g., psychodynamic, cognitive–behavioral) are based on different models of the causes of mental disorders. Case formulation includes describing a client's problems and goals, identifying the causal factors that affect a client's problems, and identifying mediating factors, such as the client's motivation or previous experiences in therapy (Haynes, 1993).

Unfortunately, the cognitive processes of clinicians engaged in treatment planning has rarely been the object of empirical study. However, results from one study (Murdock & Fremont, 1989) indicate that causal reasoning is involved in treatment planning. In this study, assignment to long-term counseling was more likely when the causes of the clients' problems were judged to be enduring rather than transient.

Use of Norms

Empirical norms are widely available for use in neuropsychological assessment (e.g., Heaton, 1992; Heaton, Grant, & Matthews, 1991). Normative data reflect the test performance of normal individuals. The results from two studies (Garb & Florio, 1997; Nadler et al., 1994), described in the chapter on neuropsychological assessment, indicate that a significant number of neuropsychologists do not attend to norms. In these studies, neuropsychologists based their ratings on demographic information (gender, education, handedness) and results from the Halstead-Reitan Neuropsychological Test Battery, the WAIS–Revised, and the Wechsler Memory Scale. In the Garb and Florio study, results from the Controlled Oral Word Association Test (F-A-S) and the Rey Auditory-Verbal Learning Test were also made available. The neuropsychologists thought that the test results were obtained by testing a 38-year-old client and a 74-year-old client, but actually the results for the "38-year-old client" were obtained from tables of normative data for 38-year-olds and the results for the "74-year-old client" were obtained from tables of normative data for 74-year-olds (Heaton et al., 1986; Russell, 1988; Spreen & Strauss, 1991; Wechsler, 1981). The results from both studies indicate that many neuropsychologists do not attend to norms when they make diagnoses. For example, in the Nadler et al. study, none of the 38-year-olds, but 23% of the 74-year-olds, were diagnosed as having dementia, even though the 74-year-olds were described by normal elderly test results.

Use of Base Rates

Clinicians sometimes attend to base rates. Meehl (1986b) gave an example from medicine: "Every general practitioner at times says to the patient, 'Well, I think you've got the winter crud; there's a lot of that going around these days,' an informal Bayesian inference" (p. 225). An example from the area of mental health can also be given. As a psychologist on an acute psychiatry inpatient unit at a V.A. medical center, I learned that the base rate for being assaulted was a great deal lower than the base rate for being threatened.

Research indicates that clinicians frequently do not attend to base rates when they make diagnoses. Instead, the representativeness heuristic seems to be descriptive (Garb, 1996b). When the representativeness heuristic is descriptive of how people make judgments, one can infer that they are not attending to base rates (Tversky & Kahneman, 1974). For example, when clinicians make diagnoses by comparing a client to the typical client with a particular disorder, it implies that they are not attending to base-rate information.

When clinicians do not attend to base rates, or when they misperceive base rates, validity may suffer. For example, in one study (Lidz et al., 1993), patients were followed for 6 months after mental health professionals made predictions of violence. The mental health professionals made more predictions of violence for the male patients than for the female patients (45% versus 22%), but the female patients were violent more often than the male patients (49% versus 42%).

When clinicians attend to base rates, they should give more weight to the base-rate information when the other information (e.g., case history information) is ambiguous or otherwise of low validity. For example, if a client is described by a case history as meeting the criteria for a mental disorder, then clinicians need not attend to base rates (e.g., they need not consider whether antisocial personality disorder occurs more frequently among males than females). However, in one study (Ford & Widiger, 1989), the effect of client gender was greater when case history information was less ambiguous. In this study, 266 psychologists made differential diagnoses after reading one of nine case histories. The case histories differed with regard to gender (male, female, or unspecified) and type of symptoms and maladaptive behaviors (antisocial, histrionic, or a combination of antisocial and histrionic). Each psychologist was given a case history that described a client with either an antisocial personality disorder or a histrionic personality disorder, or a client with antisocial and histrionic personality features. The clients with the antisocial and histrionic personality features did not meet the DSM–III criteria for antisocial personality disorder or histrionic personality disorder. The effect of client gender was statistically significant. Male clients were more likely to be diagnosed as having an antisocial personality disorder, and female clients were more likely to be diagnosed as having a histrionic personality disorder. The effect of client gender was strongest for the least ambiguous cases. That is, the effect of client gender was strongest when clients were described as having behaviors and symptoms that satisfy the criteria for the antisocial or histrionic personality disorders.

Cognitive Complexity

Variations in cognitive complexity can explain, in part, why clinicians make different judgments from one another. Cognitive complexity is "the capacity to construe behavior in a multidimensional way. A more cognitively complex person has available a more differentiated system of dimensions for perceiving others' behavior than does a less cognitively complex individual" (Bieri et al., 1966, p. 185). Research on cognitive complexity, much of which derives from the personal construct theory of George A. Kelly (e.g., Kelly, 1963), is related to schematic processing.

Using one variation of Kelly's reportory grid technique, Spengler and Strohmer (1994) were able to relate cognitive complexity to errors in judgment. To measure cognitive complexity, counseling psychologists made ratings on six scales (outgoing–shy, adjusted–maladjusted, decisive–indecisive, calm–excitable, interested in others–self-absorbed, and cheerful–ill humored) for four people (mother, friend of opposite gender, person with whom you feel most uncomfortable, and supervisor or boss). The greater the differentiation of a clinician's ratings for the four people, the greater the clinician's cognitive complexity. Spengler and Strohmer were able to show that counseling psychologists with lower cognitive complexity were less likely than counseling psychologists with higher cognitive complexity to recognize that a mentally retarded client may have an emotional disorder and may benefit from psychotherapy or psychotropic medication.

Memory and Judgment

Judgments can sometimes be invalid or biased because of the way that clinicians remember information. Research on covariation misestimation, the confirmatory bias, and the availability heuristic will be described. Covariation misestimation occurs when clinicians make systematic errors when they try to determine how events covary (e.g., when they try to remember how test results are related to diagnoses). As already noted, the confirmatory bias occurs when clinicians seek information, integrate information, or remember information that can confirm, but not refute, a hypothesis. The availability heuristic is descriptive of cognitive processes when a clinician is influenced by the ease with which instances or occurrences can be remembered (Tversky & Kahneman, 1973).

Covariation Misestimation

To accurately determine how two events covary (e.g., a test result and a diagnosis), one needs to remember instances when (a) both events occurred, (b) the first event occurred and the second event did not, (c) the first event did not occur and the second event did, and (d) neither the first event nor the second event occurred. Figure 2 depicts a prototypical situation. A clinician tries to determine if a particular test result is a strong

		Diagnosis	
		X	Not X
Test Result	Present	**A** 12 patients	**B** 6 patients
	Absent	**C** 6 patients	**D** 3 patients

Figure 2. Representation of relation between test results and diagnoses.

indicator of a particular diagnosis. For 12 patients the test result and the diagnosis co-occurred, for 6 patients the test result occurred but the diagnosis did not, for 6 patients the test result did not occur but the diagnosis did, and for 3 patients the test result did not occur and the diagnosis did not occur. The actual relation between the test result and the diagnosis is zero because the likelihood of the diagnosis does not vary as a function of the test result. However, research in the area of cognitive psychology indicates that people base their assessment of covariation largely by remembering the number of instances in Cell A (Arkes, 1981; Kayne & Alloy, 1988).

Covariation misestimation has not been studied directly in the area of psychological assessment, but one can expect that it does occur with mental health professionals. Arkes (1981) gave the following example to illustrate why one can expect covariation misestimation to occur when mental health professionals make judgments:

> Assume that you suspect that a certain MMPI profile is diagnostic of an impending psychotic break. To check this suspicion, you keep track of how many people with this profile do or do not have a subsequent psychotic episode. Would you also consider keeping track of those without that profile in order to test the hypothesis? Since the hypothesis deals only with people having a certain profile, disregarding those without it appears sensible. Yet those instances need to be recorded to test the hypothesis adequately. (p. 324)

Confirmatory Bias

After making a judgment, a clinician may selectively remember information that supports the judgment. For example, Arkes and Harkness (1980) argued that the act of making a diagnosis can influence subsequent recall of symptoms. If a symptom is associated with a diagnosis, then after a clinician makes the diagnosis for a client, the clinician may incorrectly recall the client as having the symptom. Similarly, if a symptom does not usually occur among clients having a particular diagnosis, then a clinician may forget that a client has the symptom.

Race bias, gender bias, and other client variable biases may occur because memory processes are biased. For example, if an African American patient is misdiagnosed as having schizophrenia, then a clinician may incorrectly recall the patient as having symptoms that are related to schizophrenia. Furthermore, complaints of depression or mania may not be remembered.

Empirical research indicates that the confirmatory bias does occur when clinicians remember information about clients (Lee et al., 1995; Murdock, 1988; Strohmer, Shivy, & Chiodo, 1990). That is, they tend to recall more category-consistent symptoms and traits than category-inconsistent symptoms and traits. For example, in one study (Strohmer et al., 1990), 34 master's degree counselors read one of three versions of a case history. The three versions of the case history contained (a) 12 phrases describing good self-control (e.g., "good will power") and 8 phrases describing lack of self-control (e.g., "follows own urges"), (b) 10 descriptors of good self-control and 10 descriptors of lack of self-control, and (c) 8 descriptors of good self-control and 12 descriptors of lack of self-control. One week after reading the case history, the counselors were asked to list as many factors as they could recall that "would be helpful in determining whether or not Mrs. N lacked self-control" (p. 467). For the hypothesis that the client lacks self-control, confirmatory information consisted of the phrases describing lack of self-control. The counselors listed more confirmatory information than disconfirmatory information, even when they were given the version of the case history that contained more disconfirmatory information than confirmatory information.

Availability Heuristic

The availability heuristic is descriptive of cognitive processes when clinicians are influenced by the ease with which instances or occurrences can be remembered. Several factors are related to the ease with which information can be remembered (e.g., the vividness of information and the strength of verbal associative connections between events).

The availability heuristic can be used to account for findings on illusory correlations. According to Tversky and Kahneman (1974):

> Availability provides a natural account for the illusory correlation effect. The judgment of how frequently two events co-occur could be based on the strength of the associative bond between them. When the association is strong, one is likely to conclude that the events have been frequently paired. Consequently, strong associates will be judged to have occurred together frequently. (p. 1128)

Thus, when verbal associative connections are strong, the availability heuristic is likely to be descriptive of how clinicians remember information, and this can account for findings on illusory correlations.

The strength of verbal associative connections can make it easier or more difficult to remember when a test indicator and a symptom or behavior co-occur. This can lead to poor validity when clinicians rely on their clinical experience to make judgments. Back when homosexuality was considered to be a diagnosable disorder, Chapman and Chapman (1969) had undergraduate students make ratings for 88 items including the following item:

The tendency for "homosexuality" to call to mind "rectum" and "buttocks" is:

a. Very strong
b. Strong
c. Moderate

d. Slight

e. Very slight

f. No tendency at all (p. 274)

Undergraduates' ratings of strength of verbal associative connections were related to responses clinicians made when they were asked what Rorschach signs they attend to when assessing homosexual impulses. Chapman and Chapman found that all of the Rorschach signs listed by clinicians had a strong verbal associative connection to homosexuality, even though other research studies have shown that many of the signs are not valid. In conclusion, the ease with which clinicians can remember different test results being paired with different symptoms or behaviors depends in part on the verbal associative connections between the signs and the symptoms or behaviors. When clinicians are strongly influenced by these verbal associative connections, they are likely to make invalid judgments.

AWARENESS OF COGNITIVE PROCESSES

A controversial issue in cognitive psychology and social psychology is whether people are aware of their cognitive processes (Ericsson & Simon, 1980; Nisbett & Wilson, 1977; Smith & Miller, 1978; White, 1980). The debate has continued in recent years. For example, according to Ericsson and Simon (1993), reports of cognitive processes are likely to be accurate if judges talk aloud as thoughts are attended to in short-term memory. They also argue that reports can be accurate when they are made immediately after people make their judgments as long as the task is of relatively short duration. If reports are made shortly after a judgment is made, then judges can use cues that are still in short-term memory to retrieve thoughts from long-term memory. However, according to Wilson (1994), judges' reports of their cognitive processes are likely to provide incomplete descriptions of their cognitive processes. For example, Wilson argues that asking people to say their thoughts aloud can change the way they make their judgments. Also, Wilson (1994) has argued that "a great deal of information processing occurs outside of awareness" (p. 249). Ericsson and Simon (1993) acknowledged that judges cannot describe their cognitive processes when cognitive processes are automatized and when thoughts are in a form that cannot be easily verbalized, but they also argued that only a nominal amount of information processing occurs outside of awareness (p. 15).

Are clinicians aware of how they make judgments? In some ways they are, and in other ways they are not. For example, clinicians frequently claim that they use information in a complex, configural (nonlinear) manner. As noted earlier, a recent study (Ganzach, 1995) indicates that clinicians are able to integrate information in a nonlinear manner. However, the results from this study provide only limited evidence that clinicians are aware of their cognitive processes. Information can be combined in a configural manner in a number of different ways. Though the results from Ganzach (1995) indicate that clinicians integrated information in a configural manner, it is not clear that they were aware of exactly how they integrated the information.

Results on process-tracing models suggest that awareness of cognitive processes is, at least at times, poor. As described earlier, in a study conducted by Kleinmuntz (1963), a process-tracing model was constructed to describe the cognitive processes of a clinician who made ratings of adjusted versus maladjusted based on MMPI protocols. When the data were reanalyzed by Einhorn et al. (1979), the ratings made by the clinician were predicted more accurately by a linear-regression rule than by the process-tracing model, even though the process-tracing model was derived and validated on the same protocols and the linear-regression rule was derived and cross-validated on separate sets of protocols. Correlations between the predictions of the models and the judgments of the clinician were .46 for the process-tracing model and .79 for the linear-regression model.

One can speculate about why the process-tracing model did poorly. One possibility is that the clinician may have made judgments automatically. As noted by Smith and Miller (1978), "In overlearned and routine situations, mental processes are likely to function relatively automatically and hence are inaccessible" (p. 361). A second reason the process-tracing model may have done poorly is that the experimenter may have done a poor job of constructing the model after listening to the judge's thinking-aloud statements. Because only one research investigator constructed a model from the thinking-aloud statements, interrater reliability for constructing a process-tracing model for this clinician is unknown. It should be noted that the experimenter listened to 60 hours of tape-recorded thinking-aloud statements when constructing the process-tracing model.

One can also speculate about the implications of the poor performance of the process-tracing model. If the process-tracing model did poorly because the clinician was unable to access and report appropriate thoughts, then the implications are important. For example, even when supervisors are able to make accurate judgments, they may not be able to accurately describe how they make judgments. If supervisors are able to make valid judgments but are unaware of their cognitive processes, they may not be able to provide helpful supervision.

Research on cognitive heuristics and biases also indicates that clinicians frequently may be unaware of how they make judgments. For example, when clinicians seek information that can support a hypothesis but do not seek information that can refute a hypothesis or that can support an alternative hypothesis, it is doubtful that they are aware that they have failed to consider alternative hypotheses. Similarly, clinicians are probably unaware that their judgments can be influenced by the ease with which events can be remembered. This may be a reason why some clinicians attend to invalid Rorschach signs (Tversky & Kahneman, 1974).

Results from other studies also indicate that clinicians may frequently be unaware of how they make judgments. In these studies, clinicians were asked to describe the information that they attend to when they make judgments (Chandler, 1970; Cocozza & Steadman, 1978; Fisch, Hammond, & Joyce, 1982; Gauron & Dickinson, 1966; Hoffman, 1960; Mendel & Rapport, 1969; Oskamp, 1967).

In one of the studies (Gauron & Dickinson, 1966), 12 psychiatrists and psychiatric residents made ratings for three cases. For each case, they received a list of categories of information. They were to request the information they wanted, one category at a time. After receiving each additional piece of information, they were to list diagnoses that might be correct. Also, they were to rate the probability of each of the diagnoses being correct. The most frequently requested categories of information were reason for referral, age, sex, previous episodes of illness, previous personality functioning, projective testing, school performance, and all mental-status items except proverb interpretation. After making their final diagnoses, the clinicians were to list the most important categories of information that helped them decide on the diagnoses. To determine if the clinicians were aware of how information influenced their diagnoses, the experimenters made ratings of actual category importance. The experimenters considered a category of information to be actually important if, after receiving the category of information, a clinician made a higher probability rating for the diagnosis that ended up as the final diagnosis. For example, if a clinician made a final diagnosis of schizophrenia, a score of 3 was assigned to a category of information if the probability rating for schizophrenia went up from .6 to .9 when the clinician received the information. A correlation between clinicians' ratings of importance and experimenters' ratings of actual importance was only .32. This correlation was not significantly different from zero. These results indicate that if psychiatrists and psychiatric residents are asked how they reached a diagnosis, they may not be able to accurately report the information on which they based the diagnosis.

In another study on clinicians' awareness of their judgments (Mendel & Rapport, 1969), 33 psychiatrists, psychiatric residents, psychologists, and social workers made decisions about psychiatric hospitalization for 269 individuals. They made the decisions in the course of their work at the admissions office of a university hospital. In addition to making a decision about hospitalization, when the clinicians saw the individuals in admissions they completed a clinical data form. The clinical data form contained items about the severity of symptoms, prior hospitalizations, and social resources available to the patient. Then, 4 weeks after seeing the individuals at admissions, the clinicians completed questionnaires to describe the information they believe they attend to when they make decisions about hospitalization. Decisions to hospitalize individuals were not significantly related to ratings of severity of symptoms, but were significantly related to history of previous hospitalizations. However, all of the clinicians had reported on the follow-up questionnaire that they thought severity of symptoms, and not history of previous psychiatric hospitalizations, was a major factor in deciding whether to admit someone to the hospital.

IMPEDIMENTS TO LEARNING FROM EXPERIENCE

Results from studies described in the first six chapters of this book indicate that clinicians have difficulty learning from experience. In the empirical studies, experienced clinicians were not more accurate than less experienced clinicians, clinicians were not more accurate than advanced graduate students, and presumed experts were not, in general, more accurate than other clinicians. Thus, experience with a task has not been related to the validity of judgments.

That learning from experience can be difficult is shown most clearly in two studies. In both of the studies, level of training was controlled for. In the first study (Aronson & Akamatsu, 1981), 12 clinical psychology graduate students used MMPI protocols to describe the symptoms and personality traits of patients. They made ratings at the beginning of their first year of graduate school, after they completed a course on the use and interpretation of the MMPI, and 1 year later after they had completed a year-long therapy and assessment practicum. Criterion ratings were made on the basis of interviews with the patients, interviews with close relatives of the patients, and a review of clinical records excluding psychological test reports. The graduate students were able to make more accurate judgments after they completed the training course on the MMPI (the average validity coefficient increased from .20 to .42), but accuracy did not increase after they completed the therapy and assessment practicum (the average validity coefficient was .44).

In the second study (Faust, Guilmette et al., 1988), 155 neuropsychologists reviewed results on the Halstead-Reitan Neuropsychological Test Battery, the WAIS–R, and the Wechsler Memory Scale, and they made ratings of the presence, location, process, and etiology of neurological impairment. The study is notable because many measures of training and experience were used. Measures of training included (a) hours of practicum experience in neuropsychology prior to obtaining degree, (b) percentage of internship devoted to neuropsychology, (c) completion of a postdoctoral fellowship in neuropsychology, (d) hours of supervision in neuropsychology, and (e) number of courses taken in neuropsychology and the neurosciences. Measures of experience were (a) number of years practicing neuropsychology and (b) approximate number of total lifetime hours devoted to clinical activities in neuropsychology. Training and experience were unrelated to the validity of judgments. Neuropsychologists were asked if the Halstead-Reitan was their preferred method of assessment. There was a tendency for the neuropsychologists who reported that they liked using the Halstead-Reitan to be slightly more accurate than the other neuropsychologists. However, when analyses were limited to neuropsychologists who liked the Halstead-Reitan, training and experience were again unrelated to validity.

Two impediments to learning from experience are described in the following sections. First, mental health professionals frequently do not receive feedback on whether their judgments are correct or incorrect, and when they do receive feedback the feedback can be misleading. Second, the cognitive processes of mental health professionals are sometimes inadequate.

Feedback

One reason why it can be difficult for mental health professionals to learn from their experiences is that they do not receive feedback for some tasks. For example, when psychologists describe test results for clients at case conferences, they typically do not receive definitive information about the client at the end of the conference (Meehl, 1973). In contrast, when an internist presents a case at a medical case conference, quasicriterial feedback is frequently available from a pathologist.

When mental health professionals do receive feedback, the feedback they receive from clients can be misleading. For example, when a client believes that the results of a psychological test report are accurate, the psychologist may conclude that this feedback confirms the validity of the test report. However, clients will frequently endorse a test report that is so general that it is descriptive of most clients (Snyder, Shenkel, & Lowery, 1977). This has been called the *Barnum effect* (Meehl, 1956). A test report that describes most clients can be faulted for not describing traits and symptoms that are unique to a client. Such descriptions are likely to be no more helpful than a report by an astrologer or a tea-leaf reader, assuming that they also make interpretations that are descriptive of most people.

In a recent study on the Barnum effect (Logue, Sher, & Frensch, 1992), 224 undergraduate students, half of them adult children of alcoholics, participated. Participants were told that the purpose of the study was to validate a new personality questionnaire. After they completed the personality questionnaire, participants were given a personality profile that was purportedly based on their test responses. They were then asked to rate how well the profile described themselves. Regardless of how they completed the questionnaires, participants were randomly given either a Barnum personality profile that was written so that most people would find it descriptive or an Adult Children of Alcoholics personality profile that consisted of characteristics that have been used by authors of popular books to describe adult children of alcoholics. An example of a Barnum item is: "You have a strong need for others to admire you" (p. 228). An example of an Adult Children of Alcoholics item is: "In times of crisis you tend to take care of others" (p. 228). Surprisingly, for the participants who received the Adult Children of Alcoholics profile, 71% of the adult children of alcoholics and 63% of the adult children of nonalcoholics thought that the profile described themselves very well or better. Also, for those who received the Barnum profile, 79% of the adult children of alcoholics and 70% of the adult children of nonalcoholics thought that the profile described themselves very well or better.

Feedback from clients can also be misleading because clinicians may persuade a client that an interpretation is correct, even when it is not (Snyder & Thomsen, 1988). For example, some therapists have persuaded clients that they were subjected to horrendous sexual abuse as children, even though it is not clear that they really were. As observed by Loftus (1993),

> Some contemporary therapists have been known to tell patients merely on the basis of a suggestive history or symptom profile, that they definitely had a traumatic experience. . . . Once the "diagnosis" is made, the therapist urges the patient to pursue the recalcitrant memories. . . . Evidence exists that some therapists do not take no for an answer. One therapist (who otherwise seemed sensitive to problems of memory tampering) still recommended "When the client does not remember what happened to her, the therapist's encouragement to 'guess' or 'tell a story' will help the survivor regain access to the lost material." (p. 526)

Hypnosis and the analysis of a client's bodily sensations, emotions, fantasies, and dreams have also been recommended as techniques for helping clients recall having been sexually abused. When clients incorrectly recall having been abused, clinicians will incorrectly infer that their interpretations were correct.

Feedback will also be misleading when it is received for a biased sample of clients. Harding et al. (1987) described how outcome information can lead mental health professionals to make incorrect inferences about the nature of schizophrenia:

> If a marginally functioning patient drops out of a clinician's caseload, the busy clinician often assumes that the patient has simply transferred to another clinician's caseload across town or is living a marginal existence in a single-room occupancy hotel. Rarely does the clinician assume that the patient has made a forward movement toward better functioning and reintegration into the community. There is no built-in system-

atic feedback to clinicians about eventual outcome successes. They receive only the negative messages signaled by the reappearance of patients who have relapsed. (p. 481)

Given this biased feedback, it is not surprising that many clinicians believe that the prognosis for patients with schizophrenia is uniformly poor. However, longitudinal research has shown that many individuals with schizophrenia have one or more episodes and then return to normal or near-normal functioning (e.g., Mason et al., 1995).

Feedback can also be misleading because of task characteristics such as base rates and selection ratios and because it is not possible to see the outcomes of decisions we do not make (Einhorn & Hogarth, 1978). For example, consider the task of deciding whether a psychiatric inpatient should be given a pass (e.g., should be allowed to leave the hospital grounds for a visit home). For this task, base rates refer to the percentage of successful passes and selection ratios refer to the percentage of patients that are given passes. If a modest number of patients are allowed to go on passes, and if most of the patients behave appropriately while on pass, then a clinician will probably believe that the decisions were made appropriately. The clinician will also believe that certain cues are important for making this decision. However, if most patients would do well if they were given a pass (base rate is high) and relatively few patients are given passes (selection ratio is relatively low), then one can expect that most patients given passes will behave appropriately, regardless of the cues that a clinician attends to.

Research suggests that clinicians will become more accurate when they receive unbiased feedback, but the benefits of feedback are setting specific. In a large study on clinical judgment (Goldberg & Rorer, 1965, and Rorer & Slovic, 1966, cited in Goldberg, 1968), the task was to make differential diagnoses of psychosis versus neurosis from MMPI profiles. Clinical psychologists ($n = 3$) and psychology graduate students ($n = 10$) were given feedback on over 300 MMPI profiles. After making a differential diagnosis, a clinician could turn the profile over to see the criterion diagnosis. All of the training profiles were drawn at random from one hospital setting. Clinicians made differential diagnoses, and received feedback, for these profiles on multiple occasions. They received feedback for the profiles over 4,000 times. The researchers reported that the benefits of training were almost completely setting specific. When clinicians made diagnoses for patients that were being treated in other settings, they were not able to make more accurate judgments after receiving feedback on the 300 training profiles.

The results from a second study (Graham, 1971) also indicated that clinicians become more accurate with unbiased feedback when training protocols and judgment protocols are sampled from the same setting. The task in this study was also to make differential diagnoses of neurosis versus psychosis. Apparently all of the MMPI profiles were sampled from a single setting. Judges received either correct feedback, random feedback, or no feedback. In the random feedback condition, feedback was determined according to a random schedule. Hit rates were 72% when PhD psychologists received correct feedback, 57% when they received random feedback, and 52% when they did not receive feedback. For psychology graduate students, hit rates were 61% when they received correct feedback, 58% when they received random feedback, and 58% when they did not receive feedback.

Cognitive Processes

There are several reasons why cognitive processes may be inadequate for learning from experience. First, when clinicians search for information, confirmatory bias can occur. When the confirmatory bias is descriptive of how clinicians search for information, clinicians seek information that will support, but not refute, their hypotheses, and they do not seek information that will support alternative hypotheses. When this occurs, they are unlikely to learn from experience because the information they obtain will be biased.

Second, when clinicians try to learn if a cue and a construct are related (e.g., a test result and a symptom or mental disorder), covariation misestimation can occur. Covariation misestimation is said to occur when clinicians focus on cases when the cue and construct are present and the clinicians give little attention to the other possible contingencies (e.g., the cue is not present, but the person does have the symptom or disorder). As observed by Arkes (1981), if a clinician believes that a certain MMPI profile can be used to predict that a patient is likely to have a subsequent psychotic episode, the clinician may keep track of the number of patients with this profile who subsequently have a psychotic breakdown. However, it would also be important to keep track of the number of people with other MMPI profiles who have, or do not have, a subsequent psychotic episode.

Third, when clinicians make causal judgments (e.g., case formulations), hindsight bias may occur and clinicians may draw erroneous conclusions from the feedback information. Hindsight bias occurs when clinicians receive feedback or outcome information, and they conclude that the outcome was inevitable. The following example illustrates how the hindsight bias can be an impediment to learning from experience:

> Suppose that everytime a clinician receives feedback about a patient, the clinician constructs a precise explanation for why the outcome occurred. Also, suppose that the clinician feels that the outcome was bound to happen (because the explanation is so convincing). One problem is that there may be error in the assessment information or in the feedback information. If there is a significant amount of error, then clinicians will probably draw incorrect inferences about the case (and they will not learn from this experience). A second problem is that a clinician will not know everything there is to know about the patient.

Important information can be missing because . . . a patient is trying to project a certain image and is withholding information. When the information cues that clinicians do not have access to are related to outcome, then clinicians should not feel that an outcome was inevitable on the basis of the information that they had available. (Garb, 1989, p. 393)

To learn from their experiences, clinicians need to think in probabilistic terms rather than deterministic terms (Brehmer, 1980; Einhorn, 1988). Unfortunately, thinking in probabilistic terms is something that can be very hard to do.

Fourth, when memory processes are biased, one can expect that clinicians will find it difficult to learn from their experiences. Memory processes can be biased because clinicians do not remember all of the instances when two events covary (leading to covariation misestimation), because clinicians remember information that confirms, but does not refute, a judgment, and because clinicians are influenced by the ease with which instances or occurrences can be remembered.

Finally, clinicians may also have difficulty learning from their clinical experiences because they are not always aware of their cognitive processes. Even when clinicians are accurate, they may not be aware of how they make judgments (Einhorn et al., 1979).

SUMMARY AND DISCUSSION

Statistical rules and process-tracing models have been used to model mental health professionals. When a statistical rule and a process-tracing model were used to reproduce a clinician's judgments, the statistical rule was more successful. Although statistical rules and process-tracing models can be valuable (e.g., to describe individual differences among clinicians), it is important to realize that being able to reproduce a clinician's judgments does not mean that one has described the cognitive processes of the clinician.

Different types of errors are associated with different cognitive heuristics. For example, insufficient adjustment of ratings is associated with the anchoring-and-adjustment heuristic; the confirmatory bias is associated with a tendency to seek, integrate, and remember information that can confirm but not refute a hypothesis; the neglect of base rates and the neglect of norms can be associated with the representativeness heuristic; illusory correlations are associated with the availability heuristic; the hindsight bias is associated with deterministic thinking; and covariation misestimation is associated with the biased recall of the co-occurrence of events.

The primacy effect, the anchoring-and-adjustment heuristic, and confirmatory-hypothesis testing describe how clinicians make judgments as they collect information. Clinicians make judgments quickly, the order they receive information can affect their judgments, and they may only search for information that can confirm a hypothesis.

The descriptiveness of a cognitive heuristic depends on the clinical task. For instance, with regard to diagnosis and the description of personality traits and psychiatric symptoms, the representativeness heuristic seems to be especially important for describing how clinicians make judgments. With regard to case formulation, deterministic reasoning and the representativeness heuristic are important concepts for understanding how judgments are made. For the task of behavioral prediction, causal reasoning and the past-behavior heuristic are important concepts. Finally, for the task of treatment planning, one can speculate that causal reasoning is of paramount importance.

Judgments can sometimes be invalid or biased because of the way that information is remembered. Judgments can also be invalid or biased if a clinician's knowledge structures (schemas) are biased or invalid.

Research suggests that to a surprising degree, clinicians have little awareness of their cognitive processes. For example, in a series of studies, clinicians were not able to accurately describe the information on which they base their judgments.

Mental health professionals can have trouble learning from their clinical experiences because they frequently do not receive accurate feedback and their cognitive processes are sometimes inadequate. Confirmatory hypothesis testing, covariation misestimation, deterministic reasoning, biased recall of events, and poor awareness of cognitive processes may all be involved when clinicians fail to learn from their clinical experiences.

In conclusion, formal models of judgment have been used to reproduce the judgments made by clinicians, whereas cognitive heuristics, cognitive biases, and knowledge structures have been used to describe how judgments are made, types of errors that clinicians sometimes make, and the beliefs, theories, and information that are stored in memory. To a surprising degree, clinicians have little awareness of their cognitive processes. Also, learning from clinical experience can be difficult because clinicians frequently do not receive feedback and because clinicians' cognitive processes are sometimes suboptimal.

8

COMPUTERS AND JUDGMENT

Artificial intelligence is the science of making machines do things that would require intelligence by humans (Boden, 1972, p. 4). Using computers to make judgments and decisions is an application of artificial intelligence. Progress made by computer scientists in artificial intelligence will have important ramifications for the practice of psychological assessment. This chapter discusses several of the ways in which psychological assessment and judgment interface with computer technologies.

Statistical prediction rules, automated assessment computer programs, and neural network models can be used to make diagnoses, ratings, predictions, and decisions. *Statistical prediction rules* are mathematical equations such as linear-regression equations and Bayesian rules. *Automated-assessment computer programs* (also called *computer-based test-interpretation programs*) consist of a series of if–then statements that are written by expert clinicians. They should not be confused with computer programs that are used to administer or score tests. *Neural-network models* are computing systems that are constructed to mimic how the brain works. They make use of parallel processing, and they are designed to work well with unclear or vague information.

An important distinction can be drawn between automated assessment and statistical (or actuarial) prediction and neural-network modeling. Statistical-prediction rules and neural network models are usually empirically based, whereas automated-assessment programs are based on the beliefs of expert clinicians. For example, with statistical prediction, parameters or weights for statistical rules are derived from empirical data (unit-weight linear rules, to be discussed later, are an exception). Neural-network models are also empirically derived. In contrast, automated assessment programs are not derived by collecting data. Instead, rules for making judgments or decisions are written by an expert clinician on the basis of clinical experience and knowledge of research results.

The use of computers has been controversial. One of the oldest debates in the field of clinical psychology has been over whether judgments and decisions should be made by mental health professionals or by statistical-prediction rules (e.g., Goldberg, 1968, 1974; Holt, 1958, 1970; Meehl, 1954, 1967, 1973; Sawyer, 1966; Sines, 1970). The controversy over the use of statistical prediction is concerned with whether clinicians should use statistical predictions as input data and make clinical judgments based on the statistical predictions and other information or use the statistical predictions as final diagnoses or ratings. Strong advocates of statistical prediction continue to be critical of "the failure of mental health professionals to apply in practice the strong and clearly supported empirical generalizations demonstrating the superiority of actuarial over clinical prediction" (Meehl, 1986a, p. 370, abstract; also see Dawes et al., 1989).

Automated-assessment programs are controversial because the validity of the programs has rarely been studied (Matarazzo, 1986). Automated-assessment programs exist for the interpretation of a range of tests including the MMPI, the Rorschach, the Millon Clinical Multiaxial Inventory, and the Personality Assessment Inventory (e.g., see Butcher, 1987; Fowler, 1985). As an indication of the popularity of automated assessment programs, it is interesting to note that an early automated-assessment program, developed by Fowler, was used over a 17-year period by approximately one fourth of the eligible psychologists and psychiatrists in the United States to interpret MMPI results for 1.5 million clients (Fowler, 1985). However, as observed by Snyder, Widiger, and Hoover (1990), "Remarkably few CBTI [computer-based test interpretation] validation studies have appeared in the literature, particularly when contrasted to the proliferation of computer-based testing products in the commercial market" (p. 475). The controversy is especially important because many of the consumers of computer-based test interpretation services are nonpsychologists (many are personnel workers, counselors, correctional officers, or family physicians), and they are unlikely to know about empirical results on the validity of the tests and methodological concepts that are important for test interpretation (e.g., the Barnum effect; Matarazzo, 1986). For example, if one is unaware that a test has only moderate validity, then one may accept the test interpretations at face value and not collect additional information. Similarly, if one is unaware of the Barnum effect, then one may incorrectly infer that all of the statements in a report are accurate because the client believes the report is descriptive.

As computer programs become more powerful, the controversies surrounding their use will take on greater importance. In the future, computers using artificial intelligence may be able to learn from experience; these computers will be able to modify their own programs. Computers have tremendous potential for improving the way judgments are made in the area of psychological assessment, but their proper use undoubtedly will be, and should be, the object of debate.

STATISTICAL PREDICTION

Research on statistical prediction has focused on the comparison of clinical judgment and statistical prediction and the evaluation of different types of statistical rules (e.g., linear rules versus configural rules). The research on these topics is reviewed, and present-day statistical-prediction rules are critiqued. In addition, recommendations are made for building new statistical-prediction rules.

Clinical Versus Statistical Prediction

Statistical-prediction rules have nearly always been more accurate than, or as accurate as, human judges (e.g., Dawes, 1994; Dawes et al., 1989; Garb, 1994; Kleinmuntz, 1990; Meehl, 1986a; Wiggins, 1981). This has been true for a wide range of judgment tasks, including those in the area of psychological assessment. For example, in one review of the literature (Garb, 1994), studies were included only if (a) clinical judgments were made by mental health professionals and (b) judgment tasks were related to clinical practice. Studies on the diagnosis of brain damage were not included. Forty-five studies meeting the inclusion and exclusion criteria were found. In all of these studies, the statistical rules did as well as, or better than, the mental health professionals. Even when mental health professionals had more assessment information available, they were not more accurate than the statistical-prediction rules (Astrup, 1975; Dunham & Meltzer, 1946; Edwards & Berry, 1974; Erdman, Greist, Gustafson, Taves, & Klein, 1987; Evenson, Altman, Sletten, & Cho, 1975; Gardner et al., 1996; Gustafson, Greist, Stauss, Erdman, & Laughren, 1977; Hall, 1988; Hamlin, 1934; Johnston & McNeal, 1967; Lemerond, 1977; McNiel, Binder, & Greenfield, 1988; Walters et al., 1988; Wittman, 1941; Wittman & Steinberg, 1944). However, in a study that was not included in this review (Goldstein et al., 1973), neuropsychologists were more accurate than a unit-weight linear rule.

If clinicians are given access to the predictions of a statistical rule and the information that was entered into the statistical rule, will they be able to improve on the statistical predictions? Several studies addressed this question. In these studies, mental health professionals were given the predictions of a statistical rule and the assessment data that had been used as input information for the rule (Goldberg, 1968; Leli & Filskov, 1981, 1984; Moxley, 1973; Shagoury & Satz, 1969; Young, 1972; also see Stricker, 1967). The tasks in these studies included using MMPI profiles to predict the length of psychotherapy (Moxley, 1973); using the Block Rotation Task (Satz, 1966) or the Wechsler-Bellevue Intelligence Scales to detect the presence of organic brain impairment (Leli & Filskov, 1981, 1984; Shagoury & Satz, 1969); discriminating the human figure drawings of normal and psychiatric adolescents (Stricker, 1967); and using MMPI profiles to make differential diagnoses of neurosis versus psychosis (Goldberg, 1968; Young, 1972). In all of these studies, when clinicians overrode the statistical predictions, their judgments were not significantly more accurate than the statistical predictions. In fact, they often performed worse than the statistical-prediction rules. Thus, they were not able to judge when the statistical predictions were likely to be right and when they were likely to be wrong.

When mental health professionals are given the predictions of a statistical rule, the assessment data that was used as input information for the rule, and assessment information that was not entered into the rule, will they be able to outperform the statistical-prediction rule? No studies have been conducted to answer this question, but presumably it will depend on the validity of the information that is entered into the statistical prediction rule and the validity of the additional information that the clinician has available.

Evaluation of Different Types of Statistical Rules

Research has also focused on the comparison of different types of statistical-prediction rules. Most of the research on the evaluation of different types of statistical rules has been on (a) the comparison of linear and configural statistical rules, (b) the use of linear models of judges, and (c) the comparison of unit-weight and differential-weight statistical rules. Though the comparison of Bayesian and linear rules is also important, Bayesian rules have been used to make judgments in only a few studies (e.g., Erdman et al., 1987; Gustafson et al., 1977; Hirschfeld, Spitzer, & Miller, 1974). A Bayesian rule and a linear rule were compared in only one study (Goldberg, 1969), which found that the linear rule was more accurate than the Bayesian rule.

Linear Versus Configural Statistical Prediction

A *linear* (or *additive*) *model* is an algebraic equation that contains only main-effect terms. A *configural model* is an algebraic equation that contains interaction terms (it may also contain main-effect terms). Examples of linear rules include linear-regression rules, discriminant-analysis equations, and unweighted linear composites (the sum of several items).

In nearly all of the studies that have been done on linear versus configural prediction, linear rules have done as well as, or better than, configural rules (for reviews, see Goldberg, 1968, 1974; Wiggins, 1973, 1981). In fact, in many studies, linear rules have accounted for most of the variance of the criterion variables, even when the linear rules have been cross-validated on new samples (e.g., Dawes, 1971; Giannetti, Johnson, Klingler, & Williams, 1978; Goldberg, 1965; Wiggins & Kohen, 1971).

Several well-known studies on linear versus configural statistical prediction have made use of a data set collected by Meehl (1959a). This data set was described in chapter 7, as several excellent studies on the statistical modeling of clinical judgment have made use of the same data set. The data set will be described again: 13 PhD clinical psychologists and 16 clinical psychology graduate students were given MMPI profiles for 861 psychiatric patients. The MMPI profiles were collected at seven different sites. Each patient had received a diagnosis of psychosis or neurosis. The clinicians were instructed to sort the profiles on an 11-point forced-normal distribution ranging from *neurotic* to *psychotic*.

Meehl (1959a) compared the validity of clinicians' judgments to the validity of judgments made by using a set of complex, sequential (configural) rules developed by Meehl and Dahlstrom (1960). The Meehl–Dahlstrom rules were developed using a separate sample of 402 MMPI profiles. Meehl and Dahlstrom used the derivation sample to test the validity of their ideas about scores on the MMPI that can differentiate neurotic and psychotic patients: "The skilled clinical eye was employed as a searcher and idea originator: statistical runs were employed both as searchers and as checks upon the deliverances of the clinical eye" (Meehl & Dahlstrom, 1960, p. 377). When both the Meehl–Dahlstrom rules and the clinicians were allowed to make "indeterminate" classifications, the Meehl–Dahlstrom rules achieved a hit rate of 74% while the median hit rate for clinicians was 66%.

In reanalyses of the Meehl (1959a) data, linear rules and other statistical-prediction rules have been compared to the Meehl–Dahlstrom rules. For example, Goldberg (1965) developed a number of diagnostic signs by purely empirical procedures. Using the same sample of 402 MMPI profiles that had been used to derive the Meehl–Dahlstrom rules, Goldberg entered single MMPI scales and combinations of MMPI scales in a series of linear-regression analyses. The accuracy of ratings of neurosis versus psychosis was statistically significant for 43 signs. These signs were then cross-validated on two samples. The first sample was composed of 861 MMPI profiles. The second sample was composed of 591 of the 861 profiles: When the clinicians and the statistical-prediction rules made ratings on the 11-point scale, the 270 profiles that received ratings in the middle of the rating scale (e.g., 5, 6, and 7) were eliminated from the sample of 861 profiles. Thus, different profiles were eliminated for different clinicians and different statistical-prediction

TABLE 4
Hit Rates for the Task of Diagnosing Neurosis Versus Psychosis

Predictors	Hit Rates for All Cases ($N = 861$)	Hit Rates Excluding Indeterminate Cases ($N = 591$)
Clinicians		
13 psychologists	62	66
16 trainees	61	66
29 total clinicians	62	66
Statistical-Prediction Rules		
L + Pa + Sc − Hy − Pt	70	74
Meehl–Dahlstrom rules	66	74
2-point rules	67	71
Sc − Hs − D − Hy	67	71
Number of Taulbee–Sisson signs	64	69
Pt − Sc	65	67
High-point rules	66	69
Hy − Pa	61	67
Number of Peterson signs	60	68
N − P	63	67
Pa − Hs − D − Hy	62	66
N/P	63	68
Hs − Sc	61	67
Pd + Pa − Hs − Hy	63	68

Note. Adapted from "Diagnosticians versus diagnostic signs: The diagnosis of psychosis versus neurosis from the MMPI," by L. R. Goldberg (1965), *Psychological Monographs, 79* (9, Whole No. 602). Copyright 1965 by the American Psychological Association, Adapted with permission.

rules. In this way, hit rates could be calculated for the cases of which the clinicians and the statistical-prediction rules were most certain. Hit rates for the clinicians and statistical-prediction rules are listed in Table 4. The average hit rate for the PhD psychologists was 62% for the sample of 861 MMPI profiles and 66% for the sample of 591 MMPI profiles. Hit rates for graduate students were virtually identical (they were 61% and 66%, respectively). Hit rates for the fourteen statistical-prediction rules that are listed in Table 4 are all higher than the average hit rate that was obtained by the clinicians. The first two statistical-prediction rules listed in Table 4 (the linear composite, L + Pa + Sc − Hy − Pt, and the Meehl–Dahlstrom rules) were both more accurate than the most accurate clinician. The most accurate statistical-prediction rule was the linear composite: L + Pa + Sc − Hy − Pt. Finally, in further reanalyses of the Meehl (1959a) data, the linear composite L + Pa + Sc − Hy − Pt was compared to additional configural rules (e.g., Bayesian rules). The simple linear composite continued to be the most accurate statistical-prediction rule (Goldberg, 1969).

To understand why linear rules have been successful, it is important to remember that a linear rule can be accurate even when an interaction exists in a set of data. As noted in chapter 7, in several computer-simulation studies (Birnbaum, 1974; Green, 1968; Yntema & Torgerson, 1961), a nonlinear rule was used to generate a set of data. Linear rules were able to accurately predict the numbers that were generated by using the nonlinear rules. Thus, even when an interaction exists, a linear rule may be highly successful in accounting for the variance in the data.

Though linear rules have almost always done as well as, or better than, configural rules, there may be circumstances when configural rules will outperform linear rules. First, as was described in chapter 7, scatter models have outperformed linear rules, though they have been used in only one study in the area of psychological assessment (Ganzach, 1995). In that study, scatter models were used to predict clinicians' judgments (using the data from Meehl, 1959a). Second, even when results are not analyzed using a scatter model, configural rules can do relatively well when predictors are negatively correlated. In studies that have supported the linear rule, predictors have been uncorrelated or positively correlated (e.g., Dawes, 1971; Goldberg, 1965, 1969; Giannetti et al., 1978; Rorer, 1971; Wiggins & Hoffman, 1968; Wiggins & Kohen, 1971; Yntema & Torgerson, 1961). For example, MMPI scales tend to be positively correlated (e.g., Budescu & Rodgers, 1981; Einhorn et al., 1979). In computer-simulation studies, configural rules have done relatively well when predictors have been negatively correlated (Camerer, 1985; Garb, 1995; Shanteau, 1981). For example, in one of the studies (Shanteau, 1981), 14,580 separate multiple-regression analyses were done. The larger the negative intercorrelations among predictors, the better the configural models did relative to a linear model.

Linear Models of Judges

To construct a linear model of a judge, one derives a linear-regression equation by having a judge make ratings and then using these ratings as criterion scores. The information that was given to the judges is used as input data for the linear regression rule. Once the rule has been derived, it can be used to make ratings for the construct of interest. For example, using the data set that was collected by Meehl (1959a), linear-regression equations were derived by using clinicians' ratings of neurosis versus psychosis as criterion scores (Goldberg, 1970). MMPI profiles served as assessment data for the clinicians and as input data for the linear-regression rules. Once the linear-regression rules were derived (one linear-regression equation was derived for each clinician), they were used to make diagnostic ratings of neurosis versus psychosis for a new sample of patients. The models of judges were more accurate than the judges themselves when the linear-regression rules were constructed on a small set of cases and the rules and the judges were validated on a completely new sample. The average correlation between ratings and criterion scores was .28 for clinicians and .31 for the models of judges.

Goldberg (1970) explained why models of judges can be more accurate than judges:

A clinician . . . lacks a machine's reliability. He "has his days": Boredom, fatigue, illness, situational and interpersonal distractions all plague him, with the result that his repeated judgments of the exact same stimulus configuration are not identical. . . . If we could remove some of this human unreliability by eliminating the random error in his judgments, we should thereby increase the validity of the resulting predictions. (p. 423)

Thus, a model of a judge may be more accurate than a judge because the model is more reliable.

Models of judges are valuable because it can be difficult and expensive to obtain criterion scores. If a model can account for all of the reliable variance of a clinician's judgments, then we can be confident that the model of the judge will be more accurate than the clinician (unless the clinician always makes ratings with perfect reliability, in which case they will be equally accurate). Thus, researchers can construct a statistical-prediction rule and be confident that it is more accurate than a clinician, even when criterion scores cannot be collected.

There are two problems with models of judges, however. First, if a clinician is attending to inappropriate information, then the ratings made by the clinician and the ratings made by the model of the clinician will both be inaccurate. The advantage of constructing a model of a judge is that one does not have to collect outcome information (a clinician's judgments can be used as criterion scores), but if one does not collect outcome information and if ratings made by a clinician and the model of a clinician are inaccurate, then one will not know that the ratings are inaccurate. Second, if a clinician attends to a large number of cues, it may be hard to build a model that accounts for nearly all of the reliable variance of the clinician's judgments. In empirical studies, linear models of judges have been able to account for most of the reliable variance of judges' ratings, but judges in these studies were given a small amount of information (see Dawes & Corrigan, 1974, for a review of studies on linear models of judges). For example, linear models of judges were able to account for most of the reliable variance of judges' ratings when clinicians were given MMPI results (Goldberg, 1970), but in actual clinical practice clinicians have a much larger amount of assessment information available. A strength of linear models of judges is purported to be the ease with which they can be built (Dawes et al., 1989, p. 1673), but investigators may have a difficult time building statistical rules that will predict the responses made by clinical judges when clinical judges are given all of the information that is usually available in clinical practice.

Unit Weights Versus Differential Weights

Predictors can be assigned unit weights or differential weights. When using a differential-weight linear rule, a derivation sample is used to derive weights for the predictors. For example, using multiple-regression analysis, one can derive differential weights for predictors. When using a unit-weight rule, all of the predictors are assigned unit (equal) weights. An example of a unit-weight linear rule is Goldberg's (1965) MMPI rule for diagnosing neurosis versus psychosis (L + Pa + Sc − Hy − Pt). Another well-known unit-weight linear rule, one that is used to detect neurological impairment, is the Halstead Index (Halstead, 1947). To calculate a score on the Halstead Index, one calculates the proportion of scores on seven tests that are in the brain-damaged range.

Unit-weight linear rules frequently do as well as or better than clinicians (Dawes, 1979; Dawes & Corrigan, 1974). For example, for the task of making differential diagnoses of neurosis versus psychosis, a simple linear composite did better than clinicians and other statistical-prediction rules (Goldberg, 1965). The Halstead Index has also been accurate. According to Russell (1995), no actuarial method developed for the detection of neurological impairment has been more accurate than the Halstead Index—even though the Halstead Index was developed over 50 years ago. However, ratings made by using the Halstead Index have not been as accurate as judgments made by neuropsychologists (Goldstein et al., 1973; Russell, 1995). For example, Russell (1995) reported that the average hit rate for the Halstead Index has been 76%, whereas the average hit rate for judgments made by neuropsychologists has been 85%. Clinical judgment has probably been superior because clinicians have had more information available. For example, the Trail Making Test and the Aphasia Screening Test do not contribute to the Halstead Index even though they make up part of the Halstead-Reitan battery.

The use of unit weights has been supported by mathematical proofs. Wainer (1976, also see Wainer, 1978) proved that "under very general circumstances, coefficients in multiple-regression models can be replaced with equal weights with almost no loss in accuracy on the original data sample" (p. 213). He then showed that "these equal weights will have greater robustness than least squares regression coefficients" (they can be expected to outperform differential weights when the rules are cross-validated; Wainer, 1976, p. 213). According to Wainer (1976), these results will occur when "(a) All predictor variables are oriented properly (if you don't know what direction the criterion variable lies with respect to a predictor, that predictor shouldn't be used); and (b) the predictor variables are intercorrelated positively" (p. 213). Given these results, it is clear that unit-weight linear rules can be very powerful.

Unit-weight linear rules are not as accurate when predictor variables are negatively correlated (e.g., Dawes et al., 1989, p. 1672; Einhorn & McCoach, 1977; Garb, 1995; McClelland, 1978; Newman, 1977; also see Langenbucher, Morgenstern, Labouvie, Miller, & Nathan, 1996). For example, a unit-weight linear rule did poorly in a computer-simulation study on the diagnosis of schizophrenia. In this study (Garb, 1995), differential-weight linear rules accounted for 83% to 90% of the variation of the criterion scores while the unit-weight linear rule accounted for only 41% to 50%. The unit-weight linear rule did poorly because when data were collected at a community mental health center, nearly half of the clients met five of the six *DSM–III* criteria for schizophrenia, even though they did not have schizophrenia. For these clients, the following criteria were satisfied: (a) a full depressive or manic-depressive syndrome was not prominent, (b) onset of disorder was before age 45, (c) symptoms were not due to an organic disorder or mental retardation, (d) there was a deterioration in functioning, and (e) symptoms had been present for at least 6 months. However, these clients did not meet the sixth *DSM–III* criterion for schizophrenia: They did not have specific types of delusions, hallucinations, thought disorders, and/or affective symptoms. For example, a client with a dysthymic disorder may meet five of the six criteria. To be given a diagnosis of schizophrenia using the *DSM–III* criteria, a client would have to meet all six of the criteria. Thus, the unit-weight linear rule made high ratings for the likelihood of schizophrenia for a large number of clients who did not have schizophrenia, but had, for example, dysthymic disorder instead. Negative intercorrelations among the predictors were present because for many of the clients, values for five of the criteria were in a proschizophrenia direction while for the sixth criterion the value was in the opposite direction.

Unit-weight linear rules can be constructed when criterion scores are unavailable. To construct a unit-weight linear rule, clinicians can simply be asked to list the factors that are important for a judgment task and describe how the factors are oriented to the construct that is being described. Even if clinicians say that the information should be combined configurally (nonadditively), the information would still be combined additively. If the intercorrelations among the predictors are positive or close to zero, then a unit-weight linear rule can be used to make judgments.

Should clinicians use unit-weight linear rules when criterion scores are unavailable? Unit-weight linear rules have frequently been more accurate than clinicians. However, there are several problems with unit-weight linear rules. First, as already noted, unit-weight linear rules have not always been more accurate than clinicians (Goldstein et al., 1973; Russell, 1995). Second, if invalid predictors are used, then the ratings will be inaccurate. A supposed advantage of using a unit-weight linear rule is that outcome information does not need to be collected, but if outcome information is not collected, one will not know if predictors (and ratings) are valid or invalid. Third, clinicians may not be able to accurately report the indicators that they attend to when they make ratings (see the section on awareness of cognitive processes in chapter 7). If clinicians and unit-weight linear rules are not using the same information, then one cannot assume that the unit-weight rules will be more valid than the clinicians.

Rather than using unit-weight linear rules when criterion scores are unavailable, it will be important that research investigators collect criterion scores to study the validity of the unit-weight linear rules. Of course, by the same reasoning, clinicians should not make judgments until the validity of their judgments has also been demonstrated.

Critique of Methods for Building and Evaluating Statistical Rules

Methods for building and evaluating statistical rules have been appropriate when the task has been to predict behavior, but not when the task has been to make diagnoses or describe personality traits and psychiatric symptoms. Statistical-prediction rules have only rarely been used for treatment planning and describing the causes of behaviors and symptoms. The critique in the present section is directed at the tasks of diagnosis and describing personality traits and psychiatric symptoms. Recommendations for building statistical rules for treatment planning and case formulation are described in a later section.

Limited Data Entered Into Statistical Rules

When the task has been to make diagnoses or describe personality traits and psychiatric symptoms, input data for statistical rules has usually been limited to demographic data and results from a single psychological test. This has been true of studies on clinical versus statistical prediction (Carlin & Hewitt, 1990; Danet, 1965; Exner, 1983, pp. 86–88, 88–89; Exner & Weiner, 1982, pp. 227–229; Goldberg, 1965, 1969, 1970; Grebstein, 1963; Halbower, 1955; Hiler & Nesvig, 1965; Janzen & Coe, 1975; Kleinmuntz, 1967; Lindzey, 1965; Meehl, 1959a; Oskamp, 1962; Stricker, 1967; Todd, 1954; Vanderploeg, Sison, & Hickling, 1987; Walters et al., 1988) and of studies on the incremental validity of information used by statistical-prediction rules (Archer & Gordon, 1988; Dubro, Wetzler, & Kahn, 1988; Holland & Watson, 1980; Hyer, Boudewyns, O'Leary, & Harrison, 1987; Hyer et al., 1986; Phillips, Phillips, & Shearn, 1980; Sutker, Bugg, & Allain, 1991). Though there have been exceptions (Haier et al., 1978; Hare, 1978; Hare, Frazelle, & Cox, 1978; Hart, Lahey, Loeber, & Hanson, 1994; Overall & Higgins, 1977), when statistical-prediction rules have been constructed for the tasks of diagnosis and describing traits and symptoms, there has typically been little attempt to identify and use the best available input information.

Statistical-prediction rules would probably be more powerful if there was a concerted effort to identify and use the best available input information. The addition of history and interview data to demographic data and test results would probably result in an increase in validity, at least for some tasks (e.g., making diagnoses using the DSM–IV criteria). On the other hand, the addition of marginally valid information (e.g., projective test results) to valid information will probably not lead to an increase in validity (Garb, 1984).

Limited Information Given to Clinicians

One way to validate a statistical-prediction rule is to show that it is more accurate than clinicians. However, if clinicians are given less information than they usually have available in clinical practice, researchers will not be able to determine whether statistical-prediction rules are as accurate as mental health professionals in clinical practice.

Clinicians were given extensive information in some clinical versus statistical-prediction studies, but not in others. When the task was to predict behavior, clinicians were regularly given all of the information that mental health professionals generally have available in clinical practice (Astrup, 1975; Dunham & Meltzer, 1946; Edwards & Berry, 1974; Erdman et al., 1987; Evenson et al., 1975; Gardner et al., 1996; Gustafson et al., 1977; Hall, 1988; Hamlin, 1934; Johnston & McNeal, 1967; Lemerond, 1977; McNiel et al., 1988; Wittman, 1941; Wittman & Steinberg, 1944). However, clinicians were rarely given extensive information when the task was to make psychodiagnoses or describe personality traits and psychiatric symptoms. Usually they were given results from only a single psychological test (Carlin & Hewitt, 1990; Danet, 1965; Goldberg, 1965, 1969, 1970; Grebstein, 1963; Halbower, 1955; Hiler & Nesvig, 1965; Janzen & Coe, 1975; Kleinmuntz, 1967; Lindzey, 1965; Meehl, 1959a; Oskamp, 1962; Stricker, 1967; Todd, 1954; Vanderploeg et al., 1987). They were not given much more information in other studies: In the other studies, they were given (a) brief history information and Rorschach results (Exner, 1983, pp. 86–88, 88–89; Exner & Weiner, 1982, pp. 227–229; Weinberg, 1957); (b) recordings of patients talking for 5 minutes "about anything that they want" (Oxman, Rosenberg, Schnurr, & Tucker, 1988); and (c) MMPI results and a structured interview diagnosis, but not a record of the client's responses in the interview (interviews were conducted by the research investigators) and no history or observation data (Walters et al., 1988).

Would clinicians have made more valid diagnoses and more valid ratings of personality traits and psychiatric symptoms if they had been given more information? Would they have been more accurate than statistical-prediction rules? The validity of clinical judgments does not always increase when clinicians are given additional information (Garb, 1984), but results from empirical studies indicate that the validity of clinical judgments does increase when demographic and history data are added to psychometric data (for a review, see Garb, 1984; also see Exner, 1983, pp. 86–88, 88–89; Exner & Weiner, 1982, pp. 227–229). In the absence of direct evidence, it is not known if present-day statistical-prediction rules are as accurate as clinicians in making diagnoses and describing traits and symptoms when clinicians are given extensive information.

Poor Quality of Construct Indicators

When the task has been to make diagnoses or describe personality traits and psychiatric symptoms, construct-indicator scores have frequently been made by using information that is readily available in clinical practice. For example, in many studies, clinical judges and a statistical-prediction rule were given results from a psychological test, and their ratings were compared to the ratings of a criterion judge using history and/or interview data. Diagnoses and ratings of symptoms and traits based on history and interview data can be valid, and if statistical predictions and clinical judgments are correlated with these diagnoses and ratings, it would suggest that the clinical judgments and statistical predictions are valid. On the other hand, one would like to have a statistical-prediction rule that can do more than predict ratings that are made by using information that is readily available in clinical practice.

In several studies (Dubro et al., 1988; Hyer et al., 1986; Phillips et al., 1980; Sutker et al., 1991), criterion (construct-indicator) diagnoses were made by using structured interviews. Criterion diagnoses made by using structured interviews are more valuable than criterion diagnoses made by using information that is readily available in clinical practice, but there are still problems with using these criterion diagnoses. For example, if structured interviews make use of interview and history data and a statistical-prediction rule does also, then criterion contamination can occur. Because of criterion contamination, if criterion scores are made by a structured interview, one would expect a statistical-prediction rule to do better if it weighs interview and history data more heavily than psychological test results.

Another problem with using a structured interview to evaluate the validity of a statistical-prediction rule is that we will not be able to learn if the statistical rule is more or less valid than the structured interview. As already discussed in chapter 2, the validity of diagnoses made by using structured interviews may sometimes be low. This can occur for two reasons. First, it may occur if the diagnoses are based on only interview information. Medical records can contain important information (e.g., results from a neurological exam, results from a neuroimaging procedure, results from psychological and neuropsychological testing, observations made by staff members, information obtained from family members), and validity may be low if all of these sources of information are ignored. Second, when diagnoses are based on interview information plus other information, the validity of diagnoses may be low if clinicians use their clinical judgment instead of a statistical-prediction rule to integrate the information from the structured interview with other information.

Recommendations for Building and Evaluating
Statistical-Prediction Rules

Different judgment tasks pose different problems for building and evaluating statistical-prediction rules. For each of the different types of judgment tasks that clinicians perform, recommendations will be made for improving the quality of assessment data and the quality of criterion scores. By improving the quality of criterion scores, the manner in which statistical-prediction rules are evaluated can be improved, as can methods for deriving statistical-prediction rules. In fact, for some judgment tasks, researchers may be able to build statistical-prediction rules that use more than limited data only if the quality of criterion scores can be improved.

Description of Traits and Symptoms

If statistical-prediction rules and criterion judges are given the same information, then criterion contamination will be present. Thus, when criterion judges are given history, interview, and observation data, statistical-prediction rules cannot be given the same information. Presumably this is the reason that statistical rules were usually given the results from only a single psychological test when the task was to describe personality traits and psychiatric symptoms. To enter psychometric, history, interview, and observation data into statistical-prediction rules, there will need to be new methods for obtaining criterion scores.

There are several methods for improving the way construct-indicator ratings or criterion scores are obtained for personality traits and psychiatric symptoms; these were described in chapter 1. For example, using the act-frequency approach for obtaining standardized ratings of a construct (Buss & Craik, 1986), one can follow clients over time to learn if they exhibit behaviors that exemplify traits (but also see Block, 1989). One can also use behavior sampling or psychometric methods to obtain standardized ratings of constructs. As long as the construct measures are not typically used in clinical practice, researchers will be able to enter data that are typically used in clinical practice into the statistical-prediction rules.

Psychodiagnosis

For the task of psychodiagnosis, as with the task of describing traits and symptoms, criterion diagnoses were made by criterion judges who were given history and interview data. To avoid the occurrence of criterion contamination, history and interview data were rarely entered into the statistical-prediction rules. To build statistical-prediction rules that can integrate psychometric, history, interview, and observation data, researchers will need to use new methods for obtaining criterion scores. Obtaining better criterion scores will also be important for evaluating the validity of the statistical-prediction rules.

Several methods for obtaining criterion diagnoses and evaluating validity were described in chapter 2. The methods involve the use of (a) structured interviews, (b) the LEAD standard (Spitzer, 1983), (c) the Robins and Guze criteria (Robins & Guze, 1970), (d) construct-validation procedures (e.g., Cronbach & Meehl, 1955; Widiger, 1993a, 1993c), and (e) latent class analysis (e.g., Meehl, 1995). Limitations of structured interviews have already been described, and, as already noted, the use of latent class analysis for making diagnoses requires further study. At the present time, the other three approaches are more promising. Using the LEAD approach, longitudinal data are collected and an expert clinician uses all of the data that are collected to make LEAD (criterion) diagnoses. Since criterion diagnoses are collected using this approach, one can use a derivation sample to construct statistical-prediction rules. An alternative approach is to use the Robins and Guze criteria to evaluate the validity of a set of diagnoses (e.g., one can conduct follow-up studies, family studies, or laboratory studies). Finally, the construct-validity approach provides a broader framework than the Robins and Guze criteria for evaluating the validity of a set of diagnoses. For example, using this approach, researchers can conduct follow-up, family, and laboratory studies, but can also look at additional issues such as whether diagnoses are biased. The Robins and Guze criteria and the construct-validiation approach do not require collecting criterion diagnoses, so a derivation sample to derive statistical-prediction rules cannot be used to make diagnoses.

Case Formulation

The most difficult judgment task in the area of psychological assessment is case formulation. Statistical-prediction rules have rarely been used for this task. When the validity of causal judgments made by clinicians was reviewed (see chapter 3), none of the results from any study indicated that validity was good or excellent. Meehl (1978) commented on the poverty of case formulations: "Every thoughtful clinician realizes that the standard life history that one finds in a medical chart is, from the standpoint of thorough causal comprehension, so thin and spotty and selective as to border on the ludicrous" (p. 810). Given that case formulation is so difficult, it will be hard to build statistical-prediction rules that are good at this task. At the same time, because clinicians do not do well at this task, it would be valuable to have statistical-prediction rules that can make valid judgments.

There are a number of reasons why it is difficult to construct a causal theory that can explain a client's symptoms and behaviors (Meehl, 1978). For example, the sheer number of variables for understanding a client's behavior can be huge. Also, a clinician may not know about critical events in a client's life, either because the clinician does not ask about them, or because the client does not want to talk about them or is unable to recall them. This last point was made by Meehl (1978): "I would view as an important causal source . . . inner events such as fantasies, resolutions, shifts in cognitive structure . . . that he or she may later be unable to recall" (p. 810).

Advances in statistical analysis (causal modeling), genetics, and experimental psychopathology may eventually make it possible for investigators to build statistical-prediction rules that can make valid causal judgments. For example, research suggests that anxiety sensitivity ("fear of fear") may be a causal factor in the occurrence of panic attacks (Schmidt et al., 1997). Investigators may eventually be able to explain the occurrence of panic attacks by using measures of biological and psychological factors including anxiety sensitivity.

Behavioral Prediction

When statistical rules have been used to make behavioral predictions, input data have not been limited and criterion scores have been meaningful. However, statistical-prediction rules have not achieved high levels of validity for the task of behavioral prediction. For example, statistical predictions of suicide have not been valid (Goldstein et al., 1991; Pokorny, 1983; see chapter 4). Statistical predictions have been valid when the task has been to predict violence (e.g., Gardner et al., 1996; Hall, 1988; Klassen & O'Connor, 1989), but one cannot say that a high level of validity has been achieved. For example, in one study (Lidz et al., 1993; additional analyses reported by Gardner et al., 1996), when statistical-prediction rules were used to make long-term predictions of violence, the average area under the ROC curve (AUC) for the most accurate statistical prediction rule was .74. The AUC is equal to the probability of a randomly selected violent patient being predicted to be violent more often than a randomly selected nonviolent patient. A value of .5 would represent the chance level of prediction. The average area under the ROC curve was .62 for clinicians who had all of the information that they usually use in clinical practice. Even though the AUC for the statistical-prediction rule is higher than the AUC for clinicians, the statistical-prediction rule is not highly accurate. To improve the statistical prediction of violence, new risk factors need to be identified and new techniques need to be refined to measure these risk factors (Monahan & Steadman, 1994).

Treatment Planning

Statistical-prediction rules have rarely been used to make treatment decisions. However, given that interrater reliability for treatment decisions has often been poor, statistical-prediction rules may prove to be of great value. For example, interrater reliability has been poor for some tasks in behavioral assessment and for decisions regarding psychotropic medicine and electroconvulsive therapy (see chapter 5). One way to improve reliability is to use statistical prediction rules. To build and evaluate statistical-prediction rules for treatment-planning tasks, researchers will need to conduct outcome studies.

Neuropsychological Assessment

Statistical-prediction rules in the area of neuropsychological assessment have made use of psychometric and demographic data, but not interview, history, observation, neurological, or neuroimaging data. Some of the statistical-prediction rules have been moderately valid (e.g., Mittenberg, Rotholc, Russell, & Heilbronner, 1996; Tenhula & Sweet, 1996; but also see McKinzey & Russell, 1997), but, for at least some tasks, predictions could be more accurate if extensive information is used as input data.

If extensive information is used as input data for statistical-prediction rules, then, to avoid criterion contamination, new strategies for obtaining criterion scores will need to be used. If input data for a statistical-prediction rule includes all of the information that is usually available in clinical practice, criterion scores should be based on some other source of information. To do this, one can collect longitudinal data. For example, longitudinal data can be collected to evaluate the validity of diagnoses (e.g., the validity of diagnoses of onset stage of dementia). Longitudinal data can also be collected to evaluate the validity of behavioral predictions (e.g., predictions of ability to return to work) and the validity of treatment plans (e.g., a recommendation that a client not return to independent living).

AUTOMATED ASSESSMENT

Automated-assessment programs are used more often than statistical-prediction rules, but this does not mean that they are more valid. In fact, whether automated-assessment computer programs are valid is questionable. After all, automated-assessment computer programs are not derived by collecting data. Instead, they are written by expert clinicians. Research on clinical judgment indicates that so-called expert clinicians are frequently no more accurate than advanced graduate students and other clinicians (see chapters 1, 2, 4, 5, and 6). More importantly, and more to the point, research on validity has not been done for many automated-assessment computer programs.

A strength of computer-based test reports is that they can be based on an expert clinician's knowledge of empirical research. However, when reading a computer-based test report, it is usually impossible to know which statements are based on research results and which statements are based solely on clinical experience. It is also difficult to know what percentage of the statements are based on empirical research. However, an exception can be described: National Computer Systems sponsored an independent evaluation of a computer-based test report that they distribute (Eyde, 1985). The goal of this computer-based test report (The Minnesota Report: Personnel Selection System for the MMPI) is to describe personality disorders that might interfere with an individual's functioning. According to the independent evaluation, 47% of the interpretations of 2-point code types were based on many published studies. When research did not exist for the interpretation of a 2-point code type (27% of the time), narratives were interpreted on the basis of single scales. In addition to the interpretation of 2-point code types and the interpretation of single scales, the author of the computer program used clinical judgment to develop content themes.

To evaluate an automated-assessment computer program, it would be helpful to be able to examine the if–then rules that comprise the program. One could then try to relate the rules to results from empirical studies (i.e., to results from empirical studies on the psychological test that the program is used to interpret). Unfortunately, rules comprising an automated-assessment computer program are frequently unavailable for examination.

There have been notable instances when independent reviewers have been given access to the rules that comprise an automated-assessment computer program. For example, for a review of The Minnesota Report: Personnel Selection System for the MMPI, Eyde (1985) was given access to the entire set of rules for the program and the publishers took considerable time to answer her questions. Eyde concluded that "Because the CBTI [computer-based test interpretation] may include numerous inappropriate interpretations for an applicant, the CBTI should only be *used with great care* by qualified personnel as one of several types of evidence" (pp. 1007–1008).

Studies on the validity of automated-assessment computer programs will be reviewed. Consumer-satisfaction studies and external-criterion studies have been conducted to describe the validity of the automated-assessment programs.

Consumer-Satisfaction Studies

In *consumer-satisfaction studies*, clinicians and clients rate the accuracy of automated-assessment test reports. For example, a clinician who has been working with a client may read an automated-assessment test report and rate whether the report is descriptive of the client. Moreland (1985) reviewed studies on the computerized interpretation of the MMPI and concluded that "the results of customer satisfaction studies completed to date are best viewed skeptically" (p. 819). Results from more recent studies should be viewed with similar skepticism. For example, in one study (Moreland &

Onstad, 1987), ratings of the accuracy of automated-assessment test reports were made by only eight clinicians and nearly a third of the ratings were made by only one clinician (Cash, Mikulka, & Brown, 1989; Moreland & Godfrey, 1989). Similarly, in another study (Rubenzer, 1992), half of the ratings made by the professional therapists were made by only two clinicians. Also, when more than one clinician rated the descriptiveness of the test reports, interrater reliability was horrible: A reliability coefficient of −.15 was obtained. Finally, in a third study (Guastello & Rieke, 1990), participants who took a psychological test and rated the descriptiveness of the test reports were undergraduates who participated in the study as part of a class. One cannot conclude from the results of this study that the automated-assessment computer program will be valid when used with a clinical sample.

Methodological guidelines for studying consumer satisfaction have been proposed (Snyder et al., 1990). They include (a) using a large sample of raters that is representative of clinicians who use, or are potential users of, an automated assessment test report, (b) using a large sample of test respondents that is representative of clients who can be expected to take the test, (c) controlling for the Barnum effect (having clinicians make ratings for both real automated assessment test reports and for reports that contain only statements that describe most people), (d) ensuring that rating scales are appropriate, (e) ensuring that clinicians have adequately assessed clients before they rate whether an automated-assessment test report is descriptive of the client (e.g., using structured interviews), and (f) ensuring that intra- and interrater reliability are satisfactory. Unfortunately, studies using these guidelines have not been conducted.

External-Criterion Studies

Another approach for studying the validity of automated-assessment computer programs is to compare ratings of traits, symptoms, or diagnoses made by using an automated-assessment computer program to ratings of traits, symptoms, or diagnoses made by clinicians who are given non-test information. This approach has been used in the areas of personality assessment and neuropsychological assessment.

Moreland (1985) reviewed the literature on computer-based test reports using the MMPI. As with the consumer-satisfaction studies, Moreland viewed the results skeptically because of methodological problems with the studies. In perhaps the best study (Hedlund, Morgan, & Master, 1972), two clinicians made criterion ratings after reading the discharge summaries for 100 psychiatric inpatients at a military hospital. They completed a 33-item symptom checklist for each case. These ratings were compared to statements from automated-assessment MMPI reports. The study had a number of positive features, for instance, the patient sample was large and interrater reliability for the criterion judges was good. However, the study was flawed because criterion ratings were made solely on the basis of medical records. As one might expect, symptoms and maladaptive behaviors are noted less often when ratings are made on the basis of discharge summaries than when ratings are made by clinicians using all of the information that is usually available in clinical practice (Gdowski, Lachar, & Butkus, 1980). Thus, though Hedlund et al. (1972) had reported a false positive rate of 62% for the statements contained in the automated-assessment test report, it is quite possible that many of the symptoms and behaviors described by the test report were actually present.

Computer-based test reports for other personality-assessment instruments also have been largely unvalidated. For example, in one study (Kahn, Fox, & Rhode, 1988), an automated-assessment computer program (Exner, 1985) was used to interpret the Rorschach and to make ratings of the validity of each protocol and level of functioning. The automated-assessment program made a rating of questionable validity for only one of the protocols that were obtained from six university undergraduate students who had been instructed to fake the symptoms of paranoid schizophrenia. Also, the automated assessment program made more ratings of severe psychopathology for the undergraduate students who had been instructed to fake psychopathology than for the patients with paranoid schizophrenia.

In the area of neuropsychological assessment, automated-assessment computer programs have not been as accurate as neuropsychologists and statistical-prediction rules (Adams & Heaton, 1985). For example, the most widely studied automated-assessment program in the area of neuropsychology has been the Neuropsychological Key (Russell et al., 1970). The average hit rate for the Neuropsychological Key has been about 55% when the task has been to make diagnoses of left-hemisphere, right-hemisphere, or diffuse neurological impairment (Russell, 1995). The average hit rate has been about 68% for the same task for neuropsychologists when they have also been given only neuropsychological test data (Garb & Schramke, 1996; Russell, 1995). Similarly, for the task of describing the lateralization of brain damage, statistical-prediction rules have been more accurate than the Neuropsychological Key. In studies reviewed by Russell (1995), the average hit rate for discriminant analysis rules was 66% and the average hit rate for the Neuropsychological Key was about 55%.

Ironically, one automated-assessment computer program has been more accurate than mental health professionals, but, unlike other automated-assessment programs, it has rarely been used in clinical practice. In this study (Kleinmuntz, 1963), a process-tracing model (consisting of a set of if–then rules) was constructed to describe the logic underlying a clinician's judgments (the study was described in chapter 7 and is described again here). The clinician had been more accurate than other psychologists when the task was to make ratings of level of adjustment using the MMPI. The process-tracing model was constructed by giving the clinician a set of profiles and having the clinician think aloud into a tape recorder as he sorted the profiles into adjusted and maladjusted categories. When the process-tracing model was used to make ratings for a validation sample of MMPI protocols, it tended to be more accurate than the expert judge had been, though the difference was not statistically significant. The correlation between computer ratings and criterion ratings was .52, and the correlation between the judge's ratings and criterion ratings was .45. From this study, one can infer that rather than have a presumed expert judge write an automated-assessment program, it may be better to (a) establish that a judge can make valid ratings and (b) construct the automated-assessment program by modeling the clinician. However, this may be practical when the goal is to make ratings for a single task, but not when the goal is to generate generally useful computer-based test reports. To generate computer-based test reports, one would have to model a clinician for an indefinitely large number of tasks.

Concluding Comment

When automated-assessment programs have been used in other fields (e.g., business, medicine), the results have been disappointing. Crevier (1993) has commented on this in his book on the history of artificial intelligence:

> The expert systems flaunted in the early and mid-1980s could not operate as well as the experts who supplied them with knowledge. To true human experts, they amounted to little more than sophisticated reminding lists. . . . This state of affairs has improved but slightly and is likely to endure until there is basic progress in programming common-sense, learning, and inference abilities into computers. (p. 209)

Given that most automated-assessment computer programs in the area of psychological assessment have not been validated and that the results for automated-assessment computer programs in other fields have been disappointing, current automated-assessment computer programs should be used with caution.

NEURAL NETWORKING

Neural-network models are computing systems that are constructed to mimic how the brain works (Rumelhart, McClelland et al., 1986). They are composed of interconnected parallel-processing elements (neural network technology is also called *connectionism*). Neural networks are designed to work well with large amounts of information, even when some of the information is contradictory or incomplete. Most importantly, neural networks can learn from experience. That is, they are able to modify their own programs as they are given more information.

Although there are numerous benefits to neural networks, such systems also have weaknesses. Because they have been designed to mimic the human brain, they are frequently not as powerful as other computers for undertaking some tasks, like making huge numerical computations. Also, the rules used by a neural-network model are hidden from view. If a neural-network model solves a problem (e.g., accurately predicting the onset of a psychotic episode), one cannot easily determine what information the neural-network model used to make the predictions and how the neural-network model used the information.

Neural networking has been used for a number of applications in the area of computer science (e.g., recognition tasks, image and signal processing tasks), but it has seldom been used in the area of psychological assessment (though see Zou et al., 1996). Neural-network models may be appropriate for many tasks in psychological assessment. In fact, when a large amount of assessment information is available and some of the information is incomplete or contradictory, they may be able to out-perform statistical-prediction rules. Results from empirical studies indicate that assessment information is frequently contradictory. For example, agreement has been poor for (a) descriptions of children made by parents, teachers, or children (Achenbach, McConaughy, & Howell, 1987; Frick, Silverthorn, & Evans, 1994; Greenbaum, Dedrick, Prange, & Friedman, 1994; Hart et al., 1994), (b) diagnoses made by using self-report inventories and diagnoses made by using structured interviews (Perry, 1992; Trull & Larson, 1994; Zimmerman, 1994), (c) descriptions of adult clients made by clients and significant others (Riso, Klein, Anderson, Ouimette, & Lizardi, 1994; Zimmerman, 1994), and (d) descriptions and diagnoses of psychiatric inpatients made by using either structured interviews or structured interviews and medical records (Fennig et al., 1994; Kosten & Rounsaville, 1992). Given that results in the area of psychological assessment are frequently contradictory, one can speculate that neural-network models may be valuable for making judgments.

SUMMARY AND CONCLUSIONS

Statistical-prediction rules have nearly always been as accurate as, or more accurate than, clinicians. This has been true even when mental health professionals have been given extra information.

Linear rules are surprisingly accurate, even when data have been generated by using a configural (nonlinear) rule. However, under some circumstances, linear rules may not be accurate. For example, unit-weight linear rules may not do well when predictors are negatively correlated.

The validity of statistical-prediction rules has been variable. For example, statistical rules for the prediction of violence have been impressive, though they need to be studied further before they are used in clinical practice. Statistical rules for making diagnoses and describing traits and symptoms have not been as impressive, in part because, for these tasks, there has typically been little attempt to identify and use the best input information. For the tasks of case formulation and treatment planning, statistical-prediction rules have almost never been used.

Questions have been raised about the validity of automated-assessment test reports. Automated-assessment programs are written by expert clinicians, but research has not established that expert clinicians are more accurate than advanced graduate students or other clinicians. More importantly, most automated-assessment programs have not been shown to be valid. Methodological recommendations have been made for improving the way researchers evaluate the validity of automated-assessment programs.

Neural-network models are computer models that are constructed to mimic how the brain works. They make use of a form of parallel processing, and they are designed to work well with contradictory or missing information. Because psychological-assessment information is frequently contradictory or missing, neural-network models may be appropriate for many tasks. Empirical studies need to be conducted to evaluate the validity of neural-network models.

In conclusion, the tremendous potential of computers for improving validity has not yet been realized. Most automated-assessment programs have not been shown to be valid, and the validity of statistical-prediction rules has been variable. Advances need to occur in the way we derive and validate rules. A significant advance may occur when neural-network models are used to make judgments.

9

IMPROVING PSYCHOLOGICAL ASSESSMENT

The ultimate goal of judgment research is to improve the accuracy of judgments. By learning about the reliability and validity of judgments, the occurrence of biases and errors, the cognitive processes of clinicians, and the optimal use of computers for making judgments, it should be possible to make recommendations for improving clinical practice. Some valuable recommendations based on the hundreds of judgment studies that have been conducted can already be made.

Interestingly, many mental health professionals do not believe that research investigators have fairly evaluated the reliability and validity of judgments (for results from a survey, see Rock, 1994). They are skeptical about whether judgment research can lead to improved psychological assessment. However, the mental health professionals surveyed by Rock were generally unfamiliar with research on judgment and decision making. In fact, this seems to be one area in which practitioners hold strong opinions even when they are unfamiliar with the research that has been done.

METHODOLOGICAL ISSUES

Before making recommendations for improving psychological assessment, it is helpful to explore three main issues surrounding the methodological limitations of the judgment studies: ecological validity, the criterion problem, and generalization of results.

Ecological validity refers to how representative a study is of clinical practice (e.g., Rock & Bransford, 1992; Rock, Bransford, Maisto, & Morey, 1987). There is reason to be concerned about the ecological validity of many of the studies cited in this book. As has been noted, in a majority of the studies, clinicians were not given all of the information that they usually have available in clinical practice. For example, in many studies, clinicians made their judgments after reading case histories, watching videotapes of interviews, or reviewing test results. Of course, ecological validity is not a concern for all of the studies because in many, judgments were made by mental health professionals in the course of their clinical work.

Even though ecological validity is a legitimate concern, meaningful conclusions can be reached and meaningful recommendations can be made. Such recommendations will be most useful when one is cognizant of the ecological validity of the studies. For example, in the Garb and Florio (1997) and Nadler et al. (1994) studies described in chapters 6 and 7, neuropsychologists were told that test results were obtained from real clients, but they were actually based on normative data. No diagnoses of neurological impairment or dementia should have been made. However, a substantial number of neuropsychologists did make these diagnoses. Ecological validity is not high for these studies because the neuropsychologists were not allowed to interview the clients and were given little history information. However, the results do indicate that a significant number of neuropsychologists do not attend to norms. The results also illustrate why neuropsychologists should attend to norms, especially when working with elderly clients. On the other hand, it cannot be concluded that in clinical practice the neuropsychologists would not have determined that neurological impairment was absent. For example, by interviewing clients, they can sometimes determine that neurological impairment is absent.

The criterion problem has been discussed throughout this book. It refers to the problem of being able to decide whether a judgment is correct or incorrect. The criterion problem is not relevant to studies on reliability. Also, criterion scores are not necessarily needed to determine if judgments are biased. For example, diagnoses can be considered to be biased if (a) clients clearly meet or do not meet the criteria for a mental disorder, (b) level of psychopathology is controlled for, and (c) diagnoses vary by race, gender, or another patient variable. Furthermore, in studies on the validity of behavioral predictions and treatment planning, appropriate methods have generally been used to collect criterion scores. However, when the task has been to describe personality and psychopathology, make diagnoses, or make causal judgments, the criterion problem has been vexing. Since constructs cannot be measured perfectly, any description of validity must be interpreted in relation to measures of a construct (Cronbach & Meehl, 1955). Using imperfect construct measures, inferences about the relative validity of judgments can be made, but not inferences about the absolute level of validity.

For example, as long as construct measures are moderately valid, researchers should be able to infer whether judgments made by presumed experts are more valid than judgments made by other mental health professionals, whether confidence ratings are positively related to validity, and whether judgments made by using objective personality tests are more valid than those made by using projective personality tests. On the other hand, under most circumstances, it will not be possible to describe the absolute (or "true") level of validity of a set of judgments.

When generalizing results, one needs to be aware of the limitations of the studies. For example, results on incremental validity, the appropriateness of confidence ratings, and the value of training were more positive for objective personality inventories than for projective tests. However, most of the judgment studies on the use of projective tests are over 20 years old. In only a few of the studies on the Rorschach did clinicians use the Exner scoring system (Exner, 1974, 1978, 1986, 1991, 1993; Exner & Weiner, 1994). It is possible that when clinicians use the Exner scoring system, incremental validity will be fair, confidence ratings will be appropriate, and clinicians will do better than lay judges. However, even given the limitations of the studies, it is nonetheless clear that judgments made by clinicians using projective tests have not been shown to be valid.

One also needs to be aware of the limitations of studies when generalizing from the results on bias (Garb, 1997). For example, as already discussed, judgments may not be biased when clinicians are given case histories to read, but they may be biased when clinicians collect information on their own. Similarly, bias may appear to be absent when clinicians make diagnoses based on case histories, but the judgments may be biased if the diagnostic criteria themselves are biased (Funtowicz & Widiger, 1995; Widiger & Spitzer, 1991). Diagnostic criteria are biased if adherence to the criteria results in diagnoses that are more valid for one group than another (e.g., if diagnoses are more valid for Whites than for African Americans). Also, bias may appear to be absent when clinicians are given results from a personality inventory (e.g., a clinician may interpret identical test results for a Black client and a White client in the same way), but the personality inventory itself may be biased (Lindsay & Widiger, 1995). An item from a personality inventory may be race biased if (a) it does not correlate with dysfunction, (b) people of different races score differently on it, and (c) it is included on a scale that is used as a measure of dysfunction.

Another example can be given to illustrate why caution should be exercised in generalizing from results of judgment studies. Judgments made by clinicians were compared to judgments made by advanced graduate students in 27 studies (Garb, 1989). In these studies, mental health professionals were given biographical information (Oskamp, 1965; Soskin, 1954), observational data (Garner & Smith, 1976), data from interviews (Anthony,

1968; Grigg, 1958; Schinka & Sines, 1974), data from therapy sessions (Brenner & Howard, 1976), projective drawing protocols (Levenberg, 1975; Schaeffer, 1964; Stricker, 1967), Rorschach protocols (Gadol, 1969; Turner, 1966), MMPI protocols (Chandler, 1970; Danet, 1965; Goldberg, 1965, 1968; Graham, 1967, 1971; Oskamp, 1962; Walters et al., 1988), neuropsychological testing protocols (Goldberg, 1959; Goldstein et al., 1973; Heaton et al., 1978; Leli & Filskov, 1981, 1984; Robiner, 1978), and all of the data that mental health professionals generally have available in clinical practice (Johnston & McNeal, 1967). In none of the studies were clinicians more accurate than graduate students. However, in all of the studies except one (Johnston & McNeal, 1967), the clinicians did not make judgments in the setting in which they usually work. Research on learning from feedback (discussed in chapter 7) indicates that the benefits of feedback are almost completely setting specific (Goldberg & Rorer, 1965, and Rorer & Slovic, 1966, cited in Goldberg, 1968; Graham, 1971). When clinicians received feedback for patients in one setting but then had to make ratings for patients in another setting, their ratings were not more accurate after they received the feedback. Feedback did lead to increased accuracy when the training profiles and the cross-validation profiles were sampled from the same setting. Because clinicians do not receive immediate accurate feedback in clinical practice, the results on learning from feedback do not demonstrate that clinicians learn from experience in clinical settings, but they do suggest that when clinicians learn from experience, much of what they learn will be setting specific.

IMPROVING CLINICAL JUDGMENT

Attend to Empirical Research

Mental health professionals should attend to empirical research. When methodologically sound research has been conducted, clinicians should weigh the empirical results more heavily than they weigh their own clinical experiences. For example, when clinicians interpret a test profile, they should attend to research that describes typical patients with that test profile. Clinicians should not automatically try to think of other patients they have tested who share similar test results. After all, in virtually every judgment study, experienced clinicians have not been more accurate than less experienced clinicians, and clinicians have not been more accurate than advanced graduate students. Similarly, research on illusory correlations indicates that when clinicians believe that they are basing their judgments on their clinical experiences, they may instead be responding to the verbal associations of the test indicators. Research on covariation misestimation, confirmatory bias, and the availability heuristic also suggests that clinicians can have trouble learning from their clinical experiences (because data collection is sometimes biased and because their memories are fallible).

Be Aware of, and Overcome, Cultural Biases

Race bias, social class bias, gender bias, and other biases occur in clinical practice. For example, in one study (Segal et al., 1996), Black patients, compared to other patients, were given a significantly larger number of psychotropic medications, number of doses of antipsychotic medicine, and number of injections of antipsychotic medication, even when investigators controlled for (a) the presence of a psychotic disorder, (b) the severity of psychiatric disturbance, (c) dangerousness, (d) psychiatric history, and (e) the use of physical restraints. When psychiatrists spent as much time with Black patients as they did with other patients, they were unlikely to overmedicate the Black patients. It could be recommended that clinicians talk longer with Black patients. However, until researchers and clincians address the reason why psychiatrists have spent less time talking with Black patients than White patients, race bias may continue to persist.

Describe the Client's Strengths

Mental health professionals often focus on describing a client's deficits. Empirical results indicate that these professionals are likely to (a) make overly negative ratings of personality traits and psychopathology and (b) describe normal study participants as being maladjusted or impaired. Clinicians will be less likely to describe clients as being maladjusted or impaired if they evaluate their positive behaviors as well as their behaviors that are indicative of psychopathology. Also, by describing a client's positive behaviors, clinicians will be able to design more effective treatment interventions (Evans, 1993).

Be Wary of Some Judgment Tasks

Many mental health professionals know that the prediction of violence and suicide is difficult, but they do not seem to know that other tasks are also difficult. For example, interrater reliability has been poor when clinicians have described defense mechanisms, even when concise definitions have been provided (Endler & Parker, 1995). Similarly, reliability and validity for causal judgments is poor (see chapter 3), and validity is poor for describing personality traits for clients who are depressed (Stuart et al., 1992). Clinicians should be very careful when making ratings for these tasks. In fact, it can be unethical (but financially rewarding) to make ratings that are likely to have poor validity.

Be Systematic and Comprehensive When Conducting Interviews

To improve reliability, interviews should be systematic; to improve validity, they should be comprehensive. With regard to describing psychiatric symptoms, structured interviews and rating scales can be used to improve reliability (e.g., Widiger et al., 1986). However, the use of structured interviews and rating scales will not always improve reliability (e.g., reliability has been problematic even when clinicians have used rating scales to describe defense mechanisms; Endler & Parker, 1995). Also, though reliability generally improves when structured interviews are used to make diagnoses and ratings of psychiatric symptoms, interrater reliability may still be disappointing when interviews are conducted at different sites.

Interviews should be comprehensive. Clinicians should, but do not, routinely ask clients whether they are involved in ongoing domestic violence and whether they were physically or sexually abused as children or teenagers. In one study (Malone et al., 1995), clinicians did not even document a history of suicidal behavior for 12 of 50 patients who had a history of suicidal behavior. Similarly, underdiagnosis of mental disorders occurs in some substance abuse programs and in work with the developmentally disabled, and underdiagnosis of substance abuse frequently occurs on psychiatric units. Underdiagnosis would be less likely to occur if interviews were comprehensive and standardized.

When comprehensive interviews are conducted, it becomes less likely that confirmatory bias will occur. However, it will be difficult to completely avoid the occurrence of confirmatory bias. For example, confirmatory bias may occur even when clinicians use a structured interview. For this reason, when Widiger, Frances et al. (1986) wanted to learn if personality disorders frequently co-occur, they had undergraduates conduct structured interviews because they were afraid that if clinicians conducted the interviews, it would bias the results.

Make Use of Psychological Tests and Behavioral-Assessment Methods

Psychological tests and behavioral-assessment methods can be used to improve the reliability and validity of judgments. For example, when describing a client's traits, clinicians should make greater use of well-validated scales. Thus, one can make use of intelligence tests to rate intelligence, the Revised NEO Personality Inventory and NEO Five-Factor Inventory (Costa & McCrae, 1992) to describe a client using the five-factor model of personality, and the Interpersonal Adjective Scales (Wiggins, 1995) to describe a client using the interpersonal circumplex model. Psychological tests are also valuable because they can help to prevent the occurrence of confirmatory bias. Based on an interview, a clinician may have a strong impression about the nature of a client's disorder. However, if test results suggest that another diagnosis should be considered, then the clinician will be forced to evaluate the appropriateness of this alternative or additional diagnosis.

Results from judgment studies have been substantially more favorable for objective personality tests than for projective tests. For example, judgments never became significantly more valid when projective test results were added to more readily available information (e.g., history information), confidence ratings were never positively related to validity when clinicians used projective test results, and clinicians were never more accurate than lay judges when the clinicians and lay judges were given results from projective tests. It is fair to say that the use of projective tests remains controversial (Exner, 1996; Wood, Nezworski, & Stejskal, 1996a, 1996b).

Reliability was poor when behavioral clinicians formulated treatment goals and described controlling variables that produce or maintain problem behaviors. However, for some judgments, reliability and validity may improve when clinicians use behavioral-assessment methods. For example, when working with clients who have panic disorder, one can have them keep track of the times and settings when they have a panic attack. One can also have them record the thoughts they have prior to and during the panic attack. Observational methods (e.g., time sampling) can also be used to collect information that may help clinicians make more reliable and valid judgments.

Use Debiasing Strategies

Strategies for improving the way that clinicians process information have been described by several investigators (e.g., Arkes, 1981, 1991; Arnoult & Anderson, 1988; Gambrill, 1990; Nezu & Nezu, 1993; Turk & Salovey, 1986). The most frequent recommendation is that clinicians consider alternatives when making judgments (e.g., they should consider alternative diagnoses, explanations, and treatment plans). For example, when clinicians make diagnoses, they frequently fail to consider whether an additional diagnosis may also be appropriate (e.g., substance abuse is frequently underdiagnosed among psychiatric patients). As another example, research on attribution error suggests that many clinicians tend to attribute the causes of a person's behavior to internal factors (e.g., personality traits). When making causal judgments, clinicians should ask themselves if they have given enough consideration to possible environmental influences on the client's behavior.

Empirical data suggests that clinicians can become more accurate when they consider alternative explanations. In one study (Arkes et al., 1988), hindsight bias occurred when neuropsychologists read a case history. As part of the case history, the neuropsychologists were told the client's diagnosis (e.g., "This is the case of a man with a primary diagnosis of Alzheimer's disease"). Hindsight bias occurred when the neuropsychologists were instructed to (a) pretend that they had not been told the client's diagnosis and (b) estimate the likelihood of the client having a diagnosis of alcohol withdrawal, Alzheimer's disease, or brain damage secondary to alcohol abuse. Hindsight bias is said to occur when clinicians learn about an event and then claim that they could have predicted the event if they had been asked to do so (their likelihood ratings are higher than they would be if they had not been given the outcome information). When another group of neuropsychologists performed the same task, but were instructed to list one reason why each possible diagnosis might be correct, hindsight bias was significantly less likely to occur. In another study (Tutin, 1993), when clinical psychologists read a case history, their ratings of the likelihood of suicide were higher if they were instructed to explain why the person might commit suicide. However, when they were instructed to explain why the person might, or might not, commit suicide, their ratings of the likelihood of suicide were not higher than if they were simply told to read the case history and predict the likelihood of suicide. Here too, clinicians' judgments changed after they were told to consider an alternative event.

The other recommendation that is frequently made is for clinicians to decrease their reliance on memory. Clinicians should document all of their salient observations, and they should periodically review their notes. If clinicians do not carefully prepare and review their notes, stereotype beliefs may influence how they remember a client. For example, a clinician may remember a client's diagnosis, and the clinician may then incorrectly "remember" that the client has a particular symptom because the symptom usually occurs among patients with that diagnosis (Arkes & Harkness, 1980; Kayne & Alloy, 1988, pp. 312-313).

Follow Legal and Ethical Principles

Mental health professionals should follow legal and ethical principles. For example, to prevent unfair involuntary hospitalizations, they should seek a commitment only if the necessary criteria for civil commitment are satisfied. In general, necessary criteria for civil commitment are (a) the presence of a mental disorder and (b) the inability to care for self or imminent danger to self and/or others. Results from empirical studies indicate that psychiatrists frequently do not attend to these criteria when deciding whether to seek a civil commitment (e.g., Bagby et al., 1991).

Two additional examples can be given. First, mental health professionals should be compliant with laws that require them to report child abuse. Second, when there is a threat of domestic violence, mental health professionals should help the threatened family member develop a safety plan (e.g., go to a shelter or obtain a restraining order). Unfortunately, results from empirical studies indicate that mental health professionals frequently do not report child abuse and frequently do not take steps to protect the safety of a spouse (e.g., Brosig & Kalichman, 1992; Hansen, Harway, & Cervantes, 1991).

Follow Scientific Standards

To decrease the gap between science and practice, scientific standards for clinical practice can be written to help clinicians learn about assessment methods that have been supported by empirical research. Presentations at a conference on the implications of scientific standards for clinical practice have been published (Hayes, Follette, Dawes, & Grady, 1995). The conference was sponsored by the American Association of Applied and Preventive Psychology (AAAPP), which is an affiliate of the American Psychological Society. As a result of the conference, scientific standards are being written to guide clinical practice. To the degree that the standards describe assessment methods that have been supported by empirical research, clinicians should obey the standards.

Use Decision Aids

Mental health professionals should use decision aids to help them make judgments. For example, when they make diagnoses they should attend to diagnostic criteria (e.g., *DSM–IV*), and when they interpret psychological test results they should attend to norms and base rates. However, results from empirical studies indicate that clinicians frequently do not attend to diagnostic criteria, norms, or base rates.

There are a number of reasons why clinicians should attend to diagnostic criteria. Interrater reliability would improve; labeling bias, context effects, and patient variable biases (e.g., race bias) would be less likely to occur; and secondary diagnoses would be less likely to be overlooked. For example, labeling bias is unlikely to occur if, when a clinician learns that a client has previously been given a particular diagnosis, the clinician still tries to determine if the person meets the criteria for the disorder.

Clinicians should attend to base rates when they interpret psychological test results because cutoff scores for tests should always be adjusted by using local base rates (Elwood, 1993; Finn & Kamphuis, 1995; Meehl & Rosen, 1955; Wiggins, 1973, pp. 248–253). That is, inflexible cutoff scores should not be used for any psychological test. In general, the higher the local base rate, the lower one will set the cutoff score for a test. For example, if one works primarily with veterans who suffer from posttraumatic stress disorder (i.e., if the base rate for posttraumatic stress disorder is high), then by using a lower cutoff score for a scale that identifies individuals with posttraumatic stress disorder (by making more diagnoses of posttraumatic stress disorder), one can achieve a higher overall level of accuracy.

USE OF COMPUTERS

To improve psychological assessment, it may become possible to use powerful computer programs to make, or assist in making, judgments and decisions. In the future, programs may be more powerful than most people imagine (Crevier, 1993). For example, computers of the future may be able to "comprehend" natural language and learn from experience, sit in classrooms and learn from lectures, read all of the research that is online (in the future, this may mean all of the mental health journals), and sit in clinicians' offices and learn from the interactions between clinicians and clients. Using all of this information, they may be able to detect relations and patterns that have eluded clinicians, and they may be able to make highly accurate judgments and decisions.

Though computers may transform the practice of psychological assessment, it is important to be aware that earlier predictions about the power of computers have sometimes turned out to be wrong. For example, in 1965, Simon predicted that "machines will be capable, within twenty years, of doing any work that a man can do" (Simon, 1965, p. 96). Similarly, in 1967, Minsky predicted that "Within a generation . . . few compartments of intellect will remain outside the machine's realm—the problem of creating artificial intelligence will be substantially solved" (Minsky, 1967, p. 2).

If psychological assessment is going to improve as a result of using computers to make judgments and decisions, two things will need to happen. First, advances in computer science will have to occur and more powerful computers and computer programs will need to be developed. Second, clinicians will need to accept and use the computer programs.

In reflecting on his 1954 book on clinical versus statistical prediction, Meehl (1986a) listed seven reasons why clinicians might not want to use computers to make judgments. The reasons bear repeating:

1. *Ignorance.* Without bothering to learn about studies on the validity of computer programs, some clinicians may reject the use of computers because they do not think that they can be accurate.

2. *Threat of obsolescence.* Mental health professionals may be against the use of computers because they are afraid of losing their jobs, even if they are aware that computers can be more accurate than clinicians.

3. *Threat to a clinician's self-concept.* People who believe that they are excellent clinicians may find it hard to concede that a computer should be used to make judgments.

4. *Theoretical identification.* For example, a clinician with a psychoanalytic or an existential orientation may believe that their theoretical orientation precludes them from using a computer to make judgments.

5. *The use of computers may seem dehumanizing.* A clinician may feel that by using a computer to describe or diagnose a person, one is treating a client like a rat or an inanimate object.
6. *Ethics.* Clinicians may reason that it is unethical to make judgments and decisions without allowing one's clinical judgment to modify the judgments and decisions of the computer.[1]
7. Clinicians may resent the idea that computers can be more accurate than humans. (Though as clinicians we may feel resentful, it is important that we work through our feelings and do what is best for our clients.)

TRAINING ISSUES

To improve psychological assessment, and clinical practice in general, advances need to be made in the training of mental health professionals. Changes can be made in the selection of students, training curricula, methods for evaluating the validity of training, the comparison of PhD and PsyD clinical psychology programs, licensing and accreditation, and new tools for training.

Selection of Students

If psychological assessment is to improve, admissions officers may have to change the way that they select students for graduate school programs. Snyder (1995) made the following pertinent observation:

> Are there forces attracting students to graduate training who are not predisposed toward scientific approaches to clinical psychology? ... Unless changes occur in the type of students recruited to our field and in the work environment for graduates who become practicing clinicians, my sense is that all the efforts exerted in training programs, licensure, and continuing education will not accomplish any greater emphasis on the scientific principles underlying the helping process. (p. 423)

Thus, when selecting students for graduate school, one should select not only for intelligence and personality factors that are related to clinical skill (e.g., warmth and empathy), but also for scientific mindedness. This is not to say that applicants should not be religious or even mystical. What is meant is that students should be selected who are likely to use an assessment instrument or a treatment intervention, not because a charismatic figure

---

[1]However, if judgments and decisions made by the computer are more accurate than judgments made by clinicians, then it is ethical, under carefully described circumstances, to use the computer to make judgments. In fact, under certain circumstances it may be unethical to not use computer-based judgments.

has championed it or because in their experience they have found it helpful, but because it has been repeatedly validated by careful research. Interestingly, most programs make no systematic effort to assess scientific mindedness.

Curriculum

Changes need to be made to graduate school curricula. For example, clinical psychology programs have been criticized because they typically do not include formal training in the recognition of neurological disorders (Bondi, 1992). In a study described previously (Sbordone & Rudd, 1986), clinical psychologists were given case histories that described clients with symptoms that were indicative of a neurological disease (either Huntington's disease, brain tumor, transient ischemic attack, or Alzheimer's disease). Across all of the cases, when psychologists were asked to make treatment recommendations, 33% of the time they did not recommend making a referral to a physician.

Psychology graduate school programs have also been criticized because they infrequently teach their students about judgment research (Rock, 1994), and because they typically do not offer formal training in the prediction of suicide (Bongar & Harmatz, 1989) and the prediction of violence (Borum, 1996). For example, graduate students should learn about the reliability and validity of judgments made by mental health professionals. With regard to predicting suicide and violence, they should learn about assessment instruments that have been designed to aid with data collection and with making predictions.

Graduate students in psychology should be taught about the use of semistructured and structured interviews. Currently, psychologists make diagnoses, but frequently do not attend to diagnostic criteria. By being trained in the use of semistructured and structured interviews, they would become more familiar with diagnostic criteria and hopefully would learn about the importance of adhering to criteria.

In general, it makes sense to eliminate, or at least deemphasize, training in the use of projective tests. Validity has been poor for some projective tests (e.g., for the interpretation of human figure drawings; Kahill, 1984; Motta et al., 1993; Swensen, 1957) and questionable for others (e.g., for the Rorschach; Exner, 1996; Wood, 1996a, 1996b). Also, as has already been noted, judgments made by clinicians using projective tests have rarely been shown to be valid.

Program Evaluation

As students and interns progress through graduate school and internship training programs, their performance should be evaluated. By evaluating their performance, effective and ineffective components of training programs can be identified.

There are already measures for evaluating the competence of graduate students, interns, and clinicians. For example, measures have been constructed for evaluating knowledge of diagnostic criteria (Andersen & Harthorn, 1989; Rubinson et al., 1988) treatment planning (Falvey & Hebert, 1992), and forensic issues that have a direct bearing on mental health professionals (Melton, Weithorn, & Slobogin, 1985). As another example, a behavioral instrument has recently been developed to assess the interviewing skills of graduate students (Bogels et al., 1995).

When the effect of specific training experiences has been evaluated, the results have been mixed. For example, psychiatric residents who attended a specialized 4-hour course on managing extrapyramidal syndromes were more accurate than residents who received standard psychopharmacology training: A review of medical charts revealed that they were more skilled at diagnosing extrapyramidal syndromes and using neuroleptic medicine (Dixon, Weiden, Frances, & Rapkin, 1989). On the other hand, when mental health professionals received formal training in ethics, the training did not have a significant effect on the decisions they reported they would make (Haas et al., 1988). Similarly, when PhD psychologists received formal training for working with victims of sexual abuse, the training had no discernable effect on their decisions regarding child abuse reporting (Finlayson & Koocher, 1991).

PhD versus PsyD Programs

One of the main findings of judgment research is that clinicians do not attend closely to empirical findings. Given this result, one may wonder if graduates of PhD psychology programs make more accurate judgments than graduates of PsyD psychology programs. The focus of PsyD programs is to help students become practitioners. The focus of most PhD programs is to help students become scientist–practitioners. Thus, students in a PhD program might have a greater appreciation for research than students in a PsyD program. On the other hand, students may be drawn to PhD programs because the degree holds greater prestige, not because they have an interest in research. Also, in many of the judgment studies, when disappointing results were reported, the clinicians were PhD psychologists. Of course, the results might have been even more disappointing if the clinicians were PsyD psychologists.

Additional arguments can be made regarding why PhD psychologists may, or may not, be more accurate than PsyD psychologists. For example, judgments may be more accurate for PhD psychologists than PsyD psychologists because PhD programs are more selective than PsyD programs. Getting into a PsyD program is about four times easier than getting into a research-oriented PhD program (Mayne, Norcross, & Sayette, 1994). On the other hand, judgments made by PsyD psychologists could be more accurate than judgments made by PhD psychologists because their training, unlike the training of PhD psychologists, is focused on practice.

Little research has been conducted on the relative accuracy of judgments made by PhD and PsyD psychologists (Peterson, 1985). In one study (Shemberg & Leventhal, 1981), internship supervisors saw few differences in the performance of PsyD and PhD interns. However, in a second study (Green & McNamara, 1994), clinical psychology graduate students in a PhD program scored higher than clinical psychology graduate students in a PsyD program on tests of methodology reasoning and conditional probability. The methodology-reasoning test measured "students' awareness of confounding variables and their ability to apply control group concepts to evaluate scientific research and everyday situations;" the conditional probability test measured students' ability to apply "conditional and biconditional logic, or the use of necessary and sufficient reasoning" (Green & McNamara, 1994, p. 966). PhD and PsyD students did equally well on tests of verbal reasoning and statistical reasoning, and they had similar levels of knowledge of predictors of suicide, diagnostic criteria, and treatment modalities.

Licensing and Accreditation

Psychological assessment might improve if licensing requirements were made more relevant. For example, on the national test that psychologists take for licensure, topics could be covered that have been identified as areas that clinicians need to learn more about. For example, topics might include: (a) symptoms that are related to neurological disorders, (b) the detection and treatment of spousal abuse, and (c) biases and errors that frequently occur when clinicians make judgments.

It would be beneficial to society if expert clinicians could be identified. With this goal in mind, the American Board of Professional Psychology (ABPP) offers an examination for clinicians wishing to be awarded diplomate status. As part of the examination, clinicians provide information about clients they have treated (e.g., videotapes of interviews and therapy sessions, psychological test results), and they are asked questions about the care that they provided. Unfortunately, when clinicians with the ABPP diplomate have been compared to clinicians without the ABPP diplomate, no differences in judgmental accuracy have been reported (Garb & Schramke, 1996).

Instructional Aids

By capitalizing on advances in instructional psychology, it may be possible to improve training in psychological assessment. Intelligent computer tutors can be developed to assess a judge's level of knowledge and problem-solving skills, identify things that the judge needs to learn, and then help the judge become more knowledgeable and skilled (e.g., by presenting cases that illustrate principles that clinicians are unfamiliar with). Computerized tutorial programs have been used in the area of medicine (e.g., Clancey, 1986; Clancey & Letsinger, 1984), but they have rarely, if ever, been used in the mental health fields.

Three methods can be used to develop an intelligent computer tutor. First, an expert systems approach can be used. That is, a computer tutor can be based on an expert's store of knowledge. This is the approach that has typically been used in medicine, and it may be a useful approach for some psychological assessment tasks. For example, to construct a computer tutor that could help clinicians improve their psychodiagnostic skills, one could evaluate their prototypes (their beliefs about the behaviors and symptoms that make up the diagnostic criteria for a category), identify features of their prototypes that appear to be erroneous, have the clinicians make diagnoses for cases that are selected on the basis of their seemingly erroneous beliefs, and then provide feedback to help clinicians learn when they have made a mistake. To determine whether features of a prototype are erroneous, one could compare the prototypes to a set of diagnostic criteria. Thus, the computer tutor could help clinicians learn to adhere to the criteria of a particular classification system. For other tasks, it is not as clear that presumed experts are able to make more accurate judgments than other clinicians, and thus an expert computer system approach may not be as useful.

Besides being given feedback from an expert computer system, clinicians can receive outcome feedback. For example, clinicians can be given assessment information, be instructed to make a judgment, and then be given criterion or construct-indicator information that is collected at a later time (e.g., they can be told whether the patient later became violent or suicidal). However, it is not clear how much clinicians will improve if they are given outcome information (Balzer, Doherty, & O'Connor, 1989). When clinical psychologists have been given accurate outcome feedback for a sample of patients in one setting, they have been able to make accurate judgments for additional patients from the same setting, but not for patients in other settings (Goldberg & Rorer, 1965, and Rorer & Slovic, 1966, cited in Goldberg, 1968; Graham, 1971). However, using a computer-tutorial approach, different cases could be selected for different clinicians by identifying the types of cases for which a clinician is making inaccurate judgments.

A third method for developing an intelligent computer tutor is to give clinicians cognitive feedback. Cognitive feedback refers to feedback about relations rather than outcomes (Todd & Hammond, 1965). Cognitive feedback includes information about: (a) the relations between cues and criterion (or construct) measures, (b) the interrelations among cues, (c) a judge's perceptions of the relations between cues and criterion or construct measures, (d) a judge's perceptions of interrelations among cues, and (e) the relation between a judge's perceptions and the actual relations existing in the environment. A major reason for providing clinicians with cognitive feedback is that clinicians frequently appear to lack insight into their judgment policies. If clinicians know how they make judgments, then they would not need to be told about their perceptions of the relations among cues and criterion or construct measures. By being told how they make judgments and by describing the relations that occur in the environment, clinicians should be able to improve on their judgment policies.

Providing cognitive feedback has rarely, if ever, been used as an instructional method in the mental health fields. However, cognitive feedback has been provided in studies in other fields (Balzer et al., 1989), and cognitive-feedback software exists for use in a range of fields including mental health fields (Hoffman, 1987; Rohrbaugh, 1986). When cognitive feedback has been provided, validity increased when judges were given information about the relations among cues and criterion or construct-indicator measures, but not when the judges' perceptions were described. However, the tasks in these studies were not complex. Feedback about clinicians' perceptions may prove to be valuable because tasks in mental health fields are complex (Balzer et al., 1989).

FORENSIC ISSUES

The research findings reviewed in this book put severe limitations on what forensic clinicians can ethically state to a court. First, and foremost, expert witnesses should not defend their testimony by saying that their statements are based on clinical experience. It is difficult to learn from experience because accurate feedback is frequently unavailable and because the cognitive processes of clinicians are not always optimal. Instead of giving their clinically based opinions, expert witnesses should inform the court about relevant research.

Second, when answering forensic questions, expert witnesses should make the court aware that some clinical-judgment tasks are extremely difficult and others are controversial. Difficult judgment tasks include describing defense mechanisms and making causal judgments. Controversial judgment tasks include diagnosing dissociative identity disorder (formerly *multiple personality disorder*) and concluding that a client was sexually abused even though the client has no recollection of abuse.

Third, clinicians should be careful to collect valid assessment information. Interviews should be comprehensive and standardized, and alternative hypotheses should be explicitly and systematically considered. Also, expert witnesses should be aware that the validity of projective tests has not been supported by judgment research. If they use projective tests, clinicians have an obligation to describe the controversies surrounding use of the tests.

Fourth, decision aids should be used whenever available and appropriate. For example, expert witnesses should adhere to diagnostic criteria when claiming that they use DSM–IV to make diagnoses, should explicitly incorporate base rates when setting a cutting score for a test, and should integrate the results of an automated-assessment test report with other information. Expert witnesses in neuropsychology should document that they explicitly compared patients' performances to appropriate norms when interpreting test results. Finally, expert witnesses should be aware of cultural biases. For example, when predicting violence, they should be careful to not overpredict violence among men, especially African American men.

SUMMARY AND DISCUSSION

Meaningful recommendations can be made even though limitations exist in the judgment literature. However, one must be careful how one generalizes from results, and one should evaluate the ecological validity of a study and be aware of the criterion problem when interpreting results.

Many recommendations can be made for improving clinical assessment. To become more accurate, clinicians should (a) attend to empirical research; (b) be aware of, and overcome, cultural biases; (c) describe clients' strengths; (d) be wary of some judgment tasks; (e) be systematic and comprehensive when conducting interviews; (f) make use of psychological tests and behavioral-assessment methods; (g) use cognitive debiasing strategies; (h) follow legal and ethical principles; (i) follow scientific standards; and (j) use decision aids.

Furthermore, clincians can expect that computers will transform not only clinical assessment, but also all of society. By using computers, clinicians will eventually be able to make more reliable and valid judgments. However, even when many judgments are made by computers, clinicians will continue to be involved in assessment and treatment (e.g., data collection, talking with clients about the judgments made by computers, providing psychotherapy).

To further improve clinical assessment, advances need to be made in the training of mental health professionals. Recommendations in this arena include the following: (a) Attitude toward science should be considered when selecting students for graduate school. (b) Graduate school curricula should be changed. (c) Effective and ineffective components of training programs should be identified. (d) PhD and PsyD programs should be evaluated and, if necessary, modified. (e) Licensing and accreditation requirements should be made more relevant. (f) Instructional aids (e.g., intelligent computer tutors) should be developed and used.

Several recommendations for forensic practice also should be implemented. When testifying in court, clinicians should not defend their testimony by saying that their statements are based on clinical experience.

Also, clinicians should make the court aware that some judgment tasks are extremely difficult, they should be careful to collect valid assessment information, and they should use decision aids whenever available and appropriate.

Many of the disputes in the area of clinical assessment will ultimately be resolved by the use of the scientific method. After all, by collecting and analyzing data, we as social scientists try to not be blinded by our preconceptions and theories. History has shown that there is no more generally useful method for arriving at reliable knowledge about the world. Thus, the final word should belong to, and will belong to, the scientific method.

REFERENCES

Abelson, R. P. (1985). A variance explanation paradox: When a little is a lot. *Psychological Bulletin, 97,* 129–133.

Abramowitz, C. V. (1977). Blaming the mother: An experimental investigation of sex-role bias in countertransference. *Psychology of Women Quarterly, 2,* 24–34.

Abramowitz, C. V., & Dokecki, P. R. (1977). The politics of clinical judgment: Early empirical returns. *Psychological Bulletin, 84,* 460–476.

Abramowitz, S. I., Abramowitz, C. V., Jackson, C., & Gomes, B. (1973). The politics of clinical judgment: What nonliberal examiners infer about women who do not stifle themselves. *Journal of Consulting and Clinical Psychology, 41,* 385–391.

Achenbach, T. M., Conners, K. C., Quay, H. C., Verhulst, F. C., & Howell, C. T. (1989). Replication of empirically derived syndromes as a basis for taxonomy of child/adolescent psychopathology. *Journal of Abnormal Child Psychopathology, 17,* 299–322.

Achenbach, T. M., McConaughy, S. H., & Howell, C. T. (1987). Child/adolescent behavioral and emotional problems: Implications of cross-informant correlations for situational specificity. *Psychological Bulletin, 101,* 213–232.

Achenbach, T. M., Verhulst, F. C., Baron, G. D., & Akkerhuis, G. W. (1987). Epidemiological comparison of American and Dutch children: I. Behavior and emotional problems and competencies reported by parents for ages 4 to 16. *Journal of the American Academy of Child Psychiatry, 26,* 317–326.

Adams, E. M., & Betz, N. E. (1993). Gender differences in counselors' attitudes toward and attributions about incest. *Journal of Counseling Psychology, 40,* 210–216.

Adams, K. M., & Heaton, R. K. (1985). Automated interpretation of neuropsychological test data. *Journal of Consulting and Clinical Psychology, 53,* 790–802.

Adler, D. A., Drake, R. E., & Teague, G. B. (1990). Clinicians' practices in personality assessment: Does gender influence the use of *DSM-III* Axis II? *Comprehensive Psychiatry, 31,* 125–133.

Agell, G., & Rothblum, E. D. (1991). Effects of clients' obesity and gender on the therapy judgments of psychologists. *Professional Psychology, 22,* 223–229.

Albert, S., Fox, H. M., & Kahn, M. W. (1980). Faking psychosis on the Rorschach: Can expert judges detect malingering? *Journal of Personality Assessment, 44,* 115–119.

Alexander, F. (1950). *Psychosomatic medicine: Its principles and applications.* New York: Norton.

Alford, J. D., & Locke, B. J. (1984). Clinical responses to psychopathology of mentally retarded persons. *American Journal of Mental Deficiency, 89,* 195–197.

Algozzine, B., & Ysseldyke, J. E. (1981). Special education services for normal children: Better safe than sorry? *Exceptional Children, 48,* 238–243.

Alterman, A. I., Snider, E. C., Cacciola, J. S., Brown, L. S., Jr., Zaballero, A., & Siddiqui, N. (1996). Evidence of response set effects in structured research interviews. *Journal of Nervous and Mental Disease,184,* 403–410.

Ambady, N., & Rosenthal, R. (1992). Thin slices of expressive behavior as predictors of interpersonal consequences: A meta-analysis. *Psychological Bulletin, 111,* 256–274.

American Psychiatric Association. (1968). *Diagnostic and statistical manual of mental disorders* (2nd ed.). Washington, DC: Author.

American Psychiatric Association. (1980). *Diagnostic and statistical manual of mental disorders* (3rd ed.). Washington, DC: Author.

American Psychiatric Association. (1987). *Diagnostic and statistical manual of mental disorders* (3rd ed., Rev. ed.). Washington, DC: Author.

American Psychiatric Association. (1994). *Diagnostic and statistical manual of mental disorders* (4th ed.). Washington, DC: Author.

American Psychological Association. (1985). *Standards for educational and psychological testing.* Washington, DC: Author.

Amira, S., Abramowitz, S. I., & Gomes-Schwartz, B. (1977). Socially-charged pupil and psychologist effects on psychoeducational decisions. *Journal of Special Education, 11,* 433–440.

Ananth, J., Vandewater, S., Kamal, M., Brodsky, A., Gamal, R., & Miller, M. (1989). Missed diagnosis of substance abuse in psychiatric patients. *Hospital and Community Psychiatry, 40,* 297–299.

Andersen, S. M., & Harthorn, B. H. (1989). The Diagnostic Knowledge Inventory: A measure of knowledge about psychiatric diagnosis. *Journal of Clinical Psychology, 45,* 999–1013.

Anderson, N. H. (1972). Looking for configurality in clinical judgment. *Psychological Bulletin, 78,* 93–102.

Anderson, N. H., & Shanteau, J. (1977). Weak inference with linear models. *Psychological Bulletin, 84,* 1155–1170.

Andreasen, N. C., Shore, D., Burke, J. D., Jr., Grove, W. M., Lieberman, J. A., Oltmanns, T. F., Pettegrew, J. W., Pulver, A. E., Siever, L. J., Tsuang, M. T., & Wyatt, R. J. (1988). Clinical phenomenology. *Schizophrenia Bulletin, 14,* 345–363.

Angoff, W. H. (1988). Validity: An evolving concept. In H. Wainer & H. I. Braun (Eds.), *Test validity* (pp. 19–32). Hillsdale, NJ: Lawrence Erlbaum.

Anthony, N. (1968). The use of facts and cues in clinical judgments from interviews. *Journal of Clinical Psychology, 24,* 37–39.

Appelbaum, P. S., & Hamm, R. M. (1982). Decision to seek commitment. *Archives of General Psychiatry, 39,* 447–451.

Apperson, L. J., Mulvey, E. P., & Lidz, C. W. (1993). Short-term clinical prediction of assaultive behavior: Artifacts of research methods. *American Journal of Psychiatry, 150,* 1374–1379.

Archer, R. P. (1996). MMPI-Rorschach interrelationships: Proposed criteria for evaluating explanatory models. *Journal of Personality Assessment, 67,* 504–515.

Archer, R. P., & Gordon, R. A. (1988). MMPI and Rorschach indices of schizophrenic and depressive diagnoses among adolescent inpatients. *Journal of Personality Assessment, 52,* 276–287.

Archer, R. P., & Krishnamurthy, R. (1993a). Combining the Rorschach and the MMPI in the assessment of adolescents. *Journal of Personality Assessment, 60,* 132–140.

Archer, R. P., & Krishnamurthy, R. (1993b). A review of MMPI and Rorschach interrelationships in adult samples. *Journal of Personality Assessment, 61,* 277–293.

Arieti, S. (1974). *Interpretation of schizophrenia* (2nd ed.). New York: Basic Books.

Arkes, H. R. (1981). Impediments to accurate clinical judgment and possible ways to minimize their impact. *Journal of Consulting and Clinical Psychology, 49,* 323–330.

Arkes, H. R. (1991). Costs and benefits of judgment errors: Implications for debiasing. *Psychological Bulletin, 110,* 486–498.

Arkes, H. R., Faust, D., Guilmette, T. J., & Hart, K. (1988). Eliminating the hindsight bias. *Journal of Applied Psychology, 73,* 305–307.

Arkes, H. R., & Harkness, A. R. (1980). Effect of making a diagnosis on subsequent recognition of symptoms. *Journal of Experimental Psychology: Human Learning and Memory, 6,* 568–575.

Arnoult, L. H., & Anderson, C. A. (1988). Identifying and reducing causal reasoning biases in clinical practice. In D. C. Turk & P. Salovey (Eds.), *Reasoning, inference, and judgment in clinical psychology* (pp. 209–232). New York: Free Press.

Aronson, D. E., & Akamatsu, T. J. (1981). Validation of a *Q*-sort task to assess MMPI skills. *Journal of Clinical Psychology, 37,* 831–836.

Arpino, C., Da Cas, R., Donini, G., Pasquini, P., Raschetti, R., & Traversa, G. (1995). Use and misuse of antidepressant drugs in a random sample of the population of Rome, Italy. *Acta Psychiatrica Scandinavica, 92,* 7–9.

Asarnow, R. F., Nuechterlein, K. H., & Marder, S. R. (1983). Span of apprehension performance, neuropsychological functioning, and indices of psychosis-proneness. *Journal of Nervous and Mental Disease, 171,* 662–669.

Astrup, C. (1975). Predicted and observed outcome in followed-up functional psychoses. *Biological Psychiatry, 10,* 323–328.

Atkinson, D. R., Brown, M. T., Parham, T. A., Matthews, L. G., Landrum-Brown, J., & Kim, A. U. (1996). African American client skin tone and clinical judgments of African American and European American psychologists. *Professional Psychology: Research and Practice, 27,* 500–505.

Attias, R., & Goodwin, J. (1985). Knowledge and management strategies in incest cases: A survey of physicians, psychologists, and family counselors. *Child Abuse & Neglect, 9,* 527–533.

Austad, C. S., & Aronson, H. (1987). The salience of sex role instructions to mental health professionals. *Sex Roles, 16,* 323–333.

Bagby, R. M., Thompson, J. S., Dickens, S. E., & Nohara, M. (1991). Decision making in psychiatric civil commitment: An experimental analysis. *American Journal of Psychiatry, 148,* 28–33.

Balzer, W. K., Doherty, M. E., & O'Connor, R., Jr. (1989). Effects of cognitive feedback on performance. *Psychological Bulletin, 106,* 410–433.

Bamgbose, O., Edwards, D., & Johnson, S. (1980). The effects of race and social class on clinical judgment. *Journal of Clinical Psychology, 36,* 605–609.

Barendregt, J. T. (1961). *Research in psychodiagnostics.* The Hague: Mouton.

Barlow, D. H., DiNardo, P. A., Vermilyea, B. B., Vermilyea, J., & Blanchard, E. B. (1986). Co-morbidity and depression among the anxiety disorders: Issues in diagnosis and classification. *Journal of Nervous and Mental Disease, 174,* 63–72.

Baskin, D. R., Sommers, I., Tessler, R., & Steadman, H. J. (1989). Role incongruence and gender variation in the provision of prison mental health services. *Journal of Health and Social Behavior, 30,* 305–314.

Bass, E., & Davis, L. (1988). *The courage to heal.* New York: Harper & Row.

Batson, C. D. (1975). Attribution as a mediator of bias in helping. *Journal of Personality and Social Psychology, 72,* 455–466.

Batson, C. D., & Marz, B. (1979). Dispositional bias in trained therapists' diagnoses: Does it exist? *Journal of Applied Social Psychology, 9,* 476–489.

Beck, K. A., & Ogloff, J. R. P. (1995). Child abuse reporting in British Columbia: Psychologists' knowledge of and compliance with the reporting law. *Professional Psychology, 26,* 245–251.

Becker, D., & Lamb, S. (1994). Sex bias in the diagnosis of borderline personality disorder and posttraumatic stress disorder. *Professional Psychology, 25,* 55–61.

Beiser, M., Iacono, W. G., & Erickson, D. (1989). Temporal stability in the major mental disorders. In L. N. Robins & J. E. Barrett (Eds.), *The validity of psychiatric diagnosis* (pp. 77–97). New York: Raven Press.

Beitchman, J. H., Zucker, K. J., Hood, J. E., daCosta, G. A., Akman, D., & Cassavia, E. (1992). A review of the long-term effects of child sexual abuse. *Child Abuse & Neglect, 16,* 101–118.

Bellack, A. S., & Mueser, K. T. (1993). Psychosocial treatment for schizophrenia. *Schizophrenia Bulletin, 19,* 317–336.

Benefee, L. M., Abramowitz, S. I., Weitz, L. J., & Armstrong, S. H. (1976). Effects of patient racial attribution on Black clinicians' inferences. *American Journal of Community Psychology, 4,* 263–273.

Benton, A. L. (1994). Neuropsychological assessment. *Annual Review of Psychology, 45,* 1–23.

Berman, J. (1979). Individual versus societal focus: Problem diagnoses of Black and White male and female counselors. *Journal of Cross-Cultural Psychology, 10,* 497–507.

Bernard, R., & Clarizio, H. (1981). Socioeconomic bias in special education placement decisions. *Psychology in the Schools, 18,* 178–183.

Bernstein, B. L., & LeComte, C. (1982). Therapist expectancies: Client gender and therapist gender, profession, and level of training. *Journal of Clinical Psychology, 38,* 744–754.

Berrios, G. E., & Chen, E. Y. H. (1993). Recognising psychiatric symptoms: Relevance to the diagnostic process. *British Journal of Psychiatry, 163,* 308–314.

Bickman, L., Karver, M. S., & Schut, L. J. A. (1997). Clinician reliability and accuracy in judging appropriate level of care. *Journal of Consulting and Clinical Psychology, 65,* 515–520.

Bieri, J., Atkins, A. L., Briar, S., Leaman, R. L., Miller, H., & Tripodi, T. (1966). *Clinical and social judgment: The discrimination of behavioral information.* New York: Wiley.

Bieri, J., Orcutt, B. A., & Leaman, R. (1963). Anchoring effects in sequential clinical judgments. *Journal of Abnormal and Social Psychology, 67,* 616–623.

Biklen, D. (1996). Learning from the experiences of people with disabilities. *American Psychologist, 51,* 985–986.

Bilett, J. L., Jones, N. F., & Whitaker, L. C. (1982). Exploring schizophrenic thinking in older adolescents with the WAIS, Rorschach, and WIST. *Journal of Clinical Psychology, 38,* 232–243.

Billingsley, D. (1977). Sex bias in psychotherapy: An examination of the effects of client sex, client pathology, and therapist sex on treatment planning. *Journal of Consulting and Clinical Psychology, 45,* 250–256.

Birnbaum, M. H. (1974). Reply to the devil's advocates: Don't confound model testing and measurement. *Psychological Bulletin, 81,* 854–859.

Blake, W. (1973). The influence of race on diagnosis. *Smith College Studies in Social Work, 43,* 184–192.

Blashfield, R. K., & Haymaker, D. (1988). A prototype analysis of the diagnostic criteria for *DSM-III-R* personality disorders. *Journal of Personality Disorders, 2,* 272–280.

Blashfield, R. K., & Herkov, M. J. (1996). Investigating clinician adherence to diagnosis by criteria: A replication of Morey and Ochoa (1989). *Journal of Personality Disorders, 10,* 219–228.

Bloch, P. M., Weitz, L. J., & Abramowitz, S. I. (1980). Racial attribution effects on clinical judgment: A failure to replicate among White clinicians. *American Journal of Community Psychology, 8,* 485–493.

Block, J. (1989). Critique of the act frequency approach to personality. *Journal of Personality and Social Psychology, 56,* 234–245.

Block, J. (1995). A contrarian view of the five-factor approach to personality description. *Psychological Bulletin, 117,* 187–215.

Blume, E. S. (1990). *Secret survivors: Uncovering incest and its aftereffects in women.* New York: Ballantine.

Boat, B. W., & Everson, M. D. (1988). Use of anatomical dolls among professionals in sexual abuse evaluations. *Child Abuse and Neglect, 12,* 171–179.

Boden, M. A. (1972). *Artificial intelligence and natural man.* New York: Basic Books.

Bögels, S. M., van der Vleuten, C. P. M., Blok, G., Kreutzkamp, R., Melles, R., & Schmidt, H. G. (1995). Assessment and validation of diagnostic interviewing skills for the mental health professions. *Journal of Psychopathology and Behavioral Assessment, 17,* 217–230.

Bondi, M. W. (1992). Distinguishing psychological disorders from neurological disorders: Taking Axis III seriously. *Professional Psychology: Research and Practice, 23,* 306–309.

Bongar, B., & Harmatz, M. (1989). Graduate training in clinical psychology and the study of suicide. *Professional Psychology: Research and Practice, 20,* 209–213.

Borke, H., & Fiske, D. W. (1957). Factors influencing the prediction of behavior from a diagnostic interview. *Journal of Consulting Psychology, 21,* 78–80.

Bornstein, M., Bellack, A., & Hersen, M. (1977). Social skills training for unassertive children: A multiple baseline analysis. *Journal of Applied Behavior Analysis, 5,* 443–454.

Borum, R. (1996). Improving the clinical practice of violence risk assessment: Technology, guidelines, and training. *American Psychologist, 51,* 945–956.

Bowman, P. R. (1982). An analog study with beginning therapists suggesting bias against "activity" in women. *Psychotherapy: Theory, Research, and Practice, 19,* 318–324.

Boyar, J. I., & Tsushima, W. T. (1975). Cross-validation of the Halstead-Reitan Neuropsychological Battery: Application in Hawaii. *Hawaii Medical Journal, 34,* 94–96.

Brannick, M. T., & Brannick, J. P. (1989). Nonlinear and noncompensatory processes in performance evaluation. *Organizational Behavior and Human Decision Processes, 44,* 97–122.

Brehmer, B. (1980). In one word: Not from experience. *Acta Psychologica, 45,* 223–241.

Brenner, D., & Howard, K. I. (1976). Clinical judgment as a function of experience and information. *Journal of Clinical Psychology, 32,* 721–728.

Briar, S. (1961). Use of theory in studying effects of client social class on students' judgments. *Social Work, 6,* 91–97.

Briere, J., & Zaidi, L. Y. (1989). Sexual abuse histories and sequelae in female psychiatric emergency room patients. *American Journal of Psychiatry, 146,* 1602–1606.

Brockington, I. F., Kendell, R. E., & Leff, J. P. (1978). Definitions of schizophrenia: Concordance and prediction of outcome. *Psychological Medicine, 8,* 387–398.

Brockington, I. F., & Meltzer, H. Y. (1982). Documenting an episode of psychiatric illness: Need for multiple information sources, multiple raters, and narrative. *Schizophrenia Bulletin, 8,* 485–492.

Brodsky, S. L. (1989). Advocacy in the guise of scientific objectivity: An examination of Faust and Ziskin. *Computers in Human Behavior, 5,* 261–264.

Brosig, C. L., & Kalichman, S. C. (1992). Clinicians' reporting of suspected child abuse: A review of the empirical literature. *Clinical Psychology Review, 12,* 155–168.

Broverman, I., Broverman, D., Clarkson, F., Rosenkrantz, P., & Vogel, S. (1970). Sex-role stereotypes and clinical judgments of mental health. *Journal of Consulting and Clinical Psychology, 34,* 1–7.

Brown, G. G., Del Dotto, J. E., Fiske, J. L., Taylor, H. G., & Breslau, N. (1993). Analyzing clincal ratings of performance on pediatric neuropsychological tests. *The Clinical Neuropsychologist, 7,* 179–189.

Brown, G. G., Spicer, K. B., Robertson, W. M., Baird, A. D., & Malik, G. (1989). Neuropsychological signs of lateralized arteriovenous malformations: Comparison with ischemic stroke. *The Clinical Neuropsychologist, 3,* 340–352.

Bruhn, A. R., & Reed, M. R. (1975). Simulation of brain damage on the Bender-Gestalt test by college subjects. *Journal of Personality Assessment, 39,* 244–255.

Buczek, T. A. (1981). Sex biases in counseling: Counselor retention of the concerns of a female and male client. *Journal of Counseling Psychology, 28,* 13–21.

Budescu, D. V., & Rodgers, J. L. (1981). Corrections for spurious influences on correlations between MMPI scales. *Multivariate Behavioral Research, 16,* 483–497.

Burns, C. W. (1992). Psychoeducational decision making, test scores, and descriptive data: Selected methodological issues. *Journal of School Psychology, 30,* 1–16.

Buss, D. M. (1991). The psychodiagnosis of everyday conduct: Narcissistic personality disorder and its components. In W. M. Grove & D. Cicchetti (Eds.), *Thinking clearly about psychology. Vol. 1. Matters of public interest* (pp. 333–345). Minneapolis: University of Minnesota Press.

Buss, D. M., & Craik, K. H. (1983). The act frequency approach to personality. *Psychological Review, 90,* 105–126.

Buss, D. M., & Craik, K. H. (1986). Acts, dispositions, and clinical assessment: The psychopathology of everyday conduct. *Clinical Psychology Review, 6,* 387–406.

Butcher, J. N. (Ed.). (1987). *Computerized psychological assessment: A practitioner's guide.* New York: Basic Books.

Butler, O. T., Coursey, R. D., & Gatz, M. (1976). Comparison of the Bender Gestalt Test for both Black and White brain-damaged patients using two scoring systems. *Journal of Consulting and Clinical Psychology, 44,* 280–285.

Camerer, C. (1985). Fitting linear models to interactive data when variables are intercorrelated. Unpublished manuscript, University of Pennsylvania.

Cantor, N., & Mischel, W. (1979). Prototypes in person perception. In L. Berkowitz (Ed.), *Advances in experimental social psychology* (Vol. 12, pp. 3–52). New York: Academic Press.

Cantor, N., Smith, E. E., French, R., & Mezzich, J. (1980). Psychiatric diagnosis as prototype categorization. *Journal of Abnormal Psychology, 89,* 181–193.

Carlin, A. S., & Hewitt, P. L. (1990). The discrimination of patient generated and randomly generated MMPIs. *Journal of Personality Assessment, 54,* 24–29.

Carpenter, W. T., Jr., Sacks, M. H., Strauss, J. S., Bartko, J. J., & Rayner, J. (1976). Evaluating signs and symptoms: Comparison of structured interview and clinical approaches. *British Journal of Psychiatry, 128,* 397–403.

Carroll, B. J. (1989). Diagnostic validity and laboratory studies: Rules of the game. In L. N. Robins & J. E. Barrett (Eds.), *The validity of psychiatric diagnosis* (pp. 229–244). New York: Raven Press.

Carson, R. C. (1990). Needed: A new beginning [Review of the book *Diagnosis and classification in psychiatry: A critical appraisal of DSM–III*]. *Contemporary Psychology, 35,* 11–12.

Cascardi, M., Mueser, K. T., DeGiralomo, J., & Murrin, M. (1996). Physical aggression against psychiatric inpatients by family members and partners. *Psychiatric Services, 47,* 531–533.

Casey, P. R., Dillon, S., & Tyrer, P. J. (1984). The diagnostic status of patients with conspicuous psychiatric morbidity in primary care. *Psychological Medicine, 14,* 673–681.

Cash, T. F., Mikulka, P. J., & Brown, T. A. (1989). Validity of Millon's computerized interpretation system for the MCMI: Comment on Moreland & Onstad. *Journal of Consulting and Clinical Psychology, 57,* 311–312.

Chan, D. W., & Jackson, D. N. (1982). Individual differences in the perception and judgment of psychopathology. *Multivariate Behavioral Research, 17,* 3–32.

Chandler, M. J. (1967). A process analysis of clinical inference (Doctoral dissertation, University of California, Berkeley, 1966). *Dissertation Abstracts, 27,* 3667-B.

Chandler, M. J. (1970). Self-awareness and its relation to other parameters of the clinical inference process. *Journal of Consulting and Clinical Psychology, 35,* 258–264.

Chapman, L. J. (1967). Illusory correlation in observational report. *Journal of Verbal Learning and Verbal Behavior, 6,* 151–155.

Chapman, L. J. (1990). Meehl's theory of schizotaxia, schizotypy, and schizophrenia. *Journal of Personality Disorders, 4,* 111–115.

Chapman, L. J., & Chapman, J. P. (1967). Genesis of popular but erroneous psychodiagnostic observations. *Journal of Abnormal Psychology, 72,* 193–204.

Chapman, L. J., & Chapman, J. P. (1969). Illusory correlation as an obstacle to the use of valid psychodiagnostic signs. *Journal of Abnormal Psychology, 74,* 271–280.

Chapman, L. J., Chapman, J. P., & Miller, E. N. (1982). Reliabilities and intercorrelations of eight measures of proneness to psychosis. *Journal of Consulting and Clinical Psychology, 50,* 187–195.

Chesler, P. (1972). *Women and madness.* Garden City, NY: Doubleday.

Cicchetti, D. V., & Sparrow, S. S. (1981). Developing criteria for establishing the interrater reliability of specific items in a given inventory: Applications to assessment of adaptive behavior. *American Journal of Mental Deficiency, 86,* 127–137.

Clancey, W. J. (1986). From GUIDON to NEOMYCIN and HERACLES in twenty short lessons: ONR final report 1979–1985. *AI Magazine, 7,* 40–60.

Clancey, W. J., & Letsinger, R. (1984). NEOMYCIN: Reconfiguring a rule-based expert system for application to teaching. In W. J. Clancey & E. H. Shortliffe (Eds.), *Medical artificial intelligence: The first decade.* Reading, MA: Addison-Wesley.

Clarizio, H. F., & Phillips, S. E. (1986). Sex bias in the diagnosis of learning disabled students. *Psychology in the Schools, 23,* 44–52.

Clarkin, J. F., Widiger, T. A., Frances, A., Hurt, S. W., & Gilmore, M. (1983). Prototypic typology and the borderline personality disorder. *Journal of Abnormal Psychology, 92,* 263–275.

Clavelle, P. R., & Turner, A. D. (1980). Clinical decision-making among professionals and paraprofessionals. *Journal of Clinical Psychology, 36,* 833–838.

Clayton, P. J. (1990). The comorbidity factor: Establishing the primary diagnosis in patients with mixed symptoms of anxiety and depression. *Journal of Clinical Psychiatry, 51,* 35–39.

Cloninger, C. R. (1987). A systematic method for clinical description of personality variants: A proposal. *Archives of General Psychiatry, 44,* 573–588.

Cochrane, C. T. (1972). Effects of diagnostic information on empathic understanding by the therapist in a psychotherapy analogue. *Journal of Consulting and Clinical Psychology, 38,* 359–365.

Cocozza, J. J., & Steadman, H. J. (1978). Prediction in psychiatry: An example of misplaced confidence in experts. *Social Problems, 25,* 265–276.

Coiro, M. J., & Gottesman, I. I. (1996). The diathesis and/or stressor role of expressed emotion in affective illness. *Clinical Psychology: Science and Practice, 3,* 310–322.

Coleman, D., & Baker, F. M. (1994). Misdiagnosis of schizophrenia in older, Black veterans. *Hospital and Community Psychiatry, 45,* 527–528.

Collins, W. D., & Messer, S. B. (1991). Extending the plan formulation method to an object relations perspective: Reliability, stability, and adaptability. *Psychological Assessment, 3,* 75–81.

Compas, B. E., & Adelman, H. S. (1981). Clinicians' judgments of female clients' causal attributions. *Journal of Clinical Psychology, 37,* 456–460.

Cooper, J. E., Kendell, R. E., Gurland, B. J., Sharpe, L., Copeland, J. R. M., & Simon, R. (1972). *Psychiatric diagnosis in New York and London.* London: Oxford University Press.

Cooper, R. P., & Werner, P. D. (1990). Predicting violence in newly admitted inmates: A lens model analysis of staff decision making. *Criminal Justice and Behavior, 17,* 431–447.

Copeland, J. R. M., Cooper, J. E., Kendell, R. E., & Gourlay, A. J. (1971). Differences in usage of diagnostic labels amongst psychiatrists in the British Isles. *British Journal of Psychiatry, 118,* 629–640.

Corbitt, E. M., & Widiger, T. A. (1995). Sex differences among the personality disorders: An exploration of the data. *Clinical Psychology: Science and Practice, 2,* 225–238.

Costa, P. T., Jr., & McCrae, R. R. (1992). *Revised NEO Personality Inventory (NEO-PI-R) and NEO Five-Factor Inventory (NEO-FFI) professional manual.* Odessa, FL: Psychological Assessment Resources.

Costa, P. T., Jr., & Widiger, T. A. (Eds.). (1994). *Personality disorders and the five-factor model of personality.* Washington, DC: American Psychological Association.

Cressen, R. (1975). Artistic quality of drawings and judges' evaluations of the DAP. *Journal of Personality Assessment, 39,* 132–137.

Crevier, D. (1993). *AI: The tumultous history of the search for artificial intelligence.* New York: Basic Books.

Crits-Christoph, P., Luborsky, L., Dahl, L., Popp, C., Mellon, J., & Mark, D. (1988). Clinicians can agree in assessing relationship patterns in psychotherapy. *Archives of General Psychiatry, 45,* 1001–1004.

Cronbach, L. J. (1971). Test validation. In R. L. Thorndike (Ed.), *Educational measurement* (2nd ed., pp. 443–509). Washington, DC: American Council on Education.

Cronbach, L. J., & Meehl, P. E. (1955). Construct validity in psychological tests. *Psychological Bulletin, 52,* 281–302.

Cummings, J. A., Huebner, E. S., & McLeskey, J. (1986). Psychoeducational decision making: Reason for referral versus test data. *Professional School Psychology, 1,* 249–256.

Curtis, J. T., & Silberschatz, G. (1989). *The plan formulation method: A reliable procedure for case formulation.* Unpublished manuscript, Mt. Zion Hospital and Medical Center, San Francisco, CA.

Dailey, D. M. (1980). Are social workers sexist? A replication. *Social Work, 25,* 46–50.

Dailey, D. M. (1983). Androgyny, sex-role stereotypes, and clinical judgment. *Social Work Research and Abstracts, 19,* 20–24.

Dallas, M., & Baron, R. (1985). Do psychotherapists use a confirmatory strategy during interviewing? *Journal of Social and Clinical Psychology, 3,* 106–122.

Dammers, P. M., Bolter, J. F., Todd, M. E., Gouvier, W. D., Batiansila, B., & Adams, S. G. (1995). How important is adaptive functioning in the diagnosis of dementia? A survey of practicing clinical psychologists. *The Clinical Neuropsychologist, 9,* 27–31.

Danet, B. N. (1965). Prediction of mental illness in college students on the basis of "nonpsychiatric" MMPI profiles. *Journal of Consulting Psychology, 29,* 577–580.

Davis, D. A. (1976). On being detectably sane in insane places: Base rates and psychodiagnosis. *Journal of Abnormal Psychology, 85,* 416–422.

Davis, D. A. (1979). What's in a name? A Bayesian rethinking of attributional biases in clinical judgments. *Journal of Consulting and Clinical Psychology, 47,* 1109–1114.

Davis, R. T., Blashfield, R. K., & McElroy, R. A. (1993). Weighting criteria in the diagnosis of a personality disorder: A demonstration. *Journal of Abnormal Psychology, 102,* 319–322.

Davison, K., & Bagley, C. R. (1969). Schizophrenia-like psychoses associated with organic disorders of the nervous system: A review of the literature. In R. N. Herrington (Ed.), *Current problems in neuropsychiatry* (pp. 113–184). Ashford, Kent, England: Headley Bros.

Dawes, R. M. (1971). A case study of graduate admissions: Application of three principles of human decision making. *American Psychologist, 26,* 180–188.

Dawes, R. M. (1979). The robust beauty of improper linear models in decision making. *American Psychologist, 34,* 571–582.

Dawes, R. M. (1986). Representative thinking in clinical judgment. *Clinical Psychology Review, 6,* 425–441.

Dawes, R. M. (1994). *House of cards: Psychology and psychotherapy built on myth.* New York: Free Press.

Dawes, R. M., & Corrigan, B. (1974). Linear models in decision making. *Psychological Bulletin, 81,* 95–106.

Dawes, R. M., Faust, D., & Meehl, P. E. (1989). Clinical versus actuarial judgment. *Science, 243,* 1668–1674.

Del Gaudio, A. C., Carpenter, P. J., & Morrow, G. R. (1978). Male and female treatment differences: Can they be generalized? *Journal of Consulting and Clinical Psychology, 46,* 1577–1578.

DeWitt, K. N., Kaltreider, N. B., Weiss, D. S., & Horowitz, M. J. (1983). Judging change in psychotherapy: Reliability of clinical formulations. *Archives of General Psychiatry, 40,* 1121–1128.

Diamant, J. J., & Hijmen, R. (1981). Comparison of test results obtained with two neuropsychological test batteries. *Journal of Clinical Psychology, 37,* 355–358.

DiNardo, P. A. (1975). Social class and diagnostic suggestion as variables in clinical judgment. *Journal of Consulting and Clinical Psychology, 43,* 363–368.

Dix, G. E. (1975). Determining the continued dangerousness of psychologically abnormal sex offenders. *Journal of Psychiatry and the Law, 3,* 327–344.

Dixon, L., Weiden, P. J., Frances, A. J., & Rapkin, B. (1989). Management of neuroleptic-induced movement disorders: Effects of physician training. *American Journal of Psychiatry, 146,* 104–106.

Dixon, S. P., LeLieuvre, R. B., & Walker, L. C. (1981). *Journal of Consulting and Clinical Psychology, 49,* 406–409.

Dolan, B., Evans, C., & Norton, K. (1995). Multiple Axis-II diagnoses of personality disorders. *British Journal of Psychiatry, 166,* 107–112.

Dowds, B. N., Fontana, A. F., Russakoff, L. M., & Harris, M. (1977). Cognitive mediators between patients' social class and therapists' evaluations. *Archives of General Psychiatry, 34,* 917–920.

Dowling, J. F., & Graham, J. R. (1976). Illusory correlation and the MMPI. *Journal of Personality Assessment, 40*, 531–538.

Drake, R. E., Osher, F. C., Noordsy, D. L., Hurlbut, S. C., Teague, G. B., & Beaudett, M. S. (1990). Diagnosis of alcohol use disorders in schizophrenia. *Schizophrenia Bulletin, 16*, 57–67.

Dubro, A. F., Wetzler, S., & Kahn, M. W. (1988). A comparison of three self-report questionnaires for the diagnosis of *DSM-III* personality disorders. *Journal of Personality Disorders, 2*, 256–266.

Duker, J. (1959). The utility of the MMPI atlas in the derivation of personality descriptions. *Dissertation Abstracts International, 19*, (3021). (University Microfilms No. 59–1259).

Dumont, F., & Lecomte, C. (1987). Inferential processes in clinical work: Inquiry into logical errors that affect diagnostic judgments. *Professional Psychology, 18*, 433–438.

Dunham, H., & Meltzer, B. (1946). Predicting length of hospitalization of mental patients. *American Journal of Sociology, 52*, 123–131.

Dunlap, W. P. (1994). Generalizing the common language effect size indicator to bivariate normal correlations. *Psychological Bulletin, 116*, 509–511.

Edwards, D., & Berry, N. H. (1974). Psychiatric decisions: An actuarial study. *Journal of Clinical Psychology, 30*, 153–159.

Edwards, R. (1995, January). Is hyperactivity label applied too frequently? *APA Monitor*, pp. 44–45.

Efron, B. (1983). Estimating the error rate of a prediction rule: Improvements on cross-validation. *Journal of the American Statistical Association, 78*, 316–331.

Einhorn, H. J. (1988). Diagnosis and causality in clinical and statistical prediction. In D. C. Turk & P. Salovey (Eds.), *Reasoning, inference, and judgment in clinical psychology* (pp. 51–70). New York: Free Press.

Einhorn, H. J., & Hogarth, R. M. (1978). Confidence in judgment: Persistence of the illusion of validity. *Psychological Review, 85*, 395–416.

Einhorn, H. J., Kleinmuntz, D. N., & Kleinmuntz, B. (1979). Linear regression and process-tracing models of judgment. *Psychological Review, 86*, 465–485.

Einhorn, H. J., & McCoach, W. (1977). A simple multiattribute utility procedure for evaluation. *Behavioral Science, 22*, 270–284.

Elk, R., Dickman, B. J., & Teggin, A. F. (1986). Depression in schizophrenia: A study of prevalence and treatment. *British Journal of Psychiatry, 149*, 228–229.

Elliott, T. R., Frank, R. G., & Brownlee-Duffeck, M. (1988). Clinical inferences about depression and physical disability. *Professional Psychology: Research and Practice, 19*, 206–210.

Ellis, M. V., Robbins, E. S., Schult, D., Ladany, N., & Banker, J. (1990). Anchoring errors in clinical judgments: Type I error, adjustment, or mitigation? *Journal of Counseling Psychology, 37*, 343–351.

Elovitz, G. P., & Salvia, J. (1982). Attractiveness as a biasing factor in the judgments of school psychologists. *Journal of School Psychology, 20*, 339–345.

Elwood, R. W. (1993). Psychological tests and clinical discriminations: Beginning to address the base rate problem. *Clinical Psychology Review, 13*, 409–419.

Endicott, J., & Spitzer, R. L. (1978). A diagnostic interview: The Schedule for Affective Disorders and Schizophrenia. *Archives of General Psychiatry, 35*, 837–845.

Endler, N. S., & Parker, J. D. A. (1995). Assessing a patient's ability to cope. In J. N. Butcher (Ed.), *Clinical personality assessment* (pp. 329–352). New York: Oxford University.

Epstein, S., & O'Brien, E. J. (1985). The person–situation debate in historical and current perspective. *Psychological Bulletin, 98*, 513–537.

Erdman, H. P., Greist, J. H., Gustafson, D. H., Taves, J. E., & Klein, M. H. (1987). Suicide risk prediction by computer interview: A prospective study. *Journal of Clinical Psychiatry, 48*, 464–467.

Ericsson, K. A., & Simon, H. A. (1980). Verbal reports as data. *Psychological Review, 87*, 215–251.

Ericsson, K. A., & Simon, H. A. (1993). *Protocol analysis: Verbal reports as data* (rev. ed.). Cambridge, MA: MIT Press.

Evans, C. (1984). "Draw a person . . . a whole person": Drawings from psychiatric patients and well-adjusted adults as judged by six traditional DAP indicators, licensed psychologists, and the general public (Doctoral dissertation, Temple University, 1984). *Dissertation Abstracts International, 45*, 348B.

Evans, I. (1993). Constructional perspectives in clinical assessment. *Psychological Assessment, 5*, 264–272.

Evenson, R. C., Altman, H., Sletten, I. W., & Cho, D. W. (1975). Accuracy of actuarial and clinical predictions for length of stay and unauthorized absence. *Diseases of the Nervous System, 36*, 250–252.

Exner, J. E., Jr. (1974). *The Rorschach: A comprehensive system: Vol. 1.* New York: Wiley.

Exner, J. E., Jr. (1978). *The Rorschach: A comprehensive system: Vol. 2. Current research and advanced interpretation.* New York: Wiley.

Exner, J. E., Jr. (1983). Rorschach assessment. In I. B. Weiner (Ed.), *Clinical methods in psychology* (2nd ed., pp. 58–99). New York: Wiley.

Exner, J. E., Jr. (1985). *Semantic interpretation of the Rorschach protocol utilizing the comprehensive system.* Minneapolis, MN: National Computer Systems.

Exner, J. E., Jr. (1986). *The Rorschach: A comprehensive system: Vol. 1. Basic foundations* (2nd. ed.). New York: Wiley.

Exner, J. E., Jr. (1991). *The Rorschach: A comprehensive system: Vol. 2. Interpretation* (2nd. ed.). New York: Wiley.

Exner, J. E., Jr. (1993). *The Rorschach: A comprehensive system: Vol. 1. Basic foundations* (3rd. ed.). New York: Wiley.

Exner, J. E., Jr. (1996). A comment on "The comprehensive system for the Rorschach: A critical examination." *Psychological Science, 7*, 11–13.

Exner, J. E., Jr., & Weiner, I. B. (1982). *The Rorschach: A comprehensive system: Vol. 3. Assessment of children and adolescents.* New York: Wiley.

Exner, J. E., Jr., & Weiner, I. B. (1994). *The Rorschach: A comprehensive system: Vol. 3. Assessment of children and adolescents* (2nd ed.). New York: Wiley.

Eyde, L. D. (1985). Review of the Minnesota Report: Personnel selection system for the MMPI. In J. V. Mitchell (Ed.), *The ninth mental measurements yearbook* (Vol. 2, pp. 1007–1008). Lincoln: University of Nebraska Press.

Falloon, R. H., Boyd, J. L., McGill, C. W., Williamson, M., Razani, A., Moss, H. B., Giulderman, A. M., & Simpson, G. M. (1985). Family management in the prevention of morbidity of schizophrenia: Clinical outcome of a two-year longitudinal study. *Archives of General Psychiatry, 42,* 887–896.

Fals-Stewart, W., & Angarano, K. (1994). Obsessive–compulsive disorder among patients entering substance abuse treatment: Prevalence and accuracy of diagnosis. *Journal of Nervous and Mental Disease, 182,* 715–719.

Falvey, J. E., & Hebert, D. J. (1992). Psychometric study of the Clinical Treatment Planning Simulations (CTPS) for assessing clinical judgment. *Journal of Mental Health Counseling, 14,* 490–507.

Faraone, S. V., & Tsuang, M. T. (1994). Measuring diagnostic accuracy in the absence of a "gold standard." *American Journal of Psychiatry, 151,* 650–657.

Farmer, A. E., & Griffiths, H. (1992). Labelling and illness in primary care: Comparing factors influencing general practitioners' and psychiatrists' decisions regarding patient referral to mental illness services. *Psychological Medicine, 22,* 717–723.

Faust, D., & Guilmette, T. J. (1990). To say it's not so doesn't prove that it isn't: Research on the detection of malingering. Reply to Bigler. *Journal of Consulting and Clinical Psychology, 58,* 248–250.

Faust, D., Guilmette, T. J., Hart, K., Arkes, H. R., Fishburne, F. J., & Davey, L. (1988). Neuropsychologists' training, experience, and judgment accuracy. *Archives of Clinical Neuropsychology, 3,* 145–163.

Faust, D., Hart, K., & Guilmette, T. J. (1988). Pediatric malingering: The capacity of children to fake believable deficits on neuropsychological testing. *Journal of Consulting and Clinical Psychology, 56,* 578–582.

Faust, D., Hart, K., Guilmette, T. J., & Arkes, H. R. (1988). Neuropsychologists' capacity to detect adolescent malingerers. *Professional Psychology, 19,* 508–515.

Faust, D., & Ziskin, J. (1988). The expert witness in psychology and psychiatry. *Science, 241,* 31–35.

Feinblatt, J. A., & Gold, A. R. (1976). Sex roles and the psychiatric referral process. *Sex Roles, 2,* 109–122.

Felton, J. L., & Nelson, R. O. (1984). Inter-assessor agreement on hypothesized controlling variables and treatment proposals. *Behavioral Assessment, 6,* 199–208.

Fennig, S., Bromet, E. J., Jandorf, L., Schwartz, J. E., Lavelle, J., & Ram, R. (1994). Eliciting psychotic symptoms using a semi-structured diagnostic interview: The importance of collateral sources of information in a first-admission sample. *Journal of Nervous and Mental Disease, 181,* 20–26.

Fennig, S., Craig, T. J., Tanenberg-Karant, M., & Bromet, E. J. (1994). Comparison of facility and research diagnoses in first-admission psychotic patients. *American Journal of Psychiatry, 151,* 1423–1429.

Fernando, T., Mellsop, G., Nelson, K., Peace, K., & Wilson, J. (1986). The reliability of Axis V of DSM–III. *American Journal of Psychiatry, 143,* 752–755.

Fernbach, B. E., Winstead, B. A., & Derlega, V. J. (1989). Sex differences in diagnosis and treatment recommendations for antisocial personality and somatization disorders. *Journal of Social and Clinical Psychology, 8,* 238–255.

Filskov, S. B., & Goldstein, S. G. (1974). Diagnostic validity of the Halstead-Reitan neuropsychological battery. *Journal of Consulting and Clinical Psychology, 42,* 382–388.

Finlayson, L. M., & Koocher, G. P. (1991). Professional judgment and child abuse reporting in sexual abuse cases. *Professional Psychology, 22,* 464–472.

Finn, S. E. (1982). Base rates, utilities, and DSM–III: Shortcomings of fixed-rule systems of psychodiagnosis. *Journal of Abnormal Psychology, 91,* 294–302.

Finn, S. E. (1983). Utility-balanced and utility-imbalanced rules: Reply to Widiger. *Journal of Abnormal Psychology, 92,* 499–501.

Finn, S. E., & Kamphuis, J. H. (1995). What a clinician needs to know about base rates. In J. N. Butcher (Ed.), *Clinical personality assessment: Practical approaches* (pp. 224–235). New York: Oxford University Press.

Fisch, H. U., Hammond, K. R., & Joyce, C. R. B. (1982). On evaluating the severity of depression: An experimental study of psychiatrists. *British Journal of Psychiatry, 140,* 378–383.

Fischer, J., Dulaney, D. D., Fazio, R. T., Hudak, M. T., & Zivotofsky, E. (1976). Are social workers sexists? *Social Work, 21,* 428–433.

Fischhoff, B. (1975). Hindsight foresight: The effect of outcome knowledge on judgment under uncertainty. *Journal of Experimental Psychology: Human Perception and Performance, 1,* 288–299.

Fitzgerald, L. F., & Cherpas, C. C. (1985). On the reciprocal relationship between gender and occupation: Rethinking the assumptions concerning masculine career development. *Journal of Vocational Behavior, 27,* 109–122.

Flaum, M., & Andreasen, N. (1995). The reliability of distinguishing primary versus secondary negative symptoms. *Comprehensive Psychiatry, 36,* 421–427.

Flaum, M., Arndt, S., & Andreasen, N. C. (1991). The reliability of "bizarre" delusions. *Comprehensive Psychiatry, 32,* 59–65.

Fleiss, J. L. (1981). *Statistical methods for rates and proportions* (2nd ed.). New York: Wiley.

Fliszar, G. M., & Clopton, J. R. (1995). Attitudes of psychologists in training toward persons with AIDS. *Professional Psychology, 26,* 274–277.

Foon, A. E. (1989). Mediators of clinical judgment: An exploration of the effect of therapists' locus of control on clinical expectations. *Genetic, Social, and General Psychology Monographs, 115,* 245–266.

Ford, C. V., & Sbordone, R. J. (1980). Attitudes of psychiatrists toward elderly patients. *American Journal of Psychiatry, 137,* 571–575.

Ford, M. R., & Widiger, T. A. (1989). Sex bias in the diagnosis of histrionic and antisocial personality disorders. *Journal of Consulting and Clinical Psychology, 57,* 301–305.

Fowler, R. D. (1985). Landmarks in computer-assisted psychological assessment. *Journal of Consulting and Clinical Psychology, 53,* 748–759.

Frame, R. E., Clarizio, H. F., Porter, A., & Vinsonhaler, J. R. (1982). Interclinician agreement and bias in school psychologists' diagnostic and treatment recommendations for a learning disabled child. *Psychology in the Schools, 19,* 319–327.

Frances, A., & Widiger, T. A. (1986). The classification of personality disorders: An overview of problems and solutions. In A. Frances & R. Hales (Eds.), *Psychiatry update: American Psychiatric Association annual review, 5,* 240–257.

Franklin, D. L. (1985). Differential clinical assessments: The influence of class and race. *Social Service Review, 59,* 44–61.

Freud, S. (1933). *New introductory lectures on psychoanalysis.* New York: Norton.

Frick, P. J., Silverthorn, P., & Evans, C. (1994). Assessment of childhood anxiety using structured interviews: Patterns of agreement among informants and association with maternal anxiety. *Psychological Assessment, 6,* 372–379.

Friedlander, M. L., & Phillips, S. D. (1984). Preventing anchoring errors in clinical judgment. *Journal of Consulting and Clinical Psychology, 52,* 366–371.

Friedlander, M. L., & Stockman, S. J. (1983). Anchoring and publicity effects in clinical judgment. *Journal of Clinical Psychology, 39,* 637–643.

Fromm-Reichmann, F. (1948). Notes on the development of treatment of schizophrenia by psychoanalytic psychotherapy. *Psychiatry, 11,* 263–273.

Fuller, A. K., & Blashfield, R. K. (1989). Masochistic personality disorder: A prototype analysis of diagnosis and sex bias. *Journal of Nervous and Mental Disease, 177,* 168–172.

Funder, D. C. (1987). Errors and mistakes: Evaluating the accuracy of social judgment. *Psychological Bulletin, 101,* 75–90.

Funder, D. C. (1995). On the accuracy of personality judgment: A realistic approach. *Psychological Review, 102,* 652–670.

Funtowicz, M. N., & Widiger, T. A. (1995). Sex bias in the diagnosis of personality disorders: A different approach. *Journal of Psychopathology and Behavioral Assessment, 17,* 145–165.

Gadol, I. (1969). The incremental and predictive validity of the Rorschach test in personality assessments of normal, neurotic, and psychotic subjects. *Dissertation Abstracts, 29,* (3482–B). (University Microfilms No. 69–4469).

Gambara, H., & Leon, O. G. (1996). Evidence of data and confidence in clinical judgments. *European Journal of Psychological Assessment, 12,* 193–201.

Gambrill, E. (1990). *Critical thinking in clinical practice: Improving the accuracy of judgments and decisions about clients.* San Francisco: Jossey-Bass.

Ganzach, Y. (1995). Nonlinear models of clinical judgment: Meehl's data revisited. *Psychological Bulletin, 118*, 422–429.

Garb, H. N. (1983). A conjoint measurement analysis of clinical predictions. *Journal of Clinical Psychology, 39*, 295–301.

Garb, H. N. (1984). The incremental validity of information used in personality assessment. *Clinical Psychology Review, 4*, 641–655.

Garb, H. N. (1989). Clinical judgment, clinical training, and professional experience. *Psychological Bulletin, 105*, 387–396.

Garb, H. N. (1994). Toward a second generation of statistical prediction rules in psychodiagnosis and personality assessment. *Computers in Human Behavior, 10*, 377–394.

Garb, H. N. (1995). Using computers to make judgments: Correlations among predictors and the comparison of linear and configural models. *Computers in Human Behavior, 11*, 313–324.

Garb, H. N. (1996a). Taxometrics and the revision of diagnostic criteria. *American Psychologist, 51*, 553–554.

Garb, H. N. (1996b). The representativeness and past-behavior heuristics in clinical judgment. *Professional Psychology: Research and Practice, 27*, 272–277.

Garb, H. N. (1997). Race bias, social class bias, and gender bias in clinical judgment. *Clinical Psychology: Science and Practice, 4*, 99–120.

Garb, H. N., & Florio, C. M. (1997). *Overdiagnosis of neurological impairment in the elderly*. Manuscript submitted for publication.

Garb, H. N., & Schramke, C. J. (1996). Judgment research and neuropsychological assessment: A narrative review and meta-analyses. *Psychological Bulletin, 120*, 140–153.

Gardner, W., Lidz, C. W., Mulvey, E. P., & Shaw, E. C. (1996). Clinical versus actuarial predictions of violence by patients with mental illnesses. *Journal of Consulting and Clinical Psychology, 64*, 602–609.

Garfinkle, E. M., & Morin, S. F. (1978). Psychologists' attitudes toward homosexual psychotherapy clients. *Journal of Social Issues, 34*, 101–112.

Garner, A. M., & Smith, G. M. (1976). An experimental videotape technique for evaluating trainee approaches to clinical judging. *Journal of Consulting and Clinical Psychology, 44*, 945–950.

Garvey, M. J., & Tuason, V. B. (1980). Mania misdiagnosed as schizophrenia. *Journal of Clinical Psychiatry, 41*, 75–78.

Gaudette, M. D. (1992). Clinical decision making in neuropsychology: Bootstrapping the neuropsychologist utilizing Brunswik's lens model (Doctoral dissertation, Indiana University of Pennsylvania, 1992). *Dissertation Abstracts International, 53*, 2059B.

Gauron, E. F., & Dickinson, J. K. (1966). Diagnostic decision making in psychiatry. *Archives of General Psychiatry, 14*, 225–232.

Gauron, E. F., & Dickinson, J. K. (1969). The influence of seeing the patient first on diagnostic decision making in psychiatry. *American Journal of Psychiatry, 126*, 199–205.

Gdowski, C. L., Lachar, D., & Butkus, M. (1980). A methodological consideration in the construction of actuarial interpretation systems. *Journal of Personality Assessment, 44,* 427–432.

Geertsma, R. H., & Stoller, R. J. (1960). The objective assessment of clinical judgment in psychiatry. *Archives of General Psychiatry, 2,* 278–285.

Gerardi, R. J., Keane, T. M., Calhoon, B. J., & Klauminzer, G. W. (1994). An *in vivo* assessment of physiological arousal in posttraumatic stress disorder. *Journal of Abnormal Psychology, 103,* 825–827.

Giannetti, R. A., Johnson, J. H., Klingler, D. E., & Williams, T. A. (1978). Comparison of linear and configural MMPI diagnostic methods with an uncontaminated criterion. *Journal of Consulting and Clinical Psychology, 46,* 1046–1052.

Giedt, F. H. (1955). Comparison of visual, content, and auditory cues in interviewing. *Journal of Consulting Psychology, 19,* 407–416.

Gilbert, D. T., & Malone, P. S. (1995). The correspondence bias. *Psychological Bulletin, 117,* 21–38.

Gleaves, D. H. (1996). The sociocognitive model of dissociative identity disorder: A reexamination of the evidence. *Psychological Bulletin, 120,* 42–59.

Goethe, J. W., & Ahmadi, K. S. (1991). Comparison of Diagnostic Interview Schedule to psychiatrist diagnoses of alcohol use disorder in psychiatric inpatients. *American Journal of Drug and Alcohol Abuse, 17,* 61–69.

Goldberg, L. R. (1959). The effectiveness of clinicians' judgments: The diagnosis of organic brain damage from the Bender-Gestalt test. *Journal of Consulting Psychology, 23,* 25–33.

Goldberg, L. R. (1965). Diagnosticians versus diagnostic signs: The diagnosis of psychosis versus neurosis from the MMPI. *Psychological Monographs, 79* (9, Whole No. 602).

Goldberg, L. R. (1968). Simple models or simple processes? Some research on clinical judgments. *American Psychologist, 23,* 483–496.

Goldberg, L. R. (1969). The search for configural relationships in personality assessment: The diagnosis of psychosis vs. neurosis from the MMPI. *Multivariate Behavioral Research, 4,* 523–536.

Goldberg, L. R. (1970). Man versus model of man: A rationale plus evidence for a method of improving on clinical inferences. *Psychological Bulletin, 73,* 422–432.

Goldberg, L. R. (1971). Five models of clinical judgment: An empirical comparison between linear and nonlinear representations of the human inference process. *Organizational Behavior and Human Performance, 6,* 458–479.

Goldberg, L. R. (1974). Objective diagnostic tests and measures. *Annual Review of Psychology, 25,* 343–366.

Goldberg, L. R., & Werts, C. E. (1966). The reliability of clinicians' judgments: A multitrait-multimethod approach. *Journal of Consulting Psychology, 30,* 199–206.

Goldberg, S. C., Tilley, D. H., Friedel, R. O., Hamer, R. M., Ban, T. A., Brockett, C.,

Bale, P., & Stephens, V. (1988). Who benefits from tricyclic antidepressants: A survey. *Journal of Clinical Psychiatry, 49,* 224–228.

Golden, M. (1964). Some effects of combining psychological tests on clinical inferences. *Journal of Consulting Psychology, 28,* 440–446.

Golden, R. R., & Meehl, P. E. (1979). Detection of the schizoid taxon with MMPI indicators. *Journal of Abnormal Psychology, 88,* 217–233.

Golding, S. L., & Rorer, L. G. (1972). Illusory correlation and subjective judgment. *Journal of Abnormal Psychology, 80,* 249–260.

Goldstein, G., & Hersen, M. (1984). Historical perspectives. In G. Goldstein & M. Hersen (Eds.), *Handbook of psychological assessment* (pp. 3–15). New York: Pergamon Press.

Goldstein, R. B., Black, D. W., Nasrallah, M. A., & Winokur, G. (1991). The prediction of suicide. *Archives of General Psychiatry, 48,* 418–422.

Goldstein, S. G., Deysach, R. E., & Kleinknecht, R. A. (1973). Effect of experience and amount of information on identification of cerebral impairment. *Journal of Consulting and Clinical Psychology, 41,* 30–34.

Gottesman, I. I., McGuffin, P., & Farmer, A. E. (1987). Clinical genetics as clues to the "real" genetics of schizophrenia (A decade of modest gains while playing for time). *Schizophrenia Bulletin, 13,* 23–47.

Grace, G. D., & Stiers, W. (1989). Changes in VA diagnosis of schizophrenic and affective disorders after DSM–III. *Hospital and Community Psychiatry, 40,* 277–279.

Graham, J. R. (1967). A Q-sort study of the accuracy of clinical descriptions based on the MMPI. *Journal of Psychiatric Research, 5,* 297–305.

Graham, J. R. (1971). Feedback and accuracy of clinical judgments from the MMPI. *Journal of Consulting and Clinical Psychology, 36,* 286–291.

Grant, I., Heaton, R. K., McSweeny, J., Adams, K. M., & Timms, R. M. (1982). Neuropsychologic findings in hypoxemic chronic obstructive pulmonary disease. *Archives of Internal Medicine, 142,* 1470–1476.

Grant, I., Mohns, L., Miller, M., & Reitan, R. (1976). A neuropsychological study of polydrug users. *Archives of General Psychiatry, 33,* 973–978.

Grant, M. Q., Ives, V., & Ranzoni, J. H. (1952). Reliability and validity of judges' ratings of adjustment on the Rorschach. *Psychological Monographs, 66* (2, Whole No. 334).

Grebstein, L. (1963). Relative accuracy of actuarial prediction, experienced clinicians, and graduate students in a clinical judgment task. *Journal of Consulting Psychology, 37,* 127–132.

Green, B. F., Jr. (1968). Descriptions and explanations: A comment on papers by Hoffman and Edwards. In B. Kleinmuntz (Ed.), *Formal representation of human judgment* (pp. 91–98). New York: Wiley.

Green, J. P., & McNamara, J. R. (1994). Reasoning abilities in Psy.D. and Ph.D. clinical graduate students: A preliminary study. *Journal of Clinical Psychology, 50,* 965–972.

Green, S. L., & Hansen, J. C. (1989). Ethical dilemmas faced by family therapists. *Journal of Marital and Family Therapy, 15,* 149–158.

Greenbaum, P. E., Dedrick, R. F., Prange, M. E., & Friedman, R. M. (1994). Parent, teacher, and child ratings of problem behaviors of youngsters with serious emotional disturbances. *Psychological Assessment, 6,* 141–148.

Grigg, A. E. (1958). Experience of clinicians, and speech characteristics and statements of clients as variables in clinical judgment. *Journal of Consulting Psychology, 22,* 315–319.

Griswold, P. M., & Dana, R. H. (1970). Feedback and experience effects on psychological reports and predictions of behavior. *Journal of Clinical Psychology, 26,* 439–442.

Grove, W. M. (1985). Bootstrapping diagnoses using Bayes's Theorem: It's not worth the trouble. *Journal of Consulting and Clinical Psychology, 53,* 261–263.

Grove, W. M. (1987). The reliability of psychiatric diagnosis. In C. G. Last & M. Hersen (Eds.), *Issues in diagnostic research* (pp. 99–119). New York: Plenum Press.

Grove, W. M., & Andreasen, N. C. (1986). Multivariate statistical analysis in psychopathology. In T. Millon & G. L. Klerman (Eds.), *Contemporary directions in psychopathology* (pp. 347–362). New York: Guilford.

Grove, W. M., & Andreasen, N. C. (1989). Quantitative and qualitative distinctions between psychiatric disorders. In L. N. Robins & J. E. Barrett (Eds.), *The validity of psychiatric diagnosis* (pp. 127–141). New York: Raven Press.

Grove, W. M., Andreasen, N. C., McDonald-Scott, P., Keller, M. B., & Shapiro, R. W. (1981). Reliability studies of psychiatric diagnosis. *Archives of General Psychiatry, 38,* 408–413.

Grove, W. M., Andreasen, N. C., Young, M., Endicott, J., Keller, M. B., Hirschfeld, R. M. A., & Reich, T. (1987). Isolation and characterization of a nuclear depressive syndrome. *Psychological Medicine, 17,* 471–484.

Grove, W. M., Lebow, B. S., Clementz, B. A., Cerri, A., Medus, C., & Iacono, W. G. (1991). Familial prevalence and coaggregation of schizotypy indicators: A multitrait family study. *Journal of Abnormal Psychology, 100,* 115–121.

Guarendi, R. N. (1979). Effects of information source and case picture on clinical judgments of children. *Dissertation Abstracts International, 39,* 4579-B. (University microfilms No. 79–4800).

Guastello, S. J., & Rieke, M. L. (1990). The Barnum effect and validity of computer-based test interpretations: The human resource development report. *Psychological Assessment, 2,* 186–190.

Gustafson, D. H., Greist, J. H., Stauss, F. F., Erdman, H., & Laughren, T. (1977). A probabilistic system for identifying suicide attemptors. *Computers and Biomedical Research, 10,* 83–89.

Haas, L. J., Malouf, J. L., & Mayerson, N. H. (1986). Ethical dilemmas in psychological practice: Results of a national survey. *Professional Psychology: Research and Practice, 17,* 316–321.

Haas, L. J., Malouf, J. L., & Mayerson, N. H. (1988). Personal and professional characteristics as factors in psychologists' ethical decision making. *Professional Psychology, 19,* 35–42.

Haase, W. (1964). The role of socioeconomic class in examiner bias. In F. Riessman, J. Cohen, & A. Pearl (Eds.), *Mental health of the poor* (pp. 241–247). New York: Free Press.

Haier, R. J., Rosenthal, D., & Wender, P. H. (1978). MMPI assessment of psychopathology in the adopted-away offspring of schizophrenics. *Archives of General Psychiatry, 35,* 171–175.

Halbower, C. C. (1955). *A comparison of actuarial versus clinical prediction to classes discriminated by the MMPI.* Unpublished doctoral dissertation, University of Minnesota, Minneapolis.

Hall, G. C. N. (1988). Criminal behavior as a function of clinical and actuarial variables in a sexual offender population. *Journal of Consulting and Clinical Psychology, 56,* 773–775.

Halstead, W. C. (1947). *Brain and intelligence.* Chicago: University of Chicago Press.

Hamilton, M. (1967). Development of a rating scale for primary depressive illness. *British Journal of Social and Clinical Psychology, 6,* 278–296.

Hamilton, S., Rothbart, M., & Dawes, R. M. (1986). Sex bias, diagnosis, and *DSM-III. Sex Roles, 15,* 269–274.

Hamlin, R. (1934). Predictability of institutional adjustment of reformatory inmates. *Journal of Juvenile Research, 18,* 179–184.

Hammond, K. R. (1955). Probabilistic functioning and the clinical method. *Psychological Review, 62,* 255–262.

Hammond, K. R., Hursch, C. J., & Todd, F. J. (1964). Analyzing the components of clinical inference. *Psychological Review, 71,* 438–456.

Hampton, R. L., & Newberger, E. H. (1985). Child abuse incidence and reporting by hospitals: Significance of severity, class, and race. *American Journal of Public Health, 75,* 56–60.

Hannaford, A. E., Simon, J., & Ellis, D. (1975). Criteria for special class placement of the mildly retarded—multidisciplinary comparison. *Mental Retardation, 13,* 7–10.

Hansen, F. J., & Reekie, L. (1990). Sex differences in clinical judgments of male and female therapists. *Sex Roles, 23,* 51–64.

Hansen, M., Harway, M., & Cervantes, N. (1991). Therapists' perceptions of severity in cases of family violence. *Violence and Victims, 6,* 225–235.

Harari, O., & Hosey, K. R. (1981). Attributional biases among clinicians and nonclinicians. *Journal of Clinical Psychology, 37,* 445–450.

Harding, C. M., Zubin, J., & Strauss, J. S. (1987). Chronicity in schizophrenia: Fact, partial fact, or artifact? *Hospital and Community Psychiatry, 38,* 477–486.

Hardy, D. M., & Johnson, M. E. (1992). Influence of therapist gender and client gender, socioeconomic status and alcoholic status on clinical judgments. *Journal of Alcohol and Drug Education, 37,* 94–102.

Hare, R. D. (1978). Psychopathy and electrodermal responses to nonsignal stimulation. *Biological Psychology, 6,* 237–246.

Hare, R. D., Frazelle, J., & Cox, D. N. (1978). Psychopathy and physiological responses to threat of an aversive stimulus. *Psychophysiology, 15,* 165–172.

Hart, E. L., Lahey, B. B., Loeber, R., & Hanson, K. S. (1994). Criterion validity of informants in the diagnosis of disruptive behavior disorders in children: A preliminary study. *Journal of Consulting and Clinical Psychology, 62,* 410–414.

Haverkamp, B. E. (1993). Confirmatory bias in hypothesis testing for client-identified and counselor self-generated hypotheses. *Journal of Counseling Psychology, 40,* 303–315.

Hawkins, S. A., & Hastie, R. (1990). Hindsight: Biased judgments of past events after the outcomes are known. *Psychological Bulletin, 107,* 311–327.

Hay, W. M., Hay, L. R., Angle, H. V., & Nelson, R. O. (1979). The reliability of problem identification in the behavioral interview. *Behavioral Assessment, 1,* 107–118.

Hayden, D. C. (1987). Counselor and client responses to hypothesis testing strategies. *Journal of Counseling Psychology, 34,* 149–156.

Hayes, J. A., & Mitchell, J. C. (1994). Mental health professionals' skepticism about multiple personality disorder. *Professional Psychology, 25,* 410–415.

Hayes, K. E., & Wolleat, P. L. (1978). Effects of sex in judgments of a simulated counseling interview. *Journal of Counseling Psychology, 25,* 164–168.

Hayes, S. C., Follette, V. M., Dawes, R. M., & Grady, K. E. (Eds.). (1995). *Scientific standards of psychological practice: Issues and recommendations.* Reno, NV: Context Press.

Haynes, S. N. (1993). Treatment implications of psychological assessment. *Psychological Assessment, 5,* 251–253.

Haynes, S. N., Spain, E. H., & Oliveira, J. (1993). Identifying causal relationships in clinical assessment. *Psychological Assessment, 5,* 281–291.

Heaton, R. K. (1992). *Comprehensive norms for an expanded Halstead-Reitan battery: A supplement for the WAIS-R.* Odessa, FL: Psychological Assessment Resources.

Heaton, R. K., Grant, I., Anthony, W. Z., & Lehman, R. A. W. (1981). A comparison of clinical and automated interpretation of the Halstead-Reitan Battery. *Journal of Clinical Neuropsychology, 3,* 121–141.

Heaton, R. K., Grant, I., & Matthews, C. G. (1986). Differences in neuropsychological test performance associated with age, education and sex. In I. Grant & K. Adams (Eds.), *Neuropsychological assessment of neuropsychiatric disorders* (pp. 100–120). New York: Oxford University Press.

Heaton, R. K., Grant, I., & Matthews, C. G. (1991). *Comprehensive norms for an expanded Halstead-Reitan battery: Demographic corrections, research findings, and clinical applications.* Odessa, FL: Psychological Assessment Resources.

Heaton, R. K., Smith, H. H., Jr., Lehman, R. A. W., & Vogt, A. T. (1978). Prospects for faking believable deficits on neuropsychological testing. *Journal of Consulting and Clinical Psychology, 46,* 892–900.

Hecker, L. L., Trepper, T. S., Wetchler, J. L., & Fontaine, K. L. (1995). The influence of therapist values, religiosity and gender in the initial assessment of sexual addiction by family therapists. *The American Journal of Family Therapy, 23,* 261–272.

Hedlund, J. L., Morgan, D. W., & Master, F. D. (1972). The Mayo Clinic automated MMPI program: Cross-validation with psychiatric patients in an army hospital. *Journal of Clinical Psychology, 28,* 505–510.

Henry, B., Moffitt, T. E., Caspi, A., Langley, J., & Silva, P. A. (1994). On the "Remembrance of Things Past": A longitudinal evaluation of the retrospective method. *Psychological Assessment, 6,* 92–101.

Henry, K. A., & Cohen, C. I. (1983). The role of labeling processes in diagnosing borderline personality disorder. *American Journal of Psychiatry, 140,* 1527–1529.

Herbert, D. L., Nelson, R. O., & Herbert, J. D. (1988). Effects of psychodiagnostic labels, depression severity, and instructions on assessment. *Professional Psychology, 19,* 496–502.

Herkov, M. J., & Blashfield, R. K. (1995). Clinician diagnoses of personality disorders: Evidence of a hierarchical structure. *Journal of Personality Assessment, 65,* 313–321.

Hermann, R. C., Dorwart, R. A., Hoover, C. W., & Brody, J. (1995). Variation in ECT use in the United States. *American Journal of Psychiatry, 152,* 869–875.

Herrnstein, R. J., & Murray, C. (1994). *The bell curve: Intelligence and class structure in American life.* New York: Free Press.

Heumann, K. A., & Morey, L. C. (1990). Reliability of categorical and dimensional judgments of personality disorder. *American Journal of Psychiatry, 147,* 498–500.

Hiler, E. W., & Nesvig, D. (1965). An evaluation of criteria used by clinicians to infer pathology from figure drawings. *Journal of Consulting Psychology, 29,* 520–529.

Hill, C. E., Tanney, M. F., Leonard, M. M., & Reiss, J. A. (1977). Counselor reactions to female clients: Type of problem, age of client, and sex of counselor. *Journal of Counseling Psychology, 24,* 60–65.

Hillman, J. L., Stricker, G., & Zweig, R. A. (1997). Clinical psychologists' judgments of older adult patients with character pathology: Implications for practice. *Professional Psychology: Research and Practice, 28,* 179–183.

Hirschfeld, R., Spitzer, R. L., & Miller, R. G. (1974). Computer diagnosis in psychiatry: A Bayes approach. *Journal of Nervous and Mental Disease, 158,* 399–407.

Hobfoll, S. E., & Penner, L. A. (1978). Effect of physical attractiveness on therapists' initial judgments of a person's self-concept. *Journal of Consulting and Clinical Psychology, 46,* 200–201.

Hoffman, P. J. (1960). The paramorphic representation of clinical judgment. *Psychological Bulletin, 57,* 116–131.

Hoffman, P. J. (1987). *Expert87: Artificial intelligence and decision-making support for the desk-top microcomputer* [Computer program]. Los Altos, CA: Magic7 Software.

Hoffman, P. J., Slovic, P., & Rorer, L. G. (1968). An analysis-of-variance model for the assessment of configural cue utilization in clinical judgment. *Psychological Bulletin, 69,* 338–349.

Hogan, R., & Nicholson, R. A. (1988). The meaning of personality test scores. *American Psychologist, 43,* 621–626.

Hogarty, G. E., Anderson, C. M., Reiss, D. J., Kornblith, S. J., Greenwald, D. P., Javna, C. D., & Madonia, M. J. (1986). Family psychoeducation, social skills training, and maintenance chemotherapy in the aftercare treatment of schizophrenia: I. One-year effects of a controlled study on relapse and expressed emotion. *Archives of General Psychiatry, 43,* 633–642.

Holland, T. R., & Watson, C. G. (1980). Multivariate analysis of WAIS–MMPI relationships among brain-damaged, schizophrenic, neurotic, and alcoholic patients. *Journal of Clinical Psychology, 36,* 352–359.

Hollingshead, A. B., & Redlich, F. C. (1958). *Social class and mental illness: A community study.* New York: Wiley.

Holmes, C. B., & Howard, M. E. (1980). Recognition of suicide lethality factors by physicians, mental health professionals, ministers, and college students. *Journal of Consulting and Clinical Psychology, 48,* 383–387.

Holsopple, J. Q., & Phelan, J. G. (1954). The skills of clinicians in analysis of projective tests. *Journal of Clinical Psychology, 10,* 307–320.

Holt, R. R. (1958). Clinical and statistical prediction: A reformulation and some new data. *Journal of Abnormal and Social Psychology, 56,* 1–12.

Holt, R. R. (1970). Yet another look at clinical and statistical prediction: Or, is clinical psychology worthwhile? *American Psychologist, 25,* 337–349.

Holt, R. R., & Luborsky, L. (1958). *Personality patterns of psychiatrists* (Vol. 1). New York: Basic Books.

Honigfeld, G., Gillis, R. D., & Klett, C. J. (1966). NOSIE-30: A treatment sensitive behavior scale. *Psychological Reports, 19,* 180–182.

Hooley, J. M., Rosen, L. R., & Richters, J. E. (1995). Expressed emotion: Toward clarification of a critical construct. In G. A. Miller (Ed.), *The behavioral high-risk paradigm in psychopathology* (pp. 88–120). New York: Springer-Verlag.

Horner, T. J., Guyer, M. J., & Kalter, N. M. (1992). Prediction, prevention, and clinical expertise in child custody cases in which allegations of child sexual abuse have been made: III. Studies of expert opinion formation. *Family Law Quarterly, 26,* 141–170.

Horowitz, L. M., Inouye, D., & Siegelman, E. Y. (1979). On averaging judges' ratings to increase their correlation with an external criterion. *Journal of Consulting and Clinical Psychology, 47,* 453–458.

Horowitz, L. M., Wright, J. C., Lowenstein, E., & Parad, H. W. (1981). The prototype as a construct in abnormal psychology: 1. A method for deriving prototypes. *Journal of Abnormal Psychology, 90,* 568–574.

Horowitz, M. J. (1962). A study of clinicians' judgments from projective test protocols. *Journal of Consulting Psychology, 26,* 251–256.

Houts, A. C., & Graham, K. (1986). Can religion make you crazy? Impact of client and therapist religious values on clinical judgments. *Journal of Consulting and Clinical Psychology, 54,* 267–271.

Howard, K. I. (1962). The convergent and discriminant validation of ipsative ratings from three projective instruments. *Journal of Clinical Psychology, 18,* 183–188.

Howard, K. I. (1963). Ratings of projective test protocols as a function of degree of inference. *Educational and Psychological Measurement, 23,* 267–275.

Howe, A. C., Herzberger, S., & Tennen, H. (1988). The influence of personal history of abuse and gender on clinicians' judgments of child abuse. *Journal of Family Violence, 3,* 105–119.

Hsu, L. M. (1988). Fixed versus flexible MMPI diagnostic rules. *Journal of Consulting and Clinical Psychology, 56,* 458–462.

Huebner, E. S. (1985). The influence of rural, suburban, and urban student background and school setting upon psychoeducational decisions. *School Psychology Review, 14,* 239–241.

Huebner, E. S. (1987a). Teachers' special education decisions: Does test information make a difference? *Journal of Educational Research, 80,* 202–205.

Huebner, E. S. (1987b). The effects of type of referral information and test data on psychoeducational decisions. *School Psychology Review, 16,* 382–390.

Huebner, E. S. (1990). The generalizability of the confirmation bias among school psychologists. *School Psychology International, 11,* 281–286.

Huebner, E. S., & Cummings, J. A. (1985). The impact of sociocultural background and assessment data upon school psychologists' decisions. *Journal of School Psychology, 23,* 157–166.

Huebner, E. S., & Cummings, J. A. (1986). Influence of race and test data ambiguity upon school psychologists' decisions. *School Psychology Review, 15,* 410–417.

Hurley, A. D., & Sovner, R. (1995). Six cases of patients with mental retardation who have antisocial personality disorder. *Psychiatric Services, 46,* 828–831.

Hyer, L., Boudewyns, P. A., O'Leary, W. C., & Harrison, W. R. (1987). Key determinants of the MMPI-PTSD subscale: Treatment considerations. *Journal of Clinical Psychology, 43,* 337–340.

Hyer, L., O'Leary, W. C., Saucer, R. T., Blount, J., Harrison, W. R., & Boudewyns, P. A. (1986). Inpatient diagnosis of posttraumatic personality disorder. *Journal of Consulting and Clinical Psychology, 54,* 698–702.

Hyman, I., Husband, T., & Billings, F. (1995). False memories of childhood experiences. *Applied Cognitive Psychology, 9,* 181–197.

Iacono, W. G. (1991). Psychophysiological assessment of psychopathology. *Psychological Assessment, 3,* 309–320.

Ivey, D. C. (1995). Family history, parenting attitudes, gender roles, and clinician perceptions of family and family member functioning: Factors related to gender inequitable practice. *The American Journal of Family Therapy, 23,* 213–226.

Jaccard, J., & Wan, C. K. (1995). Measurement error in the analysis of interaction effects between continuous predictors using multiple regression: Multiple indicator and structural equation approaches. *Psychological Bulletin, 117,* 348–357.

Jackson, H., & Nuttall, R. (1993). Clinician responses to sexual abuse allegations. *Child Abuse & Neglect, 17,* 127–143.

Jackson, H., & Nuttall, R. (1994). Effects of gender, age, and history of abuse on social workers' judgments of sexual abuse allegations. *Social Work Research, 18,* 105–113.

Jacobson, A., & Herald, C. (1990). The relevance of childhood sexual abuse to adult psychiatric inpatient care. *Hospital and Community Psychiatry, 41,* 154–158.

Jacobson, A., Koehler, J. E., & Jones-Brown, C. (1987). The failure of routine assessment to detect histories of assault experienced by psychiatric patients. *Hospitals and Community Psychiatry, 38,* 386–389.

Jacobson, J. W., Mulick, J. A., & Schwartz, A. A. (1995). A history of facilitated communication: Science, pseudoscience, and antiscience. *American Psychologist, 50,* 750–765.

Jacobson, J. W., Mulick, J. A., & Schwartz, A. A. (1996). If a tree falls in the woods. . . . *American Psychologist, 51,* 988–989.

James, J. W., & Haley, W. E. (1995). Age and health bias in practicing clinical psychologists. *Psychology and Aging, 10,* 610–616.

Jampala, V. C., Sierles, F. S., & Taylor, M. A. (1988). The use of *DSM–III* in the United States: A case of not going by the book. *Comprehensive Psychiatry, 29,* 39–47.

Janofsky, J. S., Spears, S., & Neubauer, D. N. (1988). Psychiatrists' accuracy in predicting violent behavior on an inpatient unit. *Hospital and Community Psychiatry, 39,* 1090–1094.

Janzen, W. B., & Coe, W. C. (1975). Clinical and sign prediction: The Draw-a-Person and female homosexuality. *Journal of Clinical Psychology, 31,* 757–765.

Jenkins-Hall, K., & Sacco, W. P. (1991). Effect of client race and depression on evaluations by White therapists. *Journal of Social and Clinical Psychology, 10,* 322–333.

John, O. P., Chaplin, W. F., & Goldberg, L. R. (1988). Conceptions of states and traits: Dimensional attributes with ideals as prototypes. *Journal of Personality and Social Psychology, 54,* 541–557.

Johnston, R., & McNeal, B. F. (1967). Statistical versus clinical prediction: Length of neuropsychiatric hospital stay. *Journal of Abnormal Psychology, 72,* 335–340.

Jones, N. F. (1959). The validity of clinical judgments of schizophrenic pathology based on verbal responses to intelligence test items. *Journal of Clinical Psychology, 15,* 396–400.

Jones, N. F., & Kahn, M. W. (1966). Dimensions and consistency of clinical judgment as related to the judges' level of training. *Journal of Nervous and Mental Disease, 142,* 19–24.

Jordan, J. S., Harvey, J. H., & Weary, G. (1988). Attributional biases in clinical decision making. In D. C. Turk & P. Salovey (Eds.), *Reasoning, inference, and judgment in clinical psychology* (pp. 90–106). New York: Free Press.

Joyce, P. R. (1984). Age of onset in bipolar affective disorder and misdiagnosis as schizophrenia. *Psychological Medicine, 14*, 145–149.

Kahill, S. (1984). Human figure drawing in adults: An update of the empirical evidence, 1967–1982. *Canadian Psychology, 25*, 269–292.

Kahn, M. W., Fox, H., & Rhode, R. (1988). Detecting faking on the Rorschach: Computer versus expert clinical judgment. *Journal of Personality Assessment, 52*, 516–523.

Kahneman, D., Slovic, P., & Tversky, A. (Eds.). (1982). *Judgment under uncertainty: Heuristics and biases.* New York: Cambridge University Press.

Kalichman, S. C., & Brosig, C. L. (1992). The effects of statutory requirements on child maltreatment reporting: A comparison of two state laws. *American Journal of Orthopsychiatry, 62*, 284–296.

Kalichman, S. C., & Craig, M. E. (1991). Professional psychologists' decisions to report suspected child abuse: Clinician and situation influences. *Professional Psychology, 22*, 84–89.

Kalichman, S. C., Craig, M. E., & Follingstad, D. R. (1989). Factors influencing the reporting of father–child sexual abuse: Study of licensed practicing psychologists. *Professional Psychology, 20*, 84–89.

Kane, R. L., Parsons, O. A., Goldstein, G., & Moses, J. A., Jr. (1987). Diagnostic accuracy of the Halstead-Reitan and Luria Nebraska neuropsychological batteries: Performance of clinical raters. *Journal of Consulting and Clinical Psychology, 55*, 783–784.

Kane, R. L., Sweet, J. J., Golden, C. J., Parsons, O. A., & Moses, J. A., Jr. (1981). Comparative diagnostic accuracy of the Halstead-Reitan and standardized Luria-Nebraska neuropsychological batteries in a mixed psychiatric and brain-damaged population. *Journal of Consulting and Clinical Psychology, 49*, 484–485.

Kaplan, H. (1983). A woman's view of *DSM–III*. *American Psychologist, 38*, 786–792.

Kaplan, H. I., Sadock, B. J., & Grebb, J. A. (1994). *Kaplan & Sadock's synopsis of psychiatry: Behavioral sciences clinical psychiatry* (7th ed.). Baltimore: Williams & Wilkins.

Kareken, D. A., & Williams, J. M. (1994). Human judgment and estimation of premorbid intellectual function. *Psychological Assessment, 6*, 83–91.

Karson, S., & Freud, S. L. (1956). Predicting diagnoses with the MMPI. *Journal of Clinical Psychology, 12*, 376–379.

Katz, M. M., Cole, J. O., & Lowery, H. (1969). Studies of the diagnostic process: The influence of symptom perception, past experience, and ethnic background on diagnostic decisions. *American Journal of Psychiatry, 125*, 937–947.

Kayne, N. T., & Alloy, L. B. (1988). Clinician and patient as aberrant actuaries: Expectation-based distortions in assessment of covariation. In L. Y. Abramson

(Ed.), *Social cognition and clinical psychology: A synthesis* (pp. 295–365). New York: Guilford Press.

Kazdin, A. (1992). *Research design in clinical psychology.* New York: Macmillan.

Keller, M. B., Klerman, G. L., Lavori, P. W., Fawcett, J. A., Coryell, W., & Endicott, J. (1982). Treatment received by depressed patients. *Journal of the American Medical Association, 248,* 1848–1855.

Keller, M. B., Lavori, P. W., Klerman, G. L., Andreasen, N. C., Endicott, J., Coryell, W., Fawcett, J., Rice, J. P., & Hirschfeld, R. M. A. (1986). Low levels and lack of predictors of somatotherapy and psychotherapy received by depressed patients. *Archives of General Psychiatry, 43,* 458–466.

Kelly, E. L., & Fiske, D. W. (1951). *The prediction of performance in clinical psychology.* Ann Arbor: University of Michigan Press.

Kelly, G. A. (1963). *A theory of personality.* New York: Norton.

Kendall-Tackett, K. A. (1992). Professionals' standards of "normal" behavior with anatomical dolls and factors that influence these standards. *Child Abuse & Neglect, 16,* 727–732.

Kendell, R. E. (1973). Psychiatric diagnoses: A study of how they are made. *British Journal of Psychiatry, 122,* 437–445.

Kendell, R. E., Cooper, J. E., Gourlay, A. J., Copeland, J. R. M., Sharpe, L., & Gurland, B. J. (1971). The diagnostic criteria of American and British psychiatrists. *Archives of General Psychiatry, 25,* 123–130.

Kennel, R. G., & Agresti, A. A. (1995). Effects of gender and age on psychologists' reporting of child sexual abuse. *Professional Psychology, 26,* 612–615.

Kenrick, D. T., & Funder, D. C. (1988). Profiting from controversy: Lessons from the person–situation debate. *American Psychologist, 43,* 23–34.

Klassen, D., & O'Connor, W. A. (1989). Assessing the risk of violence in released mental patients: A cross-validation study. *Psychological Assessment, 1,* 75–81.

Kleinmuntz, B. (1963). MMPI decision rules for the identification of college maladjustment: A digital computer approach. *Psychological Monographs, 77* (14, Whole No. 577).

Kleinmuntz, B. (1967). Sign and seer: Another example. *Journal of Abnormal Psychology, 72,* 163–165.

Kleinmuntz, B. (1990). Why we still use our heads instead of formulas: Toward an integrative approach. *Psychological Bulletin, 107,* 296–310.

Koscherak, S., & Masling, J. (1972). *Noblesse oblige* effect: The interpretation of Rorschach responses as a function of ascribed social class. *Journal of Consulting and Clinical Psychology, 39,* 415–419.

Kosten, T. A., & Rounsaville, B. J. (1992). Sensitivity of psychiatric diagnosis based on the best estimate procedure. *American Journal of Psychiatry, 149,* 1225–1227.

Kostlan, A. (1954). A method for the empirical study of psychodiagnosis. *Journal of Consulting Psychology, 18,* 83–88.

Kovacs, M., & Gatsonis, C. (1989). Stability and change in childhood-onset depressive disorders: Longitudinal course as a diagnostic validator. In L. N. Robins & J. E. Barrett (Eds.), *The validity of psychiatric diagnoses* (pp. 57–73). New York: Raven Press.

Kramer, E., & Fenwick, J. (1966). Differential diagnosis with the Bender Gestalt test. *Journal of Projective Techniques and Personality Assessment, 30,* 59–61.

Kranzler, H. R., Kadden, R. M., Burleson, J. A., Babor, T. F., Apter, A., & Rounsaville, B. J. (1995). Validity of psychiatric diagnoses in patients with substance use disorders: Is the interview more important than the interviewer? *Comprehensive Psychiatry, 36,* 278–288.

Krol, N. P. C. M., De Bruyn, E. E. J., & Van Den Bercken, J. H. L. (1995). Intuitive and empirical prototypes in childhood psychopathology. *Psychological Assessment, 7,* 533–537.

Kullgren, G., Jacobsson, L., Lynöe, N., Kohn, R., & Levav, I. (1996). Practices and attitudes among Swedish psychiatrists regarding the ethics of compulsory treatment. *Acta Psychiatrica Scandinavica, 93,* 389–396.

Kupfer, D. J., & Frank, E. (1984). The relationship of EEG sleep to vital depression. *Journal of Affective Disorders, 7,* 249–263.

Kupfer, D. J., & Thase, M. E. (1989). Laboratory studies and validity of psychiatric diagnosis: Has there been progress? In L. N. Robins & J. E. Barrett (Eds.), *The validity of psychiatric diagnosis* (pp. 177–200). New York: Raven Press.

Kurtz, N., Kurtz, R., & Hoffnung, R. (1970). Attitudes toward the lower- and middle-class psychiatric patient as a function of authoritarianism among mental health students. *Journal of Consulting and Clinical Psychology, 35,* 338–341.

Kurtz, R. M., & Garfield, S. L. (1978). Illusory correlation: A further exploration of Chapman's paradigm. *Journal of Consulting and Clinical Psychology, 46,* 1009–1015.

Kutchins, H., & Kirk, S. A. (1986). The reliability of *DSM–III:* A critical review. *Social Work Research and Abstracts, 22,* 3–12.

Langenbucher, J. W., Labouvie, E., & Morgenstern, J. (1996). Measuring diagnostic agreement. *Journal of Consulting and Clinical Psychology, 64,* 1285–1289.

Langenbucher, J. W., Morgenstern, J., Labouvie, E., Miller, K. J., & Nathan, P. E. (1996). On criterion weighting in the *DSM–IV. Journal of Consulting and Clinical Psychology, 64,* 343–356.

Langer, E. J., & Abelson, R. P. (1974). A patient by any other name . . . . : Clinician group difference in labeling bias. *Journal of Consulting and Clinical Psychology, 42,* 4–9.

Langer, E. J., & Abelson, R. P. (1981). Reply to Douglas Davis. *Journal of Consulting and Clinical Psychology, 49,* 132–133.

Leary, M. R., & Miller, R. S. (1986). *Social psychology and dysfunctional behavior: Origins, diagnosis, and treatment.* New York: Springer-Verlag.

Leary, T. (1957). *Interpersonal diagnosis of personality.* New York: Ronald Press.

Lee, D. Y., Barak, A., Uhlemann, M. R., & Patsula, P. (1995). Effects of preinterview suggestion on counselor memory, clinical impression, and confidence in judgments. *Journal of Clinical Psychology, 51,* 666–675.

Lee, D. Y., Richer, D., & Uhlemann, M. R. (1992). Effects of client preinterview information on counselors' clinical impressions and interview behavior. *Counseling Psychology Quarterly, 5,* 115–122.

Lee, S. D., & Temerlin, M. K. (1970). Social class, diagnosis, and prognosis for psychotherapy. *Psychotherapy: Theory, Research, and Practice, 7,* 181–185.

Leinhardt, G., Seewald, A. M., & Zigmond, N. (1982). Sex and race differences in learning disabilities classrooms. *Journal of Educational Psychology, 74,* 835–843.

Leli, D. A., & Filskov, S. B. (1981). Clinical-actuarial detection and description of brain impairment with the W-B Form I. *Journal of Clinical Psychology, 37,* 623–629.

Leli, D. A., & Filskov, S. B. (1984). Clinical detection of intellectual deterioration associated with brain damage. *Journal of Clinical Psychology, 40,* 1435–1441.

Lemerond, J. N. (1977). Suicide prediction for psychiatric patients: A comparison of the MMPI and clinical judgments. *Dissertation Abstracts, 38,* 5926A–5927A. (University Microfilms No. 78–01922)

Levenberg, S. B. (1975). Professional training, psychodiagnostic skill, and Kinetic Family Drawings. *Journal of Personality Assessment, 39,* 389–393.

Levinson, R. M., & York, M. Z. (1974). The attribution of "dangerousness" in mental health evaluations. *Journal of Health and Social Behavior, 15,* 328–335.

Levy, M., & Kahn, M. (1970). Interpreter bias on the Rorschach test as a function of patients' socioeconomic status. *Journal of Projective Techniques and Personality Assessment, 34,* 106–112.

Lewine, R., Burbach, D., & Meltzer, H. Y. (1984). Effect of diagnostic criteria on the ratio of male to female schizophrenic patients. *American Journal of Psychiatry, 141,* 84–87.

Lewinsohn, P. M., & Rosenbaum, M. (1987). Recall of parental behavior by acute depressives, remitted depressives, and nondepressives. *Journal of Personality and Social Psychology, 52,* 611–619.

Lewis, G., & Appleby, L. (1988). Personality disorder: The patients psychiatrists dislike. *British Journal of Psychiatry, 153,* 44–49.

Lewis, G., Croft-Jeffreys, C., & David, A. (1990). Are British psychiatrists racist? *British Journal of Psychiatry, 157,* 410–415.

Lewis, K. N., & Lewis, D. A. (1985). Impact of religious affiliation on therapists' judgments of patients. *Journal of Consulting and Clinical Psychology, 53,* 926–932.

Lidz, C. W., Mulvey, E. P., Appelbaum, P. S., & Cleveland, S. (1989). Commitment: The consistency of clinicians and the use of legal standards. *American Journal of Psychiatry, 146,* 176–181.

Lidz, C. W., Mulvey, E. P., & Gardner, W. (1993). The accuracy of predictions of violence to others. *Journal of the American Medical Association, 269,* 1007–1011.

Lindsay, K. A., & Widiger, T. A. (1995). Sex and gender bias in self-report personality disorder inventories: Item analyses of the MCMI-II, MMPI, and PDQ-R. *Journal of Personality Assessment, 65,* 1–20.

Lindsey, K. P., & Paul, G. L. (1989). Involuntary commitments to public mental institutions: Issues involving the overrepresentation of Blacks and assessment of relevant functioning. *Psychological Bulletin, 106,* 171–183.

Lindsey, K. P., Paul, G. L., & Mariotto, M. J. (1989). Urban psychiatric commitments: Disability and dangerous behavior of Black and White recent admissions. *Hospital and Community Psychiatry, 40,* 286–294.

Lindzey, G. (1965). Seer versus sign. *Journal of Experimental Research in Personality, 1,* 17–26.

Lipkowitz, M. H., & Idupuganti, S. (1985). Diagnosing schizophrenia in 1982: The effect of *DSM–III. American Journal of Psychiatry, 142,* 634–637.

Lipton, A. A., & Simon, F. S. (1985). Psychiatric diagnosis in a state hospital: Manhattan State revisited. *Hospital and Community Psychiatry, 36,* 368–373.

Li-Repac, D. (1980). Cultural influences on clinical perception: A comparison between Caucasian and Chinese-American therapists. *Journal of Cross-Cultural Psychology, 11,* 327–342.

Little, K. B., & Shneidman, E. S. (1959). Congruencies among interpretations of psychological test and anamnestic data. *Psychological Monographs, 73* (6, Whole No. 476).

Littlewood, R. (1992). Psychiatric diagnosis and racial bias: Empirical and interpretative approaches. *Social Science and Medicine, 34,* 141–149.

Livesley, W. J., Reiffer, L. T., Sheldon, A. E. R., & West, M. (1987). Prototypicality ratings of *DSM–III* criteria for personality disorders. *Journal of Nervous and Mental Disease, 175,* 395–401.

Loevdahl, H., & Friis, S. (1996). Routine evaluation of mental health: Reliable information or worthless "guesstimates"? *Acta Psychiatrica Scandinavica, 93,* 125–128.

Loewenstein, D. A., Rubert, M. P., Arguelles, T., & Duara, R. (1995). Neuropsychological test performance and prediction of functional capacities among Spanish-speaking and English-speaking patients with dementia. *Archives of Clinical Neuropsychology, 10,* 75–88.

Loftus, E. F. (1993). The reality of repressed memories. *American Psychologist, 48,* 518–537.

Logue, M. B., Sher, K. J., & Frensch, P. A. (1992). Purported characteristics of adult children of alcoholics: A possible "Barnum effect." *Professional Psychology: Research and Practice, 23,* 226–232.

Lohr, J. M. (1996). Analysis by analogy for the mental health clinician [Review of the book *Eye movement desensitization and reprocessing: Basic principles, protocols, and procedures.*] *Contemporary Psychology, 41,* 879–880.

López, S. R. (1989). Patient variable biases in clinical judgment: Conceptual overview and methodological considerations. *Psychological Bulletin, 106,* 184–203.

López, S. R., Smith, A., Wolkenstein, B. H., & Charlin, V. (1993). Gender bias in clinical judgment: An assessment of the analogue method's transparency and social desirability. *Sex Roles, 28,* 35–45.

López, S. R., & Wolkenstein, B. H. (1990). Attributions, person perception, and clinical issues. In S. Graham & V. S. Folkes (Eds.), *Attribution theory: Applications to achievement, mental health, and interpersonal conflict* (pp. 103–121). Hillsdale, NJ: Lawrence Erlbaum.

Lorenz, R. A., Christensen, N. K., & Pichert, J. W. (1985). Diet-related knowledge, skill, and adherence among children with insulin-dependent diabetes mellitus. *Pediatrics, 75,* 872–876.

Loring, M., & Powell, B. (1988). Gender, race, and *DSM–III:* A study of the objectivity of psychiatric diagnostic behavior. *Journal of Health and Social Behavior, 29,* 1–22.

Loro, B., & Woodward, J. A. (1975). The dependence of psychiatric diagnosis on psychological assessment. *Journal of Clinical Psychology, 31,* 635–639.

Lowery, C. R., & Higgins, R. L. (1979). Analogue investigation of the relationship between clients' sex and treatment recommendations. *Journal of Consulting and Clinical Psychology, 47,* 792–794.

Lueger, R. J., & Petzel, T. P. (1979). Illusory correlation in clinical judgment: Effects of amount of information to be processed. *Journal of Consulting and Clinical Psychology, 47,* 1120–1121.

Luepnitz, R. R., Randolph, D. L., & Gutsch, K. U. (1982). Race and socioeconomic status as confounding variables in the accurate diagnosis of alcoholism. *Journal of Clinical Psychology, 38,* 665–669.

Luft, J. (1950). Implicit hypotheses and clinical predictions. *Journal of Abnormal and Social Psychology, 45,* 756–760.

Lyketsos, C. G., Aritzi, S., & Lyketsos, G. C. (1994). Efectiveness of office-based psychiatric practice using a structured diagnostic interview to guide treatment. *Journal of Nervous and Mental Disease, 182,* 720–723.

Lyle, O., & Quast, W. (1976). The Bender Gestalt: Use of clinical judgment versus recall scores in prediction of Huntington's disease. *Journal of Consulting and Clinical Psychology, 44,* 229–232.

Malone, K. M., Szanto, K., Corbitt, E. M., & Mann, J. J. (1995). Clinical assessment versus research methods in the assessment of suicidal behavior. *American Journal of Psychiatry, 152,* 1601–1607.

Marks, P. A. (1961). An assessment of the diagnostic process in a child guidance setting. *Psychological Monographs, 75*(3, Whole No. 507).

Mason, P., Harrison, G., Glazebrook, C., Medley, I., Dalkin, T., & Croudace, T. (1995). Characteristics of outcome in schizophrenia at 13 years. *British Journal of Psychiatry, 167,* 596–603.

Matarazzo, J. D. (1983). The reliability of psychiatric and psychological diagnosis. *Clinical Psychology Review, 3,* 103–145.

Matarazzo, J. D. (1986). Computerized clinical psychological test interpretations: Unvalidated plus all mean and no sigma. *American Psychologist, 41,* 14–24.

Matuszek, P., & Oakland, T. (1979). Factors influencing teachers' and psychologists' recommendations regarding special class placement. *Journal of School Psychology, 17,* 116–125.

Mayne, T. J., Norcross, J. C., & Sayette, M. A. (1994). Admission requirements, acceptance rates, and financial assistance in clinical psychology programs: Diversity across the practice–research continuum. *American Psychologist, 49,* 806–811.

Mayou, R. (1977). Psychiatric decision making. *British Journal of Psychiatry, 130,* 374–376.

Mazer, D. B. (1979). Toward a social psychology of diagnosis: Similarity, attraction, and clinical evaluation. *Journal of Consulting and Clinical Psychology, 47,* 586–588.

McClelland, G. H. (1978). *Equal versus differential weighting for multiattribute decisions: There are no free lunches* (Rep. No. 207, Rev. ed.). Boulder: University of Colorado Institute of Behavioral Science, Center for Research on Judgment and Policy.

McClelland, G. H., & Judd, C. M. (1993). Statistical difficulties of detecting interactions and moderator effects. *Psychological Bulletin, 114,* 376–390.

McCollum, E. E., & Russell, C. S. (1992). Mother-blaming in family therapy: An empirical investigation. *The American Journal of Family Therapy, 20,* 71–76.

McFall, M. E., Murburg, M. M., Smith, D. E., & Jensen, C. F. (1991). An analysis of criteria used by VA clinicians to diagnose combat-related PTSD. *Journal of Traumatic Stress, 4,* 123–136.

McFarland, C., Ross, M., & DeCourville, N. (1989). Women's theories of menstruation and biases in recall of menstrual symptoms. *Journal of Personality and Social Psychology, 57,* 522–531.

McGovern, M. P., Newman, F. L., & Kopta, S. M. (1986). Metatheoretical assumptions and psychotherapy orientation: Clinician attributions of patients' problem causality and responsibility for treatment outcome. *Journal of Consulting and Clinical Psychology, 54,* 476–481.

McGuire, J., Nieri, D., Abbott, D., Sheridan, K., & Fisher, R. (1995). Do *Tarasoff* principles apply in AIDS-related psychotherapy? Ethical decision making and the role of therapist homophobia and perceived client dangerousness. *Professional Psychology, 26,* 608–611.

McKinzey, R. K., & Russell, E. W. (1997). Detection of malingering on the Halstead-Reitan Battery: A cross-validation. *Archives of Clinical Neuropsychology, 12,* 585–589.

McLaughlin, M., & Balch, P. (1980). Effects of client–therapist ethnic homophily on therapists' judgments. *American Journal of Community Psychology, 8,* 243–252.

McLellan, A. T., Luborsky, L., Cacciola, J., Griffith, J., McGahan, P., & O'Brien, C. P. (1985). *Guide to the Addiction Severity Index: Background, administration, and field testing results.* Rockville, MD: U.S. Department of Health and Human Services.

McMinn, M. R., & Wade, N. G. (1995). Beliefs about the prevalence of dissociative identity disorder, sexual abuse, and ritual abuse among religious and nonreligious therapists. *Professional Psychology, 26*, 257–261.

McNally, R. J. (1996). [Review of the book F. Shapiro's *Eye movement desensitization and reprocessing: Basic principles, protocols, and procedures.*] *Anxiety, 2*, 153–154.

McNally, R. J., Luedke, D. L., Besyner, J. K., Peterson, R. A., Bohm, K., & Lips, O. J. (1987). Sensitivity to stress-relevant stimuli in posttraumatic stress disorder. *Journal of Anxiety Disorders, 1*, 105–116.

McNiel, D. E., & Binder, R. L. (1987). Predictive validity of judgments of dangerousness in emergency civil commitment. *American Journal of Psychiatry, 144*, 197–200.

McNiel, D. E., & Binder, R. L. (1991). Clinical assessment of the risk of violence among psychiatric inpatients. *American Journal of Psychiatry, 148*, 1317–1321.

McNiel, D. E., & Binder, R. L. (1995). Correlates of accuracy in the assessment of psychiatric inpatients' risk of violence. *American Journal of Psychiatry, 152*, 901–906.

McNiel, D. E., Binder, R. L., & Greenfield, T. K. (1988). Predictors of violence in civilly committed acute psychiatric patients. *American Journal of Psychiatry, 145*, 965–970.

Mechelen, I. V., & De Boeck, P. (1989). Implicit taxonomy in psychiatric diagnosis: A case study. *Journal of Social and Clinical Psychology, 8*, 276–287.

Meehl, P. E. (1954). *Clinical versus statistical prediction: A theoretical analysis and a review of the evidence.* Minneapolis: University of Minnesota Press.

Meehl, P. E. (1956). Wanted—a good cookbook. *American Psychologist, 11*, 263–272.

Meehl, P. E. (1959a). A comparison of clinicians with five statistical methods of identifying psychotic MMPI profiles. *Journal of Counseling Psychology, 6*, 102–109.

Meehl, P. E. (1959b). Some ruminations on the validation of clinical procedures. *Canadian Journal of Psychology, 13*, 102–128.

Meehl, P. E. (1960). The cognitive activity of the clinician. *American Psychologist, 15*, 19–27.

Meehl, P. E. (1967). What can the clinician do well? In D. N. Jackson & S. Messick (Eds.), *Problems in human assessment* (pp. 594–599). New York: McGraw-Hill.

Meehl, P. E. (1973). Why I do not attend case conferences. In P. E. Meehl, *Psychodiagnosis: Selected papers* (pp. 225–302). Minneapolis: University of Minnesota Press.

Meehl, P. E. (1978). Theoretical risks and tabular asterisks: Sir Karl, Sir Ronald, and the slow progress of soft psychology. *Journal of Consulting and Clinical Psychology, 46*, 806–834.

Meehl, P. E. (1986a). Causes and effects of my disturbing little book. *Journal of Personality Assessment, 50*, 370–375.

Meehl, P. E. (1986b). Diagnostic taxa as open concepts: Metatheoretical and statistical questions about reliability and construct validity in the grand strategy of nosological revision. In T. Millon & G. Klerman (Eds.), *Contemporary directions in psychopathology* (pp. 215–231). New York: Guilford.

Meehl, P. E. (1990). Toward an integrated theory of schizotaxia, schizotypy, and schizophrenia. *Journal of Personality Disorders, 4*, 1–99.

Meehl, P. E. (1995). Bootstraps taxometrics: Solving the classification problem in psychopathology. *American Psychologist, 50*, 266–275.

Meehl, P. E. (1996). MAXCOV pseudotaxonicity. *American Psychologist, 51*, 1184–1186.

Meehl, P. E., & Dahlstrom, W. G. (1960). Objective configural rules for discriminating psychotic from neurotic MMPI profiles. *Journal of Consulting Psychology, 24*, 375–387.

Meehl, P. E., & Rosen, A. (1955). Antecedent probability and the efficiency of psychometric signs, patterns, or cutting scores. *Psychological Bulletin, 52*, 194–216.

Meeks, S. (1990). Age bias in the diagnostic decision-making behavior of clinicians. *Professional Psychology, 21*, 279–284.

Mehlman, B., & Vatovec, E. (1956). A validation study of the Bender-Gestalt. *Journal of Consulting Psychology, 20*, 71–74.

Mellsop, G., Varghese, F., Joshua, S., & Hicks, A. (1982). The reliability of Axis II of DSM–III. *American Journal of Psychiatry, 139*, 1360–1361.

Melton, G. B., Weithorn, L. A., & Slobogin, C. (1985). *Community mental health centers and the courts: An evaluation of community-based forensic services.* Lincoln: University of Nebraska Press.

Mendel, W. M., & Rapport, S. (1969). Determinants of the decision for psychiatric hospitalization. *Archives of General Psychiatry, 20*, 321–328.

Merluzzi, B. H., & Merluzzi, T. V. (1978). Influence of client race on counselors' assessment of case materials. *Journal of Counseling Psychology, 25*, 399–404.

Meyerson, A. T., Moss, J. Z., Belville, R., & Smith, H. (1979). Influence of experience on major clinical decisions: Training implications. *Archives of General Psychiatry, 36*, 423–427.

Mezzich, A. C., Mezzich, J. E., & Coffman, G. A. (1985). Reliability of DSM–III vs. DSM–II in child psychopathology. *Journal of the American Academy of Child Psychiatry, 24*, 273–280.

Miller, D. (1974). The influence of the patient's sex on clinical judgment. *Smith College Studies in Social Work, 44*, 89–100.

Miller, H. R., Streiner, D. L., & Kahgee, S. L. (1982). Use of the Golden-Meehl indicators in the detection of schizoid-taxon membership. *Journal of Abnormal Psychology, 91*, 55–60.

Miller, M. B. (1996). Limitations of Meehl's MAXCOV-HITMAX procedure. *American Psychologist, 51*, 554–556.

Mills, D. H., & Tucker, L. R. (1966). A three-mode factor analysis of clinical judgment of schizophrenicity. *Journal of Clinical Psychology, 22*, 136–139.

Minsky, M. (1967). *Computation: Finite and infinite machines.* Englewood Cliffs, NJ: Prentice Hall.

Mischel, W. (1968). *Personality and assessment.* New York: Wiley.

Mittenberg, W., Rotholc, A., Russell, E., & Heilbronner, R. (1996). Identification of malingered head injury on the Halstead-Reitan Battery. *Archives of Clinical Neuropsychology, 11,* 271–281.

Mojtabai, R., & Nicholson, R. A. (1995). Interrater reliability of ratings of delusions and bizarre delusions. *American Journal of Psychiatry, 152,* 1804–1806.

Moldin, S. O., Gottesman, I. I., Erlenmeyer-Kimling, L., & Cornblatt, B. A. (1990). Psychometric deviance in offspring at risk for schizophrenia: I. Initial delineation of a distinct subgroup. *Psychiatry Research, 32,* 297–310.

Moldin, S. O., Rice, J. P., Gottesman, I. I., & Erlenmeyer-Kimling, L. (1990a). Psychometric deviance in offspring at risk for schizophrenia: II. Resolving heterogeneity through admixture analysis. *Psychiatry Research, 32,* 311–322.

Moldin, S. O., Rice, J. P., Gottesman, I. I., & Erlenmeyer-Kimling, L. (1990b). Transmission of a psychometric indicator for liability to schizophrenia in normal families. *Genetic Epidemiology, 7,* 163–176.

Molinari, V., Ames, A., & Essa, M. (1994). Prevalence of personality disorders in two geropsychiatric inpatient units. *Journal of Geriatric Psychiatry and Neurology, 7,* 209–215.

Monahan, J. (1981). *The clinical prediction of violent behavior.* Washington, DC: US Government Printing Office.

Monahan, J., & Steadman, H. J. (Eds.). (1994). *Violence and mental disorder: Developments in risk assessment.* Chicago: University of Chicago Press.

Montgomery, R. W. (1996). [Review of the book *Eye movement desensitization and reprocessing: Basic principles, protocols, and procedures*]. *Journal of Behavior Therapy and Experimental Psychiatry, 27,* 67–69.

Moreland, K. L. (1985). Validation of computer-based test interpretations: Problems and prospects. *Journal of Consulting and Clinical Psychology, 53,* 816–825.

Moreland, K. L., & Godfrey, J. O. (1989). Yes, our study could have been better: Reply to Cash, Mikulka, and Brown. *Journal of Consulting and Clinical Psychology, 57,* 313–314.

Moreland, K. L., & Onstad, J. A. (1987). Validity of Millon's computerized interpretation system for the MCMI: A controlled study. *Journal of Consulting and Clinical Psychology, 55,* 113–114.

Morey, L. C. (1991a). Classification of mental disorder as a collection of hypothetical constructs. *Journal of Abnormal Psychology, 100,* 289–293.

Morey, L. C. (1991b). *Personality Assessment Inventory manual.* Odessa, FL: Psychological Assessment Resources.

Morey, L. C., & McNamara, T. P. (1987). On definitions, diagnosis, and *DSM–III. Journal of Abnormal Psychology, 96,* 283–285.

Morey, L. C., & Ochoa, E. S. (1989). An investigation of adherence to diagnostic criteria: Clinical diagnosis of the *DSM–III* personality disorders. *Journal of Personality Disorders, 3,* 180–192.

Morrissey, R. F., Dicker, R., Abikoff, H., Alvir, J. M. J., DeMarco, A., & Koplewicz, H. S. (1995). Hospitalizing the suicidal adolescent: An empirical investigation of decision-making criteria. *Journal of the American Academy of Child and Adolescent Psychiatry, 34,* 902–911.

Mossman, D. (1994). Assessing predictions of violence: Being accurate about accuracy. *Journal of Consulting and Clinical Psychology, 62,* 783–792.

Motta, R. W., Little, S. G., & Tobin, M. I. (1993). The use and abuse of human figure drawings. *School Psychology Quarterly, 8,* 162–169.

Mowrey, J. D., Doherty, M. E., & Keeley, S. M. (1979). The influence of negation and task complexity on illusory correlation. *Journal of Abnormal Psychology, 88,* 334–337.

Moxley, A. W. (1973). Clinical judgment: The effects of statistical information. *Journal of Personality Assessment, 37,* 86–91.

Muehleman, T., & Kimmons, C. (1981). Psychologists' views on child abuse reporting, confidentiality, life, and the law: An exploratory study. *Professional Psychology, 12,* 631–638.

Mukherjee, S., Shukla, S., Woodle, J., Rosen, A. M., & Olarte, S. (1983). Misdiagnosis of schizophrenia in bipolar patients: A multiethnic comparison. *American Journal of Psychiatry, 140,* 1571–1574.

Murdock, J. B. (1969). A procedural critique of "Bender Gestalts of Organic Children: Accuracy of Clinical Judgment." *Journal of Projective Techniques and Personality Assessment, 33,* 489–491.

Murdock, N. L. (1988). Category-based effects in clinical judgment. *Counseling Psychology Quarterly, 1,* 341–355.

Murdock, N. L., & Fremont, S. K. (1989). Attributional influences in counselor decision-making. *Journal of Counseling Psychology, 36,* 417–422.

Murray, J., & Abramson, P. R. (1983). An investigation of the effects of client gender and attractiveness on psychotherapists' judgments. In J. Murray & P. R. Abramson (Eds.), *Bias in psychotherapy* (pp. 129–167). Los Angeles: University of California Press.

Nadler, E. B., Fink, S. L., Shontz, F. C., & Brink, R. W. (1959). Objective scoring vs. clinical evaluation of the Bender-Gestalt. *Journal of Clinical Psychology, 15,* 39–41.

Nadler, J. D., Mittenberg, W., DePiano, F. A., & Schneider, B. A. (1994). Effects of patient age on neuropsychological test interpretation. *Professional Psychology, 25,* 288–295.

Nalven, F. B., Hofmann, L. J., & Bierbryer, B. (1969). The effects of subjects' age, sex, race, and socioeconomic status on psychologists' estimates of "true IQ" from WISC scores. *Journal of Clinical Psychology, 25,* 271–274.

Neer, W. L., Foster, D. A., Jones, J. G., & Reynolds, D. A. (1973). Socioeconomic bias in the diagnosis of mental retardation. *Exceptional Children, 40,* 38–39.

Neumann, M., Salganik, I., Rabinowitz, S., Bauer, A., & Kastner, M. (1990). The effect of diagnosis and educational level on therapists' treatment decisions in a regional psychiatric outpatient clinic. *Israeli Journal of Psychiatry and Related Sciences, 27,* 199–204.

New cure for ulcers often ignored. (1996, March 19). *The Washington Post.,* p. 17.

Newman, J. R. (1977). Differential weighting in multiattribute utility measurement: When it should and when it does make a difference. *Organizational Behavior and Human Performance, 20,* 312–325.

Nezu, A. M., & Nezu, C. M. (1993). Identifying and selecting target problems for clinical interventions: A problem-solving model. *Psychological Assessment, 5,* 254–263.

Nichols, D. S., & Jones, R. E., Jr. (1985). Identifying schizoid-taxon membership with the Golden-Meehl MMPI items. *Journal of Abnormal Psychology, 94,* 191–194.

Nierenberg, A. A. (1991). Treatment choice after one antidepressant fails: A survey of northeastern psychiatrists. *Journal of Clinical Psychiatry, 52,* 383–385.

Nightingale, N., & Walker, E. (1986). Identification and reporting of child maltreatment by Head Start personnel: Attitudes and experiences. *Child Abuse and Neglect, 10,* 191–199.

Nisbett, R. E., & Ross, L. (1980). *Human inference: Strategies and shortcomings of social judgment.* New York: Prentice Hall.

Nisbett, R. E., & Wilson, T. D. (1977). Telling more than we can know: Verbal reports on mental processes. *Psychological Review, 84,* 231–259.

North, C. S., Clouse, R. E., Spitznagel, E. L., & Alpers, D. H. (1990). The relation of ulcerative colitis to psychiatric factors: A review of findings and methods. *American Journal of Psychiatry, 147,* 974–981.

Nystedt, L., Magnusson, D., & Aronowitsch, E. (1975). Generalization of ratings based on projective tests. *Scandinavian Journal of Psychology, 16,* 72–78.

O'Brien, W. H. (1995). Inaccuracies in the estimation of functional relationships using self-monitoring data. *Journal of Behavior Therapy and Experimental Psychiatry, 26,* 351–357.

O'Connor, T., & Smith, P. B. (1987). The labeling of schizophrenics by professionals and lay-persons. *British Journal of Clinical Psychology, 26,* 311–312.

Ofshe, R., & Watters, E. (1994). *Making monsters: False memories, psychotherapy, and sexual hysteria.* New York: Scribner's.

O'Leary, K. D., Vivian, D., & Malone, J. (1992). Assessment of physical aggression against women in marriage: The need for multimodal assessment. *Behavioral Assessment, 14,* 5–14.

Oskamp, S. (1962). The relationship of clinical experience and training methods to several criteria of clinical prediction. *Psychological Monographs, 76* (28, Whole No. 547).

Oskamp, S. (1965). Overconfidence in case-study judgments. *Journal of Consulting Psychology, 29,* 261–265.

Oskamp, S. (1967). Clinical judgment from the MMPI: Simple or complex? *Journal of Clinical Psychology, 23,* 411–415.

Overall, J. E., & Higgins, C. W. (1977). An application of actuarial methods in psychiatric diagnosis. *Journal of Clinical Psychology, 33,* 973–980.

Oxman, T. E., Rosenberg, S. D., Schnurr, P. P., & Tucker, G. J. (1988). Diagnostic classification through content analysis of patients' speech. *American Journal of Psychiatry, 145,* 464–468.

Oyster-Nelson, C. K., & Cohen, L. H. (1981). The extent of sex bias in clinical treatment recommendations. *Professional Psychology, 12,* 508–515.

Ozer, D. J. (1985). Correlation and the coefficient of determination. *Psychological Bulletin, 97,* 307–315.

Pain, M. D., & Sharpley, C. F. (1989). Varying the order in which positive and negative information is presented: Effects on counselors' judgments of clients' mental health. *Journal of Counseling Psychology, 36,* 3–7.

Pat-Horenczyk, R. (1988). Attitudes of psychotherapists towards diagnosis and treatment of depression in old age. *Israeli Journal of Psychiatry and Related Sciences, 25,* 24–37.

Paul, G. L. (Ed.). (1987). *Observational assessment instrumentation for service and research—the Time-Sample Behavioral Checklist: Assessment in residential treatment settings, Part 2.* Champaign, IL: Research Press.

Pavkov, T. W., Lewis, D. A., & Lyons, J. S. (1989). Psychiatric diagnoses and racial bias: An empirical investigation. *Professional Psychology, 20,* 364–368.

Payette, K. A., & Clarizio, H. F. (1994). Discrepant team decisions: The effects of race, gender, achievement, and IQ on LD eligibility. *Psychology in the Schools, 31,* 40–48.

Perlick, D., & Atkins, A. (1984). Variations in the reported age of a patient: A source of bias in the diagnosis of depression and dementia. *Journal of Consulting and Clinical Psychology, 52,* 812–820.

Perrett, L. F. (1971). *Immediate and background contextual effects in clinical judgment.* Unpublished doctoral dissertation, University of California, Los Angeles.

Perry, J. C. (1992). Problems and considerations in the valid assessment of personality disorders. *American Journal of Psychiatry, 149,* 1645–1653.

Perry, J. C., & Cooper, S. H. (1989). An empirical study of defense mechanisms. I. Clinical interview and life vignette ratings. *Archives of General Psychiatry, 46,* 444–452.

Perry, S. W., & Tross, S. (1984). Psychiatric problems of AIDS inpatients at the New York Hospital: Preliminary report. *Public Health Report, 99,* 200–205.

Persons, J. B., Mooney, K. A., & Padesky, C. A. (1995). Interrater reliability of cognitive–behavioral case formulations. *Cognitive Therapy and Research, 19,* 21–34.

Peterson, D. R. (1985). Twenty years of practitioner training in psychology. *American Psychologist, 40,* 441–451.

Pfohl, B., Blum, N., Zimmerman, M., & Stangl, D. (1989). *The structured interview for DSM–III–R personality disorders (SIDP–R).* Iowa City: University of Iowa Hospital and Clinics.

Pfohl, S. J. (1978). *Predicting dangerousness: The social construction of psychiatric reality.* Lexington, MA: Lexington Books.

Phillips, W. M., Phillips, A. M., & Shearn, C. R. (1980). Objective assessment of schizophrenic thinking. *Journal of Clinical Psychology, 36,* 79–89.

Pilkonis, P. A., Heape, C. L., Ruddy, J., & Serrao, P. (1991). Validity in the diagnosis of personality disorders: The use of the LEAD standard. *Psychological Assessment, 3,* 46–54.

Piotrowski, C., & Zalewski, C. (1993). Training in psychodiagnostic testing in APA-approved PsyD and PhD clinical psychology programs. *Journal of Personality Assessment, 61,* 394–405.

Plous, S. (1993). *The psychology of judgment and decision making.* New York: McGraw-Hill.

Plous, S., & Zimbardo, P. G. (1986). Attributional biases among clinicians: A comparison of psychoanalysts and behavior therapists. *Journal of Consulting and Clinical Psychology, 54,* 568–570.

Pokorny, A. D. (1983). Prediction of suicide in psychiatric patients: Report of a prospective study. *Archives of General Psychiatry, 40,* 249–257.

Polusny, M. A., & Follette, V. M. (1996). Remembering childhood sexual abuse: A national survey of psychologists' clinical practices, beliefs, and personal experiences. *Professional Psychology: Research and Practice, 27,* 41–52.

Poole, D. A., Lindsay, D. S., Memon, A., & Bull, R. (1995). Psychotherapy and the recovery of memories of childhood sexual abuse: U.S. and British practitioners' opinions, practices, and experiences. *Journal of Consulting and Clinical Psychology, 63,* 426–437.

Pope, H. G., Jr., & Hudson, J. I. (1995). Can memories of childhood sexual abuse be repressed? *Psychological Medicine, 25,* 121–126.

Potts, M. K., Burnam, M. A., & Wells, K. B. (1991). Gender differences in depression detection: A comparison of clinician diagnosis and standardized assessment. *Psychological Assessment, 3,* 609–615.

Potts, M. K., Daniels, M., Burnam, M. A., & Wells, K. B. (1990). A structured interview version of the Hamilton Depression Rating Scale: Evidence of reliability and versatility of administration. *Journal of Psychiatric Research, 24,* 335–350.

Prentice, D. A., & Miller, D. T. (1992). When small effects are impressive. *Psychological Bulletin, 112,* 160–164.

Propping, P. (1983). Genetic disorders presenting as "schizophrenia." *Human Genetics, 65,* 1–19.

Prout, H. T., & Frederickson, A. K. (1991). Sex bias in clinical judgment among school psychologists. *Psychology in the Schools, 28,* 226–229.

Pruitt, J. A., & Kappius, R. E. (1992). Routine inquiry into sexual victimization: A survey of therapists' practices. *Professional Psychology, 23,* 474–479.

Pulver, A. E., Carpenter, W. T., Adler, L., & McGrath, J. (1988). Accuracy of the diagnoses of affective disorders and schizophrenia in public hospitals. *American Journal of Psychiatry, 145,* 218–220.

Quinsey, V. L. (1975). Psychiatric staff conferences of dangerous mentally disordered offenders. *Canadian Journal of Behavioral Science, 7,* 60–69.

Quinsey, V. L., & Ambtman, R. (1979). Variables affecting psychiatrists' and teachers' assessments of the dangerousness of mentally ill offenders. *Journal of Consulting and Clinical Psychology, 47*, 353–362.

Rabinowitz, J., & Lukoff, I. (1995). Clinical decision making of short- versus long-term treatment. *Research on Social Work Practice, 5*, 62–79.

Rabinowitz, J., Massad, A., & Fennig, S. (1995). Factors influencing disposition decisions for patients seen in a psychiatric emergency service. *Psychiatric Services, 46*, 712–718.

Rapaport, D., Gill, M., & Schafer, R. (1946). *Diagnostic psychological testing.* (Vols: 1–2). Chicago: Year Book.

Ray, D. C., McKinney, K. A., & Ford, C. V. (1987). Differences in psychologists' ratings of older and younger clients. *The Gerontologist, 27*, 82–86.

Ray, D. C., Raciti, M. A., & Ford, C. V. (1985). Ageism in psychiatrists: Associations with gender, certification, and theoretical orientation. *The Gerontologist, 25*, 496–500.

Reade, W. K., & Wertheimer, M. (1976). A bias in the diagnosis of schizophrenia. *Journal of Consulting and Clinical Psychology, 44*, 878.

Realmuto, G. M., & Wescoe, S. (1992). Agreement among professionals about child's sexual abuse status: Interviews with sexually anatomically correct dolls as indicators of abuse. *Child Abuse and Neglect, 16*, 719–725.

Reiss, S., Levitan, G., & Szyszko, J. (1982). Emotional disturbance and mental retardation: Diagnostic overshadowing. *American Journal of Mental Deficiency, 86*, 567–574.

Reiss, S., & Szyszko, J. (1983). Diagnostic overshadowing and professional experience with mentally retarded persons. *American Journal of Mental Deficiency, 87*, 396–402.

Reitan, R. M. (1964). Psychological deficits resulting from cerebral lesions in man (pp. 295–312). In J. M. Warren & K. A. Akert (Eds.), *The frontal granular cortex and behavior.* New York: McGraw-Hill.

Rey, J. M., Stewart, G. W., Plapp, J. M., Bashir, M. R., & Richards, I. N. (1988). DSM–III Axis IV revisited. *American Journal of Psychiatry, 145*, 286–292.

Rice, M. E., & Harris, G. T. (1995). Violent recidivism: Assessing predictive validity. *Journal of Consulting and Clinical Psychology, 63*, 737–748.

Rich, B. E., Paul, G. L., & Mariotto, M. J. (1988). Judgmental relativism as a validity threat to standardized psychiatric rating scales. *Journal of Psychopathology and Behavioral Assessment, 10*, 241–257.

Ridley, C. R. (1986). Diagnosis as a function of race pairing and client self-disclosure. *Journal of Cross-Cultural Psychology, 17*, 337–351.

Riemann, B. C., McNally, R. J., & Cox, W. M. (1992). The comorbidity of obsessive–compulsive disorder and alcoholism. *Journal of Anxiety Disorders, 6*, 105–110.

Riso, L. P., Klein, D. N., Anderson, R. L., Ouimette, P. C., & Lizardi, H. (1994). Concordance between patients and informants on the Personality Disorder Examination. *American Journal of Psychiatry, 151*, 568–573.

Robertson, J., & Fitzgerald, L. F. (1990). The (mis)treatment of men: Effects of client gender role and life-style on diagnosis and attribution of pathology. *Journal of Counseling Psychology, 37,* 3–9.

Robiner, W. N. (1978). *An analysis of some of the variables influencing clinical use of the Bender-Gestalt.* Unpublished manuscript.

Robins, E., & Guze, S. B. (1970). Establishment of diagnostic validity in psychiatric illness: Its application to schizophrenia. *American Journal of Psychiatry, 126,* 107–111.

Robins, L. N., & Barrett, J. E. (Eds.). (1989). *The validity of psychiatric diagnosis.* New York: Raven Press.

Robins, L. N., Helzer, J. E., Croughan, J., & Ratcliff, K. S. (1981). National Institute of Mental Health Diagnostic Interview Schedule. *Archives of General Psychiatry, 38,* 381–389.

Robins, L. N., & Regier, D. A. (Eds.). (1991). *Psychiatric disorders in America.* New York: Free Press.

Rock, D. L. (1994). Clinical judgment survey of mental health professionals: I. An assessment of opinions, ratings, and knowledge. *Journal of Clinical Psychology, 50,* 941–950.

Rock, D. L., & Bransford, J. D. (1992). An empirical evaluation of three components of the tetrahedron model of clinical judgment. *Journal of Nervous and Mental Disease, 180,* 560–565.

Rock, D. L., Bransford, J. D., Maisto, S. A., & Morey, L. C. (1987). The study of clinical judgment: An ecological approach. *Clinical Psychology Review, 7,* 645–661.

Rohrbaugh, J. R. (1986). *Policy PC: Software for judgment analysis* [computer program]. Albany, NY: Executive Decision Services.

Rorer, L. G. (1971). A circuitous route to bootstrapping. In H. B. Haley, A. G. D'Costa, & A. M. Schafer (Eds.), *Conference on personality measurement in medical education.* Washington, DC: Association of American Medical Colleges.

Rorer, L. G., & Widiger, T. (1983). Personality structure and assessment. *Annual Review of Psychology, 34,* 431–463.

Rosen, G. M. (1975). On the persistence of illusory correlations associated with the Rorschach. *Journal of Abnormal Psychology, 84,* 571–573.

Rosen, G. M. (1976). "Associative homogeneity" may affect the persistence of illusory correlations but does not account for their occurrence. *Journal of Abnormal Psychology, 85,* 239.

Rosenberg, S. E., Silberschatz, G., Curtis, J. T., Sampson, H., & Weiss, J. (1986). A method for establishing reliability of statements from psychodynamic case formulations. *American Journal of Psychiatry, 143,* 1454–1456.

Rosenfield, S. (1982). Sex roles and societal reactions to mental illness: The labeling of "deviant" deviance. *Journal of Health and Social Behavior, 23,* 18–24.

Rosenhan, D. L. (1973). On being sane in insane places. *Science, 179,* 250–258.

Rosenhan, D. L. (1975). The contextual nature of psychiatric diagnosis. *Journal of Abnormal Psychology, 84,* 462–474.

Rosenthal, A. (1982). Heterosexism & clinical assessment. *Smith College Studies in Social Work, 52,* 145–159.

Rosenthal, R. (1995). Progress in clinical psychology: Is there any? *Clinical Psychology: Science and Practice, 2,* 133–150.

Rosenzweig, N., Vandenberg, S. G., Moore, K., & Dukay, A. (1961). A study of the reliability of the mental status examination. *American Journal of Psychiatry, 117,* 1102–1108.

Rosnow, R. L., & Rosenthal, R. (1995). "Some things you learn aren't so": Cohen's paradox, Asch's paradigm, and the interpretation of interaction. *Psychological Science, 6,* 3–9.

Ross, M. (1989). Relation of implicit theories to the construction of personal histories. *Psychological Review, 96,* 341–357.

Routh, D. K., & King, K. M. (1972). Social class bias in clinical judgment. *Journal of Consulting and Clinical Psychology, 38,* 202–207.

Rowden, D. W., Michel, J. B., Dillehay, R. C., & Martin, H. W. (1970). Judgments about candidates for psychotherapy: The influence of social class and insight-verbal ability. *Journal of Health and Social Behavior, 11,* 51–58.

Rowe, D. C. (1987). Resolving the person–situation debate: Invitation to an interdisciplinary dialogue. *American Psychologist, 42,* 218–227.

Rubenzer, S. (1992). A comparison of traditional and computer-generated psychological reports in an adolescent inpatient setting. *Journal of Clinical Psychology, 48,* 817–827.

Rubinson, E. P., & Asnis, G. M. (1989). Use of structured interviews for diagnosis. In S. Wetzler (Ed.), *Measuring mental illness: Psychometric assessment for clinicians* (pp. 45–66). Washington, DC: American Psychiatric Press.

Rubinson, E. P., Asnis, G. M., & Friedman, J. M. H. (1988). Knowledge of diagnostic criteria for major depression: A survey of mental health professionals. *Journal of Nervous and Mental Disease, 176,* 480–484.

Rumelhart, D. E., McClelland, J. L., & the PDP Research Group. (1986). *Parallel distributed processing: Explorations into the microstructure of cognition, Volumes 1 and 2.* Cambridge, MA: MIT Press.

Russell, E. W. (1988). Renorming Russell's version of the Wechsler Memory Scale. *Journal of Clinical and Experimental Neuropsychology, 10,* 235–249.

Russell, E. W. (1995). The accuracy of automated and clinical detection of brain damage and lateralization in neuropsychology. *Neuropsychology Review, 5,* 1–68.

Russell, E. W., Neuringer, C., & Goldstein, G. (1970). *Assessment of brain damage: A neuropsychological key approach.* New York: Wiley-Interscience.

Sandifer, M. G., Hordern, A., & Green, L. M. (1970). The psychiatric interview: The impact of the first three minutes. *American Journal of Psychiatry, 126,* 968–973.

Sartorius, N., Kaelber, C. T., Cooper, J. E., Roper, M. T., Rae, D. S., Gulbinat, W., Üstün, T. B., & Regier, D. A. (1993). Progress toward achieving a common language in psychiatry: Results from the field trial of the clinical guidelines accompanying the WHO classification of mental and behavioral disorders in ICD–10. *Archives of General Psychiatry, 50,* 115–124.

Sartorius, N., Üstün, T. B., Korten, A., Cooper, J. E., & van Drimmelen, J. (1995). Progress toward achieving a common language in psychiatry, II: Results from the International Field Trials of the *ICD–10 Diagnostic Criteria for Research for Mental and Behavioral Disorders. American Journal of Psychiatry, 152,* 1427–1437.

Sattler, J. (1977). The effects of therapist–client racial similarity. In A. S. Gurman & A. M. Razin (Eds.), *Effective psychotherapy: A handbook of research* (pp. 252–290). New York: Pergamon Press.

Sattler, J. M., & Kuncik, T. M. (1976). Ethnicity, socioeconomic status, and pattern of WISC scores as variables that affect psychologists' estimates of "effective intelligence." *Journal of Clinical Psychology, 32,* 362–366.

Satz, P. (1966). A block rotation task: The application of multivariate and decision theory analysis for the prediction of organic brain disorder. *Psychological Monographs, 80*(21, Whole No. 629).

Sawyer, J. (1966). Measurement and prediction, clinical and statistical. *Psychological Bulletin, 66,* 178–200.

Sbordone, R. J., & Rudd, M. (1986). Can psychologists recognize neurological disorders in their patients? *Journal of Clinical and Experimental Neuropsychology, 8,* 285–291.

Schaeffer, R. W. (1964). Clinical psychologists' ability to use the Draw-a-Person Test as an indicator of personality adjustment. *Journal of Consulting Psychology, 28,* 383.

Schank, R., & Abelson, R. P. (1977). *Scripts, plans, goals, and understanding: An inquiry into human knowledge structures.* Hillsdale, NJ: Lawrence Erlbaum.

Schinka, J. A., & Sines, J. O. (1974). Correlates of accuracy in personality assessment. *Journal of Clinical Psychology, 30,* 374–377.

Schmidt, L. D., & McGowan, J. F. (1959). The differentiation of human figure drawings. *Journal of Consulting Psychology, 23,* 129–133.

Schmidt, N. B., Lerew, D. R., & Jackson, R. J. (1997). The role of anxiety sensitivity in the pathogenesis of panic: Prospective evaluation of spontaneous panic attacks during acute stress. *Journal of Abnormal Psychology, 106,* 355–364.

Schofield, W., & Balian, L. (1959). A comparative study of the personal histories of schizophrenic and nonpsychiatric patients. *Journal of Abnormal and Social Psychology, 59,* 216–225.

Schover, L. R. (1981). Male and female therapists' responses to male and female client sexual material: An analogue study. *Archives of Sexual Behavior, 10,* 477–492.

Schreiber, D. J., Goldman, H., Kleinman, K. M., Goldfader, P. R., & Snow, M. Y. (1976). The relationship between independent neuropsychological and neurological detection and localization of cerebral impairment. *Journal of Nervous and Mental Disease, 162,* 360–365.

Schwartz, G. S., Friedlander, M. L., & Tedeschi, J. T. (1986). Effects of clients' attributional explanations and reasons for seeking help on counselors' impressions. *Journal of Counseling Psychology, 33,* 90–93.

Schwartz, H. I., Appelbaum, P. S., & Kaplan, R. D. (1984). Clinical judgments in the decision to commit. *Archives of General Psychiatry, 41,* 811–815.

Schwartz, J. M., & Abramowitz, S. I. (1975). Value-related effects on psychiatric judgment. *Archives of General Psychiatry, 32,* 1525–1529.

Schwartz, J. M., & Abramowitz, S. I. (1978). Effects of female client physical attractiveness on clinical judgment. *Psychotherapy: Theory, Research, and Practice, 15,* 251–257.

Segal, S. P., Bola, J. R., & Watson, M. A. (1996). Race, quality of care, and antipsychotic prescribing practices in psychiatric emergency services. *Psychiatric Services, 47,* 282–286.

Segel, R. H. (1952). *A study of the ability to predict the self-concept of an individual from four different media.* Unpublished doctoral dissertation, University of Chicago.

Seitz, P. F. D. (1966). The consensus problem in psychoanalytic research. In L. Gottschalk & A. H. Auerbach (Eds.), *Methods of research in psychotherapy.* New York: Appleton-Century-Crofts.

Seligman, M. R. (1968). The interracial casework relationship. *Smith College Studies in Social Work, 39,* 84.

Settin, J. M. (1982). Clinical judgment in geropsychology practice. *Psychotherapy: Theory, Research, and Practice, 19,* 397–404.

Settin, J. M., & Bramel, D. (1981). Interaction of client class and gender in biasing clinical judgment. *American Journal of Orthopsychiatry, 51,* 510–520.

Shagoury, P., & Satz, P. (1969). The effect of statistical information on clinical prediction. *Proceedings of the 77th Annual Convention of the American Psychological Association, 4,* 517–518.

Shanteau, J. (1981). *Detection of multiplicative synergisms in simulated data for nonorthogonal designs: What lies beyond linearity?* (Rep. No. 235). Boulder: University of Colorado Institute of Behavioral Science, Center for Research on Judgment and Policy.

Shapiro, F. (1995). *Eye movement desensitization and reprocessing: Basic principles, protocols, and procedures.* New York: Guilford Press.

Sharkey, J. (1994). *Bedlam: Greed, profiteering, and fraud in a mental health system gone crazy.* New York: St. Martin's.

Sharpe, L., Gurland, B. J., Fleiss, J. L., Kendell, R. E., Cooper, J. E., & Copeland, J. R. M. (1974). Some comparisons of American, Canadian, and British psychiatrists in their diagnostic concepts. *Canadian Journal of Psychiatry, 19,* 235–245.

Shemberg, K. M., & Leventhal, D. B. (1981). Attitudes of internship directors toward pre-internship training and clinical training models. *Professional Psychology: Research and Practice, 12,* 639–646.

Shenkel, R. J., Snyder, C. R., Batson, C. D., & Clark, G. M. (1979). Effects of prior diagnostic information on clinicians' causal attributions of a client's problems. *Journal of Consulting and Clinical Psychology, 47,* 404–406.

Shneidman, E. S. (1971). Perturbation and lethality as precursors of suicide in a gifted group. *Life-Threatening Behavior, 1,* 23–45.

Shortliffe, E. H., Buchanan, B. G., & Feigenbaum, E. A. (1979). Knowledge engineering for medical decision making: A review of computer-based clinical decision aids. *Proceedings of the IEEE, 67,* 1207–1224.

Shullman, S. L., & Betz, N. E. (1979). An investigation of the effects of client sex and presenting problem in referral from intake. *Journal of Counseling Psychology, 26,* 140–145.

Silverman, L. H. (1959). A Q-sort study of the validity of evaluations made from projective techniques. *Psychological Monographs, 73*(7, Whole No. 477).

Simon, H. A. (1965). *The shape of automation for men and management.* New York: Harper & Row.

Simon, H. A. (1978). Information-processing theory of human problem solving. In W. K. Estes (Ed.), *Handbook of learning and cognitive processes* (Vol. 5). Hillsdale, NJ: Erlbaum.

Simon, R. J., Fleiss, J. L., Gurland, B. J., Stiller, P. R., & Sharpe, L. (1973). Depression and schizophrenia in hospitalized Black and White mental patients. *Archives of General Psychiatry, 28,* 509–512.

Sines, J. O. (1970). Actuarial versus clinical prediction in psychopathology. *British Journal of Psychiatry, 116,* 129–144.

Sines, L. K. (1959). The relative contribution of four kinds of data to accuracy in personality assessment. *Journal of Consulting Psychology, 23,* 483–492.

Skinner, H. (1981). Toward the integration of classification theory and methods. *Journal of Abnormal Psychology, 90,* 68–87.

Skodol, A. (1989). *Problems in differential diagnosis: From DSM–III to DSM–III–R in clinical practice.* Washington, DC: American Psychiatric Press.

Skodol, A., Oldham, J., Rosnick, L., Kellman, H., & Hyler, S. (1991). Diagnosis of *DSM–III–R* personality disorders: A comparison of two structured interviews. *International Journal of Methods in Psychiatric Research, 1,* 13–26.

Skodol, A., Williams, J. B. W., Spitzer, R. L., Gibbon, M., & Kass, F. (1984). Identifying common errors in the use of *DSM–III* through diagnostic supervision. *Hospital and Community Psychiatry, 35,* 251–255.

Smith, E. R., & Miller, F. D. (1978). Limits on perception of cognitive processes: A reply to Nisbett and Wilson. *Psychological Review, 85,* 355–362.

Smith, M. L. (1974). Influence of client sex and ethnic group on counselor judgments. *Journal of Counseling Psychology, 21,* 516–521.

Smith, M. L. (1980). Sex bias in counseling and psychotherapy. *Psychological Bulletin, 87,* 392–407.

Snyder, C. R. (1977). "A patient by any other name" revisited: Maladjustment or attributional locus of problem? *Journal of Consulting and Clinical Psychology, 45,* 101–103.

Snyder, C. R. (1995). Clinical psychology building inspection: Slipping off its science-based foundation. [Review of the book *House of cards: Psychology and psychotherapy built on myth*]. *Contemporary Psychology, 40*, 422–424.

Snyder, C. R., Shenkel, R. J., & Lowery, C. R. (1977). Acceptance of personality interpretations: The "Barnum effect" and beyond. *Journal of Consulting and Clinical Psychology, 45*, 104–114.

Snyder, D. K., Widiger, T. A., & Hoover, D. W. (1990). Methodological considerations in validating computer-based test interpretations: Controlling for response bias. *Psychological Assessment, 2*, 470–477.

Snyder, J. C., & Newberger, E. H. (1986). Consensus and difference among hospital professionals in evaluating child maltreatment. *Violence and Victims, 1*, 125–139.

Snyder, M., & Thomsen, C. J. (1988). Interactions between therapists and clients: Hypothesis testing and behavioral confirmation. In D. C. Turk & P. Salovey (Eds.), *Reasoning, inference, and judgment in clinical psychology* (pp. 124–152). New York: Free Press.

Soskin, W. F. (1954). Bias in postdiction from projective tests. *Journal of Abnormal and Social Psychology, 49*, 69–74.

Soskin, W. F. (1959). Influence of four types of data on diagnostic conceptualization in psychological testing. *Journal of Abnormal and Social Psychology, 58*, 69–78.

Spanos, N. P. (1994). Multiple identity enactments and multiple personality disorder: A sociocognitive perspective. *Psychological Bulletin, 116*, 143–165.

Spengler, P. M., & Strohmer, D. C. (1994). Clinical judgmental biases: The moderating roles of counselor cognitive complexity and counselor client preferences. *Journal of Counseling Psychology, 41*, 8–17.

Spengler, P. M., Strohmer, D. C., & Prout, H. T. (1990). Testing the robustness of the overshadowing bias. *American Journal on Mental Retardation, 95*, 204–214.

Sperber, Z., & Adlerstein, A. M. (1961). The accuracy of clinical psychologists' estimates of interviewees' intelligence. *Journal of Consulting Psychology, 25*, 521–524.

Spitzer, R. L. (1975). On pseudoscience in science, logic in remission, and psychiatric diagnosis: A critique of Rosenhan's "On Being Sane in Insane Places." *Journal of Abnormal Psychology, 84*, 442–452.

Spitzer, R. L. (1983). Psychiatric diagnosis: Are clinicians still necessary? *Comprehensive Psychiatry, 24*, 399–411.

Spitzer, R. L., First, M. B., Kendler, K. S., & Stein, D. J. (1993). The reliability of three definitions of bizarre delusions. *American Journal of Psychiatry, 150*, 880–884.

Spitzer, R. L., & Forman, J. B. W. (1979). DSM–III field trials: Initial experience with the multiaxial system. *American Journal of Psychiatry, 136*, 818–820.

Spitzer, R. L., Forman, J. B. W., & Nee, J. (1979). DSM–III field trials: Initial interrater diagnostic reliability. *American Journal of Psychiatry, 136*, 815–817.

Spitzer, R. L., Williams, J. B. W., Gibbon, M., & First, M. B. (1987). *Structured*

Clinical Interview for DSM–III–R *Personality Disorders (SCID–II)*. New York, Biometrics Research, New York State Psychiatric Institute.

Spitzer, R. L., Williams, J. B. W., Gibbon, M., & First, M. B. (1990). *Structured Clinical Interview for* DSM–III–R *(SCID): User's guide*. Washington, DC: American Psychiatric Press.

Spreen, O., & Strauss, E. (1991). *A compendium of neuropsychological tests: Administration, norms, and commentary*. New York: Oxford University.

Stack, L. C., Lannon, P. B., & Miley, A. D. (1983). Accuracy of clinicians' expectancies for psychiatric rehospitalization. *American Journal of Community Psychology*, *11*, 99–113.

Starr, B. J., & Katkin, E. S. (1969). The clinician as an aberrant actuary: Illusory correlation and the Incomplete Sentences Blank. *Journal of Abnormal Psychology*, *74*, 670–675.

Stearns, B. C., Penner, L. A., & Kimmel, E. (1980). Sexism among psychotherapists: A case not yet proven. *Journal of Consulting and Clinical Psychology*, *48*, 548–550.

Stein, L. S., Del Gaudio, A. C., & Ansley, M. Y. (1976). A comparison of female and male neurotic depressives. *Journal of Clinical Psychology*, *32*, 19–21.

Steiner, J. L., Tebes, J. K., Sledge, W. H., & Walker, M. L. (1995). A comparison of the Structured Clinical Interview for *DSM–III–R* and clinical diagnoses. *Journal of Nervous and Mental Disease*, *183*, 365–369.

Stelmachers, Z. T., & McHugh, R. B. (1964). Contribution of stereotyped and individualized information to predictive accuracy. *Journal of Consulting Psychology*, *28*, 234–242.

Stelmachers, Z. T., & Sherman, R. E. (1990). Use of case vignettes in suicide risk assessment. *Suicide and Life-Threatening Behavior*, *20*, 65–84.

Stenson, H., Kleinmuntz, B., & Scott, B. (1975). Personality assessment as a signal detection task. *Journal of Consulting and Clinical Psychology*, *43*, 794–799.

Stevens, G. (1981). Bias in the attribution of hyperkinetic behavior as a function of ethnic identification and socioeconomic status. *Psychology in the Schools*, *18*, 99–106.

Stoller, R. J., & Geertsma, R. H. (1963). The consistency of psychiatrists' clinical judgments. *Journal of Nervous and Mental Disease*, *137*, 58–66.

Stott, D. H. (1958). Some psychosomatic aspects of causality in reproduction. *Journal of Psychosomatic Research*, *3*, 42–55.

Stricker, G. (1967). Actuarial, naive clinical, and sophisticated clinical prediction of pathology from figure drawings. *Journal of Consulting Psychology*, *31*, 492–494.

Stricker, G. (1977). Implications of research for psychotherapeutic treatment of women. *American Psychologist*, *32*, 14–22.

Strickland, T. L., Jenkins, J. O., Myers, H. F., & Adams, H. E. (1988). Diagnostic judgments as a function of client and therapist race. *Journal of Psychopathology and Behavioral Assessment*, *10*, 141–151.

Strohmer, D. C., & Chiodo, A. L. (1984). Counselor hypothesis testing strategies: The role of initial impressions and self-schema. *Journal of Counseling Psychology*, *31*, 510–519.

Strohmer, D. C., & Newman, L. J. (1983). Counselor hypothesis testing strategies. *Journal of Counseling Psychology*, *30*, 557–565.

Strohmer, D. C., Shivy, V. A., & Chiodo, A. L. (1990). Information processing strategies in counselor hypothesis testing: The role of selective memory and expectancy. *Journal of Counseling Psychology*, *37*, 465–472.

Stuart, S., Simons, A. D., Thase, M. E., & Pilkonis, P. (1992). Are personality assessments valid in acute major depression? *Journal of Affective Disorders*, *24*, 281–290.

Sutker, P. B., Bugg, F., & Allain, A. N. (1991). Psychometric prediction of PTSD among POW survivors. *Psychological Assessment*, *3*, 105–110.

Sutton, R. G., & Kessler, M. (1986). National study of the effects of clients' socioeconomic status on clinical psychologists' professional judgments. *Journal of Consulting and Clinical Psychology*, *54*, 275–276.

Sweet, J. J., Moberg, P. J., & Westergaard, C. K. (1996). Five-year follow-up survey of practices and beliefs of clinical neuropsychologists. *The Clinical Neuropsychologist*, *10*, 202–221.

Swensen, C. H. (1957). Empirical evaluations of human figure drawings. *Psychological Bulletin*, *54*, 431–466.

Swiercinsky, D. P., & Leigh, G. (1979). Comparison of neuropsychological data in the diagnosis of brain impairment with computerized tomography and other neurological procedures. *Journal of Clinical Psychology*, *35*, 242–246.

Temerlin, M. K. (1968). Suggestion effects in psychiatric diagnosis. *Journal of Nervous and Mental Disease*, *147*, 349–353.

Temerlin, M. K., & Trousdale, W. W. (1969). The social psychology of clinical diagnosis. *Psychotherapy: Theory, Research, and Practice*, *6*, 24–29.

Tenhula, W. N., & Sweet, J. J. (1996). Double cross-validation of the Booklet Category Test in detecting malingered traumatic brain injury. *The Clinical Neuropsychologist*, *10*, 104–116.

Teri, L. (1982). Effects of sex and sex-role style on clinical judgment. *Sex Roles*, *8*, 639–649.

Terman, L. M. (1940). Psychological approaches to the biography of genius. *Science*, *92*, 293–301.

Thomas, A. H., & Stewart, N. R. (1971). Counselor response to female clients with deviate and conforming career goals. *Journal of Counseling Psychology*, *18*, 352–357.

Thompson, J. S., & Ager, J. W. (1988). An experimental analysis of the civil commitment recommendations of psychologists and psychiatrists. *Behavioral Sciences & the Law*, *6*, 119–129.

Todd, F. J. (1954). *A methodological analysis of clinical judgment*. Unpublished doctoral dissertation, University of Colorado, Boulder.

Todd, F. J., & Hammond, K. R. (1965). Differential effects in two multiple-cue probability learning tasks. *Behavioral Science, 10,* 429–435.

Tomlinson-Clarke, S., & Cheatham, H. E. (1993). Counselor and client ethnicity and counselor intake judgments. *Journal of Counseling Psychology, 40,* 267–270.

Trachtman, J. P. (1971). Socio-economic class bias in Rorschach diagnosis: Contributing psychological attributes of the clinician. *Journal of Projective Techniques and Personality Assessment, 35,* 229–240.

Tranebjærg, L., & Ørum, A. (1991). Major depressive disorder as a prominent but underestimated feature of Fragile X syndrome. *Comprehensive Psychiatry, 32,* 83–87.

Trueblood, W., & Binder, L. M. (1997). Psychologists' accuracy in identifying neuropsychological test protocols of clinical malingerers. *Archives of Clinical Neuropsychology, 12,* 13–27.

Trull, T. J., & Larson, S. L. (1994). External validity of two personality disorder inventories. *Journal of Personality Disorders, 8,* 96–103.

Tseng, W., McDermott, J. F., Jr., Ogino, K., & Ebata, K. (1982). Cross-cultural differences in parent–child assessment: U.S.A. and Japan. *International Journal of Social Psychiatry, 28,* 305–317.

Tsujimoto, R. N., & Berger, D. E. (1986). Situational influences on the predictive value of client behavior: Implication for Bayesian prediction. *Journal of Consulting and Clinical Psychology, 54,* 264–266.

Turk, D. C., & Salovey, P. (1986). Clinical information processing: Bias inoculation. In R. E. Ingram (Ed.), *Information processing approaches to clinical psychology* (pp. 305–322). Orlando, FL: Academic Press.

Turk, D. C., & Salovey, P. (Eds.). (1988). *Reasoning, inference, and judgment in clinical psychology.* New York: Free Press.

Turner, D. R. (1966). Predictive efficiency as a function of amount of information and level of professional experience. *Journal of Projective Techniques and Personality Assessment, 30,* 4–11.

Tutin, J. (1993). The persistence of initial beliefs in clinical judgment. *Journal of Social and Clinical Psychology, 12,* 319–335.

Tversky, A., & Kahneman, D. (1973). Availability: A heuristic for judging frequency and probability. *Cognitive Psychology, 5,* 207–232.

Tversky, A., & Kahneman, D. (1974). Judgments under uncertainty: Heuristics and biases. *Science, 185,* 1124–1131.

Tymchuk, A. J., Drapkin, R., Major-Kingsley, S., Ackerman, A. B., Coffman, E. W., & Baum, M. S. (1982). Ethical decision making and psychologists' attitudes toward training in ethics. *Professional Psychology, 13,* 412–421.

Uhlenhuth, E. H., Balter, M. B., Mellinger, G. D., Cisin, I. H., & Clinthorne, J. (1983). Symptom checklist syndromes in the general population. *Archives of General Psychiatry, 40,* 1167–1173.

Umbenhauer, S. L., & DeWitte, L. L. (1978). Patient race and social class: Attitudes and decisions among three groups of mental health professionals. *Comprehensive Psychiatry, 19,* 509–515.

Vail, S. (1970). The effects of socioeconomic class, race, and level of experience on social workers' judgments of clients. *Smith College Studies in Social Work, 40,* 236–246.

Van den Bosch, R. J., Rozendaal, N., & Mol, J. M. F. A. (1987). Symptom correlates of eye tracking dysfunction. *Biological Psychiatry, 22,* 919–921.

Vanderploeg, R. D., Sison, G. F. P., Jr., & Hickling, E. J. (1987). A reevaluation of the use of the MMPI in the assessment of combat-related Posttraumatic stress disorder. *Journal of Personality Assessment, 51,* 140–150.

Veit, C. T., & Ware, J. E., Jr. (1983). The structure of psychological distress and well-being in general populations. *Journal of Consulting and Clinical Psychology, 51,* 730–742.

Vitiello, B., Malone, R., Buschle, P. R., Delaney, M. A., & Behar, D. (1990). Reliability of DSM–III diagnoses of hospitalized children. *Hospital and Community Psychiatry, 41,* 63–67.

Wadsworth, R. D., & Checketts, K. T. (1980). Influence of religious affiliation on psychodiagnosis. *Journal of Consulting and Clinical Psychology, 48,* 234–246.

Wagner, E. E. (1969). A reply to Mordock's "Critique." *Journal of Projective Techniques and Personality Assessment, 33,* 492.

Wagner, E. E., & Murray, A. Y. (1969). Bender-Gestalts of organic children: Accuracy of clinical judgment. *Journal of Projective Techniques and Personality Assessment, 33,* 240–242.

Wainer, H. (1976). Estimating coefficients in linear models: It don't make no nevermind. *Psychological Bulletin, 83,* 213–217.

Wainer, H. (1978). On the sensitivity of regression and regressors. *Psychological Bulletin, 85,* 267–273.

Walker, B. S., & Spengler, P. M. (1995). Clinical judgment of major depression in AIDS patients: The effects of clinician complexity and stereotyping. *Professional Psychology, 26,* 269–273.

Walker, C. E., & Linden, J. D. (1967). Varying degrees of psychological sophistication in the interpretation of sentence completion data. *Journal of Clinical Psychology, 23,* 229–231.

Walker, E., & Lewine, R. J. (1990). Prediction of adult-onset schizophrenia from childhood home movies of the patients. *American Journal of Psychiatry, 147,* 1052–1056.

Wallach, M. S., & Schooff, K. (1965). Reliability of degree of disturbance ratings. *Journal of Clinical Psychology, 21,* 273–275.

Waller, R. W., & Keeley, S. M. (1978). Effects of explanation and information feedback on the illusory correlation phenomenon. *Journal of Consulting and Clinical Psychology, 46,* 342–343.

Wallsten, T. S., & Budescu, D. V. (1981). Additivity and nonadditivity in judging MMPI profiles. *Journal of Experimental Psychology: Human Perception and Performance, 7,* 1096–1109.

Walters, G. D., White, T. W., & Greene, R. L. (1988). Use of the MMPI to identify malingering and exaggeration of psychiatric symptomatology in male prison inmates. *Journal of Consulting and Clinical Psychology, 56,* 111–117.

Wanderer, Z. W. (1969). Validity of clinical judgments based on human figure drawings. *Journal of Consulting and Clinical Psychology, 33,* 143–150.

Warner, R. (1978). The diagnosis of antisocial and hysterical personality disorders: An example of sex bias. *Journal of Nervous and Mental Disease, 166,* 839–845.

Warner, R. (1979). Racial and sexual bias in psychiatric diagnosis. *Journal of Nervous and Mental Disease, 167,* 303–310.

Watkins, C. E., Jr., Campbell, V. L., Nieberding, R., & Hallmark, R. (1995). Contemporary practice of psychological assessment by clinical psychologists. *Professional Psychology: Research and Practice, 26,* 54–60.

Watson, C. G. (1967). Relationship of distortion to DAP diagnostic accuracy among psychologists at three levels of sophistication. *Journal of Consulting Psychology, 31,* 142–146.

Watson, M. A., Segal, S. P., & Newhill, C. E. (1993). Police referral to psychiatric emergency services and its effect on disposition decisions. *Hospital and Community Psychiatry, 44,* 1085–1090.

Waxer, P. (1976). Nonverbal cues for depth of depression: Set versus no set. *Journal of Consulting and Clinical Psychology, 44,* 493.

Wechsler, D. (1981). *Wechsler Adult Intelligence Test–Revised.* New York: The Psychological Corporation.

Wedding, D. (1983). Clinical and statistical prediction in neuropsychology. *Clinical Neuropsychology, 5,* 49–55.

Weinberg, G. H. (1957). Clinical versus statistical prediction with a method of evaluating a tool. *Dissertation Abstracts, 17* (1602). (University Microfilms No. 57-2577)

Weintraub, W., Harbin, H. T., Book, J., Nyman, G. W., Karahasan, A., Krajewski, T., & Regan, B. L. (1984). The Maryland plan for recruiting psychiatrists into public service. *American Journal of Psychiatry, 141,* 91–94.

Weiss, J., Sampson, H., & The Mount Zion Psychotherapy Group (1986). *The psychoanalytic process: Theory, clinical observations, and empirical research.* New York: Guilford Press.

Weiss, J. H. (1963). The effect of professional training and amount and accuracy of information on behavioral prediction. *Journal of Consulting Psychology, 27,* 257–262.

Weist, M. D., & Ollendick, T. H. (1991). Toward empirically valid target selection with children: The case of assertiveness. *Behavior Modification, 15,* 213–227.

Weist, M. D., Ollendick, T. H., & Finney, J. W. (1991). Toward the empirical validation of treatment targets in children. *Clinical Psychology Review, 11,* 515–538.

Weller, R. A., Weller, E. B., Tucker, S. G., & Fristad, M. A. (1986). Mania in prepubertal children: Has it been underdiagnosed? *Journal of Affective Disorders, 11,* 151–154.

Wells, K. B., Katon, W., Rogers, B., & Camp, P. (1994). Use of minor tranquilizers and antidepressant medications by depressed outpatients: Results from the Medical Outcomes Study. *American Journal of Psychiatry, 151*, 694–700.

Werner, P. D. (1992, September). *The quest for mental health practitioners' special expertise in predicting violence.* Paper presented at the Third European Conference of Law and Psychology, Oxford, England.

Werner, P. D., Rose, T. L., & Yesavage, J. A. (1983). Reliability, accuracy, and decision-making strategy in clinical predictions of imminent dangerousness. *Journal of Consulting and Clinical Psychology, 51*, 815–825.

Wetzler, S., & van Praag, H. M. (1989). Assessment of depression. In S. Wetzler (Ed.), *Measuring mental illness: Psychometric assessment for clinicians* (pp. 70–88). Washington, DC: American Psychiatric Press.

White, P. (1980). Limitations on verbal reports of internal events: A refutation of Nisbett and Wilson and of Bem. *Psychological Review, 87*, 105–112.

Whitley, B. E. (1979). Sex roles and psychotherapy: A current appraisal. *Psychological Bulletin, 86*, 309–321.

Widiger, T. A. (1983). Utilities and fixed diagnostic rules: Comments on Finn. *Journal of Abnormal Psychology, 92*, 495–498.

Widiger, T. A. (1993a). Issues in the validation of the personality disorders. In L. J. Chapman, J. P. Chapman, & D. C. Fowles (Eds.), *Progress in experimental and psychopathology research. Volume 16* (pp. 117–136). New York: Springer.

Widiger, T. A. (1993b). Personality and depression: Assessment issues. In M. H. Klein, D. J. Kupfer, & M. T. Shea (Eds.), *Personality and depression: A current view* (pp. 77–118). New York: Guilford.

Widiger, T. A. (1993c). Validation strategies for the personality disorders. *Journal of Personality Disorders* (Suppl.), 34–43.

Widiger, T. A., Cadoret, R., Hare, R., Robins, L., Rutherford, M., Zanarini, M., Alterman, A., Apple, M., Corbitt, E., Forth, A., Hart, S., Kultermann, J., Woody, G., & Frances, A. (1996). DSM–IV antisocial personality disorder field trial. *Journal of Abnormal Psychology, 105*, 3–16.

Widiger, T. A., & Frances, A. (1987). Definitions and diagnoses: A brief response to Morey and McNamara. *Journal of Abnormal Psychology, 96*, 286–287.

Widiger, T. A., Frances, A., Warner, L., & Bluhm, C. (1986). Diagnostic criteria for the borderline and schizotypal personality disorders. *Journal of Abnormal Psychology, 95*, 43–51.

Widiger, T. A., Freiman, K., & Bailey, B. (1990). Convergent and discriminant validity of personality disorder prototypic acts. *Psychological Assessment, 2*, 107–113.

Widiger, T. A., Sanderson, C., & Warner, L. (1986). The MMPI, prototypal typology, and borderline personality disorder. *Journal of Personality Assessment, 50*, 540–553.

Widiger, T. A., & Settle, S. A. (1987). Broverman et al. revisited: An artifactual sex bias. *Journal of Personality and Social Psychology, 53*, 463–469.

Widiger, T. A., & Spitzer, R. L. (1991). Sex bias in the diagnosis of personality disorders: Conceptual and methodological issues. *Clinical Psychology Review, 11*, 1–22.

Widiger, T. A., & Trull, T. J. (1985). The empty debate over the existence of mental illness: Comments on Gorenstein. *American Psychologist, 40*, 468–470.

Wiggins, J. S. (1973). *Personality and prediction: Principles of personality assessment.* Reading, MA: Addison-Wesley.

Wiggins, J. S. (1981). Clinical and statistical prediction: Where are we and where do we go from here? *Clinical Psychology Review, 1*, 3–18.

Wiggins, J. S. (1995). *Interpersonal Adjective Scales: Professional manual.* Odessa, FL: Psychological Assessment Resources.

Wiggins, J. S., & Trobst, K. K. (1997). Prospects for the assessment of normal and abnormal interpersonal behavior. *Journal of Personality Assessment, 68*, 110–126.

Wiggins, N., & Hoffman, P. J. (1968). Three models of clinical judgment. *Journal of Abnormal Psychology, 73*, 70–77.

Wiggins, N., & Kohen, E. S. (1971). Man versus model of man revisited: The forecasting of graduate school success. *Journal of Personality and Social Psychology, 19*, 100–106.

Wildman, R. W., & Wildman, R. W., II. (1975). An investigation into the comparative validity of several diagnostic tests and test batteries. *Journal of Clinical Psychology, 31*, 455–458.

Wilkins, J. N., Shaner, A. L., Patterson, C. M., Setoda, D., & Gorelick, D. (1991). Discrepancies between patient report, clinical assessment, and urine analysis in psychiatric patients during inpatient admission. *Psychopharmacology Bulletin, 27*, 149–154.

Williams, L. M. (1994). Recall of childhood trauma: A prospective study of women's memories of child sexual abuse. *Journal of Consulting and Clinical Psychology, 62*, 1167–1176.

Wills, T. A. (1978). Perceptions of clients by professional helpers. *Psychological Bulletin, 85*, 968–1000.

Wilson, C. A., & Gettinger, M. (1989). Determinants of child abuse reporting among Wisconsin school psychologists. *Professional School Psychology, 4*, 91–102.

Wilson, F. E., & Evans, I. M. (1983). The reliability of target-behavior selection in behavioral assessment. *Behavioral Assessment, 5*, 15–32.

Wilson, S. A., Becker, L. A., & Tinker, R. H. (1995). Eye movement desensitization and reprocessing (EMDR) treatment for psychologically traumatized individuals. *Journal of Consulting and Clinical Psychology, 63*, 928–937.

Wilson, T. D. (1994). The proper protocol: Validity and completeness of verbal reports. *Psychological Science, 5*, 249–252.

Wittman, M. P. (1941). A scale for measuring prognosis in schizophrenic patients. *Elgin Papers, 4*, 20–33.

Wittman, M. P., & Steinberg, L. (1944). Follow-up of an objective evaluation of prognosis in dementia proecox and manic-depressive psychoses. *Elgin Papers*, 5, 216–227.

Wood, J. M., Nezworski, M. T., & Stejskal, W. J. (1996a). The Comprehensive System for the Rorschach: A critical examination. *Psychological Science*, 7, 3–10.

Wood, J. M., Nezworski, M. T., & Stejskal, W. J. (1996b). Thinking critically about the Comprehensive System for the Rorschach: A reply to Exner. *Psychological Science*, 7, 14–17.

Worthington, R. L., & Atkinson, D. R. (1993). Counselors' responsibility and etiology attributions, theoretical orientations, and counseling strategies. *Journal of Counseling Psychology*, 40, 295–302.

Wright, J. A., & Hutton, B. O. (1977). Influence of client socioeconomic status on selected behaviors, attitudes, and decisions of counselors. *Journal of Counseling Psychology*, 24, 527–530.

Wrobel, N. H. (1993). Effect of patient age and gender on clinical decisions. *Professional Psychology*, 24, 206–212.

Wyatt, G. E., Powell, G. J., & Bass, B. A. (1982). The survey of Afro-American behavior: Its development and use in research. In B. A. Bass, G. E. Wyatt, & G. J. Powell (Eds.), *The Afro-American family: Assessment, treatment, and research issues* (pp. 13–33). New York: Grune & Stratton.

Wyatt, R. J., Alexander, R. C., Egan, M. F., & Kirch, D. G. (1988). Schizophrenia, just the facts. What do we know, how well do we know it? *Schizophrenia Research*, 1, 3–18.

Yapko, M. D. (1994). Suggestibility and repressed memories of abuse: A survey of psychotherapists' beliefs. *American Journal of Clinical Hypnosis*, 36, 163–171.

Yesavage, J. A., Werner, P. D., Becker, J. M., & Mills, M. (1982). Short-term civil commitment and the violent patient: A study of legal status and inpatient behavior. *American Journal of Psychiatry*, 139, 1145–1149.

Yntema, D. B., & Torgerson, W. S. (1961). Man-computer cooperation in decisions requiring common sense. *IRE Transactions on Human Factors in Electronics*, HFE-2, 20–26.

Young, L. M., & Powell, B. (1985). The effects of obesity on the clinical judgments of mental health professionals. *Journal of Health and Social Behavior*, 26, 233–246.

Young, R. C. (1972). Clinical judgment as a means of improving actuarial prediction from the MMPI. *Journal of Consulting and Clinical Psychology*, 38, 457–459.

Ysseldyke, J., Algozzine, B., Regan, R., & McGue, M. (1981). The influence of test scores and naturally-occurring pupil characteristics on psychoeducational decision making with children. *Journal of School Psychology*, 19, 167–177.

Zellman, G. L. (1990). Report decision-making patterns among mandated child abuse reporters. *Child Abuse and Neglect*, 14, 325–336.

Zellman, G. L. (1992). The impact of case characteristics on child abuse reporting decisions. *Child Abuse & Neglect*, 16, 57–74.

Zellman, G. L., & Bell, K. (1989). *The role of professional background, case characteristics, and protective agency response in mandated child abuse reporting*. Santa Monica, CA: Rand.

Zimmerman, M. (1994). Diagnosing personality disorders: A review of issues and research methods. *Archives of General Psychiatry, 51,* 225–245.

Zimmerman, M., Coryell, W., & Black, D. W. (1993). A method to detect intercenter differences in the application of contemporary diagnostic criteria. *Journal of Nervous and Mental Disease, 181,* 130–134.

Zimmerman, M., Coryell, W., Pfohl, B., & Stangl, D. (1985). Four definitions of endogenous depression and the dexamethasone suppression test. *Journal of Affective Disorders, 8,* 37–45.

Ziskin, J., & Faust, D. (1988). *Coping with psychiatric and psychological testimony* (Vols. 1–3, 4th ed.). Venice, CA: Law and Psychology Press.

Ziskin, J., & Faust, D. (1991). Reply to Matarazzo. *American Psychologist, 46,* 881–882.

Zou, Y., Shen, Y., Shu, L., Wang, Y., Feng, F., Xu, K., Qu, Y., Song, Y., Zhong, Y., Wang, M., & Liu, W. (1996). Artificial neural network to assist psychiatric diagnosis. *British Journal of Psychiatry, 169,* 64–67.

Zygmond, M. J., & Denton, W. (1988). Gender bias in marital therapy: A multidimensional scaling analysis. *The American Journal of Family Therapy, 16,* 262–272.

AUTHOR INDEX

Meltzer, B., 209
Meltzer, H. Y., 47, 60
Memon, A., 123
Mendel, W. M., 199
Merluzzi, B. H., 62
Merluzzi, T. V., 62
Messer, S. B., 91, 122
Meyerson, A. T., 70
Mezzich, A. C., 90
Mezzich, J. E., 90, 187
Michel, J. B., 131
Mikulka, P. J., 225
Miley, A. D., 113, 115
Miller, D. T., 22
Miller, E. N., 52
Miller, F. D., 179, 197, 198
Miller, H., 193
Miller, H. R., 52
Miller, K. J., 215
Miller, M., 76, 156
Miller, M. B., 52, 65, 135
Miller, R. G., 210
Miller, R. S., 5
Mills, D. H., 174
Minsky, M., 240
Mischel, W., 20, 21, 22, 187
Mitchell, J. C., 78
Mittenberg, W., 68, 223, 232
Moberg, P. J., 157
Moffitt, T. E., 47
Mohns, L., 156
Mojtabai, R., 12
Mol, J. M. F. A., 52
Moldin, S. O., 50
Molinari, V., 53, 65, 75
Monahan, J., 107, 222
Montgomery, R. W., 150
Mooney, K. A., 119
Moore, K., 12
Moreland, K. L., 224, 225
Morey, L. C., 11, 43, 44, 46, 51, 66, 68, 81, 232
Morgan, D. W., 225, 226
Morgenstern, J., 40, 215
Morin, S. F., 31, 34, 67, 135, 137
Morrisey, R. F., 135
Morrow, G. R., 132
Moses, J. A., Jr., 156, 158, 159
Moss, J. Z., 70
Mossman, D., 107, 108, 109, 111
Motta, R. W., 24, 242
Mount Zion Psychotherapy Group, 91

Mowrey, J. D., 25
Moxley, A. W., 210
Muehleman, T., 145
Mueser, K. T., 89, 111
Mukherjee, S., 61, 113, 127
Mulick, J. A., 149
Mulvey, E. P., 104, 107, 108, 109, 111, 114, 222
Murburg, M. M., 188
Murdock, J. B., 158
Murdock, N. L., 186, 191, 195
Murray, A. Y., 158
Murray, C., 131
Murray, J., 64, 133, 134, 140
Murrin, M., 89
Myers, H. F., 28, 62

N

Nadler, E. B., 166
Nadler, J. D., 68, 167, 168, 191, 232
Nalven, F. B., 27, 30, 31, 32
Nasrallah, M. A., 106
Nathan, P. E., 215
Nee, J., 41
Neer, W. L., 63
Nelson, K., 43
Nelson, R. O., 35, 72, 119, 120
Nesvig, D., 57, 217
Neubauer, D. N., 104, 105
Neumann, M., 131
Neuringer, C., 158
Newberger, E. H., 129, 130, 136, 146, 147
Newhill, C. E., 143
Newman, F. L., 99
Newman, J. R., 215
Newman, L. J., 186
Nezu, A. M., 237
Nezu, C. M., 237
Nezworski, M. T., 237
Nichols, D. S., 52
Nicholson, R. A., 12, 51
Nieberding, R., 158
Nierenberg, A. A., 121
Nieri, D., 137
Nightingale, N., 147
Nisbett, R. E., 173, 197
Nohara, M., 144, 238
Noordsy, D. L., 77
Norcross, J. C., 244
North, C. S., 93
Norton, K., 76

Nuechterlein, K. H., 52
Nuttall, R., 129, 136, 139, 146
Nystedt, L., 11, 13

O

Oakland, T., 129, 130
O'Brien, E. J., 20
O'Brien, W. H., 94
Ochoa, E. S., 43, 44, 66, 68
O'Conner, W. A., 222
O'Connor, R., Jr., 245
O'Connor, T., 35
Ofshe, R., 78, 149
Ogino, K., 29
Ogloff, J. R. P., 145, 147
Olarte, S., 61
Oldham, J., 54
O'Leary, K. D., 89
O'Leary, W. C., 217
Oliveira, J., 100
Ollendick, T. H., 150
Onstad, J. A., 225
Orcutt, B. A., 185
Ørum, A., 74
Osher, F. C., 77
Oskamp, S., 15, 16, 17, 19, 56, 57, 184, 199, 217, 233, 234
Ouimette, P. C., 228
Overall, J. E., 217
Oyster-Nelson, C. K., 65, 133, 134
Ozer, D. J., 22

P

Padesky, C. A., 120
Pain, M. D., 185
Parad, H. W., 187
Parker, J. D. A., 12, 235, 236
Parsons, O. A., 156, 158, 159
Pat-Horenczyk, R., 68, 138
Patsula, P., 35
Patterson, C. M., 77
Paul, G. L., 126, 185
Pavkov, T. W., 61, 67, 68, 113
Payette, K. A., 129, 136
Peace, K., 43
Penner, L. A., 31, 32, 115
Perlick, D., 68, 138
Perrett, L. F., 185
Perry, J. C., 12, 228
Perry, S. W., 74

Persons, J. B., 119
Peterson, D. R., 244
Petzel, T. P., 25
Pfohl, B., 41, 65, 75, 190
Phelan, J. G., 18
Phillips, A. M., 217
Phillips, S. D., 185
Phillips, S. E., 67, 136
Phillips, W. M., 217, 219
Pichert, J. W., 151
Pilkonis, P., 13, 235
Pilkonis, P. A., 49, 50
Piotrowski, C., 158
Plapp, J. M., 90
Plous, S., 98, 99, 173
Pokorny, A. D., 106, 222
Polusny, M. A., 95, 123
Poole, D. A., 123, 189
Pope, H. G., Jr., 149
Porter, A., 27, 30, 130
Potts, M. K., 67, 152
Powell, B., 33, 61, 66, 116, 140
Powell, G. J., 27
Prange, M. E., 228
Prentice, D. A., 22
Propping, P., 45
Prout, H. T., 64, 65, 74, 135
Pruitt, J. A., 88
Pulver, A. E., 79, 80

Q

Qu, Y., 228
Quast, W., 158
Quay, H. C., 69
Quinsey, V. L., 110, 124, 190

R

Rabinowitz, J., 112, 114, 115, 128, 130, 131, 132, 137
Rabinowitz, S., 131
Raciti, M. A., 115
Randolph, D. L., 63
Ranzoni, J. H., 72
Rapkin, B., 243
Rapport, S., 199
Ratcliff, K. S., 46, 151
Ray, D. C., 115, 138
Rayner, J., 47
Reade, W. K., 71
Realmuto, G. M., 87

Young, L. M., 33, 116, 140
Young, R. C., 57, 210
Ysseldyke, J., 130, 136, 140, 141

Z

Zaidi, L. Y., 88
Zalewski, C., 158
Zellman, G. L., 129, 130, 136, 139, 146,
    147

Zhong, Y., 228
Zigmond, N., 129
Zimbardo, P. G., 98, 99
Zimmerman, M., 41, 65, 228
Ziskin, J., 4, 71, 80
Zivotofsky, E., 31
Zou, Y., 228
Zubin, J., 110
Zucker, K. J., 100
Zweig, R. A., 68, 115, 138
Zygmond, M. J., 115

SUBJECT INDEX

Behavioral prediction (*continued*)
  experience and training, 110
  historical perspective on, 103
  idiographic and nomothetic
    approaches to, 111
  interrater reliability of
    for suicide, 104
    for violence, 104
  person–environment interaction in,
    103
  reliability of, 104
  representativeness heuristic in, 189
  schizophrenia prognosis, 109–110
  statistical rules in, 222
  suicide and, 105–106, 118
  validity and reliability of
    mental health professionals versus
      lay judges, 110
  validity of
    clinical experience and, 110
    training and, 110
  violence and, 107–109
Bias. *See also specific, e.g., Racial bias*
  in case history data, 87–88
  in psychodiagnosis, 59–63
    base rate information and, 80–82

C

Case formulation
  case history data in, 85–89. *See also*
    Case history data
  causal inferences in, 89–100
  cognitive processes in, 189
  statistical prediction rules in, 221–222
Case history data
  accuracy of clients' statements in, 85–
    86
    implicit theories and memory, 86–
      87
    motivation and, 87
  biases in, 87–88
    confirmatory hypothesis testing
      and, 87–88
  comprehensiveness of, 88–89
    omission of sexual and physical
      abuse data in, 88–89
Causal inferences
  empirical derivation of, 99–100
  reliability of, 89–92, 100–101
    primary versus secondary negative

symptoms of schizophrenia and,
  92
psychodynamic formulations and,
  90–92
psychosocial stressor ratings and,
  89–90
validity of, 92–93, 100, 101
  attribution theory and, 98–99
  behavioral assessment and, 94–95
  context effects on, 97–98
  patient variable biases and, 95–97
  psychoanalytic formulation, 93–94
Causal reasoning
  and prediction, 190–191
Child abuse
  mandatory reporting of, 145–147
    clinician differences and, 146–147
    demographic characteristics and,
      146
    ethical principles and, 146–147
    situational factors and, 147
    underreporting and, 145
    unfamiliarity with laws and, 145–
      146
  reporting of
    gender bias and, 136
    social class bias in, 130, 152
  reporting of age bias in, 139
Civil commitment
  criteria for, 144–145
    appropriate and inappropriate
      judgment in, 144–145
  factors in
    legal, 144–145
Classification system(s)
  in assessment of personality and psy-
    chopathology, 39–43
  DSM-III, 41, 42–43
  DSM-IV, 39–43
  *International Classification of Diseases
    (ICD-10)*, 41–42
  studies of validity of, 54–55
  validity of psychodiagnosis and, 54–
    55
Client statements
  in case history
    memory and, 86–87
    motivation and, 87
Clinical judgment
  Adult Children of Alcoholics person-
    ality profile in, 202
  approaches to study of, 173

awareness of cognitive processes in, 197–200

clinician awareness of
in decision for psychiatric hospitalization, 199–200

cognitive biases in
examples of, 183

cognitive heuristics in
examples of, 182–183

cognitive processes of clinicians in, 173

data collection for
anchoring and adjustment in, 184–185

confirmatory hypothesis testing, 185–186

primacy effect in, 184

feedback from clients and, 202

formal models of
comparison of, 179–182

process-tracing, 177–179

statistical, 174–177

impediments to learning from experience, 200–205

integration of information for
base rates in, 192–193

case formulation and treatment planning and, 191

cognitive complexity in, 193

confirmatory hypothesis testing in, 186

deterministic reasoning and hindsight bias in, 189–200

norms in, 191–192

past-behavior heuristic, causal reasoning, and prediction in, 200–201

representativeness and knowledge structures in, 186–189

and learning from experience
client feedback and, 202–204

in clinical psychology graduate students study, 200

cognitive processes in, 204–205

in neuropsychologists, 200–201

memory and judgment
availability heuristic and, 196–197

confirmatory bias in, 195–196

covariation misestimation and, 194–195

schematic processing of knowledge structures in, 183–184

unawareness of clinician and, 198–199
in study of diagnoses, 197

Clinicians
comparison of diagnoses
with LEAD procedure diagnoses, 82

with structured interview diagnoses, 82

versus graduate students
prognostic ratings of, 117

psychodiagnoses of
validity of, 55

Cognitive complexity
in clinical judgments, 193

Cognitive processes
clinician awareness of judgments
nonlinear integration of information, 197–198

talking aloud and, 197

results on process-tracing models, 198

Computer-based test-interpretation programs. See Automated-assessment computer programs

Computers and judgment
automated assessment and. See Automated assessment

neural networking and. See Neural networks

statistical predication and. See Statistical prediction; Statistical prediction rules

Confidence ratings
in malingering versus neurological impairment, 165

validity of, 164–165
with forced-choice tests of malingering, 165

in localization of impairment, 165

overconfidence of neuropsychologists and, 165–166

underconfidence of neuropsychologists and, 166

Confirmatory bias
in clinical judgment, 183

in memory and judgment, 195–196

Confirmatory hypothesis testing
and case history data collection, 87–88

in clinical judgment
for data collection, 185–186

integration of information in, 186

Construct validation
of psychodiagnoses, 51, 53

LEAD (longitudinal, expert, all data) procedure
    validation of
        Robins and Guze criteria for, 49–51
    in validation of psychodiagnoses
        advantages of, 48, 52
        clinician expertise and, 48–49
        longitudinal data in, 48

M

Malingering
    detection of
        in fabricated studies, 162–163
        pseudoimpaired and head trauma patients, 163
Memory and judgment
    covariation misestimation and, 194–195
Memory(ies)
    accuracy of client's, 86–87
    false memories of childhood, 149, 202
    recovery of lost, 149
        child abuse and, 122–123, 149
    traumatic
        eye movement desensitization and reprocessing for, 149–252
Mental retardation
    treatment decisions for, 139, 162

N

Neural-network models
    benefits of, 228
    definition of, 227–228
    in psychological assessment, 228
Neuroleptic medication
    racial bias in use of, 127–128
Neurological impairment, 168–170
    overperception and underperception of, 168
Neuropsychological assessment. *See also* Malingering; Neurologic impairment
    intertest reliability in, 156–157
    interrater reliability in
        describing cognitive strengths and weaknesses, 156
        detection of impairment in, 155–156
        for localization of brain impairment, 156

judgment tasks in, 155
reliability of, 156–157
reliability studies of, limitations of, 157
results of, versus personality assessment results, 155
statistical rules in, 223
validity of, 157–168
    appropriateness of confidence ratings, 164–166
    for detection of impairment, 157–159
    for detection of malingering, 162–163
    for etiology of impairment, 162
    for level of adaptive functioning, 163–164
    for localization of impairment, 159–161
    overperception of impairment and client variable biases, 168
    for process of impairment, 161–162
    training experience and, 166–167
Neuropsychological impairment
    detection of
        by clinical psychologists, 158
        correct negatives in, 159
        false negatives in, 159
        false positives in, 159
        by neuropsychologists, 158–159
    etiology of
        validity of judgments, 162, 169
    localization of
        judgment tasks in, 159–160
        neuropsychologists and, 160
        rating scales for, 160
        reason for testing normal participants, 160
        validity of, 160–161
    process of
        neuropsychologist description of, 161–162, 169
Norms
    in clinical judgments, 191–192

O

Obesity
    effect on client assessment, 32–33
    effect on psychodiagnosis, 69
    treatment decisions and, 140

Psychological assessment improvement
issue(s) (*continued*)
use of decision aids, 239
use of psychological tests and behavior assessment methods for,
236–237
wariness of some judgment tasks,
225
computer use, 240–241
limitations of, 240
necessity of advances in computer
science for, 240
reasons to not use computer for
judgments, 240–241
forensic, 246–247
methodologic, 231–234
criterion problem, 232–233
ecological validity, 231–232
study limitations in generalization,
233–234
training, 241–242
graduate school curriculum,
242
instructional aids, 244–246
licensing and accreditation, 244
PhD versus PsyD, 243–244
program evaluation in, 242–243
selection of students, 241–242
Psychological tests
in psychodiagnosis, 55–59, 82
validity of
clinician confidence and, 57
discussion of test results on test validity and diagnosis, 58–59
experience and, 56
expertise and, 55–56
incremental, 57–58
psychologists verus lay judges and,
56–57
training and, 56, 57
Psychopathology
clinician bias in judgment of, 35–36
clinician versus lay person judgments
of, 35–36
Psychosocial stressors and *DSM-IV* Axis
IV, 29–30, 89–90
Psychotropic medicine
reliability of treatment decision for,
121–122
use and misuse use of for depression,
151

R

Racial bias
in behavioral prediction, 112–113
for children, 112
clinician differences and, 112–113
prognostic ratings in, 112–113
for violence, 113–114
in case formulations, 96
interaction of client's and clinician's, 96
in diagnosis of schizophrenia and psychotic affective disorders, 82–
83
in differential diagnosis of schizophrenia and affective disorders, 60–
62
African Americans and Hispanics
versus Whites, 60–61
Blacks and Puerto Rican Hispanics
versus Whites, 61
Blacks versus White and schizophrenia, 61–62
in psychodiagnosis
for adjustment level and severity of
disturbance, 62
conditions for insignificance of, 62
in rehospitalization prediction, 113
for social maturity, 27–28
studies of Asian American, White
American, and Japanese clients, 29–30
studies of Whites, African Americans,
and Mexican Americans
adults, 27–28
children, 27
for depression, 28
insignificance of client race in, 28–
29
for psychopathology, 28
social maturity assessment, 27–28
in trait and symptom assessment, 26–
29
in treatment decisions
for adults, 126–128, 152
in cannabis psychosis, 127
for children and adolescents, 129
for hospitalization or commitment,
126
for neuroleptic medication, 127–
128

for psychotherapy, 128
for psychotropic medication, 127
for type of psychotherapy, 128
of White clinicians, 27
Referrals
appropriateness of and treatment outcome, 148
Reliability
of adjustment ratings
DSM-III field trials, 42–43
DSM-IV trials, 43
in assessment of personality and psychopathology, 10–14
of behavioral assessment
in treatment decisions, 119–120
breach of confidentiality and, 123
calculation of kappa or intraclass correlation for, 10
of civil commitment decision, 124
convergence in, 13–14
with International Classification of Diseases (ICD-10), 41–42
interrater
of defense mechanisms, 12
of personality traits, 11
same versus different hospitals, 12
of mental status ratings, 11–12
structured interview in, 12
of older studies, 10–11
of psychodiagnosis
adherence and nonadherence to criteria for, 43–44
DSM-III and, 41, 42–43
of personality disorder in adults, 41
research improvements in, 40–41
stability of ratings over time, 13
of treatment decisions
for level of care, 122
for psychodynamic psychotherapy, 122
for recovering memories of child sexual abuse, 122–123
for somatotherapy and psychotherapy, 121–122
Religion, effect of on case formulation, 97
Religious bias in treatment decisions, 141
Representativeness heuristic and knowledge structures
in behavioral prediction, 189

in case formulation, 189
clinician prototypes and, 186–187
in diagnosis, 188–189
in integrating information, 186–187
in traits and symptoms ratings, 187
Robins and Guze criteria
research in evaluating diagnostic criteria and
phases in, 49
in validation of psychodiagnoses
comparison with LEAD approach, 50–51
family studies, 50
follow-up studies, 49–50
laboratory tasks and biological tests, 50
Rosenhan study of context effects
in case formulation, 97–98
in psychodiagnosis, 70–71

S

Schizophrenia
diagnosis of versus affective disorder, 79–80
racial bias in, 60–62
diagnostic controversy and, 79–80
diagnostic criteria for
in DSM-IV, 39–40
etiology of
psychoanalytic formulation of, 93–94
negative symptoms of
distinguishing primary versus secondary, 92
overdiagnosis of, 79–80
prediction of, criterion validity for, 109–110
Sex role, effect on client assessment, 33, 34
Sex role bias
in behavioral prediction, 116
versus gender bias, 136–137
in psychodiagnosis, 68
in treatment decisions
for gay men or lesbians, 137
in vocational counseling, 137
Sexual abuse
child
reliability of recovering memories of, 122–123

ABOUT THE AUTHOR

Howard N. Garb is a full-time staff psychologist at the Pittsburgh V.A. Health Care System, Highland Drive Division. He is the coordinator for the Anxiety and Adjustment Disorders Clinic, sees clients for assessment and individual therapy, and is a member of the hospital psychiatric emergency team.

Dr. Garb received a double-major PhD in Clinical Psychology and "Research Methodology and Psychological Measurement" from the University of Illinois at Chicago. He completed an NIMH postdoctoral fellowship in Clinical Psychology and "Research Methodology and Program Evaluation" at Northwestern University. He has published extensively in the areas of psychological assessment and clinical judgment, and as a scientist practitioner he has devoted himself to integrating scientific research with clinical work.